the gentle art *of* preserving

Katie & Giancarlo Caldesi

the gentle art *of* preserving

Photography by Chris Terry

Kyle Books

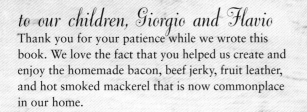

to our children, Giorgio and Flavio
Thank you for your patience while we wrote this book. We love the fact that you helped us create and enjoy the homemade bacon, beef jerky, fruit leather, and hot smoked mackerel that is now commonplace in our home.

Contents

introduction

Curing, smoking, freezing, pickling, bottling, fermenting, drying... these time-honored skills for preserving food have never been so topical. More and more we are growing uneasy with our throwaway and fast-living society and becoming actively concerned about food costs and waste, air miles and additives, and looking for ways to become more self-sufficient. Sometimes the way forward is to look back, and so we have spent two years delving into long-cherished traditions of home-conserving foods. In the process we have converted our old playhouse and barbecue grill into smokeries, turned our wine fridge into a curing chamber for hanging bacon and sausages, packed the freezer with homemade sauces, festooned the kitchen with bunches of drying herbs, and covered every surface with jars of chutney and bottles of fruit and scrumptious hedgerow booze. It has been a journey into sometimes familiar territory—for example, making use of the freezer and microwave—and sometimes unknown territory, in terms of curing and smoking. However, everyone in the family has made a contribution—and you know what? It has changed all of our lives.

Both my husband, Giancarlo, and I thought we were pretty good at valuing and preserving food. Giancarlo grew up in a family in Tuscany which never, ever, wasted food and yet there was no fridge in the house. They kept their own pig and butchered it each November, and every part of the animal would be used—some for eating fresh, the rest for curing as ham or salami. And in every appropriate season there would be food—from tomatoes to porcini— that could be conserved for the rest of the year. I grew up in an English seaside town, watching my mother make chutneys, jams, and marmalades throughout the year and helping my father pack apples and potatoes into boxes to store in winter. And our whole family have always enjoyed foraging. But during these last few years, I realize I had only scratched the surface of the enormous world of preserving. Even Giancarlo has admitted that there are so many more fascinating things to discover about self-sufficiency than he ever dreamt of. In the course of writing this book, we have worked alongside expert artisans, collected long-standing family recipes and techniques from friends, and tapped into diverse preserving traditions from Thailand and Italy to France, Sri Lanka, Japan, Sweden, and America.

There is something about preserving, I have discovered, that forges a link with other people—perhaps it is the sense that we have been doing these things throughout the history of mankind, so wisdom is handed down and passed on. Around the world, groups of friends and family come together to preserve their fresh produce—whether in Korea to make *kimchi*, in Sri Lanka to salt and dry fish or in Italy to make the annual tomato *passata*. It is quite special to spend time chatting and chopping, spreading the workload and sharing the rewards. I had friends around for a "marmalade morning" and we had great fun. The oranges were cut up in no time, we were able to have three preserving pans on the go at once, and now we all have jars of marmalade that taste better than anything you could buy. Next up a piccalilli party, sharing our surplus of vegetables or supermarket bargain buys! I often give courses at our cooking school, showing people how to cook quick, but tasty and nutritious, meals. However, now I also encourage people to sometimes allow themselves a few hours to slow down, unwind and enjoy some simple aspect of preserving food— and, of course, the two often go hand in hand: what you preserve today makes for a quick meal tomorrow.

Though I never really considered myself wasteful, writing this book has made us, as a family, much more conscious of all the things we could do to be more food-thrifty. There are appalling statistics from Wrap, the UK government-backed Waste and Resources Action Programme, that flag up the fact that as a nation we throw away around one-third of the food we buy (much of which ends up in landfill, producing the greenhouse gas methane). This is largely because we don't plan our shopping trips, or end up leaving food at the back of the fridge until it has passed its sell-by date. Our grandparents' generation knew how to budget and eke out food, and that is what working on this book has taught me too.

These two years have changed my attitude so much that I can't bear to throw anything away. Trimmings of carrot, parsley, and celery leaves are in bags in my freezer for making into stock, along with shrimp shells, vacuum-bagged so that they stack neatly. Potato peelings get turned into chips, squeezed lemons are stored in the freezer for adding to the bathtub at the end of the day.

After writing this book, I have also become more aware of gluts of seasonal fruits and vegetables—from zucchini to strawberries—that can be snapped up for preserves. And our two boys now know all the best local paths for blackberries, wild pears, little apples, herbs, elderberries, rowans, rosehips, sloes, and nettles, depending on the season. Even if there is not much to be had on one trip, we pick what we can find—for example, blackberries— and put them in the freezer until eventually there is enough for a pie and some bottles of fruit liqueur. Even Giancarlo, who was raised on bottles and jars of homemade tomato *passata*, preserved vegetables, and home-cured salami, has found himself experimenting with very English chutneys and Asian pastes to make the best use of the basketfuls of seasonal fruit and vegetables we have picked.

Without these time-honored preservation techniques our population could not have survived. However, over the generations, people have also conserved food not just out of necessity, but also for pure pleasure—as a way of evoking the joys of summer on a drizzly winter day, or to rekindle autumnal pleasures long after the hedgerows are bare—and that is what our whole family has found so enjoyable. And there really is added satisfaction when you are savoring and relishing food that you have produced yourself, since you understand in a completely different way the time and care that goes into such processes.

It was never our intention to produce a bible on the subject—as there are so many wonderful, detailed books on different aspects of preserving already out there. Rather we wanted to produce something personal and celebratory, full of simple techniques that hopefully every family can draw some inspiration from—even if it is just one aspect of conserving food. We promise that once you give some of the ideas a try, you will begin to rethink your whole attitude to cooking, eating, and shopping.

As I have mentioned, one of the joys of curing, bottling, freezing, and generally stockpiling food is that you can make your life easier and make a meal in a hurry, without compromising what you are feeding the family. And if friends or family turn up unexpectedly, no panic, you can feed them without even having to go to the store. Imagine a cocktail before dinner made with your own cordials; homemade vegetable chips to nibble; a quick lunch of home-cured fish or salami; supper of pasta with the bottled tomato sauce that you made in the summer; little tubs of spicy Asian sauces, frozen and ready to go for a speedy curry; or a dessert made with the preserved plums you bottled when the trees were laden.

All this might seem like a lot of work, but I have found that once you change your mindset and begin to take a different approach to food, you can happily build preserving food into a busy lifestyle.

GENERAL ADVICE AND INSTRUCTIONS

trusting your instincts

Preserving is a science, but not an exact science, and there is no foolproof way of preserving in the home environment. However, what I have discovered on this journey is to learn to trust my instincts—the more I pickle, cure, air-dry, and smoke, the more I understand how to spot problems and adapt, and also to accept the occasional failure.

Our grandparents knew how to judge for themselves whether a food was spoiled, whereas in our supermarket-dominated world, governed by use-by and sell-by dates, it is easy to abandon the fundamental sensual skills of looking and smelling. But once you enter the world of preserving, it is important to re-hone your senses, as well as to understand and feel comfortable with what you are doing.

food safety

All around us in the air, on the surface of our food, on our equipment, and ourselves are microorganisms such as yeasts, molds, and bacteria. Some of these are good and we encourage them to grow in our food, such as *Lactobacillus* in yogurt and the typical green mold in cheese. However, some are positively harmful, such as *Clostridium botulinum*, and the rest are just downright unpleasant. This is why we have to be as clean as possible and take every care that we do not encourage unwanted microorganisms also known as "spoilers."

Washing, blanching, and peeling fruit can help remove spoilers. Heat-processing jars of food, if done correctly, destroys the spoilers that would naturally cause food to decay. This also creates a vacuum in the jar by driving the air out of it. When the jars cool after heating, this vacuum sucks the lid on tight and prevents other spoilers getting in.

the four spoilers

ENZYMES

Enzymes are in all living things, be they plants or animals. Their activity can cause food to change color, flavor, and texture. They are discouraged by blanching and inhibited by cooking or processing at about 285°F.

MOLDS AND YEASTS

Molds and yeasts are fungi; they are usually visible as fur, patches, or specks on the food. Mold thrives in acidic conditions—hence why you sometimes see white fur appear on old tomato sauce or green patches on yogurt. Yeasts cause food to ferment, which might be positively encouraged in the fermenting chapter, but is usually discouraged. Acidic environments create a hostile atmosphere for most bacteria, but they offer no protection against molds or yeast.

BACTERIA

Yes I know it is an ugly word and no one wants to think about it when making beautiful jars of peaches suspended in a rich cinnamon syrup, but some molds and yeasts are good and are actively encouraged when you want to ferment something. Once you understand about bacteria, you can begin to discern when to encourage and when to avoid them. Bacteria are not so easily destroyed as molds and yeast. Salmonella is destroyed when foods are held at 140°F for a specific time, depending on their acidity level. *Staphylococcus aureus* or "staph" is destroyed at 240°F when held for a specific time. Botulism, caused by *Clostridium botulinum*, is destroyed by boiling, but the spores that cause it are not. They are anaerobic, meaning they do not need air to survive. They need to be heated to 240°F for a period of time to destroy them. Since water boils at 212°F at sea level (and at a lower temperature in areas over 1,000ft), you can see that processing food in boiling water isn't going to do the job of destroying them. Temperatures such as this can only be achieved in a pressure canner due to the pressurized steam. *Clostridium botulinum* spores flourish in low-acid environments; this means they are quite at home in a jar of food such as canned vegetables.

USE YOUR EYES, NOSE, AND TASTE

If you see mold, be bold and discard your pot of preserves. Although many of us have scraped mold off jam before and lived to tell the tale, the mycotoxins from mold can go deep into the jam. The same goes if you smell the product and it has an unpleasant or "off" smell. If it fizzes when you unscrew the lid, but looks and smells normal, throw it away.

QUALITY OF INGREDIENTS

Fresh, undamaged produce is key to a good preserve. If it is not in tip-top condition when it is preserved, it will not be good when you come to eat it.

STERILIZING JARS AND LIDS

Make sure all jars and bottles are in pristine condition. Scrape off old labels with a knife under hot water and finish with a metal scourer to get off any glue.

To sterilize jars in the oven the temperature we recommend is 285°F for a minimum of 20 minutes. Dishwashers don't generally heat to adequate temperatures to sterilize jars—most cycles are 122°F or 140°F—however they are useful for washing them. We recommend that you sterilize bottles and jars in an oven, microwave, or waterbath instead.

sterilizing in the oven

This is our preferred method for sterilizing jars. Give them a good wash with hot soapy water, followed by a very good rinse to get rid of any odors. Put them upside down into the oven at 285°F for a minimum of 20 minutes. Store in a warm oven until they are ready to be filled. They will dry as they sterilize.

sterilizing in the microwave

Fill up to four jars with water so they are quarter full. Heat on high until the water boils. Remove wearing oven gloves and pour out the water. Turn the jars over to dry on a clean rack. Fill while still warm.

sterilizing in a waterbath

Wash the jars in hot soapy water and rinse very well. Put them upright onto a rack in a stockpot, pressure cooker, or canner without the lid. Fill the jars and pot with warm water to cover the jars by 1in. Bring the water to a boil and continue to boil for 10 minutes; reduce the heat and keep the jars in the hot water until you are ready to fill them.

sterilizing lids

Either use new clean lids or immerse old ones in boiling hot water in a large saucepan for 10 minutes. Remove them from the water and drain, inside facing downward, on a clean rack. Make sure they are dry before fastening them onto the jars. Note: Preserves made with vinegar should be sealed with vinegar-proofed lids—i.e. ones that are plastic-coated.

vinegar

Vinegar is highly acidic and most harmful to bacteria, which cannot survive in acidic environments. Even a teaspoon of standard strength vinegar (6 percent) in an 8oz glass of water will create too much acidity for most bacteria to survive. Vinegar can be measured by the percentage of acetic acid in it and this varies according to what it is made from—rice vinegar being the mildest, followed by beer and cider, with wine and distilled vinegar being the strongest. Usually the acetic acid percentage is written on the bottle.

The sophisticated Babylonians in 4,000 BC used vinegar from fermented raisin and date wines to preserve vegetables and meats. They even flavored the vinegar with spices and herbs just as we do today. The Romans too enjoyed a dressing made from honey and vinegar, and drank it with water in a drink called *posca*, while the ancient Chinese created vinegar from fermented plums and a dark, complex vinegar from rice and wheat.

Recent studies have shown that although vinegar is high in acid and does not support the growth of *Clostridium botulinum* bacteria it could support the growth of *Escherichia coli bacteria*. To avoid this use dried spices and herbs or cook anything fresh that you add to vinegar to a boil, including herbs, fruit, and flavorings.

This chapter concentrates on chutneys, pickles, and sauces that are made with vinegar, as well as vegetables that are preserved in vinegar to make them crisp and sour.

which vinegar?

Always use reasonable quality vinegar for preserving with an acetic acid content of at least 5 percent. Most chutney recipes call for malt vinegar, but it is possible to use spirit, cider or wine vinegar for certain recipes, depending on the flavor and color wanted in the finished product. If you don't like a sharp acidic flavor to a recipe you can always add a little sugar; it will balance the flavor but it won't take away the acidity required to make the product safe.

herb-flavored vinegar

Herbs such as tarragon completely change mediocre white wine vinegar into a savory, mouthwatering potion, which is wonderful in sauces such as hollandaise, dressings, and creamy sauces that need some acidity to cut through the fat. Store in bottles with corks or plastic lids. Swing-top bottles with rubber seals are ideal.

METHOD For best results, pick the herbs first thing in the morning when their essential oils are at their height. Four sprigs about the length of your hand are enough to flavor a 16fl oz bottle of white wine vinegar. Shake and wash the herbs to make sure that there are no insects clinging to them. Put the sprigs and the vinegar into a saucepan and bring to a boil for 2 minutes. Pull the sprigs out of the vinegar with tongs and put into a warm, sterilized bottle, pour in the vinegar and close the lid. Store in a cool, dark place for 3–4 weeks, and then strain the vinegar through a sieve lined with cheesecloth to remove the herbs and pour it back into the bottle. Keep in a cool, dark place or the fridge and use within 3 months.

Variation

Heat a mixture of rosemary, sage, and thyme leaves in white wine vinegar. Use in salad dressings with extra virgin olive oil, drizzle over sautéed zucchini or add to sauces.

USES My friend Karin Piper makes a delicious chicken recipe with tarragon vinegar: brown the chicken pieces in a large frying pan and set aside; sauté some finely chopped onion, pour in a splash of tarragon vinegar and reduce so the onion takes on the flavor; add a good splash of white wine or vermouth and reduce a little, then add a little stock; return the chicken to the pan to cook over low heat for about 15–20 minutes; finish with a dash of cream and some freshly chopped tarragon and cook on low heat for another couple of minutes or until the chicken is cooked through.

shallot vinegar

This has bite and sweetness without the overpowering odor of raw onion.

METHOD Finely chop a shallot or half a banana shallot and mix it with 10fl oz red wine vinegar. Bring to a boil in a saucepan and then remove from the heat. Leave it to infuse for 2 hours, then strain, discarding the onion. Store the vinegar in a sealed bottle in the fridge and use within a month.

USES Shallot vinegar makes a wonderful vinaigrette mixed with extra virgin olive oil and mustard for use in salads. Alternatively serve it on its own as a traditional dressing for oysters.

fruit vinegars

Historically fruit vinegars were used not only for cooking but also as drinks diluted with water. Fruit vinegars are easy to produce and make a great addition to sauces, gravy, and salad dressings. Use anywhere you might use balsamic vinegar.

Raspberry and blackberry vinegar are our favorites as we enjoy berry picking in the summer. To use, simply pour them directly over salad or mix them with an equal quantity of extra virgin olive oil and a pinch of salt and freshly ground black pepper.

BLACKBERRY VINEGAR

makes 1 bottle (approx. 2½ cups)
**1lb 10oz blackberries, stalks and
  leaves removed**
**about 2 cups cider vinegar, white wine
  vinegar, or red wine vinegar**
**up to 1 cup superfine sugar,
  to taste**

Put the blackberries in a nonreactive bowl and crush them gently with a potato masher. Pour 1¾ cups vinegar over the fruit making sure it covers them, adding more if not. Cover the dish with plastic wrap or a lid and set aside to infuse for 3–5 days (or longer, if you wish, to impart a stronger flavor).

Strain the blackberries through a jelly bag or a sieve lined with two layers of cheesecloth; this is best done overnight. Measure the strained juice and calculate the quantity of sugar needed, allowing ¼ cup sugar per ½ cup juice, according to taste. Pour the juice (and any additional spices and flavorings) into a heavy-bottomed saucepan and set over medium heat. Bring to a simmer for 2 minutes then reduce the heat and add the sugar, stirring to dissolve. Skim off any scum that forms on the surface. Taste and adjust the sugar as necessary. Remove from the heat and pour into a warm, sterilized bottle. Leave to cool and store in a cool, dark place or the fridge for up to a year.

Variations
You can use strawberries or raspberries in place of the blackberries; just make sure you adjust the quantity of sugar to taste. Ripe figs also work well if cut into quarters first. Fig vinegar is good sweetened with maple syrup instead of sugar.

For spiced fruit vinegar, add a few spices with the crushed fruit at the beginning. We love raspberry vinegar infused with a sprig of rosemary and a teaspoon of crushed pink peppercorns. To give the blackberry vinegar a kick, try adding a teaspoon of allspice berries and a few black peppercorns.

ELDERFLOWER VINEGAR

On a dry and sunny spring day take yourself on a foraging trip to pick young heads of elderflowers. Try to pick the flowers early on a sunny morning when their essential oils are at their best. This delicate, flowery vinegar is ideal for salads, hollandaise sauce, or for pickled elderberries (see right).

makes 2½ quarts
2½ quarts English cider vinegar
20–30 elderflower heads

Pour a little vinegar out of the container to use another day or pour all the vinegar into a nonreactive container with a lid.

Check for any insects in the flower heads, but do not be tempted to wash them or they will spoil. Using scissors, trim the flowers from the stems into a funnel so that they fall into the vinegar. Put the lid on the container and leave in a cool, dark place for up to 3 weeks.

Taste the vinegar and if you are happy that the flavor is strong enough, strain it through cheesecloth to get rid of the flowers. If the flavor is weak, add some more flowers and repeat as above. Pour the vinegar into a saucepan and bring to a boil. Let it bubble for 5 minutes and then remove from the heat. Allow to cool. The vinegar can then be left in the container or bottled and labeled. It will keep in a cool, dark place for up to a year.

PICKLED ELDERBERRIES

These tiny, poky little berries are somewhere between a caper and a green peppercorn. They make a great spicy sauce or add a little kick to salads and pasta dishes. I couldn't resist trying them with a cream and white wine sauce for lemon sole and Giancarlo scatters them onto pizza with anchovies.

makes 2 cups
2–3 handfuls of green elderberries
2 teaspoons fine sea salt
**approx. 1 cup elderflower vinegar
  (see left)**

Pick the elderberries while still green and underripe. Use a fork to strip the berries off the stalks. Scatter in the salt and stir through. Leave them in a cool, dark place, covered, overnight.

The following day, rinse the salt off the berries and dry them on paper towels. Put the berries into a sterilized jar and top up with the vinegar to the top of the jar. Close the lid—remember to use a rubber seal or a vinegar-proof lid. Store in a cool, dark place and use after a month and for up to a year.

PONTACK SAUCE

This old English sauce made with elderberries is named after Monsieur Pontack, who owned the famous Pontack's Head Tavern in Lombard Street, London, in the 17th century. This was said to be London's first fashionable eating house and this sauce would have been served with roasted meat and game.

Pontack sauce is said to improve with age, rather like a vintage red wine. Our version changed in the bottle and is still improving after a year—see how long you can wait before you sample yours! Serve drizzled over steak that has been cut into strips straight after cooking or stir into a gravy or hearty casserole.

makes 1½ cups
4 cups elderberries
2 cups cider vinegar
¼ cup superfine sugar
1 red onion, finely chopped
5 tsp bruised fresh ginger (gently squeezed with your fist)
1 tablespoon black peppercorns
6 allspice berries, lightly crushed in a mortar and pestle
6 cloves
fine salt and freshly ground black pepper, to taste

Use a fork to strip the berries off the stalks. (Don't wear your best white clothes, the juice stains horribly.) Put all the ingredients into a casserole, stir together and cover. Cook in a low oven (approx. 220°F) for 4 hours, stirring occasionally. Strain the vinegar through a piece of cheesecloth over a sieve into a saucepan, pushing down on the fruit to release as much juice as possible. Bring to a boil for 5 minutes and adjust the seasoning if necessary. Pour the sauce into a sterilized pitcher and pour into a sterilized bottle. Seal. Keep for several years in a cool, dark place. Wait at least 3 months before tasting.

spiced vinegar

Spiced vinegar is used as a base in many of the chutney recipes in this book. According to my sister Louise and our friend Penny Wragg, in order to make the very best spiced vinegar you should put your spices into bottles of cold vinegar a year before you need them. Apparently if you shake the bottles from time to time you will encourage the flavor of the spices to really penetrate the vinegar. I am hopelessly impatient, but I am going to try this in the future as the ingredients are not expensive and once made the vinegar can be left in the garage and forgotten about for a year.

Of course, not everyone will have the foresight to make their spiced vinegar a year in advance, so here is a shortcut that involves heating the ingredients to speed up the process.

QUICK SPICED VINEGAR

This is my speedy version for people who need their spiced vinegar in a hurry.

makes 1 quart
1 quart vinegar of your choice (make sure it is at least 5 percent acetic acid)
2in cinnamon stick
1 teaspoon cloves
½ teaspoon mace (optional)
pinch of cayenne pepper
2 teaspoons allspice
1 teaspoon black peppercorns
1 teaspoon mustard seeds
2–3 bay leaves

Put the vinegar and spices in a saucepan, cover with a lid and bring to just below boiling point—do not allow it to bubble. Remove from the heat and set aside for a minimum of 2 hours (preferably overnight). The longer you leave it, the better the flavor. Strain the vinegar through a sieve lined with cheesecloth and bottle once cold if not using immediately. Store in a cool, dark place for up to a year.

LOUISE'S PICKLED EGGS

My sister Louise remembers pickling eggs with our grandmother in her cramped little kitchen. She would traditionally make the eggs in autumn to give as Christmas presents later in the year. Our grandmother used malt vinegar, but any vinegar is fine. My sister always uses spiced vinegar (see left), which imparts a lovely flavor to the finished dish. Homemade pickled eggs are so much nicer than the commercially made versions you can buy. We eat them with slices of cold ham, pâté, cheese, or curries.

makes 2 x 18-oz Mason jars
14 medium, organic fresh eggs
1 quart Spiced or Quick spiced vinegar (see left) or white wine vinegar and the chile below
1 teaspoon salt
2 teaspoons roughly crushed black peppercorns
2 small pieces of dried chile (optional)

Hard-boil the eggs for about 10 minutes. Put the cooked eggs under cold water to cool and give each one a quick tap to break the shells (this should stop the blue ring appearing around the outside of the yolk). Peel off the shells. Put the eggs into your Mason jars and top up with the cold vinegar, salt, peppercorns, and chile, if using, making sure they are completely submerged. Seal with nonreactive lids and store in a cool, dark place. Leave for 1 month before opening and consume within 6 months. Once opened, store in the fridge and eat within a week.

Variation
For a really pretty version of pickled eggs, add 1 cup pasteurized beet juice to the pan with the vinegar.

PICKLED VEGETABLES

Most recipes require you to soak your vegetables in brine or layer them with dry salt before immersing them in vinegar. This preliminary process removes excess moisture in the veggies, improves their texture, and helps destroy bacteria. As a general rule, brining is used for vegetables such as onions to soften them, while dry salt is used for brassicas such as cabbage to keep them crisp. After brining or salting you must rinse your veggies in clean, cold water and drain them thoroughly before packing them into jars and covering with vinegar.

For best results, always pickle fresh vegetables or fruit as soon as possible after harvesting and never be tempted to use bruised produce. Make sure your vegetables are totally immersed in the vinegar solution at all times to stop them from becoming contaminated. I always allow 1in headroom above the vegetables to leave plenty of space for the vinegar. Don't be tempted to squash the vegetables down inside the jar or they will bruise and the vinegar won't be able to reach all the surfaces.

As a general rule, use cold vinegar for making crisp pickles and warm vinegar for soft pickles, so that it lightly cooks the food before it cools. Always use nonreactive (vinegar-proof) lids.

PICKLED ONIONS

Pickled onions remind me of the Sunday evenings of my childhood. After a big roast lunch and a walk along the blustery seaside of Eastbourne we would settle down for a simple supper in front of the TV consisting of Cheddar cheese, bread, butter, and my mum's homemade pickled onions—heaven!

makes 2 x 18-oz Mason jars and 1 x 9-oz jar

1 quart medium brine (see page 86)
2¼lbs small pickling onions, unpeeled
½ cup superfine sugar (optional)
2–2¾ cups cold Quick spiced vinegar (see page 19), to cover the onions

Make up the brine and set aside to cool. Meanwhile peel the onions. The easiest way to do this is to cut off the tops and roots (just the very tips and ends to keep them intact and so not to waste too much of the onion) and plunge them into a bowl of boiling water. Set aside for 1 minute, then drain and plunge into cold water. You should now be able to peel off the skins easily along with any tough leathery layers.

Put the onions into a mixing bowl and cover them with the cold brine, weighing them down with a plate so that they are fully submerged. Set aside for 12 hours in a cold place. Meanwhile, dissolve the sugar (if using) in the vinegar and set aside to cool.

Drain the onions and pat dry on paper towels. Pack the onions into sterilized jars and cover with the cold, spiced vinegar, making sure they are totally submerged. Put on the nonreactive lids tightly and store in a cold, dark place for up to a year, however you can start eating them after a month.

Variation

To make the jars look pretty and add a little more spice, put a couple of bay leaves, a few black peppercorns, and either a dried red chile or a teaspoon of mustard seeds into each jar.

PICKLED RED CABBAGE

This is great with roasted pork belly, cold turkey or ham, or as part of a stir-fry. My favorite way to eat pickled cabbage is slightly warm with homemade British or Italian sausages (see page 107).

You can vary the texture of the finished cabbage by pickling it in hot or cold vinegar (see below). Use hot vinegar for a softer texture or cold vinegar if you like a bit of crunch.

makes approx. 2¼lbs
1 small red cabbage, shredded
3 tablespoons fine salt
¾–1 quart Quick spiced vinegar
  (see page 19)
1 teaspoon cumin seeds
10 black peppercorns, lightly crushed

Mix the shredded cabbage with the salt in a nonmetallic bowl. Weigh it down with a plate and set aside overnight.

Meanwhile, put the vinegar and spices in a saucepan and heat to boiling point; remove from the heat and set aside to infuse. Depending on whether you like your cabbage soft or crunchy, you can either use the vinegar immediately or leave it to cool. Drain

through a sieve, reserving the spices.

Squeeze out the cabbage and give it a good rinse in cold water, discarding any juice from the bowl. Drain it well and turn onto paper towels to dry. Pack the cabbage into sterilized jars, sprinkling it with the reserved seeds and peppercorns. Pour in the vinegar to cover the cabbage completely and then poke it several times with a clean chopstick or wooden skewer to release any air bubbles. Seal with nonreactive lids. Store in a cool, dark place. It should be ready to enjoy after a week but will keep for up to 3 months. Once opened, store in the fridge and eat within 2 weeks.

SWEDISH PICKLED CUCUMBERS

My Swedish friend Pernilla gave this recipe to me. Her sister-in-law, Lotta Gustafsson, loves to grow her own vegetables and forage for herbs. Each time Pernilla goes home to Sweden she comes back laden with jars of pickled vegetables.

makes approx. 2¼lbs
approx. 1lb 12oz small cucumbers
1 tablespoon fine sea salt
a handful of dill
2 tablespoons white mustard seeds
½ cup superfine sugar
½ quart distilled white vinegar

Wash the cucumbers, removing any blossom from the ends. Dry on paper towels and cut into 2in slices. Put them into a nonmetallic bowl and use your hands to mix them with the salt. Cover with a saucer and leave in the fridge or a cold room overnight.

The following day, rinse the cucumbers really well in cold water and pat dry with paper towels. Cut them into 2in slices and layer them with the

dill, mustard seeds, and sugar in a clean nonmetallic bowl. Pour the vinegar over the top and set aside to steep for a further 24 hours, stirring occasionally with a wooden spoon to encourage the sugar to dissolve so it comes into contact with all of the cucumber slices.

The following day, put the cucumbers into sterilized jars and top them up with the vinegar. Seal with vinegar-proof lids and store in a cool, dark place for up to 6 months. You can start eating them within a week.

GARLIC RELISH

This recipe is from our friend Kam Degun. It was her mother's recipe and she serves the relish with samosas, spring rolls, and lentil curry. She kindly gave us a jar and we loved it. We discovered it goes really well with many European foods—try it spread thinly on hot sourdough toast, mixed into mashed potatoes, stirred into hot, steamed green beans, or added to stir-fries and marinades (see Dragon chicken, pages 37–38). Use it wherever you see garlic being used: a teaspoon is equal to one garlic clove.

makes 9oz
4 whole heads of garlic
½ cup extra virgin olive oil
1 tablespoon apple cider vinegar
1 tablespoon lemon juice
½ teaspoon chili powder or paprika
1 level teaspoon superfine sugar
good pinch of salt, to taste

Peel the garlic cloves and grind them to a coarse or smooth paste in a mortar and pestle or using an immersion blender. Stir in the olive oil, vinegar, lemon juice, chili powder (or paprika), sugar, and salt. Scoop into a cold, sterilized jar with a lid and store in the fridge. Consume within a month.

MALAYSIAN PICKLED VEGETABLES

This is our friend and chef Caroline Mili Artiss' recipe. She serves the pickled vegetables at parties as a pre-dinner nibble or as an accompaniment to curries. They also work really well on a board of charcuterie and cheeses.

makes approx. 4½lbs

2¼lbs mixed vegetables such as cauliflower, carrots, red bell pepper, baby onions, green beans, celery, cucumber (discard the soft middle and seeds)
⅓ cup fine sea salt

For the dressing
1 tablespoon sunflower oil
1 tablespoon mustard seeds
1 heaping teaspoon turmeric powder
1 heaping teaspoon chili powder
3 garlic cloves, peeled and finely sliced
1in piece of fresh ginger, finely sliced
1 quart distilled white vinegar
3 cups superfine sugar
1 heaping teaspoon salt

Chop the vegetables into small bite-sized pieces—batons, wedges, or florets, the choice is yours. Put them into a large plastic or glass bowl and scatter the fine sea salt over the top. Toss carefully with your hands to coat the vegetables evenly in the salt. Place a plate on top so it rests directly on the vegetables and weigh it down with something heavy. Set the bowl aside for approx. 8 hours in a cool place. A garage is ideal, just make sure it doesn't attract pests or flies.

Meanwhile make the dressing. Heat the oil in a large saucepan and add the mustard seeds. Once they start to pop, add the turmeric and chili powder, garlic, and ginger and let them cook for 1 minute. Pour in the vinegar and stir in the sugar and salt. Bring slowly to a boil, stirring to dissolve the sugar, and then reduce to a simmer for 3 minutes. Set aside to cool. (At this stage you can store the dressing in a sterilized bottle in the fridge for up to 1 month.)

Put the vegetables into a colander and rinse really well with plenty of cold water. Put them into a bowl of clean, cold water and leave them to soak for a few minutes before rinsing again. Repeat this process to get rid of the salt. Taste the vegetables to make sure they are not too salty and rinse again if necessary. Drain really well and pat dry on paper towels.

Put the vegetables in a glass or ceramic bowl, pour in the dressing, and set aside to marinate in the fridge for about an hour.

You can either serve the vegetables immediately or pack them into sterilized glass jars and seal with sterilized nonreactive lids—just make sure the vegetables are fully submerged in the dressing or they will spoil. Store in a cool, dark pantry for up to 6 months. Once opened, the jars should be kept in the fridge and eaten within a month.

PICKLED GRAPES

This is based on a recipe by Patrick Eude, Le Havre, from the fascinating book *Preserving Food Without Freezing or Canning*. Pickled grapes are really unusual; they have an initial acidity followed by an intense sweetness as you eat them. We have increased the sugar content from the original recipe to tone down the mouth-puckering vinegar shock and to allow for my sweet tooth. We serve pickled grapes alongside pâté or rillettes to counteract the richness or with cold meats.

makes 1 x 18-oz Mason jar
1⅓lbs mixed seedless white and red grapes in bunches
⅓ quart white wine vinegar
1¼ cups superfine sugar
6 white peppercorns
4 cloves
2 sprigs of tarragon

Wash the grapes while still on the bunch and snip them off individually with scissors keeping a very short stalk. Put the vinegar and sugar in a large saucepan, add the peppercorns and cloves and bring to a boil to dissolve the sugar. Reduce the heat to a very gentle simmer and add the grapes and tarragon. Simmer very gently for 3 minutes, then remove the grapes with a slotted spoon into a sterilized jar. Allow the vinegar mixture to cool to room temperature before pouring it over the grapes. Tuck the tarragon sprigs and spices in among the grapes and ensure that the grapes are pushed down under the level of the vinegar. Seal with nonreactive lids and store in a cool, dark place for up to a year. Leave for 3 months before opening.

Variation
Use gooseberries or cherries in season in place of the grapes.

PICKLED NECTARINES

These have a delightful flavor—sweet fruit with the sourness of vinegar and a hint of spice. A bit like Marmite, they might not be everyone's cup of tea, but we love them with cold smoked ham or roasted duck. The recipe also works with peaches or pears.

makes 1 x 2¼-lb Mason jar
10 just ripe but firm nectarines (approx. 1lb 14oz)
⅔ cup water
½ quart white wine vinegar or apple cider vinegar
2in cinnamon stick
1 teaspoon allspice berries
5 cloves
2in piece of fresh ginger, peeled and cut into julienne sticks
1 teaspoon freshly ground black peppercorns
2 cups superfine sugar

Peel the nectarines, cut into quarters, and remove the seeds. Put the remaining ingredients into a large saucepan and bring to a boil. Add the nectarine quarters and poach them very gently until just tender, approx. 6–8 minutes. Remove the fruit with a slotted spoon and pack into a warm, sterilized jar. Return the poaching liquid to the heat and boil up vigorously for 5 minutes to reduce a little. Pour it over the nectarines, including the spices, making sure they are totally submerged, and seal immediately with a nonreactive lid. Store in a cool, dark place for up to a year. Allow at least 6 months before opening.

PICKLED CHILES

Mexican pickled chiles, also known as *chiles en escabeche*, are a spicy addition to fajitas (see page 254), enchiladas, cheeses, or cut small to pep up a salad. Often this recipe is made with jalapeños but any chiles such as habaneros, long Hungarian chiles, and the typical green and red chiles in most supermarkets are fine to use; they will all have their individual stengths of heat. I have also used red bell peppers and cauliflower in this recipe and they are both delicious.

makes 2¼lbs
1lb chiles
3 medium carrots, peeled and cut into batons
3 medium onions, peeled and cut into eighths
3 tablespoons extra virgin olive oil
6 garlic cloves, peeled
1 teaspoon oregano
2 bay leaves
2 teaspoons majoram
10 black peppercorns, lightly crushed
3 tablespoons granulated cane sugar
2 teaspoons salt
½ quart apple cider vinegar, plus a little extra for topping up the jars
¾ cup water

Wash all the vegetables. Leave the stems intact but cut a cross in the tip of each chile to allow the vinegar to penetrate. Add the oil to a saucepan over medium heat and cook the chiles, carrots, onions, and garlic for 10 minutes, turning the vegetables frequently to avoid burning. Add the herbs, peppercorns, sugar, and salt and stir through. Pour in the vinegar and water and bring to a boil. Reduce the heat to a simmer and cook for an additional 10 minutes. Bottle hot into sterilized jars, topping up with extra vinegar if necessary to make sure that all the vegetables are covered. Seal and allow to cool. Store in the fridge for up to 2 months or waterbath for 15 minutes following the hot-pack method on page 253.

PICKLED WALNUTS

Our good friends Dee and Barrie at Chalfont Chillies gave me this recipe. Apparently their local vicar asked them to make some for him and they were so popular they have continued making them. Eat pickled walnuts with cheese or ham to make a more interesting ploughman's lunch. Barrie's favorite way to eat them is in the charmingly named dish of beef collops.

makes approx. 4 x 12-oz jars

3¾ quarts water
6 tablespoons fine sea salt,
  for the brine
2lbs green walnuts, in their husks
2 tablespoons whole black
  peppercorns
1 tablespoon allspice berries
2 teaspoons whole cloves
1 teaspoon whole yellow mustard
  seeds
2 garlic cloves, peeled and sliced
4 thin slices of fresh ginger
1¾ quarts malt vinegar
2¼ cups light brown sugar

DAY ONE First make the brine. Heat 1¼ quarts of water with 2 tablespoons of sea salt in a saucepan over medium heat, stirring to dissolve; pour into a glass or plastic bowl and set aside to cool to room temperature.

Wearing rubber gloves, top and tail the walnuts, pierce each one several times with a large needle and drop them into the brine. Set aside for 3 days, covered loosely, at room temperature.

DAY FOUR Make up a fresh solution of brine: dissolve 2 tablespoons of sea salt in 1¼ quarts of boiling water and set aside to cool. Drain the walnuts, discarding the old brine, and transfer them to the new brine. Set aside for a further 3 days.

DAY SEVEN Make up a fresh solution of brine: dissolve 2 tablespoons of sea salt in 1¼ quarts of boiling water and set aside to cool. Drain the walnuts, discarding the old brine, and transfer them to the new brine. Set aside for a further 3 days.

DAY TEN Drain the walnuts one final time and spread them out on a tray lined with newspaper to dry. In good weather you can place the walnuts outside to dry, protected with a net, or you can put them inside on a sunny windowsill. Set aside for 2–3 days, turning occasionally, until they blacken.

DAYS 12–13 Lightly crush the spices in a mortar and pestle to bruise them slightly. Wrap them in a piece of cheesecloth, putting in the garlic and ginger as well, and tie with a knot. Heat the vinegar and sugar with the spice bag in a large saucepan to dissolve the sugar. Bring to a boil and then reduce to a simmer for 15 minutes. Set aside to cool before removing the spices.

Pack the walnuts into dry, sterilized jars, cover with the vinegar and seal immediately. Store for 8–12 weeks before using. Pickled walnuts will keep for a year. Refrigerate after opening and use within 2 months.

HORSERADISH SAUCE

Horseradish grows easily in the UK and it is often a problem to get rid of in gardens. We stumbled across a patch near where we live and occasionally go and dig a root up. The white root buries itself deep in the ground and can be hard to dig up, but even a little piece goes a long way.

To preserve fresh horseradish for a few weeks in the fridge, finely grate it and spoon into a small jar or container adding enough white wine vinegar to cover. When grating horseradish, do it at arm's length and don't take a big sniff of the root as it is really powerful stuff. Wash your hands well afterward and avoid touching your eyes.

serves 4

2 heaping tablespoons finely grated
  fresh horseradish
2–3 teaspoons white wine vinegar
1–2 teaspoons lemon juice, to taste
1–2 teaspoons superfine sugar,
  to taste
good pinch of salt
2–3 tablespoons Crème fraîche (see
  page 223) or heavy cream

Mix all the ingredients together to taste. Store in the fridge for up to 3 days in a sealed jar or plastic container. This is not just to be eaten with roast beef—try it stirred into buttery mashed potato, with steak or with the Peppered mackerel (page 168).

CHRAIN

This was introduced to us by a group of lovely women from the Cooking Lunch Girls, a group of foodie Jewish women from North London. We taught them about Italian food and in return they took us on a tour of the Golders Green delicatessens and introduced us to the tastiest versions of their typical food. I relished the soft just-baked challah bread, tangy cream cheese, subtle smoked salmon, pickled gherkins, slivers of pastrami and salt beef, but I had never seen chrain before and just loved it.

This pickle combines the strong flavor of horseradish with the sweetness of beets. Horseradish grows in wild abundance where we live, so occasionally we take a trowel and go and dig some up. It always needs a good wash afterward and you must take care when grating it as it can sting your eyes and take your breath away. This is why I make a little of this at a time. Chrain is lovely on toasted bagels or rye bread with cream cheese, or with Salt beef (see page 118). Beet takes a long time to roast in the oven (up to 2 hours to become tender), but the end result is sweeter tasting than boiled beets. Feel free to experiment with the quantities, according to taste, and don't worry about exact measurements.

makes approx. 10oz

10–10½oz boiled or roasted beets (approx. 4 medium beets) – I wrap them in foil and roast them in a hot oven until tender
2–3 heaping tablespoons grated horseradish
4–6 teaspoons white wine vinegar
4 teaspoons lemon juice
4–6 teaspoons superfine sugar
fine sea salt, to taste

Put all the ingredients in a food processor (or use an immersion blender) and purée to a smooth paste. Adjust the seasoning to taste with salt and sugar. Store in a covered container in the fridge for up to a month.

JAPANESE PICKLED GINGER

Pickled ginger is usually served with sushi and is called *gari*. Try to find fresh young ginger (*shin shoga*) for this—look out for the yellow-skinned tender ones with a tinge of pink at the end of the roots. If you use old ginger root it might not turn pink naturally. Sometimes coloring is added to alter the appearance, however I think that is a shame. For best results use a mandolin to cut the ginger into transparent slices. This is also lovely with steamed or grilled fish for a simple supper or shredded or tossed into stir-fries and salads. Try it in the marinade for Beef jerky (see page 138) in place of raw ginger and marinate beef or fish in it before grilling.

makes 2¼ lbs

1lb 12oz young fresh ginger
2 teaspoons sea salt
¾ quart rice vinegar
1 cup superfine sugar

Cut the woody ends off the ginger roots and scrape off the skin using a teaspoon. Slice the ginger really thinly using a mandolin or a very sharp knife and mix with the salt in a bowl. Set aside for an hour at room temperature, covered with a cloth.

Remove the ginger from the bowl, dry the slices with paper towels and transfer them to a sterilized jar. Put the rice vinegar and sugar in a saucepan and bring to a boil to dissolve the sugar. Pour the hot liquid over the ginger slices in the jar and set aside to cool, loosely covered with a piece of cheeseloth to allow the heat to escape but nothing to fall in. The ginger will turn light pink as it cools. Put a nonreactive lid on the jar and store in the fridge for up to 3 weeks.

PICKLED FISH

MARINATED ANCHOVIES

These remind me of being on vacation by the sea in Italy. The sun shines, the white wine is crisp and cold and a little dish of silver vinegary fish is presented before the meal to eat with bread. Heaven. However, marinated anchovies still taste good in a cloudy, cold climate (so I tell myself). In fact, our son Giorgio gobbles them up even before I have a chance to lay them on a plate.

Marinated anchovies look really pretty dressed with parsley and red onion, and make great antipasti. Fresh small sprats can also be used if you can't find anchovies. To economize, it is perfectly fine to use sunflower oil, but do drain them well and dress with extra virgin olive oil for serving.

makes 18oz (serves 8–10)
14oz fresh anchovies, filleted
¼–⅓ quart white wine vinegar
½ cup extra virgin olive oil or
   sunflower oil

To serve
1 red onion, cut into thin strips
a small handful of fresh parsley,
   roughly chopped
extra virgin olive oil, for drizzling
salt and freshly ground black pepper

Place the anchovy fillets side by side on a nonmetallic tray and pour over enough white wine vinegar to cover them completely. Set aside in the fridge to marinate (preferably overnight) or until the flesh turns white.

Drain the anchovies, discarding the vinegar, and pat dry on paper towels. Lay them side by side in a plastic container and pour over enough oil to cover them completely. Put the lid on and transfer the container to the fridge, where the anchovies will keep for up to 3 weeks.

To serve, remove the anchovies from the oil and lay on a plate. Rinse the onion strips in water to soften the flavor and scatter them over the fish with the parsley. Drizzle with olive oil and season with salt and pepper.

Variation
This dish can also be made with the Salted anchovies on pages 90–91— just make sure you give them a good rinse under cold water and pat dry before use, and avoid adding any extra salt later.

SWEET MARINATED MACKEREL WITH BABY LEEKS

This recipe is from Anton Edelmann, who was head chef at the Savoy for 21 years. This is one of his mother's recipes. She used to make this dish using trout or herring when he was a child growing up in a small village in Bavaria, Germany. We thought it was quite easy to make and really delicious.

serves 4
2 small carrots, peeled and cut into
   thin slices
a bunch of baby leeks, trimmed with
   leaves removed but kept whole
2 shallots, peeled and finely sliced
5 tablespoons extra virgin olive oil
1 cup water
½ cup superfine sugar
1 cup apple cider vinegar
a sprig of thyme
4 juniper berries
1 bay leaf
4 medium mackerel, filleted
fine sea salt and freshly ground
   black pepper
1 teaspoon ground coriander
½ cup "00" or all-purpose flour
1 tablespoon golden raisins, soaked in
   water for 30 minutes
a small handful of chives, finely
   chopped

Blanch the carrots in boiling water for 3 minutes and the leeks for 2 minutes. Drain, refresh under cold running water and drain again once cold; set aside. Cook the shallots in 2 tablespoons of the olive oil over low heat until softened but still pale. Meanwhile, place the water, sugar, vinegar, thyme, juniper berries, and bay leaf in a saucepan and boil for 5 minutes; remove from the heat. Season the mackerel fillets with salt, pepper, and coriander and toss in the flour. Shake well to get rid of the excess.

Heat the remaining 3 tablespoons of olive oil in a nonstick frying pan. Add the mackerel fillets, skin-side down first, and fry until golden brown and just cooked through. Drain on paper towels. Combine the shallots, carrots, leeks, and golden raisins in a large dish and top with the fish. Strain the hot vinegar over the top, so the fillets are completely submerged, and then set aside to cool. Once cold, cover with plastic wrap and transfer to the fridge to marinate overnight. It will keep for 3 days.

Serve at room temperature: spoon the leeks onto a plate, top with the mackerel fillets and garnish with the carrots, golden raisins, shallots, and chives. Accompany with wheat toast.

SCANDINAVIAN PICKLED HERRINGS

"Silver darlings," as herrings were once known, have brought wealth, health, and prosperity to the shores of the UK from the Middle Ages right up until the present day. In Scotland, in particular, towns grew on their herring trade and railway lines were extended to places like Wick, Ullapool, and Mallaig to allow for their transportation south.

The Scandinavians and Dutch, too, ate and sold herrings in massive quantities, fishing for them in the Baltic Sea from the 10th century onward. It is said that Amsterdam was built on the bones of herrings and historian Jules Michelet referred to it as the place where "herring fishers transmuted their stinking cargo into gold."

Herrings are "pelagic," meaning they are continually on the move, similar to sardines and mackerel. And like them they are oily fish rich in omega 3, so they are really good for you. Herrings don't keep for long in their fresh form, which is why they are often preserved by being smoked, when they become known as "kippers," or pickled and stored in jars as they are in this recipe.

Herrings continued in popularity right up until the mid-20th century, so much so that they were overfished and stocks became dangerously low. However, we are now seeing quantities return to levels that are sustainable and for now, at least, we can enjoy them free from guilt. This Swedish recipe was given to me by Lotta Gustafsson. Pickled herrings are delicious served plain with toasted rye or pumpernickel bread, or hot boiled potatoes and hard-boiled eggs, or you can chop them up and serve them with the Dill, mustard and honey sauce on page 92.

serves 4 as a main course (or 8 as a starter)
2 cups distilled white vinegar
2½ quarts water
¾ cup fine sea salt
1 heaping tablespoon sugar
5½lbs herrings, filleted
1 small white onion, finely sliced into rings (optional)
Dill, mustard, and honey sauce (see page 92), to serve (optional)
1 tablespoon crème fraîche

Pour the vinegar and water into a large shallow dish, such as one you would use for lasagna, and stir in the salt and sugar to make a brine. Lay the fish and the onion rings (if using) in the liquid, making sure they are totally submerged. Cover the dish with plastic wrap and set aside to marinate in the fridge for 24 hours.

Drain the herrings and onions and either serve them plain or chop into bite-sized pieces and mix with the dill sauce, adding a couple of tablespoons crème fraîche. If you want to preserve them for longer, mix with the dill sauce (omitting the crème fraîche) and pack into sealed jars. Like this, they will keep in the fridge for up to 4 weeks.

CHUTNEY

Chutney, which derives from the Hindi word *chatni*, was traditionally used to describe the range of relishes that were brought back to Europe during the colonial era. The brand Major Grey was famous for its mango chutney during this time. Today chutneys take on various forms and the term is used to describe both a simple mixture of fresh ingredients to be eaten on the day, as well as slow-cooked fruit or vegetables sweetened with honey or sugar and preserved with vinegar.

TOMATO KASUNDI

This spicy Indian chutney also works as a quick sauce. My favorite way to serve it is heated with halved boiled eggs, dollops of Greek yogurt, and a generous scattering of cilantro. It is so tasty and pretty, I'm going to make three times the amount next time tomatoes are in season.

makes approx. 6 x 12-oz jars
6¾lbs ripe tomatoes
2 tablespoons black mustard seeds
2 tablespoons cumin seeds
7oz fresh ginger, peeled
3½oz garlic, peeled
2–3 red chiles, depending on the heat
  you prefer
1 tablespoon turmeric powder
⅔ quart malt vinegar
4 tablespoons sunflower oil
1 tablespoon salt
2½ cups light brown sugar

First prepare the tomatoes. Make a cross in the bottom of each tomato and remove the green core. Plunge into boiling water for 30 seconds–1 minute, remove with a slotted spoon and plunge immediately into very cold water. Peel off the skins, cut each tomato in half, scoop out the seeds, and set aside.

Toast the mustard seeds and cumin seeds in a dry pan for 3–4 minutes until they start to pop and release their aroma. Put them into a mortar and pestle and grind to a rough powder. Place the ginger, garlic, and chiles together in a food processor and blend to a coarse purée. Add the spices to the food processor along with approx. 1 cup of the vinegar and blend again.

Heat the sunflower oil in a heavy-bottomed pan, scoop in the paste, and cook for a few minutes to release the fragrance. Add the remaining vinegar with the salt and sugar followed by the tomatoes. Bring to a boil, stirring to dissolve the sugar, and then reduce the heat and simmer for approx. 2 hours, stirring occasionally to prevent it sticking on the bottom. The chutney is ready when it reaches the trail stage (see page 34). Taste and adjust the salt and chile as necessary before bottling into warm, sterilized jars. Once cold, seal with nonreactive lids and store in a cool, dark place for up to a year.

MRS. WISHDISH'S PLUM AND GINGER CHUTNEY

This recipe is adapted from Delia Smith's Spiced Plum Chutney in her *Complete Illustrated Cookery Course*. I noticed when making this with our friend, Mrs. Wishdish, that her recipe book is marked with lots of check marks made with a pencil so that she knows she has added that ingredient; she can then erase her markings next time she uses the recipe. Good idea, I thought. She and I decided to add a little heat in the form of red chile and some fresh ginger. We made this recipe together when the plums were ripe and falling from the trees in summer.

makes approx. 3 quarts
3⅓lbs firm, ripe plums
18oz apples (cooking apples are
  ideal but you can make the
  weight up with some of each)
3 large yellow onions
1⅓ quarts malt vinegar
2¼ cups dark brown sugar
2¼ cups raw sugar
12oz golden raisins
4 fat garlic cloves, peeled and grated
3oz fresh ginger, peeled and cut into
  short julienne strips
1 red chile, finely chopped
2 heaping tablespoons salt

For the spice bag
1oz allspice berries
2 teaspoons cloves
2 x 2in cinnamon sticks

Cut the plums into quarters, remove the pits, and discard. Core the apples and cut into small pieces, leaving the skin on, either using a sharp knife or in a food processor. Peel and chop the onions in the same way. Put the plums, apples, and onions in a large, heavy-bottomed saucepan along with the remaining ingredients (except the spices in the spice bag). Put the loose spices into a small spice bag or wrap in a piece of cheesecloth and tie with string. Fasten the spice bag onto the handle of the pan, letting it fall inside. Bring everything to a boil, stirring to dissolve the sugar, and simmer for 2–3 hours, stirring frequently to prevent sticking. When the chutney reaches the trail stage (see page 34), pour into warm, sterilized jars and seal immediately. Store in a cool, dark place and allow at least 3 months before tasting. Unopened, the chutney will keep for a year. Once opened, store in the fridge and consume within a month.

CHUTNEY-MAKING TIPS

Equipment

When some metals are combined with the acids in vinegar, fruit juices, and wine they can form an unpleasant taste. It is better to use glass, plastic, or stainless-steel pans, bowls, and utensils for chutney-making.

Use vinegar-proofed lids, which are usually plastic coated; never be tempted to reuse old lids if they are damaged or rusty.

Preserving or Maslin pans are wider at the top than the bottom to allow steam to escape from a large surface area, hastening the cooking of your chutney. They also have a heavy base so that your preserves don't burn easily.

It is a good idea to keep one large wooden spoon for chutney-making and another one for jam-making, so the flavors cannot be confused. My favorite spoon is one with a hook on it that stops it from falling into the pan.

Ingredients

Make sure vegetables and fruit are in perfect condition; if possible use them as soon as possible after harvesting.

Cut vegetables and fruit into similar-sized pieces so they have the same cooking time.

To peel ginger, scrape the skin off with a teaspoon.

Always use whole herbs and spices rather than ground ones; powdered spices tend to make the chutney go cloudy; whole spices are easy to pick out if necessary.

Spice bags, which can be bought online or from kitchen stores, are really useful and the advantage is they can be reused. To make your own spice bag, wrap your spices in a circle of cheesecloth and tie with string.

Bottling

Chutney is ready for bottling when it reaches the "trail stage." To test, draw a wooden spoon across the mixture in the pan and see if it leaves a furrow or trail; it should last for a few seconds before refilling with syrupy juices.

Bottle chutney immediately after it reaches the trail stage. Ladle through a jam funnel or pour from a sterilized pitcher into sterilized jars and seal immediately with vinegar-proofed sterilized lids.

Use sterilized jars and lids for chutney, always pouring hot chutney into a hot jar. For tips on sterilizing jars and bottles, see page 12.

When packing your chutney into the jar, make sure the fruit and vegetables are fully submerged in the sauce and not exposed to the air to prevent spoiling.

Fill the jars to ¼in from the top, which might seem quite high but the chutney will shrink.

Label all pickles and chutneys as soon as they are cool in the jars; you really won't remember what they are a few months later!

Tasting

Remember that flavors tend to mellow over time, so don't judge an acidic-tasting pickle immediately after cooking. As I have learned from experience, flavors really change in the jars. For best results, store them for at least 3 months before tasting.

Storing

Store chutneys and pickles in a cool, dark place.

GREEN TOMATO CHUTNEY

No matter what we do, we always seem to suffer with gluts of green tomatoes that simply refuse to be moved by the sun's rays to change their hue. I have tried frying them, inspired by the famous film's title, putting them into ratatouille or making them into soup—but their sharp and acidic personality seems to overpower everything else. At last, good news, I have tamed them by tempering them with spices and sweetness. This delicious sweet, and tangy chutney pairs with a wide variety of foods—from curries and cold meats to hot sausages or cheese. Our friend Vivien Lloyd adds bananas to her Green tomato chutney for sweetness.

makes 2½ quarts

3⅓lbs green tomatoes, skinned and roughly chopped into ½in dice
1¼lbs onions, peeled and roughly chopped into ½in dice
18oz cooking or eating apples, cores removed and cut into small pieces, leaving the skins on (it will be sweeter with the latter)
3 bananas, diced into ½in cubes (optional)
1½ quarts distilled white vinegar
1 tablespoon salt
2½ cups demerara sugar
1½ cups granulated sugar
1 red chile, finely chopped
3 fat garlic cloves, peeled and finely chopped
1 tablespoon ground ginger
3½oz preserved ginger, chopped into little cubes (see pages 74–75)

For the spice bag
3 star anise
10 cardamom pods, husks removed and seeds lightly crushed
1 teaspoon cloves
1 tablespoon allspice berries

Put the spices into a spice bag or wrap them in a piece of cheesecloth and fasten with string. Tie the bag onto the handle of a preserving pan, allowing the bag to hang inside. Put the remaining ingredients into the pan and bring to a boil, stirring to dissolve the sugar. Reduce the heat to a simmer and continue to cook for approx. 2–2½ hours until the chutney reaches the trail stage (see page 34). Bottle into warm, sterilized jars and put on the lids immediately. Store in a cool, dark place for at least 3 months before tasting. Unopened, the chutney will keep for a year. Once opened, keep in the fridge and consume within a month.

MANGO CHUTNEY

We eat a lot of mango chutney in our house and we are quite fussy about the brands we buy. We love it to be mild and sweet, but packed with flavor and spices, so it took a lot of trial runs before we were happy with this homemade version. Now we make it in big batches so there is always plenty for the five of us to enjoy. We enjoy it served with curry and sometimes with cheese, however my elderly father likes it with almost everything including eggs, soup, fish pie, and even Giancarlo's pasta with *ragù* —to his horror!

makes approx. 3¼lbs

6 firm but ripe mangoes (approx. 5¾lbs in weight)
1 medium onion, finely chopped
⅔ quart white wine vinegar
2oz fresh ginger, peeled and finely chopped
1 small dried chile, crushed
6 garlic cloves, peeled and finely chopped
1 teaspoon cloves
1 teaspoon cumin seeds
8 cardamom pods

1 tablespoon coriander seeds
good pinch of fenugreek seeds
2¾ cups light brown sugar
1 teaspoon salt, to taste
3 teaspoons poppy seeds (optional)

Peel the mangoes with a potato peeler and slice the flesh from the stone into approx. 1in pieces. Put the mango, onion, vinegar, ginger, chile, and garlic in a large, heavy-bottomed saucepan and cook over low heat for approx. 10 minutes.

Meanwhile, toast the spices (not including the poppy seeds) in a dry pan until they release their aroma. Put them immediately onto a plate to cool (don't leave them in the pan or they will continue cooking).

Once cold, grind the spices in a mortar and pestle or spice grinder to a coarse powder; remove the cardamom husks after they have released their seeds. Add the spices to the pan along with the sugar and salt. Bring to a boil, stirring to dissolve the sugar, and then reduce the heat and simmer gently for 2–3 hours or until the chutney reaches the trail stage (see page 34). Stir in the poppy seeds. Spoon into warm, sterilized jars and put on the lids immediately. Store in a cool, dark place and allow 3 months before tasting. Unopened, the chutney will keep for a year. Once opened, store in the fridge and consume within a month.

DEBI'S TOMATO, CHILE, AND GINGER JAM

A regular customer at Caldesi in Campagna, our restaurant in Bray, Debi Peppin told us about a chile jam she had bought at a farmers' market and loved. She was never able to find the stallholder again, so she ended up developing her own recipe. Debi serves the jam with grilled halloumi, on a cheese board, with cold meat or with fried chicken. She gave us the recipe and it is so good we now keep a jar permanently in our fridge. Every time I serve it people ask me for the recipe, so here it is.

makes approx. ⅔ quart
2¼ cups superfine sugar
½ cup water
16 medium tomatoes
½ cup white wine vinegar
4 medium red chiles, seeded and chopped
2oz fresh ginger, peeled and finely chopped
2 teaspoons fine sea salt

Dissolve the sugar in the water over medium heat in a large, heavy-bottomed saucepan. Meanwhile prepare the tomatoes. Make a cross in each one at either end. Drop them into boiling water for 1 minute, or until the skins start to split, and then remove them with a slotted spoon and peel. Discard the green cores and dice the flesh into ½in cubes. Remove most of the seeds, but don't worry about some of them being included.

Add the tomatoes to the sugar syrup in the pan, pour in the vinegar, and add the chile and ginger. Season with salt and pepper. Bring to a boil, stirring, and then reduce the heat and simmer for 30–45 minutes or until the jam reaches the trail stage (see page 34). Spoon into warm, sterilized jars and seal immediately. Put on the lids and store in a cool, dark place for up to a year. Once opened, keep in the fridge.

DAWID'S SWEET CHILE JAM

Dawid Bakowski is the patisserie chef at our restaurant, Caldesi in Campagna. He is a real stickler for detail and loves to do things properly—including cutting the chiles for this recipe by hand, which not only takes time but must also sting your hands and eyes. However, he likes the fact that all the little pieces of chile end up almost the same size, which you could never achieve in a food processor. If you do follow his method, make sure you wear protective gloves.

Note: Do taste the chiles first to gauge their strength, as it is impossible to tell the difference between a blow-your-socks-off chile and a mild, sweet and cuddly one just by looking at them. This recipe is meant to be hot, so adjust your chiles accordingly by adding some dried chile flakes if they are particularly mild in flavor.

makes approx. 1 quart
1⅓lbs long medium-hot red chiles
1 quart malt vinegar
1 tablespoon finely grated fresh ginger
2 tablespoons tomato paste
6 cups light brown sugar

Remove the stalks and tips of the chiles. To seed them, roll them between your palms with the tips facing down. Chop the chiles by hand or, if Dawid isn't looking, put them into a food processor and work until finely chopped. Place the chopped chiles in a heavy-bottomed saucepan with the remaining ingredients and set over medium heat, stirring to dissolve the sugar. Simmer for 2–3 hours, stirring occasionally to stop everything sticking, or until the trail stage is reached (see page 34). Spoon into warm, sterilized jars and seal immediately. Store in a cool, dark place for up to a year. Once opened, keep in the fridge.

DRAGON CHICKEN

This is our younger son Flavio's recipe for his favorite way of cooking spicy chicken. It is one of my favorites too, as it is so easy—in fact, every member of my family likes it. We serve it with a simple vegetable stir-fry and noodles. When I asked Flavio why it should be called Dragon chicken, he told me to say: "Enjoy it or a dragon will come and get you!" You can't argue with that.

serves 6

1¼lbs lean chicken (preferably a mixture of thigh and breast meat), cut into bite-sized pieces
1 garlic clove, peeled and finely chopped or 1 heaping teaspoon Garlic relish (see page 21)
4 tablespoons extra virgin olive or vegetable oil
1 teaspoon pink or black peppercorns, crushed
1 heaping tablespoon Dawid's sweet chile jam (page 37)

Put all the ingredients in a bowl and mix together thoroughly. Cover the bowl with plastic wrap and set aside to marinate in the fridge for up to an hour (preferably overnight).

To cook the chicken pieces, either put them into a nonstick frying pan with a little oil or thread them onto skewers and cook under a hot broiler for about 15 minutes until cooked through and golden.

PAPA'S BANANA AND DATE CHUTNEY

"Soft and sweet and easy to eat": this is my 88-year-old father's mantra. He could eat oodles of this chutney, as well as the mango one, on almost anything. We find the mellowness of the fruit marries beautifully with hot curries. This is a great way to use up overripe bananas that are turning brown.

makes approx. 2¼–2¾lbs

9oz cooking apples, peeled and roughly chopped
7oz white or yellow onions, peeled and roughly chopped
1 cup malt vinegar
8 ripe bananas (approx. 1⅔lbs), peeled and roughly chopped
3½oz preserved ginger, finely chopped
1 cup dark brown sugar
9oz pitted dates, roughly chopped
1 teaspoon fine sea salt
½ cup water

For the spice bag
4 allspice berries
1 small cinnamon stick
4 cloves
2 pieces of orange peel

Put the apples and onions in a large, heavy-bottomed saucepan, pour in the vinegar, and cook over low to medium heat until soft, approx. 20 minutes. Stir in the remaining ingredients and bring to a boil, stirring to dissolve the sugar. Reduce the heat to a simmer and bubble away gently for 1–2 hours or until the chutney reaches the trail stage (see page 34). Spoon into warm, sterilized jars and put on the lids immediately. Store in a cool, dark place for up to a year. Once opened, keep in the fridge and consume within a month.

APPLE AND GINGER CHUTNEY

A great way to use up windfall. Eating apples are fine to use and will give a sweeter result.

makes approx. 4½lbs

2¼lbs cooking or eating apples
12oz onions
1oz garlic cloves
3½oz golden raisins
3½oz fresh ginger
½ tablespoon salt
3 cups apple cider vinegar
3 cups dark brown sugar

For the pickling spice
4 teaspoons coriander seeds
1 teaspoon mustard seeds
1 teaspoon fennel seeds or aniseed
6 cloves
2 teaspoons black peppercorns
2 teaspoons cumin seeds

Peel, core, and chop the apples, cutting away any bruised areas. Peel the onions and garlic and chop finely. Mince or chop the golden raisins. Peel and grate the ginger. Put the pickling spices into a piece of cheesecloth. Tie the cheesecloth up and add it to a large un-lidded preserving pan with the chopped apples, onion, garlic, ginger, salt, and golden raisins. Pour in the apple cider vinegar.

Bring the pan slowly to a boil, reduce the heat, and simmer gently until the contents of the pan are pulpy and soft, stirring occasionally. Add the sugar and dissolve it carefully. Continue to cook gently until you reach the trail stage (see page 34). This will take about 1½–2 hours. Stir frequently to prevent the chutney sticking to the bottom of the pan.

Remove the pan from the heat, and ladle the chutney into a glass or plastic pitcher. Pour the chutney into hot, sterilized jars and seal immediately. Store in the pantry for 2–3 months before opening and consume within a year. Once opened keep in the fridge.

SPICED RED ONION MARMALADE

This Anglo-Sri-Lankan recipe is based on the flavors of British red onion marmalade and *Sini Sambal*, a spicy condiment eaten with Sri Lankan hoppers and curry. It is also a good sweet partner to

sharp Cheddar and goat cheese. I also use it to enrich gravies. The Sri Lankans use tamarind paste but we found that chopped prunes added the same rich body and tang.

To limit unnecessary crying, you can use a food processor for speed to chop up the onions but open the doors. While the chutney was cooking, our house filled with the smell of spices, and the end product was well worth a few tears.

makes approx. 4½lbs
6 tablespoons sunflower oil
4½lbs red onions, peeled and thinly sliced
7oz prunes, diced into 1cm cubes
⅓ quart balsamic vinegar
1⅔ cups water
4 level teaspoons fine sea salt
1 cup dark brown sugar
1–2 dried red chiles, to taste
2in cinnamon stick

Heat the oil in a large preserving pan and gently cook the onions over low heat until soft and translucent, approx. 1½ hours, partially covered. Stir them frequently to stop them burning or sticking to the bottom. You can add a little more oil to prevent them from burning, but the key to successful onion marmalade is slow cooking to maximize the sweetness of the onions.

Add the remaining ingredients and bring to a boil, stirring to dissolve the sugar. Immediately after it comes to a boil, reduce the heat to a simmer and bubble very gently for 30–45 minutes or until the chutney reaches the trail stage (see page 34). Taste for seasoning; remember the vinegar taste will subside with time. Spoon into warm, sterilized jars and put on the lids immediately. Store in a cool dark place for up to a year; taste after at least 3 months. Once opened, store in the fridge and consume within 1 month.

ZUCCHINI AND RED PEPPER CHUTNEY

This is a good all-rounder of a chutney—you can bring it to the table with cold meats, serve it with grilled fish, or burgers and dollop it onto cheese sandwiches and it will never let you down. Every year one of our neighbors puts a little table outside her driveway, topped with zucchini from the surplus in her garden in summer. This year our children carried a few home for us, despite the weight, as they couldn't believe you could get something for free! As we already had our fair share of zucchini in our garden, I wasn't overjoyed with more but then I worked on this recipe. By grating the zucchini in the food processor, we soon had chutney where there had previously been huge green monster vegetables.

makes approx. 4½lbs
3⅓lbs zucchini
3 red bell peppers
1 large red onion, peeled and finely chopped
⅔ quart white wine vinegar
1 tablespoon allspice berries, lightly crushed
1 tablespoon black peppercorns, lightly crushed
1½ cups superfine sugar

Cut the ends off the zucchini and peel them. Grate the flesh in a food processor using the grater attachment or by hand. Cut the red bell peppers into ½in dice, discarding the pith and seeds. Place all the ingredients in a large, heavy-bottomed saucepan and bring to a boil, stirring to dissolve the sugar. Simmer gently for 2½–3 hours or until the chutney reaches the trail stage (see page 34), stirring occasionally to prevent sticking. Spoon into warm, sterilized jars and put on the lids immediately. Store in a cool, dark place for up to a year. Taste after

3 months and keep in the fridge once opened.

PICCALILLI

Piccalilli, or "Paco-Lilla" or Indian Pickle as it was also known, can be traced back to a cookbook by Mrs. Raffald published in 1772. It is based on a traditional Indian pickle and the name could be a mixture of "pickle" and "chile."

This is a great way to use up surplus vegetables, which are kept crisp in the sauce rather than being cooked until soft. Mrs. Raffald recommends: "You may put in fresh pickles, as things come into season, and keep them covered with vinegar." However, I think it is safer to make it in one go—although her method does demonstrate you can happily alter the ingredients to suit whatever is in season.

makes approx. 3⅓lbs
2¼lbs mixed vegetables such as cauliflower, green beans, cucumber, zucchini, pearl onions, peppers, carrots
3 tablespoons fine sea salt
⅔ quart white wine vinegar
1½ cups superfine sugar
¼ cup cornstarch
¼ cup turmeric powder
¼ cup English mustard powder
1 teaspoon ground coriander
2 tablespoons ground ginger

Peel the vegetables and chop them into even bite-sized pieces. Imagine eating the finished pickle in a sandwich and you will gauge the size of each piece correctly. Layer the vegetables in a plastic or glass bowl, sprinkling each layer with salt. Using your hands, mix everything together to ensure the vegetables are evenly covered, and then cover the bowl with a dish towel. Set aside in a cool place overnight.

The following day, wash the

vegetables under plenty of cold running water and set aside to drain. Meanwhile, pour the vinegar into a large saucepan, add the sugar, and stir over medium heat until dissolved. Combine the cornstarch with the spices in a small bowl, pour in a ladleful of the hot vinegar and mix to a smooth paste. Scoop the paste into the saucepan and whisk thoroughly to remove any lumps. Bring to a boil, stirring, and then reduce the heat. Simmer for approx. 8 minutes, stirring frequently. Remove the pan from the heat and carefully fold in the drained vegetables so they are evenly coated in the sauce. Spoon into warm, sterilized jars, topping up with the hot sauce so the vegetables are completely submerged. Put on the lids immediately. Store in a cool, dark place for up to a year. Taste after at least 6 weeks. Once opened, keep in the fridge and consume within a month.

SALLY DAVIDSON'S RATHER SPECIAL LEMON CHUTNEY

Sally makes chutney for her local farmers' market in Ruislip, Middlesex. I love her produce and asked her for this lovely lemon chutney recipe. It is great with fish such as salmon or trout, but also with chicken curry. I warned you at the beginning of this section not to judge your chutney until it has had time to mature, and this is especially true with this one. The lemons really mellow after a couple of months, so be patient and wait for at least 3 months before tasting.

makes 3lbs
4 large organic lemons
8oz onions
1⅓ tablespoons fine sea salt
2 cups apple cider vinegar
3½oz golden raisins

1 oz mustard seeds or roughly crushed coriander seeds
1 teaspoon cayenne pepper
1 heaping teaspoon finely chopped red chile
2 cups demerara sugar

Wipe the lemons with a damp cloth but don't wash them. Chop finely, skins and all, removing the seeds as you see them. Peel and finely chop the onions. Combine the lemons and onions in a plastic or glass bowl, sprinkle with the salt and set aside in the fridge overnight.

The following day, put the contents of the bowl into a preserving pan and cook over medium heat for 15–20 minutes until the onions are soft but the lemons still have a little bite to the them. (If the pan starts to dry out, add a little water if necessary.) Add the remaining ingredients and simmer for 1 hour, stirring occasionally, until the chutney reaches the trail stage (see page 34). Spoon the hot chutney into warm, sterilized jars and seal immediately. Store in a cool, dark place for 6–9 months. Refrigerate once opened and consume within a month.

CORN RELISH

As a child I used to love corn in sandwiches with Cheddar cheese and sliced tomatoes. Now we eat it with homemade hamburgers or sausages. The sweetness is great with grilled meat, chicken, or vegetables. We grow corn in our garden at home and I can't believe how different and sweet it tastes when it is cooked straight from the plant.

Note: This is another relish that really mellows with time. After 3 months in the jar the sweetness of the corn will really come through.

makes 4lbs
6 cobs of corn
2 teaspoons mustard seeds
2 teaspoons cumin seeds
1 dried red chile
1 teaspoon allspice berries
4 ripe but firm, medium tomatoes, diced into ½in cubes
1 green bell pepper, diced into ½in cubes
1 red bell pepper, diced into ½in cubes
1 medium onion, finely chopped
2 garlic cloves, peeled and finely chopped
1 apple, core removed and diced into ½in cubes
2 cups distilled white vinegar
1 cup superfine sugar
approx. 1 teaspoon fine sea salt, to taste

Boil the cobs in plenty of salted water for 8–10 minutes or until just tender. Remove from the pan and set aside to cool.

Meanwhile, toast the mustard and cumin seeds in a dry frying pan for 2 minutes until they pop and release their aroma. Put into a mortar and pestle or spice grinder and grind them with the dried chile and allspice berries to a fine powder.

Remove the kernels from the corn with a sharp knife by cutting downward onto a board. Scoop them into a large, heavy-bottomed saucepan and add the remaining ingredients. Bring to a boil, stirring to dissolve the sugar, and then reduce the heat. Simmer for about an hour until the relish reaches the trail stage (see page 34). Bottle immediately into warm, sterilized jars and put on the lids. The relish will keep for up to a year in a cool, dark place. Wait at least 3 months before trying it and store in the fridge once opened.

MISCELLANEOUS

CHINESE PLUM SAUCE

This is my take on the classic Chinese sauce. According to my Chinese friends, I will never make it like they do back home in China because our plums are completely different. However, we love to make this sauce with a mixture of Victoria plums and the little wild ones that grow near our home. We cooked our version in the oven because we wanted to concentrate the flavor of the plums without burning them. Any slight caramelization adds to the flavor.

makes 2 x 12-oz jars
18oz ripe plums of your choice
1 cup dark brown sugar
2 tablespoons grated fresh ginger
½ dried red chile
1 teaspoon fine sea salt
1 fat garlic clove, peeled and finely grated
1 small onion, peeled and finely chopped
2 star anise
1 small cinnamon stick
2 tablespoons soy sauce
2 tablespoons rice wine or red wine vinegar

Preheat the oven to 350°F. Wash and quarter the plums, discarding the pits. Put them in an ovenproof dish and bake in the oven for 45 minutes. (If you prefer, you can do this on the stove in a heavy-bottomed saucepan over low heat, however keep an eye on them in case they stick, in which case add a few tablespoons water.)

Pass the roasted plums through a sieve to remove the skins. Put the plum purée into a preserving pan with the remaining ingredients and bring to a boil, stirring to dissolve the sugar.

Reduce the heat to a simmer and cook very slowly for 1 hour, stirring frequently, until it reaches the trail stage (see page 34). Spoon into warm, sterilized jars and seal. Store in a cool dark place for up to a year. Wait at least 4 months before tasting and store in the fridge once opened.

MUSHROOM KETCHUP

This curious condiment has been in use in the UK for centuries. It can be added to recipes almost anywhere you see soy or Worcestershire sauce mentioned. It works a little like a liquid flavor enhancer, offering a kick of umami where it is needed such as in gravies, stir-fries, beef stews, or simply drizzled over grilled steak or lamb. The choice of flavorings is up to you—I sometimes include a touch of lemon zest or a little grated ginger for a bit of punch, and it is equally delicious. For a really intense mushroom flavor, use your own home-dried mushrooms (see page 126), preferably porcini.

make approx. 6oz
2¾lbs fresh, flavorful mushrooms such as portabello or crimini
1 tablespoon fine sea salt
⅔oz (2 large handfuls) dried porcini and/or crimini mushrooms
⅔ cup cold water
1 white or yellow onion, finely chopped
1 cup malt or apple cider vinegar
a small sprig of rosemary
2in cinnamon stick
5 cloves
5 allspice berries

Do not wash the fresh mushrooms but wipe them clean, and then roughly chop into 1in pieces. Put them in a plastic, glass, or stainless-steel bowl and sprinkle over the salt, tossing it through with your hands. Cover with a small plate and set aside in a cool place for 24 hours. Meanwhile, place the dried mushrooms in a bowl with the water and set aside to rehydrate in a cool place overnight, covered.

The following day, place all the mushrooms along with their juices in a heavy-bottomed saucepan. Add the remaining ingredients and bring to a boil, stirring. Reduce the heat and simmer over low heat for 30 minutes, covered. Remove from the heat and set aside to cool overnight, covered with a dish towel.

The following day, strain the mushroom mixture through a sieve lined with cheesecloth into a clean saucepan. Squeeze out as much of the liquid as you can from the cheesecloth. Place the saucepan over medium heat and allow the liquid to reduce by one-third. Taste and adjust the seasoning if necessary. Pour into warm, sterilized bottles. If you are going to keep the ketchup for longer that 2 months, you should waterbath the bottle for 10 minutes at this stage (see page 253). Alternatively, store in the fridge and consume within 2 months.

TOMATO KETCHUP

The word "catsup" comes from the Chinese *ke-tsiap*, a term used to describe a brine leftover from pickling fish. In Europe, catsup has been made for centuries using the leftover vinegary brine from pickled walnuts and mushrooms. However, it was the Americans who first added tomatoes to their catsup and a man called Joshua Davenport from Massachusetts who became the first person to add sugar. He bravely added two cups of sugar to a gallon of tomato stock and half a pint of flavored vinegar and began to sell it. Now ketchup is a worldwide phenomenon.

We love making our own ketchup at home, and enjoy playing with the sweetness and spices. Do use the best flavored tomatoes you can find, as this will affect the final flavor. I often end up using a mixture of cherry and large tomatoes, with any bruised parts cut away.

makes approx. 18oz

4½lbs ripe but not soft tomatoes, cut in half if large
18oz white or yellow onions, roughly chopped
2 celery stalks
1½oz fresh ginger, peeled and grated
4 garlic cloves, peeled
2 teaspoons fine sea salt, or to taste
½ cup superfine or granulated sugar
3 tablespoons apple cider or red wine vinegar

For the spice bag
1 teaspoon cloves
1 teaspoon allspice berries
2in cinnamon stick
6 cardamom pods

Put the tomatoes in a food processor with the onions, celery, ginger, and garlic. Pulse until roughly chopped—you may have to work in batches—or chop by hand with a knife. Scoop the contents into a large preserving pan, add the salt and bring to a boil.

Meanwhile, put the spices into a spice bag (see page 34) and give them a bash with a rolling pin to lightly crush them. Add the spice bag to the simmering tomatoes. As soon as the tomato mixture starts to bubble, reduce the heat and simmer gently for 1–1½ hours, stirring frequently, or until the vegetables are soft.

Pass the softened tomato mixture through a food mill or sieve to get rid of the tomato skins, seeds, and cores; discard. Pour the strained juice back into the preserving pan, stir in the sugar and vinegar, and return to the heat. Bring to a boil, stirring to dissolve the sugar, and then reduce the heat to very low and let the ketchup bubble away gently for about an hour, stirring frequently so it doesn't stick on the bottom of the pan. The sauce should reduce in this time by about half to leave a bright red, thick velvety sauce. Taste and add more salt or sugar if you feel it needs it. Pour into warm, sterilized bottles and seal immediately. (If you want to keep the ketchup longer than 3 months, it is safest to waterbath the warm bottles for 10 minutes at this stage, see page 253.) Alternatively, store in a dark, cool place for up to 3 months. Once open, store in the fridge and consume within a month.

sugar

Afternoon tea may be more of a chic treat these days than a regular meal for most families, but that hasn't stopped our love of jams, particularly homemade. And breakfast just isn't right without marmalade—I have even got Giancarlo eating it on toast before he goes to work after years of skipping the first meal of the day. And, of course, there are so many other things you can do with fruit and sugar, from making cordials and syrups to sauces. Our favorite quick dessert is homemade Greek-style yogurt layered with raspberry sauce and sliced bananas: simple and utterly delicious.

According to Sue Shephard's brilliant and fascinating book, *Pickled, Potted and Canned*: "The earliest kind of jam-making dates back to pre-Roman times when fruit pulp was mixed with honey and spices and dried in the sun." The Greeks followed suit in the first century AD by stuffing peeled quinces into jars filled with honey. After a year they became soft and the resulting treat was known as *melomeli*. Many centuries later this transformed into *marmelada*, a quince preserve made by the Portuguese with sugar and flavored with rosewater. In the 16th century, wooden boxes of *marmelada* were transported to England where the locals reproduced the idea, using other fruits such as damsons, plums, and pears. Eventually, oranges became the main fruit of choice, and the name of the preserve became marmalade.

It wasn't until the 17th and 18th centuries that people started to make preserves on a larger scale, as sugar became available and affordable to a wide population.

JAM

The word "jam" appeared in a cookbook by Mrs. Eales in 1718 in which she described apricot, raspberry, and cherry jams. *The Oxford English Dictionary* suggests that the word may have come from the process of jamming—i.e. bruising or crushing fruit. It also suggests that it may have derived from the French *j'aime*, meaning "I love," which is what might have been said about this delicious substance! At some point in Britain, the division was made between preserves made with citrus (marmalade) and other fruit/sugar concoctions (jam)—whereas the rest of continental Europe tend to retain one term for all sweet preserves, for example *mermelada* in Spain, *confiture* in France, and *marmellata* in Italy.

In the US and Canada, "jelly" also became a term that commonly referred to a fruit preserve, although strictly speaking a jelly is made by crushing fruit and straining out everything but the fruit, while jam is simply made from crushed fruit. In jellies, the juice is boiled and sugar and pectin are added to create a thicker consistency for spreading. Jams often contain less pectin and sometimes none at all as the mashed fruit provides a good thickness for spreading.

One of the defining specifications for jams and related products is the total sugar content. This includes the sugar present in the fruit and the sugar added through cane sugar or concentrates and syrups. The FDA considers jams and preserves to be the same thing and rules that they must contain at least 55 percent sugar and 45 percent fruit. If a product contains less sugar, then it is not considered a jam or a preserve but a fruit spread. Similarly, a jelly must contain at least 65 percent sugar and be made with fruit juices or concentrates.

In the UK, however, the ratios are a little different. In 1929 the Agriculture and Food Research Centre produced a book called *Home Preservation of Fruit and Vegetables*. This was based on a study of sugar-based preserves conducted by a research center in Bristol, England, and is still regarded as the bible of preserving fruit and vegetables today. It was the AFRC that came up with the 60/40 percent ratio of sugar to fruit that is necessary to keep jam out of the fridge and today in the UK, by law, "jams" must contain 60 percent sugar (including natural fruit sugars of up to 5 percent). As this allows jams to be made with a good shelf life and pure fruit flavors, it is with these guidelines in mind that we have written this book.

how jam works

The idea of jam-making is to stop the natural decay of fruit due to microorganisms, so that you can enjoy it for months ahead. To find out more about the science behind the process and how to avoid problems, please read the information below.

Here is the process in a nutshell:
First you cook the fruit. During this time, moisture is evaporated away in the perfumed clouds of steam that are produced, concentrating sugar levels. The high concentration of sugar that results, along with the acid from the fruit, creates an environment that is inhospitable to bacteria. Next the jam is boiled, destroying any microorganisms. Finally it is bottled in sterilized airtight jars; the vacuum prevents the regrowth of bacteria and yeasts.

calculating the ratio of fruit to sugar

Experimenting or playing with fruit and sugar is fun, simple, and very tasty. If you take fruit and start mixing it gradually with sugar, you will go through many stages and create many delicious combinations—from simple sweetened fruit to fruit coulis and low-sugar jams. However, until you reach a ratio of 60/40 sugar to fruit, the sugar is simply acting as a sweetener and flavor enhancer, not a preservative. Since bacteria find it hard to flourish in an environment that is this acidic and high in sugar, preserves made with at least 60 percent sugar can be bottled and left out of the fridge. Typically jams are made with equal or near equal quantities of sugar and fruit; after boiling the sugar levels increase as the moisture is evaporated off so that they end up closer to 60 percent. This includes an amount of fructose, the natural sugar from the fruit.

Of course, if you want to increase the ratio of fruit to sugar that is fine, it's just that you will have to store your produce in the fridge. This applies to low-sugar jams (see page 56), which should either be made in small batches and kept in the fridge or freezer, or heat-treated after bottling (see page 52) to extend their shelf-life.

tips on jam-making

Once you start making preserves, it is more than likely that you will find yourself hooked. Of course, most of us make jam for our own enjoyment and we are not too fussed about winning competitions, but if you want to take your jam-making to the next level here are some tips from jam-making expert Vivien Lloyd, who teaches jam judges how to judge for the Women's Institute:

1) **CHOOSE A GOOD RECIPE**. According to Vivien Lloyd, many beginners win prizes with a good recipe while many experienced jam-makers fail to succeed with a bad one.

2) **COOKING THE FRUIT**. This should be done over low heat to drive off water before adding the sugar. Cooking times vary between 10 minutes for raspberries to up to 2 hours for oranges.

3) **ACHIEVING A GOOD SET**. The point at which you add the sugar to form a "gel" is key in jam-making. For best results, the sugar should be added after the fruit has been cooked thoroughly to avoid toughening it. Keep the heat low to begin with, stirring to dissolve the sugar. Only once the sugar has completely dissolved should you increase the heat to a rolling boil. As a rule of thumb, boil the fruit and sugar together for as little time as possible to discourage any caramelization of the sugar that could darken the jam—Vivien suggests 5–7 minutes. Obviously large quantities will take longer to reach setting point, however Vivien suggests making jam in small batches so you reach setting point more quickly, in a matter of minutes, as this results in a better flavor and color.

jam jars and lids

Most of the time it is fine to reuse old jam jars as long as they are washed thoroughly and sterilized before use (see page 12). Providing the lids are in perfect condition, all you need to do is sterilize them first by boiling them for 10 minutes. If your lids are rusty or you have lost them, you can always seal your jars with cellophane lids instead. If using cellophane lids, make sure you cover the surface of the jam first with wax paper, wax-side down. To create a good seal, wet one side of

the cellophane only and put it on top of the jar, wet-side up. Secure tightly with elastic bands or ribbon.

The only time I wouldn't recommend recycling jars is if you plan to waterbath your produce after bottling, since most don't have thick enough glass to withstand heat-processing. For this, my advice is to buy Mason jars (or similar) that come with two-part lids with a metal disk that you replace each time. This is held in place with a screw band that is fitted after the disk has formed a good seal. For more information on waterbathing, see page 252.

perfect produce

As with all forms of preservation, choose fruit and vegetables in tip-top condition, as bruised and damaged foods are more likely to harbor spoilers. For best results, choose ripe (but not overripe) fruit, since unripe will affect the sugar levels of your finished product. Ideally, fruit should be processed as quickly as possible after picking.

acidity

Acid helps bring out the pectin in fruits, which is needed to achieve a good set. Most fruits are naturally high in acid, however those that are not can be helped along by adding lemon juice or citric acid—recipes for strawberry preserve, for example, always contain added lemon juice. In order to extract as much pectin as possible, make sure you add the acid at the start of the recipe while the fruit is cooking, before you put in the sugar. This should speed up the setting process, so that you avoid the caramelization and subsequent darkening of the sugar that occurs with excessive boiling. As a rule of thumb, allow 3 percent lemon juice to your weight of low-acid fruit.

FRUIT	PECTIN	ACID
Apples (cooking)	High	High
Apples (dessert)	Medium	Low
Apricots	Medium	Low
Blackberries (early)	Medium	Low
Blackberries (late)	Low	Low
Black currants	High	High
Cherries (dessert)	Low	Low
Cherries (tart)	Medium	High
Cherries (sweet)	Low	Low
Citrus fruits	High-Medium	High-Medium
Crabapples	High	High
Cranberries (ripe)	High	Medium
Currants (red, black, and white)	High	High
Damsons	High	High
Elderberries	Low	Low
Figs	Low	Low
Gooseberries	High	High
Grapes (unripe)	Medium	Medium
Greengages	Medium	Medium
Loganberries	Medium	High
Nectarines	Low	Low
Peaches	Low	Low
Pears	Low	Low
Plums (sweet)	Medium	Medium
Plums (tart)	High	High
Quince	High	Low
Raspberries (ripe)	Medium	Medium
Raspberries (unripe)	Medium	Low
Rhubarb	Low	Low
Sloes	Medium	High
Strawberries	Low	Low

THE PECTIN TEST

To determine the amount of pectin in your fruit, remove 1 teaspoon of the cooked juice only (with no seeds or fruit pieces) from the simmered fruit and put into a small jar or ramekin. Add 1 tablespoon of denatured alcohol and swirl them both together.

If the mixture comes together into a jellified lump, the juice is high in pectin; if it forms small clumps, the juice has medium levels of pectin; if it forms tiny lumps or no lumps at all, your fruit is low in pectin.

pectin

Pectin is needed to make jam, jellies, and marmalade set. It occurs naturally in fruit and is released during cooking. Pectin levels are high in underripe fruit as well as specific types, such as apple, citrus fruit, quince, and damsons, which are all quite sour to the taste, as they are all high in acid too. These fruits have no problem setting and are therefore good to mix with low-pectin or low-acid fruits or they can be made into stock to add to your jam at a later stage.

We discovered in Pam Corbin's book, *Preserves*, that there is less pectin in the seeds of fruit than in the pith and peel. Many recipes tell you to collect the seeds of the fruit when making marmalade to put into a bag and boil up with the fruit while Pam suggests you discard them. We put this to the test and couldn't see any difference between the batch of marmalade with seeds in and the one without. However the choice is yours.

making your own pectin stock

Homemade pectin stock is very easy to make and useful for adding to low-pectin fruits such as strawberries, pineapple, and passion fruit. It is made from the juice extracted from high-pectin fruits such as apples, crabapples, gooseberries, and red currants. You can use commercial liquid pectin instead, but we prefer not to because it contains sulfur dioxide.

HOMEMADE PECTIN STOCK

This is made in the same way as fruit jelly and strained afterward to obtain a stock. Apples and crabapples make a slightly murky stock. Red currants leave a clear stock. To calculate the amount needed, allow ½ cup pectin stock for every 18oz low-pectin fruit.

2¼lbs of each the following or a mixture of cooking or crabapples, gooseberries, and red currants
1–1½ quarts water (enough to cover the fruit)

Chop the fruit into bite-sized pieces (including the peel and core, but discarding the stems). Put in a saucepan and cover with the water. Put a lid on the pan and bring to a boil, and then simmer until the fruit is really soft and pulpy, up to 1 hour.

Transfer the pulp to a jelly bag and set aside to hang for at least 5 hours (preferably overnight), covering with a dish towel to keep out fruit flies. The following day, measure out the clear juice (your pectin stock) and use immediately, or freeze in small amounts, allowing ½ cup pectin stock per 18oz low-pectin fruit used in the recipe.

sugar

We prefer our cooking to be as natural as possible, therefore we use pure sugar and fruit in most of the recipes. We prefer to use granulated cane sugar for jam-making.

Preserving sugars, in our opinion, are an unnecessary expense and our recipes are not designed to use them. Jam sugar has added pectin, which gives the jam an uncharacteristically bright color and also changes the flavor—the resulting jam often doesn't have a cooked fruit flavor. Be aware that it can make the jam too firm in consistency and it does leave an aftertaste.

Often the sugar is warmed beforehand in an oven: this is useful because it means the sugar will dissolve more quickly and come to a boil rapidly.

TESTING FOR A SET

There are three ways of checking for a set: the flake test, the cold saucer test, and the thermometer test. In my opinion, the temperature test is the least reliable method, although it is helpful as a guide alongside the other methods.

The flake test

I tend to use this method. Dip a wooden spoon into the jam and then hold it above the surface. Twist it three times and watch the drops. Do they fall frequently as individual drops or do they slowly come together into one large, long drip? If the latter is the case, your jam will set.

The cold saucer test

Put a saucer or small plate into the

It is vital that the sugar is completely dissolved before you bring your jam to the boil or it could crystallize.

setting points

Three things are needed to achieve a good set: pectin, sugar, and acid. Setting point is reached after the rolling boil stage—this is when the heat is high and the bubbles are foamy, plentiful, and cover the surface. If you put a spoon through the surface the bubbles don't stop.

When checking for a set, always remove the jam from the heat as those vital few minutes may result in overcooked jam. If necessary, you can always put the jam back on the heat again afterward if you are not there yet. You can repeat this process until

freezer until chilled. When you feel you are close to setting point, drip a few drops of jam onto the cold saucer. Return it to the freezer and wait a couple of minutes. Remove the plate from the freezer and push your finger across the surface. If wrinkles form, your jam has reached setting point.

The temperature test

Take the temperature of your jam using a digital thermometer. Supposedly, if it reads 220°F your jam will set, however I have read this temperature in the past in a very liquid-looking jam and found that it didn't set. Saying that, it certainly shouldn't be lower than this temperature, so use this method as a guide only and double-check using the flake or cold saucer method.

you are confident you have reached setting point.

Never continue with the rolling boil for more than 15 minutes—if you reach 10 minutes and you haven't achieved a set, there is probably something wrong with your ingredients. Overboiling ruins the fresh flavor of most jams and also caramelizes the sugar, resulting in a darker jam with a bitter taste. A runny jam can always be used as a sauce for ice cream or yogurt.

when to bottle and when to waterbath?

Waterbathing is a form of heat-processing that is carried out after bottling to extend the shelf-life of certain preserves, especially ones that are low in sugar (see page 48). If you follow the 60/40 rule (that is, 60 percent sugar to 40 percent fruit), there is no need to waterbath jam after bottling. The only time you need to waterbath is if you reduce the quantity of sugar to under 60 percent and plan to store your produce outside of the fridge.

bottling

Have your jars, lids, and jam funnel sterilized and hot before you start to make jam (see page 12). When setting point is reached (see above) it is time to bottle your jam.

Have a ladle in the jam for the last few minutes so that it sterilizes in the jam. Some jams need to be left to settle before bottling—if this is the case, we have stated it in the recipe.

Remove any scum before bottling. I find the best method is to allow the jam to settle in the pan for 5 minutes to form a skin, and then simply scrape it back with a sterilized spoon and discard. Remove the jam from the heat and take out your first warmed jar, put the funnel into the jar and ladle out the jam into the jar. Some people prefer to use a pitcher for this, in which case you need to sterilize that in the oven too and hold it firmly with a cloth. Fill to the neck of the jar and put on the lid tightly.

Leave the jars to cool. Check the seals are depressed and tighten the lids if necessary.

jam-making equipment

I always find that jam-making is much more fun if I have the right tools. All of the following can be bought from cooking stores or online (see page 290):

PRESERVING OR MASLIN PAN—this is essential for preserving because it has a heavy base that protects the jam from burning. A lid is a good idea to bring the fruit up to a boil quickly (although this should be removed once the jam comes to a boil).

LONG WOODEN SPOON—keep a long wooden spoon specially for jam-making and a separate one for chutneys and pickles. My favorite spoon has a hook halfway down the handle to stop it falling into the pan.

JAM FUNNEL—this avoids lots of mess, enabling you to fill your jars quickly without the jam going everywhere.

SUGAR THERMOMETER—this has a higher range than most thermometers, enabling you to check the temperature of your jam as setting point is reached.

LADLE—this is useful for spooning your jam into the jars.

WIDE, PLASTIC-COATED TONGS—for gripping the jars from the oven.

MAGNETIC PRONG—to pick up lids.

PLASTIC STICK—for prodding fruit into jars and releasing air bubbles.

HEATPROOF GLOVE (OR WELL-FITTING OVEN GLOVE)—to maneuver hot jars, funnels, and lids into position.

jam-making tips

Fruit—pick fruit when the weather is dry; avoid using wet fruit or you will dilute your jam.

Mrs. Wishdish (see page 32) warms lemons in the microwave for 1 minute on high to make them more juicy and easier to squeeze.

Heat the fruit first before adding the sugar (unless it has been pre-mixed with the sugar the night before). The less you heat the sugar the less likely you are to get caramelization—when the sugar darkens in color.

When the color of your bubbling jam darkens, it indicates the sugar is starting to caramelize.

Add alcohol later to a jam or marmalade so that you do not get rid of the flavor and alcohol.

Remove the scum at the end by pushing it to one side and discarding it; there is no need to use butter to disperse it.

Put newspaper down when decanting the jam from pan to pot to absorb sticky splashes.

Use a jam funnel to avoid wastage.

Keep jam in a cool, dark cupboard for up to a year unless we have specified otherwise in the recipe.

RASPBERRY AND VANILLA JAM

This recipe is from Vivien Lloyd, a food writer and WI judge who also teaches the judges. Giancarlo and I were lucky enough to be taught by her and loved this classic recipe with Vivien's addition of vanilla. She uses ndali vanilla, which comes from Uganda and is organic and ethically farmed. The pods are fat and oily and full of seeds, hence the amazing flavor. When we make this jam the house fills with the wonderful aroma of comfort food and summer scents. Vivien prefers to use the later voluptuous autumn raspberries that are packed with flavor. If using frozen fruit, add 10 percent more fruit. Raspberries are medium-pectin and therefore do not need lemon juice, however it is a good idea to do a pectin test to make sure (see page 50). If the pectin is weak, you can add a little pectin stock to compensate (see page 51).

makes approx. 3lbs

2¼lbs raspberries
1 vanilla pod or 1 teaspoon organic vanilla powder or extract
5 cups superfine sugar

Put the raspberries in a large, heavy-bottomed saucepan. Split the vanilla pod, scrape out all of the seeds and add them to the pan. Cut the pod into four and add to the pan (or add the vanilla powder or extract). Simmer the fruit and vanilla gently for about 10 minutes. Meanwhile, warm the sugar in a low oven at 275°F.

If using a vanilla pod, remove the pieces from the pan. Add the warmed sugar to the pan and stir until it has dissolved. Bring the jam to a rolling boil and boil hard until setting point is reached (see page 52).

Start testing for a set after 4 minutes using the flake, thermometer, or cold plate test (see page 52). As soon as setting point is reached, remove the pan from the heat and leave it to stand for a few minutes. Push any scum from the surface of the pan to the side and remove it with a metal spoon.

Gently stir the jam and pour it into warm, sterilized jars, up to the brim. Seal the jars immediately. Store in a cool, dark place for up to a year.

Below
Testing for a set: jam thermometer
(left); the wrinkle test (middle); the
flake test (right).

microwave jam

I find this method is perfect for small amounts of jam. When I tested microwave jam against jam made on the stove, I couldn't perceive any real difference in taste or texture. For small amounts such as this, there isn't an awful lot of difference in cooking times—the microwave only saves a few minutes—but it is the ease of making it that I like, as well as the lack of washing up. If you make the jam in a large glass pitcher, all you need to do is simply pour it straight into a sterilized jar (even the sterilizing can be done in the microwave, see page 12). Do get to know your settings on the microwave and equipment. Practice makes perfect, as they say, and now I can make jam the way I like it with a low sugar content in 15 minutes start to finish. I use a large measuring jug that is large enough that the fruit can move around and lose the water easily. The handle is very thick and doesn't get too hot. I turn the power back and forth between full (900 watts) and medium (600 watts) so that the fruit doesn't boil over and yet it is a strong enough heat to get a hard boil to reach setting point at the end.

Most recipes work in the microwave, but this method is obviously not ideal for large quantities. The jug or bowl may become hot in the microwave, so do use oven gloves to remove it. Below is an example of a recipe made in the microwave.

SWEDISH LOW-SUGAR RASPBERRY JAM

Strictly speaking, a jam low in sugar should contain at least 25 percent sugar and no more than 50 percent sugar to be sold as "reduced-sugar" jam. This recipe comes from Lotta Gustafsson from Sweden. She makes small amounts of this jam at a time with fresh or frozen berries. Often this style of jam is soft set so it is ideal for pouring, however it can be cooked for longer to become firmer, the choice is yours. Bear in mind that the more you boil away the water to achieve a set, the higher the concentration of added and natural sugar, so you may defeat the purpose of a low-sugar jam. This recipe will work with any juicy berries such as raspberries, strawberries, loganberries, etc. As the jam is low in sugar, it should be stored in the fridge or waterbathed for a longer shelf-life.

makes approx. 10½oz
14oz fresh or frozen raspberries
6 tablespoons granulated cane sugar
juice of ½ lemon

MICROWAVE METHOD Put the berries and lemon juice together into a nonmetal jug or bowl and microwave on medium to full power for about 5 minutes or until the fruit has softened. Stir halfway through. Add the sugar and return to the microwave on medium heat for another 5 minutes or until the sugar has dissolved. Now increase the heat to high and boil rapidly until setting point is reached, approx. 5 minutes, stirring every 2 minutes. Stop cooking when you are happy with the consistency—either runny enough to pour over yogurt and oats or firm to spread on toast. Pour into a warm, sterilized jar, seal and set aside to cool. Store in the fridge for up to 2 weeks or waterbath in 9–18oz Mason or two-part lid jars using the hot-pack method for 10 minutes (see page 253) for a longer shelf-life.

STOVE METHOD Put the berries and lemon juice together into a heavy-bottomed saucepan and cook over low heat for about 5–7 minutes or until the fruit has softened, stirring frequently. Add the sugar and stir over medium heat until it has dissolved. Now increase the heat to high and boil rapidly until setting point is reached, approx. 5 minutes. Stop cooking when you are happy with the consistency—either runny enough to pour over yogurt and oats or firm to spread on toast. Pour into a warm, sterilized jar, seal and set aside to cool. Store in the fridge for up to 2 weeks or waterbath in 9–18oz Mason or two-part lid jars using the hot-pack method for 10 minutes for a longer shelf-life (see page 253).

APRICOT NO-SUGAR, NO-COOK JAM

Keep no-sugar jams in the fridge or freezer and only make small quantities because they don't keep. If you want to store them for longer than 2 weeks, you should heat-process the jars afterward by waterbathing (see page 253). Often no- and low-sugar jams are sweetened with apple juice and have no added sugar, although strictly speaking they shouldn't be sold as jam unless they contain a certain percentage of sugar. Note that no-sugar jams do contain fruit sugars, so they are not suitable for diabetics.

makes 4 x 9-oz Mason jars
18oz dried organic apricots, chopped
 into ½in cubes
2 cups apple juice
juice of 1 lemon
2 teaspoons honey

Put the chopped apricots in a bowl, cover with the apple juice and set aside to soak overnight.

The next day, add the lemon juice and honey to the apricot mixture and purée to a smooth paste with an immersion blender. Bottle into cold, sterilized jars and keep in the fridge or heat-process by waterbathing using the hot-pack method for 10 minutes (see page 253).

STRAWBERRY AND WHITE PEACH JAM

White peaches come into season at the same time as strawberries. Both flavors shine through equally in this jam, which is lovely on fresh scones with cream. As both fruits are low in pectin it is necessary to add pectin stock to achieve a good set. Ideally the pectin stock should be made of red currants as it will be clear and pink in color. Apple pectin stock will cloud the preserve but taste just as good.

makes approx. 2lbs

4½ cups granulated cane sugar
18oz strawberries, hulled and halved if small, or quartered if large
18oz white peaches or nectarines, peeled, pitted, and cut into pieces the same size as the strawberries
1 cup pectin stock (see page 51)
juice of 2 lemons

Preheat the oven to 275°F. Line a baking sheet with parchment paper, pour in the sugar and put into the oven to warm for 20 minutes. Put the fruit in a large preserving pan with the pectin stock and lemon juice. Simmer the mixture over low to medium heat to soften the fruit, approx. 15 minutes. Pour in the sugar and stir until dissolved. Increase the heat and bring to a rolling boil. Boil hard until setting point is reached (see page 52). Bottle into warm, sterilized jars (see page 52) and keep in a cool, dark place for up to a year.

Variations
STRAWBERRY AND RED PLUM JAM

Hard red plums have good acidity and pectin levels, so they help the strawberries to set and mean that you won't need the pectin stock.

makes approx. 1½lbs

18oz strawberries, hulled and halved if small, or quartered if large
2 cups superfine sugar
6 small, round, hard red plums, quartered and pitted
juice of 1 lemon

Make as for Strawberry and white peach jam (above), substituting the plums for peaches.

STRAWBERRY, RED PLUM, AND LIME JAM

Make as for Strawberry and red plum jam (left), omitting the lemon juice and replacing it with the juice of 2 limes and the zest of 1 lime.

RHUBARB AND GINGER JAM

This jam is often made with preserved ginger, however we have used grated fresh ginger to give a pleasant kick of heat.

makes approx. 18oz

1lb rhubarb, roughly chopped cut into ¾in lengths
1 heaping tablespoon finely grated fresh ginger
1¾ cups superfine sugar
juice of 1 lemon

Follow the instructions for Strawberry and white peach jam (left), including the ginger with the macerated fruit.

HEDGEROW JAM

A walk in the country is never the same once you start picking wild berries. The finished product is different every time we make Hedgerow jam, but that is part of the fun. As long as you include one-third apples in your mix you will have enough pectin for a set. Bump up your load of wild berries with bought berries such as red currants and raspberries. The spices make this great on toast or with goat cheese, lamb, and game.

makes 2lbs

12oz apples, peeled, cored and roughly chopped
1⅓lbs hedgerow fruit, such as haws, hips, blackberries, elderberries etc.
2 cups water
3½ cups superfine sugar
1 heaping teaspoon black peppercorns, lightly crushed
1 heaping teaspoon juniper berries, lightly crushed
¾ cup red wine

Put the apples, haws, and hips into a large, heavy-bottomed saucepan and pour over the water. (If you don't want blackberry seeds in your finished jam, you can put in the blackberries now too.) Bring to a boil and simmer until the fruit is tender, approx. 10–20 minutes. Pass through a food mill or sieve to remove the skins and large seeds. Put the strained fruit back into the pan along with the rest of the fruit. Add the sugar and stir over low heat to dissolve. Put the peppercorns and juniper berries into a spice bag, fasten with string and drop into the pan, securing it to the handle. Add the wine and bring to a boil. Boil hard until setting point is reached (see page 52). Bottle into warm, sterilized jars (see page 52). Store in a cool, dark place for up to a year.

ITALIAN DAMSON OR PLUM JAM

Stefano Borella is the head teacher at our cooking school, La Cucina Caldesi. His grandmother lived on a farm in the hills near Parma, northern Italy. Every year she and the family collected *susine*, a type of small, dark red plum to make *marmellata di susine*, a sweet black jam. She would cook the jam for ages, ignoring any worries about caramelization of the sugar, as that was the way she liked it. Giancarlo's family in Tuscany did the same and the result was eaten in a jam tart or on bread. There is a bittersweet quality to this jam that we love.

makes approx. 3⅓lbs
4lbs damsons or plums
2¼lbs superfine sugar

Wash and pick over the plums and put them into a pan with the sugar. Put over medium heat and stir until the water comes out of the fruit. Reduce the heat to a mere simmer and continue to cook, stirring occasionally, for 2 hours. Scoop out the pits with a slotted spoon when they pop up to the surface. Keep cooking until the jam is thick, dark and firm, by which time it should set easily when you test it (see page 252). If you want a smooth finish, put the jam through a food mill before bottling into warm, sterilized jars (see page 52). Store in a cool, dark place for up to a year.

CLAUDIA'S TOMATO AND APPLE JAM

This is a Portuguese recipe from Claudia Moreira. Sometimes orange peel is included as a flavoring, however Claudia and her partner Gregorio prefer it plain to enjoy with Brie or Robiola.

makes approx. 1lb 10oz–1 quart
2¼lbs round, ripe, flavorful tomatoes
2 cooking apples, peeled, cored, and roughly chopped
3¾ cups superfine sugar

First prepare the tomatoes. Make a cross in the bottom of each one and remove the stalk from the other end. Plunge into boiling water for 20–30 seconds, remove with a slotted spoon, and immerse immediately into cold water. Peel off the skins, cut each tomato into quarters, and scoop out the seeds with a teaspoon or knife. Put the tomatoes and apples into a blender and whizz until smooth. Transfer the mixture into a large, heavy-bottomed saucepan and bring to a boil. Simmer until the mixture has reduced by one-third, approx. 45 minutes depending on the water content of the fruit. Add the sugar, stir over low heat to dissolve and bring to a rolling boil. Cook until setting point is reached (see page 52). Bottle into warm, sterilized jars (see page 52) and keep in a cool, dark place for up to a year.

LIVIA'S OVEN-BAKED QUINCE JAM

I adore the floral perfume of quinces and this baked jam really concentrates their flavor. It is normally cooked to a soft set and used as a jam for bread or for filling jam tarts. Our friend Livia Cecuzzi runs a smallholding in Tuscany and makes this jam every year. Nello, her husband, uses a wood-burning oven for cooking and often makes the jam in it. He likes the fact that when it is cooked in the oven Livia doesn't ask him to stir it constantly, which he ends up having to do if she makes it on the stove. It won't catch on the bottom if it is made in the oven, but it may get a little discolored on the top if you don't stir it occasionally.

makes approx. 2¼lbs
2 lemons
2⅔lbs quinces
1 quart water
4 cups superfine sugar
2 cups white wine

Cut the lemons in half and squeeze out the juice; set the juice aside for later. Peel the quinces and cut them into quarters. Remove the cores with a sharp knife and cut the flesh into small pieces, approx. ¾in in size. To stop the pieces discoloring, place them in a bowl of cold water with the lemon halves.

STOVE METHOD Drain the quinces, discarding the lemon halves and water. Put them in a large, heavy-bottomed saucepan with 1 quart fresh water, the reserved lemon juice and the rest of the ingredients. Bring to a boil, reduce the heat to medium, and cook for 1 hour, stirring every now and again, until the fruit is really tender. Remove the pan from the heat and set aside to cool slightly before puréeing with an immersion blender (being careful not to splash yourself). Return the pan to the heat and simmer until setting point is reached, approx. 30 minutes. Bottle into warm, sterilized jars (see page 52). Store in a cool, dark place for up to a year.

OVEN METHOD Preheat the oven to 400°F. Drain the quinces, discarding the lemon halves and water. Place them in a large, ovenproof dish with 1 quart fresh water, the reserved lemon juice and the rest of the ingredients. Bake in the oven for 1 hour, stirring occasionally to stop the fruit from sticking. Remove the quinces from the oven and purée to a smooth paste in a food processor or with an immersion blender. Return to the oven or put the mixture into a saucepan and cook until setting point is reached (see page 52). Bottle and keep as above.

Wimalarathne, an energetic teacher in her late seventies, worked furiously to show me how to make this delicious, exotic jam. It is not only glorious on scones, but also it is wonderful scooped onto meringues with soft whipped cream for a quick dessert. Pineapple and passion fruit have very little pectin in them, so it is necessary to add some here. We have given the quantities for homemade pectin stock, however you could use liquid or powdered pectin and follow the manufacturer's instructions instead.

makes 1½ quarts
2 medium pineapples
6 passion fruit
approx. 5–6 cups superfine sugar
juice of 1 lemon
approx. 1–1⅓ cups pectin stock
  (see page 51)

Peel the pineapples and cut out any "eyes" so there are no dark areas. Discard the hard cores from the center and chop the flesh into approx. ½in cubes. This can be done in a food processor. Scoop out the flesh and seeds from the passion fruit and put with the chopped pineapple in a bowl. Weigh the fruit to calculate the correct amount of sugar, allowing equal quantities of sugar to fruit. Also calculate the amount of pectin stock, allowing ½ cup pectin stock per 1⅔ cups pulp.

Put the sugar in an ovenproof dish and warm in a low oven (275°F) while you cook the fruit.

Put the fruit in a large preserving pan with the lemon juice and pectin stock. Cook over medium heat for approx. 15–20 minutes until the fruit is just soft. Add the warmed sugar, stirring until it dissolves. Bring the mixture to a rolling boil and boil hard until setting point is reached, approx. 10–15 minutes. Bottle into warm, sterilized jars (see page 52). Store in a cool, dark place and use within a year.

GREENGAGE AND VANILLA JAM

As the greengage season is fairly short, I make the most of them by preserving their wonderful flavor and color in jam.

makes approx. 3⅓lbs
5 cups superfine sugar
2¼lbs ripe (but not soft) greengages
½ cup water
juice of 1 lemon
½ organic vanilla pod or a few drops
  of vanilla extract

Preheat the oven to 275°F. Line a baking sheet with parchment paper, pour in the sugar, and put into the oven to warm for 20 minutes.

Meanwhile halve the greengages, discarding the pits, and put into a preserving pan with the water, lemon juice, and vanilla. Bring to a boil, stirring, and then reduce the heat to a simmer. Simmer until the fruit is tender and soft, approx. 10–15 minutes. Pour in the warmed sugar and stir over low heat to dissolve. Bring the jam to a rolling boil and boil hard until setting point is reached (see page 52). Leave to stand for 5 minutes, and then scrape off the scum with a sterile spoon and remove the vanilla pod. Bottle into warm, sterilized jars (see page 52). Store in a cool, dark place for up to a year.

PINEAPPLE AND PASSION FRUIT JAM

This rich, bright yellow jam was shown to us in Sri Lanka during our visit there. Mrs.

CONSERVES

A conserve has whole or large pieces of fruit suspended in a thick syrup. Unlike most jams, conserves should be allowed to rest and settle for up to 10 minutes before bottling; this ensures an even dispersion of fruit in the jar. Usually when making a conserve, the fruit is layered with the sugar and lemon juice in a bowl and left to macerate in the fridge overnight. This process helps to firm up the fruit and draws out some of the liquid and pectin. However with strawberries I don't find the sugary juices helpful, so I leave out that stage. Any alcohol should be added after boiling and before bottling.

STRAWBERRY CONSERVE

Small whole strawberries picked during summer burst in your mouth when you eat them. Strawberries are low in pectin, so this is a tricky preserve to set. We have added homemade pectin stock to counteract this.

makes approx. 3⅓lbs
2¼lbs superfine sugar
2¼lbs strawberries, stalks removed
1 cup pectin stock (see page 51)
juice of ½ lemon

Preheat the oven to 275°F. Line a baking sheet with parchment paper, pour in the sugar, and put into the oven to warm for 20 minutes.

If the strawberries are large, cut them in half, otherwise leave them whole.

Put the fruit, pectin stock and lemon juice into a preserving pan and slowly bring to a boil. Cook until just tender. Reduce the heat and add the warmed sugar. Stir to dissolve. Bring to a rolling boil and cook until setting point is reached (see page 52). Remove from the heat and allow the jam to settle for 10 minutes before bottling into warm, sterilized jars (see page 52). Store in a cool, dark place for up to a year.

APRICOT CONSERVE

This reminds me of my favorite French jam. I like this jam to be soft set with large pieces of fruit; ideal for eating with warm croissants and huge cups of café au lait. Peeling away the skins is a sticky job so do omit this stage if you don't mind leaving them on.

makes approx. 1lb 14oz
2¼lbs apricots
5 cups superfine sugar
juice of 1 lemon

Cut the fruit into quarters and put the pits to one side. Layer the apricots with the sugar and lemon juice in a bowl, cover with plastic wrap and set aside to macerate in the fridge for 2 hours.

Meanwhile, crack the pits inside a plastic bag using a meat mallet or small saucepan. This will release the almondy kernels inside. Gather them into a muslin bag and put this with the apricots. Discard the shells.

Put the macerated fruit mixture into a large preserving pan, along with the muslin bag. Cook over medium heat until the sugar dissolves, stirring frequently but gently so as not to break up the fruit. Once the sugar has dissolved completely, bring the conserve to a boil. Remove from the heat and leave to cool. Pour through a sieve, reserving the liquid for later.

Peel the skins off the apricots. Put the fruit and liquid back into the pan and boil hard until setting point is reached (see page 52). Discard the muslin bag and allow the conserve to settle for 10 minutes before bottling into warm, sterilized jars (see page 52). Store in a cool, dark place for up to a year.

Variation
DELUXE APRICOT AND ALMOND CONSERVE
To make a deluxe version, add 3oz shelled almonds to the pan and ¼ cup brandy after setting point is reached. Stir through to disperse.

FIG AND MUSCAT CONSERVE

This conserve is perfect for eating with cheese or cold ham. It also makes a great canapé, generously spread onto hot toast and topped with soft goat cheese.

makes approx. 2⅔lbs
2¼lbs figs, peeled and quartered, stems removed
3¼ cups superfine sugar
4 cloves
2in cinnamon stick
sprig of thyme
1 cup pectin stock (see page 51)
1⅓ cups sweet wine, such as muscat, Sauternes, or port
3½oz toasted walnuts (optional)

Put the figs and sugar in a bowl, cover with plastic wrap and set aside to macerate in the fridge for a minimum of 5 hours (preferably overnight). Meanwhile, put the cloves, cinnamon, and thyme together in a muslin bag.

Put the macerated fruit mixture into a large preserving pan, put in the spice bag and the pectin stock and stir over medium heat until the sugar dissolves. Add the wine and bring to a rolling boil and boil hard until setting point is reached (see page 52). Discard the muslin bag and stir in the walnuts, if using. Remove from the heat and allow the conserve to settle for 10 minutes before bottling into warm, sterilized jars (see page 52). Store in a cool, dark place for up to a year.

marmalade

There are two methods for making marmalade—the first involves cooking the whole fruits in water first and then cutting up the tender flesh to cook with sugar and the second involves slicing the raw fruit and cooking it with sugar in a similar way to jam. Both methods work well, however we find the first method results in a softer texture and a better set as the longer cooking time releases more pectin and acid.

We love to make marmalade with Seville oranges. Their joyous fragrance is like no other fruit and the bittersweet flesh means they make perfectly balanced marmalade. Besides, the smell of sweet oranges cooking in mid-winter cheers up a cold household no end. We like to look for organic fruit.

MRS. BUN'S MARMALADE

Our friend Paul Wilson makes his own sourdough and we are frequently swapping tips. On one of our visits to see his bread he gave us some to try with his homemade marmalade. It was divine and so, of course, we asked him to show us how he made it. This marmalade is one he has been making for years and it was shown to him by his mother, affectionately known as Mrs. Bun.

Like Mrs. Bun, we prefer thick-cut marmalade, so to make this version we cut diagonally across each quarter of skin to give long lengths of peel. However, if you prefer, you can cut the peel into very small pieces. Paul got us to pick out the seeds—Giancarlo preferred to use the point of the knife to do this and I preferred to use my fingers. Giancarlo didn't agree and proceeded to tell me his way of doing it, so we said we would race the next orange. Paul said this was just what he didn't want ... competitive Seville

orange cutting! He said this was why he preferred to make marmalade alone! (By the way, I won.) Paul also said his mom made a delicious Seville orange sorbet from the oranges so we have included that recipe in Cold (see page 286).

Mrs. Bun always warms the sugar so that it dissolves into the fruit and liquid more quickly. Cold sugar brings the temperature right down and for this quantity it takes a long time to get the oranges boiling. As a rough guide, you will need twice the amount of sugar to cooked oranges.

makes 6¾–9lbs
3⅓lbs Seville oranges
juice of 2 lemons
approx. 15 cups superfine sugar

Scrub the oranges and put them into a preserving pan with the lemon juice. Cover them with cold water and weigh them down with a plate and a weight to keep them submerged or use a lid. Bring to a boil and simmer for about 2 hours or until the skins are soft and tender when poked with a sharp knife or skewer. (This stage can be done the night before and the oranges left to cool overnight.)

Preheat the oven to 275°F. Remove the oranges one by one from the water and, using a sharp knife, cut them into quarters. Reserve the cooking liquid for later. Separate the skins from the flesh and remove the seeds, saving these for later. Cut the skins into thick or fine shreds depending on your preference. I do this by hand, however you can do it in a food processor if you wish. The flesh becomes soft and breaks up but any remaining large pieces should be cut small. Weigh the shredded skin and flesh, along with any juice that came out of the oranges. You will need 10 cups sugar and 3 cups water to every 2¼lbs fruit.

Put the skins, flesh, juice and cooking liquid in a large preserving pan. Put the sugar in an ovenproof dish and put into the oven for about 20–30 minutes to warm through.

Meanwhile make the pectin stock. Put the reserved seeds in a small saucepan with enough water to just cover them and bring to a boil. Simmer for 10 minutes and then strain the liquid into the pan with the oranges.

Bring the ingredients in the preserving pan to a boil. Add the warmed sugar, ladleful by ladleful, and bring back to a boil. It should dissolve immediately. Skim any scum from the surface. Boil hard until setting point is reached (see page 52), during which time you should resist the temptation to stir or you will only create more bubbles and scum.

Once your marmalade has reached setting point, remove from the heat and leave it to stand for 10 minutes to allow the fruit to settle. Stir through once to disperse the fruit, and then bottle into warmed, sterilized jars (see page 52).

MERRY MARMALADE

Another of WI jam judge Vivien Lloyd's award-winning marmalades, and too good to miss out. This one is from her excellent book, *First Preserves*. The color is vibrant orange with thin-cut skins suspended in a perfect gel. It is "merry" due to the addition of whisky.

During the 1950s it was fashionable to add alcohol to marmalade. Rum, brandy, Cointreau, and even Campari can be added instead of whisky: as a rule of thumb, allow 1 tablespoon of alcohol to each 14oz jar, stirring it in at the end just before bottling—so you can mix and match as you please. Our favorite is whisky—I like it so much I put 2 teaspoons into each jar!

makes approx. 5lbs

1½lbs Seville oranges
juice of 1 large lemon
1¾ quarts water
7 cups superfine sugar
alcohol of your choice (optional)

Cut the oranges in half, squeeze out the juice, and combine with the lemon juice and water in a large preserving pan with a lid. Scrape out the inner membranes and seeds of the oranges with a small knife; do not remove the bitter pith. Finely chop the inner membranes by hand or use a food processor. Put the chopped membranes, seeds, and any stray parts of the oranges left on the juicer into a 13in square cheesecloth square. Tie this up tightly with string and add to the pan, securing it to one of the pan handles.

Quarter the orange skins, turn them peel-side down and shred them evenly into thin strips with a sharp knife. Add them to the pan. If time allows, cover the pan with a lid and set the fruit aside to soak overnight, which will help soften the peel.

Bring the lidded pan to a boil, reduce the heat and simmer gently for 2 hours. Meanwhile warm the sugar in a low oven at 275°F for 20 minutes. After the marmalade has cooked for 2 hours, remove the cheesecloth bag and squeeze out all the juices into the pan—place it in a sieve and press down hard with a wooden spoon or potato masher to extract all the juices. Check the volume level in the pan—it should have reduced by one-third.

Add the warmed sugar to the pan and stir over low heat to dissolve. Bring the pan to a rolling boil and start testing for a set after 5 minutes (see page 52). Once setting point is reached, remove the pan from the heat and set aside to cool for 5 minutes. Remove any scum by pushing it to the side of the pan with a metal spoon and

removing it. Gently stir the marmalade to distribute the peel. Ladle into a pitcher and pour into warm, sterilized jars or pour directly into the jars using a jam funnel. Add 1 tablespoon of alcohol to each jar and stir in before sealing the jars (see pages 53–54). Store in a cool, dark place for up to a year.

VIVIEN LLOYD'S LEMON AND LIME MARMALADE

We loved the zing of this marmalade as well as the color. Not only is it zesty enough to grace any breakfast table, but we also find it makes a delicious topping for lemon cheesecake.

makes approx. 5lbs

1lb limes
8oz lemons
7 cups superfine sugar
1¾ quarts water

Follow the instructions for Merry marmalade (left), using limes and lemons instead of oranges. Shred the lemon and lime skins and set aside to soften in the water and juice for 12 hours before simmering them in water and then boiling with the sugar.

COMPOTES

A compote is made from whole fruit or pieces of fruit in a sugar syrup. Generally it is runnier than a conserve or jam, and often it is served with yogurt or poured over ice cream. It can contain nuts and alcohol, and spices are frequently used as flavorings. Compotes were developed in France during the 17th century, when they would have been served in the afternoon with sour cream and cookies. (A compote is also the name for a long, stemmed dish that holds fruit.) Traditionally compotes used to be very sweet, however as tastes have changed they are more often made with minimal amounts of sugar, meaning they don't last as long and therefore need to be kept in the fridge. Because of this they are best made in small amounts. We regularly make them from rhubarb, plums, figs, and berries and eat them for breakfast most days with homemade Greek yogurt or oatmeal.

To turn a compote into a "fool," a rich and creamy dessert, ripple the compote through softly whipped cream and serve with crumbly shortbread cookies. My mother's favorite variety was made with gooseberries. She would add a little grated lemon zest to the mix and it was utterly delicious.

FIG AND ORANGE COMPOTE

This is great for breakfast when good figs are in season. In winter we like it heated for a quick dessert with crème fraîche or whipping cream. If you wish to waterbath the compote use either Mason or two-part lid jars and do stick to the recipe with the same amount of lemon juice. It is there to increase the level of acidity to make it safe to waterbath.

makes approx. 18oz (use either 2 x 8-oz or 1 x 16-oz Mason jar or two-part lid jars)

1¼lbs figs (approx. 20 small figs)
juice of 2 oranges
1 tablespoon lemon juice
⅓ cup superfine sugar
1 vanilla pod, split

Trim the hard stalks off the tops of the figs. Peel and cut them into quarters. Remove three long strips of orange zest from the oranges using a vegetable peeler and squeeze out the juice. Put the zest and juice into a saucepan with the figs, sugar, and vanilla pod and slowly bring to a boil, stirring to dissolve the sugar. Reduce the heat and stir frequently until the fruit has softened, approx. 10–15 minutes. Spoon into warmed, sterilized jars and seal. Heat-process by waterbathing, according to the instructions on page 253 for 45 minutes for either size of jar and store in a cool, dark place for up to 6 months. (If you choose not to waterbath, store in the fridge and consume within 2 weeks.)

Variation
RHUBARB AND GINGER COMPOTE

makes 1¼lbs

18oz rhubarb, tough ends removed and cut into 1in lengths
1 length of orange zest
juice of 1 lemon
⅔–1 cup soft brown sugar, to taste
1¼in piece of fresh ginger, grated or preserved ginger (see pages 74–75)

Follow the instructions for the Fig and orange compote (left), using rhubarb instead of figs and flavoring with ginger instead of vanilla.

CRANBERRY SAUCE

My mom always made her cranberry sauce with port and orange. It was rich, sticky, and looked just like Christmas, all shiny and red. For this recipe, I followed Glynn Christian's advice and added the sugar after the berries had softened, and I was very pleased with the result.

makes 2¼lbs sauce

1¼lbs fresh cranberries
¾ cup port or red wine
thinly sliced zest and juice of 1 orange
1¾ cups dark muscovado sugar

Combine the cranberries in a medium saucepan with the port and orange zest and juice. Bring to a boil, reduce the heat to a simmer, and allow the cranberries to bubble away merrily while you listen to Christmas carols and the skins soften on the fruit and begin to burst, approx. 10–15 minutes. Remove the pan from the heat and add the sugar, stirring to dissolve. If it is very runny, return the pan to the heat and let the sauce boil away rapidly until it thickens to your liking. Allow to cool then bottle into clean jars and store in the fridge for up to 2 weeks.

JELLIES

Jellies are simple to make. Providing you have the right amount of pectin to set the jelly, you can use a variety of fruits to obtain an array of flavors. Often apples or crabapples are used as a base because they are high in pectin.

to make a jelly

Cook the fruit over low heat with water until it is soft and easily squashed against the side of the pan with a wooden spoon. If there is any resistance, cook a little longer. Seeds and skin can all be left in at this stage. Fruits containing a lot of juice, such as strawberries and blackberries, will need approx. 1 cup water per 2¼lbs of fruit. Fruits with less water, such as hard plums and damsons, will need approx. 2 cups water per 2¼lbs of fruit. Harder fruit, such as apples and quinces, simply need to be cooked with just a covering of water (although you can add more if the fruit starts to stick to the bottom of the pan). This initial cooking stage will probably take 30 minutes–1 hour to achieve a soft, wet pulp.

Once the fruit is soft, you need to strain the pulp overnight to remove the seeds and skins, etc. You can either use a sterilized sieve lined with two layers of cheesecloth, a clean stocking, or a jelly bag suspended over a bowl to catch the drips. I usually set my cheesecloth or jelly bag up and pour through a kettle of boiling water first to sterilize everything before filling it with the fruit pulp.

When the last drip has dropped, do not be tempted to squeeze the bag or you will cloud the jelly. Discard the pulp (or use it to make fruit leather or fruit cheese, see page 135 and page 69) and measure the strained juice to calculate the amount of sugar needed. Traditionally jellies are made with equal parts fruit juice and sugar so for every ⅓ cup juice you will need ½ cup superfine sugar (you can use other types of sugar, however they will change the jelly's color). For a lower sugar jelly, you can take the ratio down to 75 percent: for every ⅓ cup juice you will need ⅓ cup sugar. This may give you a slightly more wobbly jelly.

Pour the juice into a saucepan and bring to a boil, add the sugar, and stir to dissolve. Bring the jelly to a boil and boil hard until you achieve a set (see page 52), approx. 10–15 minutes. Note: The less you boil the sugar the lighter in color your jelly will be; if you boil your jelly long and hard, the sugars will start to caramelize and the jelly could take on a bitter taste. Skim the jelly with a spoon, immediately pour into warm, sterilized containers and seal (see page 52). Leave to cool and set.

jelly bags

Jelly bags can be bought easily and inexpensively online or from kitchen shops. However, to make your own you simply need a couple of squares of cheesecloth tied over an upturned chair or stool like the one in our kitchen (right), or use an old but clean pillowcase. Have a bowl ready under your jelly bag to catch the drips. Make sure that you cover the pulp and bag with another cloth to protect it from fruit flies.

HEDGEROW AND PORT JELLY

Blackberries are ideal for making into jelly as the straining process removes all of the annoying seeds. For this jelly, you can either use just blackberries or mix them with other foraged fruits from the list below. Crabapples are included to give the necessary pectin for a set. I love this jelly with duck or venison and also use it for sweetening gravy.

makes approx. 1½lbs

2¼lbs mixed berries and hedgerow fruits, such as blackberries, elderberries, rosehips, blueberries, and haws
2¼lbs crabapples or cooking apples
1 quart water
⅔ cup port
approx. 5 cups superfine sugar

Wash the fruit well and remove any stalks. Cut the apples in half and combine them with the rest of the fruit in a heavy-bottomed saucepan. Pour in the water, bring to a boil, and simmer until the fruit is really soft and pulpy and can be crushed easily against the side of the pan. Put into a jelly bag, suspended over a sterile bowl, and set

aside to drip overnight. For this jelly only, you can gently squeeze the bag to extract all the juices. (Normally we don't advise this as it makes the jelly cloudy, but in this case the jelly is so dark it doesn't really matter, and anyway we hate to waste the valuable hedgerow juice—so go ahead and squeeze!)

Pour the juice into a measuring jug and weigh out the sugar. You will need the same quantity of sugar as juice *and* port combined (although don't add the port yet).

Put the sugar and juice into a medium, heavy-bottomed saucepan and set over low heat to dissolve the sugar. Bring to a boil and boil hard until setting point is reached (see page 52). Remove the pan from the heat, skim the surface, and stir in the port. Bottle into warm, sterilized jars (see page 52).

Variation
ROSEHIP AND ROSÉ JELLY
Follow the recipe for Hedgerow and port jelly (see pages 65–66), replacing the foraged berries with rosehips. For best results, either freeze them beforehand to soften them or pick after the first frost. Rosehips are full of vitamin C and the finished jelly is supposed to soothe sore throats. The port can be omitted if you wish or substituted with white or rosé wine.

APPLE AND ROSEMARY JELLY

We hate waste and so it seems a really good deal to get lovely gleaming jars of crystal clear jelly in return for a load of peel and cores. We often have apple cores and skins left over from making crumbles and pies. If you don't want to use them there and then, freeze them until you have enough. You can use the whole apple for this, but you won't have the same sense of satisfaction. This jelly is delicious with roasted pork and lamb.

makes 1½lbs
3⅓lbs apple peel and cores
2⅔ cups water
2 long sprigs of rosemary
3 tablespoons cider vinegar
up to 5 cups superfine sugar

Put the apple bits into a large preserving pan with the water, rosemary, and vinegar. Bring to a boil and then reduce the heat to a simmer. Cook gently until the fruit is soft and squashes easily with a wooden spoon. Pour the mixture into a jelly bag, cover with a cloth to keep out flies, and set aside to drip overnight into a container underneath. Measure the strained juices. To calculate the amount of sugar needed and finish the jelly, follow the general instructions on page 65.

Variations
CHILE AND APPLE JELLY
Follow the recipe for Apple and rosemary jelly, omitting the rosemary and cider vinegar and adding a crushed chile instead. Taste the jelly toward the end of cooking and add further heat in the form of more crushed chile as necessary. We love this on a cheese board or with roast pork belly.

QUINCE JELLY
Follow the recipe for Apple and rosemary jelly, substituting the apples for quinces—include the skins, flesh, cores, seeds, and all. Omit the rosemary and cider vinegar and add the juice of 2 lemons at the beginning, when you cook the quinces, to stop them becoming brown.

RED CURRANT JELLY

This bright, ruby-colored jelly is one of the most beautiful preserves to make. I think I would make it even if I never ate it, just to have a jar sitting on my shelf to look at. Actually it is one of the most useful preserves to have in your pantry, so we make a large batch over summer for use in sauces and gravies, or for serving with baked Camembert or Brie. The bittersweet flavor also makes it the perfect partner to accompany lamb or ham.

Note: You don't need to include any other fruit with the red currants because they are naturally high in pectin.

makes approx. 1¼lbs
2¼lbs red currants
approx. 1⅔ cups water
approx. 2½ cups superfine sugar

Wash the berries and pick off any long stalks, but don't worry about removing the tiny stems as they will be strained out later.

Boil the fruit with the water until soft and pulpy. Strain through a jelly bag overnight (see page 65), resisting the temptation to squeeze the jelly bag or your jelly will be cloudy. Weigh the strained juices and calculate the amount of sugar needed, allowing equal quantities of fruit to sugar.

Return the strained juices to the pan with the sugar and stir over low heat to dissolve. Bring to a boil and boil hard until setting point is reached (see page 52). Bottle into warm, sterilized jars (see page 52). Store in a cool, dark place for up to a year.

FRUIT CHEESE

Fruit cheeses are high in sugar and set to a solid consistency similar to soft cheese made with milk. Fruit cheese is one of the earliest preserves. In the 16th century it was traditionally made out of quinces by the Portuguese and called *marmelada*. Fruit cheese can be made using the pulp left over in the jelly bag after making jelly (unless it contains the cores and seeds).

Fruit cheese is traditionally potted into molds and turned out whole, and served cut into slices. You can either use silicone molds for potting the cheese or individual ramekins. If using ramekins, coat the sides of the container with liquid glycerine beforehand to make them easier to turn out and cover with waxed paper and plastic wrap; store in the fridge for up to 3 months. If you want to keep the cheese for longer than this, bottle into sterilized jam jars and seal with screw-cap lids; store in a cool, dark place for up to a year.

CRABAPPLE AND CHILE CHEESE

Individual little pots of Crabapple and chile cheese make wonderful homemade presents—we often give them as gifts with a wedge of good Cheddar or goat cheese. The first mouthful of this fruit cheese is soft, sweet, and innocent but it is soon followed by a punch of chile making it irresistible.

makes approx. 2¼lbs
2¼lbs crab or cooking apples
3 red chiles
approx. 4–5 cups superfine sugar

Wash the apples very well and chop them in half. Put them into a saucepan with a covering of cold water and bring to a boil. Reduce the heat to a simmer and cook for 30 minutes until the fruit squashes easily with a fork and is very soft. Strain through a sieve or a food mill to obtain a purée.

Measure the purée and put into a saucepan. Add the same quantity of sugar (give or take ½ cup, depending on the tartness or ripeness of the fruit). Put over low heat, stirring frequently, until the sugar dissolves and the mixture has reduced to a thick paste; this could take up to an hour. If a skin forms during this time, remove it with a spoon and discard. The cheese is done when it is really thick and a line can be drawn across the bottom of the pan with a spoon and it doesn't disappear quickly. Spoon into containers and seal (see pages 52–53). Serve with cheese or roasted pork.

Variations
DAMSON CHEESE
Follow the recipe for Crabapple and chile cheese (left), omitting the chile and replacing the crabapples with damsons. You can leave the seeds in the fruit to begin with, as they will all be strained out later in the sieve. Warm the sugar in a low oven at 275°F for 15–30 minutes before adding; this will help it dissolve more quickly. Watch over it as it thickens, approx. 40 minutes. Serve with lamb or duck or layered into a chocolate cake.

QUINCE JELLY
Follow the recipe for Crabapple and chile cheese (left), omitting the chile and replacing the crabapples with quinces. To achieve a deep, pink color, allow the cooked quinces to stand overnight before straining. Serve with roasted pork or Manchego or goat cheese.

CURDS

Always bottle curd into sterilized containers and seal with waxed paper and plastic wrap to stop it forming a skin. This recipe comes from Stefano Borella, Head Teacher at our cooking school.

STEFANO'S LEMON CURD

This hits the spot where mouth-puckering citrus acidity meets sugary sweetness. We love it stirred into Greek yogurt but it is also great mixed into ice cream.

makes 1lb
9 tablespoons unsalted butter
1¼ cups superfine sugar
juice and zest of 3 lemons
3 eggs and 1 egg yolk

Put the butter, sugar, lemon juice and zest in a saucepan over low heat. Meanwhile whisk up the whole eggs and egg yolk in a bowl with an electric mixer until very smooth. When the butter mixture has melted, pour in the frothy egg mixture. Keep whisking until the mixture starts to thicken, increasing the heat gradually. As soon as you hear the first "gloop" sound, remove the pan from the heat. Strain the curd through a nylon sieve to obtain a smooth texture. Bottle into sterilized jars, taking care to fill them absolutely full. Press a waxed disk on top, waxed-side down, and set aside to cool. Once cold, seal the pots with plastic wrap disks and secure with rubber bands. Store in the fridge and consume within 2 weeks.

Variation
PASSION FRUIT CURD
Follow the recipe for Stefano's lemon curd (above), replacing the lemons with the pulp and seeds of 4 passion fruit.

FRUIT BUTTER

Fruit butter is low in sugar and really delicious spread on toast or hot pancakes. We have given two methods for making it, one on the stove and one in the oven. Both work well, however I do think the oven version gives a slightly better flavor. Either bottle into sterilized glass jars and store in the fridge for up to 3 weeks, or heat-process by waterbathing and store in a cool, dark place for up to a year (see page 253).

APPLE AND CINNAMON BUTTER

This butter is spiced with cinnamon and it is wonderful served with cheese or as a sauce for roasted pork or with homemade British pork and leek sausages (see page 107). Alternatively spread it onto hot pancakes and top with homemade Crème fraîche (see page 223).

makes approx. 2¼lbs
6¾lbs eating apples
⅔ cup water
zest and juice of 1 lemon
2in cinnamon stick
4 cloves
¾ cup dark brown sugar

Quarter the apples, leaving the peel and core intact, and put into a large saucepan with the water, lemon zest and juice and spices. Cover with a lid and simmer until tender, approx. 20 minutes. Put the apple mixture through a food mill or a sieve to strain out the spices and separate the skins and seeds from the pulp.

Combine the purée with the sugar in a heavy-bottomed saucepan, stirring over low heat to dissolve the sugar. Cook until the purée is really thick and a spreadable consistency, stirring frequently, approx. 1 hour. Check for a set by placing a teaspoonful of the butter on a plate; if it is properly set it shouldn't "weep" at the edges. Spoon immediately into warmed, sterilized 9oz Mason or two-part lid jars, seal and waterbath for 10 minutes using the hot-pack method on page 253. It will keep for up to a year in a cool, dark place. If not waterbathed, store in sterilized containers, after cooling, in the fridge for up to 3 weeks.

ROASTED PEACH AND VANILLA BUTTER

This is a delightful combination that is heightened and concentrated by the roasting of the peaches. I have used the oven method for this recipe, but you can cook it on the stove if you wish. Enjoy it mixed into bread and butter pudding or simply on hot toast.

makes 1¼lbs
2¼lbs ripe but firm peaches
approx. ¼ cup soft brown sugar, to taste
1 vanilla pod or ½ teaspoon vanilla extract

Preheat the oven to 350°F. Wash the peaches and dry them with paper towels. Quarter the peaches, discarding the pits, and arrange in an ovenproof dish, skin-side up. Roast in the oven for up to 45 minutes or until the skins have shriveled and the flesh is soft.

Remove from the oven and put into a food processor, or use an immersion blender, to blitz the peaches to a paste. Taste the purée and sweeten with sugar if you feel it needs it—we normally add approx. ¼ cup because we never seem to have really sweet peaches.

Return the purée to the ovenproof dish and put it back into the oven for a further 30 minutes to reduce some more and dissolve the sugar, stirring it halfway through. If the spread is watery after this time, continue to cook until the water has disappeared. Remove from the oven and spoon immediately into warmed, sterilized 9oz Mason or two-part lid jars. Seal and waterbath for 10 minutes using the hot-pack method on page 253. It will keep for up to a year in a cool, dark place. If not waterbathed, store in sterilized containers, after cooling, in the fridge for up to 3 weeks.

CORDIALS, COULIS, AND ELIXIRS

The term "cordial" derives from the Latin word *cordialis*, which describes a medicinal drink made from herbs, fruits, honey, and often alcohol. Over time, alcoholic cordials have become known as "liqueurs," while the term "cordial" is more widely used to describe nonalcoholic syrups diluted with water. One of the most famous cordials is Rose's Lime Cordial, which was patented in 1867 and originally made for British sailors to prevent scurvy.

An elixir or syrup is another name for these sweet, medicinal mixtures. Nowadays all the words seem to be interchangeable, for all of them are fruity and sweet (the sugar content helps them to last). We have grouped all the runny syrups that need diluting together, and called them "cordials."

To make a coulis, which is a thin purée served as a sauce, push the fruit through a sieve instead of cheesecloth.

clear and cloudy cordials—to squeeze or not to squeeze!

Syrups and cordials are both made by straining the juice through a jelly bag or two layers of cheesecloth. If you want a crystal clear liquid, allow plenty of time to let the juices drip overnight. If you're in a hurry, and not fussed if the resulting liquid isn't crystal clear—and you can't bear the thought of wasting all that precious pulp—the only choice is to squeeze the bag or push it through a sieve with a spatula; this way you will gain more liquid, but it will be cloudy. The choice is yours!

SPICED BLACK FRUIT ELIXIR

Foraging for autumn fruit is always lots of fun, however this recipe actually works really well with frozen fruits of the forest. In fact, the fruit releases the juice better after being frozen (or after the first frost if picked outside), so you could include a mixture of summer and autumn berries.

This elixir is loosely based on an old Carluccio recipe. It is great heated in a mug with boiling water for a warming winter drink, mixed with Prosecco or used as a base for Bramble cocktails. To turn it into a cocktail, combine 2 tablespoons elixir with ½ cup gin or sloe gin, a teaspoon of lemon juice and a little tonic. Serve over crushed ice, garnished with mint leaves (see page 200).

makes approx. 1⅓ cups

2¼lbs black fruit, such as elderberries, blackberries, blueberries, cherries, etc.
1⅔ cups water
2 long strips of lemon or orange peel, or 1 of each
4 cloves
3 cardamom pods
2½in cinnamon stick
superfine sugar or honey

Wash the fruit well and remove any stalks. Put into a heavy-bottomed saucepan with the water and flavorings. Bring to a boil and simmer until all the fruit is tender, approx. 30 minutes—it should crush easily when you press it against the side of the pan with a wooden spoon.

To strain the juice, pour into a jelly bag and leave it to drip overnight. For this recipe, it is perfectly fine to gently squeeze the bag. (Normally we don't advise this as it makes the cordial cloudy, but in this case the elixir is so dark you won't notice it, and anyway it's a shame to waste all that valuable juice.)

Measure the juice and calculate the amount of sugar needed, allowing 1¼ cups sugar or ⅓ cup honey per 1⅔ cups juice. Combine the juice and sugar or honey in a medium, heavy-bottomed saucepan and stir over low heat** to dissolve. Pour into warm, sterilized bottles and keep in the fridge for up to a month.

** To make the elixir last longer, bring the heat up to over 185°F when dissolving the sugar, pour into sterilized bottles and waterbath according to the instructions on page 253.

cordials

RASPBERRY CORDIAL

For a bright, fruity drink, simply dilute this with cold sparkling water. It is also versatile as a base for cocktails—try it mixed with Prosecco or Cava. For a gin-based drink that tastes like summer in a glass, add a generous dash of raspberry cordial and muddle with crushed ice, a wedge of lime and a few mint leaves. If you leave out the gin it works as a great mocktail for the kids too. Another favorite of mine is Raspberry gin fizz—raspberry cordial mixed with a bruised stick of lemongrass, some crushed ice, lime juice, gin, and sparkling water.

makes approx. 1⅓ cups clear cordial using a jelly bag or 1½ cups cloudy cordial using a sieve

18oz raspberries
juice of ½ lemon
1 cup superfine sugar

Put the fruit, lemon juice, and sugar in a saucepan over medium heat until the sugar dissolves and the raspberries give up any resistance if you squeeze them against the side of a pan with a wooden spoon, approx. 10 minutes. Strain through a sieve or jelly bag into a sterilized pitcher or bowl. Pour into a sterilized bottle and keep in the fridge for up to 10 days.

If you wish to make larger quantities of this to keep out of the fridge, you will need to waterbath the bottles according to the instructions on page 253.

STRAWBERRY CORDIAL

Follow the method for Raspberry cordial (left) with strawberries instead of raspberries. To make a coulis push the fruit through a sieve instead of through cheesecloth.

RHUBARB CORDIAL

We love our pink rhubarb from the garden. It is one of the first edible plants that greet us with color and flavor straight after a cold winter. This early rhubarb gives a great color, but you could also use the later, greener variety too. We mix this with Prosecco, pour it over Greek yogurt or ice cream or serve it with vanilla panna cotta.

makes approx. 2½ cups

2¼lbs rhubarb (approx. 10 stalks),
 roughly cut into 1in chunks
juice of 1 lemon
⅓ cup water
approx. 2 cups superfine sugar

Combine the rhubarb, lemon juice, and water in a saucepan and cook until soft, approx. 40 minutes. Strain the liquid through cheesecloth. To achieve a very clear liquid, let it drip through slowly overnight, covered to prevent insects joining it. If you don't mind it being cloudy, push it through with a spatula. Dilute with water if the juice is very thick.

Pour the strained rhubarb into a saucepan and sweeten with sugar to taste. Boil up the rhubarb and sugar together briefly until the sugar dissolves, and then pour into warm, sterilized bottles. Keep in the fridge for up to 2 weeks.

Boil the sugar and water together in a large pan. When bubbling rapidly, push the flower heads into it, stems upward. Leave to boil for a few minutes and then add the lemon juice, chopped lemon flesh, and citric acid (if using). Remove from the heat and leave to cool in the pan, covered, overnight.

The following day, strain the syrup through cheesecloth into a pitcher and then into sterilized bottles. Keep in the fridge for up to 3 weeks. To preserve the cordial for longer, reheat after straining until boiling hot. Pour into warm, sterilized bottles and waterbath according to the instructions on page 253.

CANDIED FRUITS

Candied fruits, also known as glacé and crystallized fruits, were known in Ancient China but were made popular by the Arabs who served candied citrus fruits at important occasions. Known in Europe since the 16th century candying works by repeatedly soaking fruits in a sugar syrup. The fruit becomes saturated in sugar and is therefore resistant to spoilage bacteria and molds that cannot survive in a sugary environment.

ELDERFLOWER CORDIAL

Enjoy this cordial diluted with sparkling water, with a slice of lime and even a sprig of fresh mint. Our friend Hannah's tip is to pour it over ice, using 2 tbsps gin, 2 tbsps cordial, and a splash of lemon or lime juice and top up with tonic. Try to pick young elderflowers early in the morning when it is dry. Before putting them in the pan, have a good look for insects. Citric acid can be hard to buy but it helps preserve the cordial and adds a pleasant sour flavor.

makes ¾–1 quart
3½ cups superfine sugar
2½ cups water
15–20 elderflower heads (depending on size)
1 lemon, juiced and roughly chopped (including the skin)
1 tablespoon citric acid powder (optional)

PRESERVED GINGER

Every year at Christmas our family had a spread of treats adorning the Christmas table including preserved ginger in syrup, chocolates, and Turkish delight displayed in Victorian glass dishes. I don't remember liking the ginger as a child, but it is definitely something I have grown into. Now we cut the pieces up into small dice and use them and the syrup to flavor ice cream or stir through rhubarb compote. It is spicy and warming when poured over vanilla cheesecake or served with strong cheeses such as Pecorino. It can also be cut into lengths and covered with melted chocolate.

makes approx. 2¾lbs
18oz fresh ginger
3½ cups superfine sugar

Peel the ginger with the edge of a teaspoon, discarding the rough, dry ends and skin. Cut the ginger into small pieces about the size of a quail's egg, place in a bowl of cold water, and set aside to soak overnight.

The following day, drain the ginger and discard the water. Put the ginger into a saucepan with enough cold water to cover and bring to a boil. Reduce the heat to a simmer, cover with a lid, and continue to cook until the ginger is tender when poked with a skewer, approx. 2 hours. Add a little more water if necessary to ensure the ginger is always covered. Remove the pan from the heat and set aside to cool overnight at room temperature.

The following day, remove the ginger from the pan and set aside in a heatproof bowl. Measure out ¾ cup of the cooking liquid making up the amount with cold water if necessary and discarding the rest if too much. Pour into a saucepan and add 1¼ cups of the sugar. Bring the water and sugar to a boil to dissolve the sugar, and then pour the resulting sugar syrup over the ginger. Set aside to cool overnight. This will allow the sugar to permeate through the fruit and the syrup to become flavored with the ginger.

The following day, strain the ginger out of the syrup and set aside. Put the syrup into a saucepan and bring to a boil with another 1¼ cups sugar; pour over the ginger and set aside overnight.

Repeat the process again on the fourth day, using up the rest of the sugar. Boil the syrup until you are happy with the consistency, it should be thick but easily pourable. Combine the syrup and ginger in the bowl and bottle immediately into warm sterilized jars (see page 52). Seal with lids and store in a cool, dark place for up to a year.

ORANGE PEEL SPOON SWEETS

This is a recipe from our lovely friend Gloria Mylona who is Greek Cypriot and mother to our friend Soulla. Gloria showed me some of the ways she was taught to preserve fruits by her mother. As a child, she and her siblings would stand on a chair to get into the high cupboard where her mother kept these sticky sweets for special occasions. They would dare to take out a couple each, blaming one another for instigating the stealth if they were ever caught!

Use sweet oranges for this when they are at their best, fresh and young. You can also use watermelon, lemons, and grapefruit. Traditionally, these sweets are eaten with strong Greek coffee. This recipe uses the pith of the oranges, which sounds bizarre but it makes great use of an otherwise discarded part of the fruit.

makes approx. 2¼lbs
6 medium oranges
approx. 2¾ cups water
rose geranium leaf (optional)
approx. 3½ cups superfine sugar

Using a vegetable peeler or sharp knife, peel away the dark zest from the oranges leaving the white pith intact; discard. Top and tail the oranges and make four vertical, shallow cuts into the orange pith as if you were about to divide it into quarters. Now carefully peel away the four pieces of pith separating them from the flesh as neatly as possible trying to get smooth surfaces. The flesh can now be eaten or saved for another recipe. Any raggedy edges should be tidied up and cut away. Curl the neatened pieces of pith up tightly into rolls and tie with a length of cotton thread or secure them with a toothpick. Soak the rolls in water overnight, changing the water three times to rid them of the bitterness.

The next day, put the rolls and the geranium leaf into a saucepan and cover with cold water. Bring to a boil and cook until they are tender when poked with a thin skewer, approx. 45 minutes–1 hour. Remove the pan from the heat and set aside to cool.

Remove the rolls with a slotted spoon and set aside in a bowl. Pour 2¾ cups of the cooking liquid back into a saucepan, discarding the rest. Add 3½ cups sugar to the pan and bring to a boil. Simmer gently for approx. 20 minutes until the sugar syrup thickens, then add the orange rolls. Boil the oranges for 3 minutes, then remove the pan from the heat. Set aside to cool overnight.

The next day, return the pan to the heat and boil the oranges again for 3 minutes; set aside to cool overnight.

On the fourth day, boil the mixture again for 3 minutes or until the liquid has reduced to a thick syrup. Spoon the rolls into hot sterilized jars leaving 1¼in headroom. Top up with the syrup, making sure the rolls are completely covered. Seal the jars and leave to cool before storing in a cool, dark place for up to a year. Once the jars are opened, consume within a month and store in the fridge ensuring the rolls are always covered in syrup.

Variation
Do the same with black cherries, flavoring with a cinnamon stick instead of the rose geranium leaf.

MUSTARD FRUITS

Mostarda di Frutta, as this is known in Italian, is a condiment made from candied fruit in mustard syrup that has been made in Cremona, northern Italy, for centuries. It is eaten particularly with cheeses and sliced boiled meats. To make the real thing you need to get hold of mustard essence, also known as mustard oil. This is banned in the US but available from specialist food stores in Europe. We bought ours at a wonderful old pharmacy in Rome called Antica Erboristeria Romana, which is worth a visit just to see the interior dating back to 1752. The owner told us to be really careful of the mustard essence. He told us to open it at arm's length so that you don't breathe too much in and to avoid getting it near your eyes. Apparently mustard oil available from Asian shops is just as good but I haven't tried it.

As for the fruits, *Mostarda di Frutta* is made out of a variety of fruits, such as quinces, apricots, oranges, cherries, apples, and pears.

makes approx. 3⅓lbs

4 large pears, e.g. 'William'
1 lemon
14oz mini clementines or kumquats
7oz glacé cherries
2¾ cups water
3¾ cups superfine sugar
8–10 drops of mustard essence,
according to the strength

Peel the pears, cut into quarters, and discard the cores. Put them in a saucepan and poach until just tender in gently simmering water. Remove the pears from the pan with a slotted spoon, keeping the cooking liquid, and place them in a heatproof bowl. Squeeze over the lemon juice to stop them discoloring and put the hollowed out shells into the pan with the cooking liquid. Make a small cross in the top and bottom of the clementines or kumquats and prick them a few times all over. This ensures that the cooking liquid gets inside. Poach them in the cooking liquid for 5 minutes, remove them with a slotted spoon and add to the pears. Add the cherries as well.

Measure the cooking liquid and make up to 2¾ cups with cold water. Return to the saucepan with 1¼ cups of the sugar and heat to dissolve. Pour the resulting sugar syrup over the fruits. Stir it through and leave the mixture to cool, covered, overnight.

The following day, drain the fruits from the syrup and set aside. Put the syrup into a pan and bring to a boil with another 1¼ cups of the sugar to form a thicker sugar syrup. Pour over the candied fruits and stir to combine. Set aside to cool, covered, overnight.

The following day, repeat the method above using up the remaining sugar. Boil the syrup until you are happy with the consistency, it should be thick but easily pourable. Pour over the fruits and add the mustard essence from arm's length; don't be tempted to have a sniff of it. Take a small piece of fruit out and after cooling taste for the strength of mustard. Add a few more drops if necessary. Immediately pour into warm, sterilized jars (see page 52). Store in a cool, dark place for up to a year. Any leftover syrup can be used to pour over hot ham steaks or toasted cheese for a delicious combination. If the spicy heat dissipates with time, add a few more drops of essence before serving.

MARRONS GLACÉS

I love to eat these in France or Italy, but wanted to make my own variety with homegrown chestnuts. Our local variety is smaller than the bulging French ones, but nonetheless sweet and tender.

makes approx. 4 x 8-oz jars

1lb chestnuts
1⅛ cups superfine sugar
½ cup water
¾ cup liquid glucose
1 vanilla pod, cut into 1in pieces
3 tablespoons brandy

Pierce each chestnut through the tough brown skin in about four places and put into a large saucepan. Cover with cold water and bring to a boil. Reduce the heat to low and simmer for 5 minutes. Remove the pan from the heat, remove the chestnuts one by one and peel off the outer shell and inner skins. Try to do this quickly as possible because they are easier to peel when they have been in the hot water for 5 minutes only. Don't be tempted to remove them all and let them cool or the skin will become like glue and it will be harder to remove.

Put the sugar, water, glucose, and vanilla into a saucepan and bring to a boil to dissolve the sugar. Add the chestnuts to the pan and simmer gently for 5 minutes. Remove the pan from the heat and set aside to stand for 24 hours.

The next day, return the pan to the heat and simmer the chestnuts for 2–3 minutes. Remove from the heat and set aside to cool overnight.

On the third day, repeat the process, simmering the chestnuts again for 2–3 minutes in the syrup. Remove the pan from the heat, stir in the brandy and decant the syrup and chestnuts into warm, sterilized jars (see page 52). Store in a cool, dark place for up to a year.

salt

Salt "cures" and extends the life of food by stopping bacteria and mold from reproducing. In foods such as bacon, ham, and cured salmon it draws out moisture by the process of osmosis, and flavors it at the same time, rendering it delicious as well as long-lasting. Salt curing alters the texture of fish or meat, making it firmer and less delicate to handle, so this process is beneficial for produce that needs to be hung.

Brine (salt mixed with water) can also be used to add moisture to food—for example, to plump up poultry. The purpose of brining poultry is not only to preserve, but to open up the proteins in the meat so that it becomes more spongelike so it can absorb flavors better. In America, most people brine their turkeys before roasting them for Thanksgiving. I tried this and the meat was so tasty and succulent that I couldn't understand why we don't all do it regularly. Now, even when I am going to roast a chicken I leave it in 40 percent brine overnight and dry it for a few hours in the fridge before cooking it. This way, it is just how we like it—flavorful and juicy inside with a savory, crispy skin.

Nearly all food is salted in some way before being smoked. This adds flavor, makes it firmer in texture, and protects it from decay during the smoking process (see Smoke, page 153). The combination of salty and smoky food is quite irresistible—perfect examples are smoked salmon and bacon.

Salting has a long history. It was an ancient and preferred method of preserving food in China, and in the Mediterranean the preservation of fish with salt goes back to 3,500 BCE. The process of salting meat—hams in particular—and then hanging them in breezy climates to cure, is fundamental to the food of Italy and Spain.

Many of the cured foods were easier to make than we expected, such as smoked salmon and bacon, others took patience and months if not years of experimentation to get right, such as *prosciutto*. Our advice would be to start small: begin with two pounds of pork belly before you progress to a whole piece, or try a mackerel first rather than a whole salmon until you get used to your new skills and equipment.

watch your meat!

You will have to tend to your produce almost daily, watching for mold, humidity, and temperature changes, so don't start making cured ham before venturing off on a world trip.

where to cure

Many smaller items can be cured in your kitchen fridge. However, before you undertake any of the large or long-term salt cures in this chapter, such as cured ham or salami, bear in mind that salting is only the first stage of the production process. After curing, you will need somewhere to hang and dry your meat while it cures.

Professional curers are not allowed to hang meat and fish together and logic tells me this should be avoided at home as well, as the flavor of one could taint the other. I have also learned from experience not to hang too many things in my "curing chamber" (wine fridge) at once, as this can raise humidity levels and encourage the wrong sorts of molds to grow. Air needs to move around the produce easily and so the curing foods should not touch one another. (In the past, I have had to cut out an area of tackiness from a small piece of *prosciutto* because it was touching another meat and the air couldn't get to it.) Strings of sausages are slightly problematic because they naturally rest against each other, however I find tying them up in between the hooks, rather like a garland, keeps them apart for efficient airflow and drying. Cured foods should be checked daily for mold growth.

Ideally, you want to create your own "curing chamber"—words that probably conjure up horrible images of torture! In our house, this is our very friendly wine fridge that has now taken on the pleasant aroma of a French charcuterie. If you have a pantry against a north-facing wall, that is ideal—but we will go into this in more detail in the next chapter, Air, see pages 141–143.

how long to cure for?

One phrase that popped up constantly during our quest to learn more about the fine art of curing was "well, how long is a piece of string?" Infuriating as it was, that was the response I always seemed to get when I asked various curers how long a piece of meat or fish should be cured for. In my experience, if I cured it for too long it ended up overly salted and if I didn't cure it for long enough it never seemed to preserve properly and then it didn't taste as good either.

We have included approximate curing times in each recipe, however please be aware that curing is not a precise science. Like many forms of preservation, timings will be affected by many factors, including the temperature of your fridge, the size and shape of your cut, and whether or not the meat is on the bone. Usually it is better to err on the side of caution and leave your meat in the curing salts or brine for longer to be on the safe side, rather than removing it too quickly. If you find your meat is too salty (as happens to the best of us when we start curing), excess salt can be removed by soaking your cut in cold water for an hour or two; if necessary you can repeat the process several times. However, remember that some salt is always needed to kill bacteria.

sanitation and hygiene

Cleanliness is next to butchery, as someone once told me. Imagine a shiny-tiled, immaculately scrubbed butcher's shop, and that is what you need to recreate at home. Before you start work, move all your clutter away from the worksurfaces, wipe them down with vinegar (I prefer this to breathing in antibacterial sprays) and wash or sterilize your equipment. Keep bowls and equipment cold, where possible, by putting them in the fridge. Make sure your hands are washed at all times.

equipment

Many of the recipes don't call for anything other than a few plastic boxes with lids and some salt. For more complicated recipes, I have listed the equipment at the beginning of each recipe.

labels

Always label your meat and sausages before hanging them up to cure. Put what they are, the date you made them, and their weight so you can check them regularly and easily.

THE CURES

There are three basic methods: dry-salting, also known as dry-curing, wet-curing or brining, and bag-curing. Dry-curing involves rubbing the food with salt, sometimes with the addition of flavorings such as black pepper, juniper, cloves, nutmeg, molasses, or dark brown sugar (see page 82). Wet-curing involves soaking the food in a salt solution (brine), often with the addition of sugar and spices (see page 84). There is also a technique known as bag-curing, which is somewhere between the two, which works well for small things like bacon (see pages 94–96).

which salt?

Rock salt is found inland from fossilized seabeds, while sea salt comes directly from an existing sea. Table salt is usually sea salt that has gone though an industrial process to refine it to pure sodium chloride.

We originally, and rather romantically, wanted to use flakes of Maldon sea salt, beautiful orange Himalayan rock salt, or stunning Hawaiian black salt for all our curing projects. However, we soon discovered it was very expensive and not necessary for an excellent result—although it was fine for using on small items such as fillets of fish, etc.

We recommend using ordinary fine or coarse sea salt for most of the recipes. For best results, look for natural salt without anti-caking agents or iodine. Some recipes specifically call for large grain salt, as it encourages water to leach out more easily and flow away—for example, for making *prosciutto* and smoked salmon. For other recipes, it is better to use fine sea salt. Many of the meat recipes are cured with specialist curing salts that contain nitrates to control the spread of bacteria.

nitrates and nitrites

Sooner or later when you delve into salt-curing you will come across the words nitrates and nitrites. Nitrates with an "a" are a form of saltpetre— the original curing salt that was used for centuries and can still be seen in old recipes. Nowadays we know that nitrates can be highly toxic if used in large quantities, so they are no longer sold on their own. Nitrites with an 'i' are what nitrates turn into during the curing process, and since these are far stronger, and much more reliable to use, most curing salts rely entirely on them— though some combine nitrites with a small quantity of nitrates, especially when the salts are required for curing meats like salami, which require longer hanging times. In these cures, the initial nitrites in the curing salts will come to an end more quickly than the nitrates, which will gently keep the process going, producing more nitrites during the long curing.

Ultimately safety is the most important thing, and the safest and most consistent route is to use curing salts, which are a mixture of salt, nitrates, and/or nitrites. Curing salts are the only reliable way of eliminating the risk of botulism caused by the bacterium *Clostridium botulinum*. Nitrates prevent *botulinum* spores from transforming into toxins, eliminating the possibility of food poisoning. They also prevent rancidity in the fat. Curing salts preserve the natural, pinky-red color of the meat that we associate with bacon and salami and give firmness to the food, making it easier to cut.

The two brands of curing salt I recommend are Prague Powder No. 1 and No. 2 and Quickcure (see page 290 for suppliers). The reason I have stuck to these brands is because the percentage of nitrates and nitrites varies between different brands, and I want you to achieve consistent results every time. Other curing salts can be used, but you will have to follow the manufacturer's instructions.

Note: Both nitrates and nitrites have endured something of a bad name in the press over recent years, as people have become concerned with anything chemical that we add to our food. However, it is only fairly recently that we have come to understand the way both nitrates and nitrites work. Today the amounts that can be used in commercial curing are strictly controlled—and actually less than those found naturally in many green leafy vegetables. Ultimately, if you decide not to use curing salts, your cured produce will not last as long and carries a greater risk of spoilage and contamination. Having said that, in some of the recipes we have given instructions for using ordinary sea salt, but this is principally for foods like bacon that will not hang around for long. Saying that, we always use curing salts at home because we like the texture and color they impart, but if you don't mind gray bacon and a short shelf-life then feel free to leave them out.

sugar

Sugar can help to balance the salty flavor in cured produce, and since bacteria feeds on sugar its presence helps promote good bacteria at the beginning of the curing process—once these are established, they will fight off bad bacteria. The drawback of using sugar is it can soften the texture of the product, so this needs to be taken into consideration.

DRY-CURING

Most artisan curers of bacon and ham will tell you that dry-curing is best, because it allows the salt to dissolve slowly into the meat or fish and cures it from outside to inside, over a period of hours or days, depending on what you are curing, and the size and thickness.

how much salt to use?

The amount of salt used in each recipe depends upon its task. When it is used merely for flavor, a small amount can be used, however when it is used to preserve, more is needed. An excess of salt used to keep the food safe during drying or smoking might make the

food unpalatable but it can be removed before we eat the results.

A thin fillet of fish that is going to be eaten quickly might only need a light covering of salt to give it flavor and firm up the flesh. It will cure quickly due to its size.

Salami might have 2.5 percent salt in it, a low amount. This is because the salt is spread evenly and quickly through the ground meat before it is made into sausages. The salami are preserved partly by the salt but also by their fermentation and drying. Through weight loss the percentage of salt in the finished product could be 3–4.5 percent.

Bacon by contrast has between 3–4 percent salt added from the beginning. The salt has to travel from the outside to the middle of the pork. It is only hung for a short amount of time and is not eaten raw.

Conversely a huge ham that is to be cured in a rainy country might have large amounts of salt added to it to carry it safely through the curing and possible smoking stages. English country hams can have as much as 8–9 percent salt in them but they are traditionally soaked to remove this before cooking or are at least boiled with several changes of water so that the end result is actually rather mild.

Left: Salami, *coppa, speck* and more salami.

DRY-CURING—
A BASIC GUIDE

Timing I have indicated approximate curing times in each recipe, however these are a guide only. Actual times will be influenced by many factors, including the temperature of your room/fridge, and the size and age of the product you are curing. For more information on dry-curing times, see below right.

Feel Once cured for long enough, the fish/meat will become firmer and take on a bacony texture. Test by prodding regularly with clean fingers to see if it is firm to the touch or still wobbly like jelly.

Taste It is safe to taste all salted products except raw pork or chicken. If salted correctly, they should have a salty tang but still taste of the product.

Weight loss Meat should lose at least 5 percent of its weight and up to 40 percent for cured pork such as salami after it has been air-dried. This method of testing is less reliable for fish fillets, which dry out anyway as they age without salting.

Practice Through trial and error you will soon get the hang of curing and there is no better way to practice than on small fish. These cure in minutes, allowing you to see the changes quickly—i.e. a floppy fillet of mackerel will become firm and less flexible under a fine covering of salt in 15–30 minutes.

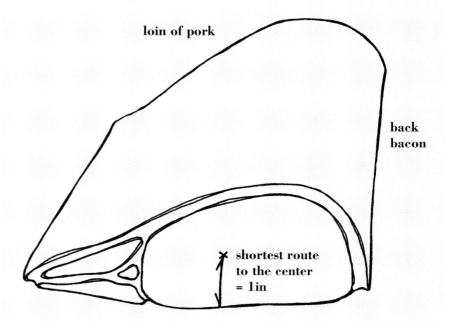

loin of pork

back bacon

✕ shortest route to the center = 1in

7 days for every 1in to the center via the shortest route

DRY-CURING TIMES

We have worked out the approximate curing times for you, based on the theory learned from our friend Jasper Aykroyd, aka "The Bacon Wizard," who cures bacon primarily but also most things under the sun. He suggests you work out how long to dry-cure your produce using this simple scale: allow 7 days for every 1in to the middle of the cut via the shortest route.

The reason Jasper has developed this formula, rather than one based on weight, is because it takes longer for the salt to penetrate to the center of thicker cuts than thinner ones. Using this formula, a standard pork belly, approx. 1¼in thick, will usually takes about 4½ days to cure, whereas back bacon, which is thicker, would normally take about 7 days. If the half-day timing falls at an inconvenient moment, midnight say, leave it until the morning and don't worry. Always err on the side of caution, curing for slightly too long rather than too short a time.

WET-CURING (BRINING)

Most industrial curers employ the "multi-needle" injection method of curing, which is done on a vast scale and is especially designed to add water. This has the effect of plumping up the meat, which is why bacon that has been cured in this way leaches out that familiar white liquid when it goes into a hot pan. You pay for the water as part of the weight of your purchase—rather expensive water! Some manufacturers even include polyphosphates that form a jellylike substance at cold temperatures in order to keep the water in there until you cook the product. These modern processes are often done to speed up the whole curing process so that bacon can be made in less than an hour.

Stitch-brining is an older form of curing that involves injecting the meat by hand with a single needle. This is a more skilled technique than the industrial process mentioned above. It can be done at home with a brine pump, and does speed up brining times, however it takes a lot of practice to get uniform results and we have rarely found it necessary.

Traditional wet cures, where the meat is soaked in brine, are something quite different and this method is much older than injection curing. Wet-brining introduces juiciness and flavor during the curing stage. Old-fashioned wet-brining recipes, which vary from region to region, may include flavorings such as black strap molasses, molasses, brown sugar, bay leaves, juniper, wine, cider, or buttermilk with the basic salt and water mixture.

The traditional method of determining whether you have enough salt in your brine is to drop in a potato or an egg: when it floats, there is enough

BRINING—A BASIC GUIDE

Timing As a rule of thumb, the stronger the brine the shorter the brining time for the same result. Large pieces of meat and fish take more time to absorb the brine than lean, thin ones.

Temperature The temperature of the brine is important. Meat and fish must be put into cold brine, about 37°F is ideal, and this temperature should be maintained throughout the curing process, so leave it in the fridge or a cool place below 41°F.

salt. This occurs when the brine is made up of 4½oz salt to 1 quart water and this is a good all-purpose brine. Today, most people use a brineometer to measure the correct level of salt, or you can follow the table on page 86.

brining times

We give curing times with each recipe, but if using strong brine i.e. in order to cure for preserving, the rule is to allow 4 days for every half inch to the center of the meat via the shortest route. This means a 9lbs pork leg could take about a month; the strength of salt will protect it from decay during this time.

calculating how much brine you need

A simple method of calculating the quantity of brine needed is to place your meat/fish in a plastic container that is roughly the same size and shape. Cover

Containers For best results, choose a container of a similar size and shape to fit your cut, so that you use as little brine and storage space as possible. Meat or fish should always be submerged below the level of the brine. If necessary, weigh it down with weights to prevent any part from protruding.

Precautions If white scum appears on the surface of the brine, this should be removed. If the brine turns milky, blue, slimy, or sticky—or smells foul—discard it straight away. Do not reuse brine; discard after one use.

with cold water, adding one quart at a time, until the meat is submerged. Then you know how much brine to make up. As a rough guide, you will need roughly the same amount in quarts as the weight of your produce.

hot brine or cold brine?

There are two methods for making the brine, depending on whether you use hot or cold water. The good thing about cold brine is it can be made up quickly. With this method, the salt isn't heated but gradually dissolves over a few days. The drawback of this method is you have to turn the foods frequently, and stir up the brine, to ensure the salt is evenly distributed around the meat or fish. This method of brining is only suitable for longer brining times—i.e. greater than a day—because the salt needs time to dissolve.

Hot brines need to be made in advance and left to cool before use. With this method, the salt is dissolved in hot liquid (with or without sugar and

spices) and then chilled. The advantage of a hot brine is the salt is completely dissolved and any spices have a chance to release their flavor into the brine; the drawback is you need to allow time for the brine to chill (preferably overnight) before use.

method for making hot brine

Work out how much brine you need (see page 84) and calculate the correct percentage of water, salt, and sugar/flavorings needed. Combine the salt and sugar with 1 quart of the water in a saucepan over medium heat, stirring to dissolve. Herbs and spices can also be included at this stage, since the cooking helps release the flavors. Once the sugar and salt have dissolved, set aside to cool to room temperature (over a bowl of ice to speed things up). Combine with the remaining cold water and transfer the brine to the fridge to chill.

adding sugar and spices

Traditionally, hot brines are flavored with sugar, herbs, and spices—see Bradenham-style ham, pages 99–100. As a general rule of thumb, allow half the amount of sugar, maple syrup, or honey to the amount of salt in the cure. Note that you must always stick to the exact ratio of salt and water stated.

Feel free to experiment with additional flavorings, although in our experience they are never really detectable in the final product. Choose flavorings that go well together out of the following: 2 sprigs of rosemary, 1 tablespoon of crushed juniper berries, 1¼in cube of grated ginger, 2 x 2½in strips of orange peel, 2 bay leaves, a handful of parsley, and 2 crushed garlic cloves to 1 quart of water.

BRINING STRENGTHS

These are the three strengths of brine we recommend for the recipes in this book; we refer to them in this chapter and in Smoke.

Note: We initially found it very confusing that a so-called 40 percent brine didn't actually contain 40 percent salt to water! Instead it is to do with the way brine is measured with using a brineometer or salinometer, which measures the percentage saturated solution of brine in water.

Many curers develop their own preferred brine strengths based on individual tastes. You might decide after experimenting that you prefer a saltier taste to your produce or a longer brining time to suit your schedule. However, bear in mind that if you alter the strength, or the timings, it could affect the shelf-life of your produce.

Weak 20 percent brine:
2oz salt to 1 quart water.
This is ideal for already salty foods, such as mussels, or for items that need brining overnight such as whole turkeys or chickens.

Medium 40 percent brine:
4½oz salt to 1 quart water. This is ideal for curing smallish pieces of meat such as bacon or a small ham. At this ratio, an egg or potato should float in the brine; this was the old way of determining the strength of a brine.

Strong 70 percent brine:
8oz salt to 1 quart water.
This will work more quickly than the weaker brines and is useful for smaller pieces of meat or fish—such as pheasant or duck breasts, or whole medium fish—that only need a short curing time, i.e. less than 2 hours.

WET-BRINED TURKEY OR CHICKEN

Wet-brining poultry results in a more flavorful and succulent bird after roasting. You can use large brining or roasting bags for this method—use two just in case one splits—or a sanitized cooler or large, nonreactive container that fits inside your fridge. If the weather is cold, you can carry out this process in an outdoor room (providing it stays below 41°F).

METHOD Make up a weak, 20 percent hot brine solution (see left) and set aside to cool in the fridge. Place the poultry in a container and top up with the cold brine so that it is completely submerged. Cover the container with a lid or plastic wrap and transfer to the fridge to cure for 8 hours or overnight.

Discard the brine and rinse the poultry briefly under cold running water; pat dry on paper towels.

Set aside to dry on a wire rack in a cool place (covered with a fly net) or in the fridge to form a pellicle for a minimum of 3 hours and up to a day.

To cook, either roast in a conventional oven at 350°F or hot smoke until the internal temperature reaches 185°F (see page 173). Eat straight away or store in the fridge for up to 5 days.

WET-BRINED FISH OR SHELLFISH

This method is ideal for fish that are going to be smoked or broiled, as the brining imparts moisture to the fish and stops it from drying out. Brining also affects the texture of the fish, firming it up so the flesh is less likely to fall apart on the grill. It is certainly a great way to get fish seasoned all the way through, and the salt also helps to preserve it. Always make sure the fish is fresh and sustainably caught.

METHOD Make up a weak, 20 percent hot brine solution (see left) and set aside to cool in the fridge. Arrange the fish in a single layer, skin-side down, in a large lasagne dish or similar. Pour the cold brine over the fish and cover the container with plastic wrap.

If necessary, weigh the fish down so that it is completely submerged in the brine. Transfer the fish to the fridge for a period of time depending on the strength of the brine and the size of the fish, see the box below. Discard the brine and rinse the fish briefly under cold running water; pat dry on paper towels.

Arrange the fish on a wire rack and set aside to dry in a cool place (covered with a mesh food cover) or in the fridge to form a pellicle for a minimum of an hour and up to a day.

Cook the fish under a hot broiler, flesh-side up, until cooked through. Alternatively, hot smoke until the internal temperature reaches 145°F. Eat straight away or store in the fridge for up to 2 days. For advice on cold smoking, see pages 152–154.

BRINING CHART – A QUICK REFERENCE GUIDE

Product	% brine	Time	Additional Flavorings
whole turkey, whole chicken, fish	20	overnight	sugar, maple syrup, honey, garlic cloves, parsley, bay leaves, onion
pork chops	40	4 hours	replace half the water with apple juice; rosemary
tuna, mackerel, salmon, white fish	20	1 hour for thin fillets up to ¾in; 6–8 hours for thicker fillets over ¾in.	orange peel, lemon peel, ginger
turkey breast	40	4–6 hours	sugar, maple syrup, or honey
chicken or duck breast	40	3–4 hours	sugar, maple syrup, or honey; orange peel
shrimp, scallops, crawfish	70	15 minutes for small, peeled shellfish; 1 hour for really large shrimp	orange or lemon zest, dill—not much time for flavors to penetrate

BAG-CURING

Bag-curing sits somewhere between dry-curing and wet-curing. Usually when dry-curing meat you leave it on a slope or rack so that the water that is drawn out of it can drain away. However, many recipes use a bag, such as a vacuum or freezer bag, to hold the meat and its cure instead. With this method, the water is not emptied out; instead the water leaching from the product makes its own brine (sometimes confusingly called "pickle"). Although the rack method is preferable because it partially dries the product and concentrates the flavor, bag-curing is easy and quick to do. Care needs to be taken when hanging bag-cured produce as they are more likely to suffer molds due to their humidity. It is ideal for bacon however as it doesn't have a long hanging time. We make our bacon and *Petit salé* using this method. A two pound piece of belly will fit perfectly into a medium-sized freezer bag, I can keep it in the fridge easily and turn it daily. The dosages for bag-curing are the same as dry-curing.

FRUIT

Salting citrus fruit is a method of preserving lemons, limes, grapefruit, and kumquats well after their season has expired. This method of preserving was originally used to transport citrus fruit in the days before refrigeration. Indian pickled or salted lemons were regularly brought back from India to Europe by travelers centuries ago. Nowadays we don't need to preserve these fruits as they are available all year round, but it is the distinct flavor of preserved fruits that we enjoy—especially in Middle Eastern and Asian cuisines. This flavor is partly achieved by the "healthy" bacteria, *lactobacillus*, that thrive in the salty environment and ferment the fruit. After a few weeks, the salt draws the water out of the fruit, creating a brine; this can be reused for brining meats—see Duck with salted kumquats on pages 116–117. Preserved citrus flesh and rind can be used in tagines, etc.

SALTED KUMQUATS

We have grown kumquats in the past without ever really knowing what to do with them. These salted kumquats not only look pretty in the jar, but are really delicious in a lamb or chicken tagine. Don't waste the salty brine that collects in the jars; it makes a great citrusy cure for the duck breasts on pages 116–117.

makes approx. 3 x 12-oz jars
18oz kumquats
1 tablespoon black peppercorns
2in cinnamon stick
1⅓–1¾ cups coarse sea salt
juice of 4–5 lemons

Wash the kumquats and dry well. Cut off the very end of each kumquat where it was attached to the stalk. Make a

SALTED LEMONS

These are a favorite ingredient in Moroccan tagines.

makes approx. 2¼ lbs
18oz lemons
1⅓–1¾ cups coarse sea salt
juice of 4–5 lemons

Follow the method for Salted kumquats (left), omitting the cinnamon and pepper.

USES FOR SALTED FRUITS Finely chop the preserved lemons and combine with olives to serve as a canapé.

To make a delicious citrus rub for fish, jumbo shrimp, or chicken, finely chop them with some scallions and parsley and combine with olive oil or butter.

Preserved lemons are also used in the impressive Italian topping *gremolata* for *osso buco*; here they are finely chopped with parsley and garlic.

Marc Frederic, known as the English Charcutier, told us his tip for curing salmon with lemon salt: use one part lemon salt to one part normal salt to impart a delicious citrus flavor.

Variation
SALTED LIMES
Follow the recipe for Salted lemons using limes instead.

cross in each fruit using a small knife, starting at the stalk end and cutting halfway down the side of the fruit; be careful not to cut all the way through. Place the kumquats in a mixing bowl. Lightly crush the peppercorns in a mortar and pestle or pepper grinder and add these to the bowl. Break the cinnamon stick into two or three pieces and add to the bowl with the salt. Mix the ingredients together with your hands, pressing the salt into the cuts in the kumquats to penetrate the flesh. Divide the mixture between sterilized jars and top them up with lemon juice. Make sure the kumquats are completely covered with the lemon juice and salt to protect them from the air. Put on the lids and transfer to a sunny spot for up to a week. After a week, move to a cool, dark place for approx. 3 months. Salted kumquats will keep for up to a year. Once opened, store in the fridge for up to 6 months.

FISH

Few foods go off quicker than fish, which is probably one of the reasons we are sometimes afraid of cooking and eating it as much as we should. Fish has been salted, dried, and smoked for centuries to preserve it, and to enable it to travel to areas away from the coast. Although refrigeration has made fresh fish easily accessible, many of us still end up throwing it away occasionally because we haven't used it up quickly enough. However, simply by rubbing salt into fish you can extend its life by a few more days.

Fresh fish contains about 80 percent water, but if it is cured with salt and dried this percentage can be reduced to below 25 percent, creating a hostile environment for bacteria. If you take the water content under 15 percent, molds will struggle to survive. This is the science behind salt cod or *baccalà*, as it is also known, and this is the way people have preserved fish for centuries.

Most of us are unlikely to try salting a whole cod in the kitchen sink, but it is fulfilling to experiment with fish on a smaller scale.

SALTED COD FILLETS

Salting cod gives the fish a wonderful flavor and texture. It also preserves the shelf-life of the fish. This recipe produces a similar flavor to *baccalà*, but it is not as intense since less salt is used and the cod is not dried. Use these salted cod fillets in any recipe that calls for salt cod. One of my favorite recipes is simply to steam the fish and serve it with aioli and vegetables. However, do make sure it has had a good soak in cold water beforehand to remove the salt. If you are worried it might be too salty, cut off a small piece and quickly cook it to taste, bearing in mind the outside will be slightly saltier than the inside. This preserving method is also suitable for other fish in the cod family such as pollock.

serves 4
fine sea salt
4 x 7oz cod, haddock, or pollock fillets

Scatter some salt over the base of a shallow dish and put in the fish, skin-side down. Cover the tops and sides of the fish completely with salt so you cannot see the fish—this can be in a thin layer. Cover the dish with plastic wrap and set aside overnight in the fridge (or a cold place below 41°F).

The following day, give the fish a quick rinse under cold running water and pat dry with paper towels. Wrap the fish in plastic wrap and store in the fridge until needed, for up to 1 week. Before use, soak the fish for 24 hours in cold water, changing the water twice during this time.

MARINATED BLACK COD IN MISO

Miso preserves and enhances the flavor of the fish. This is our friend, and teacher of Japanese cookery, Reiko Hara's recipe. Black cod done in a similar way was made famous by Nobu Matsuhisa at the renowned London restaurant that bears his name. This recipe also works well with mackerel, sea bass, and salmon.

serves 4
fine sea salt
4 x 3½–4½oz black cod fillets
⅓ cup mirin
⅓ cup sake
1lb white miso
1¼ cups sugar
1 teaspoon ginger juice (squeezed from grated fresh ginger)
4 slices of pickled preserved ginger, to decorate (see page 74–75)

Sprinkle some salt over the base of a large dish, put in the cod fillets, skin-side down, and cover with a thin layer of salt. Set aside in the fridge for 1 hour.

Meanwhile make the marinade. Pour the mirin and sake into a saucepan and bring to a boil to burn off the alcohol. Add the miso and stir vigorously over low heat to make a smooth paste, taking care not to let it burn. Add the sugar and stir well to dissolve. Remove the pan from the heat and set aside to cool to room temperature.

Add the ginger juice to the marinade and mix well. Rinse the cod to remove the salt and pat it dry with paper towels. Spread half of the marinade evenly over the base of a large, shallow, rectangular container. Spread a clean piece of cheesecloth over the top, put in the cod fillets, and then place another piece of cheesecloth on top. (The cheesecloth stops the miso sticking to the fish.) Spread the rest of the marinade over the cheesecloth, cover with a lid or plastic wrap and set aside to marinate in the fridge for 3–4 days.

To serve, remove the cod fillets from the container and wipe each one with damp paper towels. Broil the fish on both sides for a few minutes until golden brown. Serve hot, garnished with ginger (see pages 74–75), accompanied by steamed rice.

SALTED ANCHOVIES

Anchovies or sprats are often packed in layers of salt to preserve them for long periods of time, and this is how they have been transported for centuries. The Romans loved anchovies and used the juices released from packing them in salt as a flavor enhancer called *garum*. To this day, anchovies are packed and pressed down in salt in Cetara, on the Amalfi coast of Italy, to release brine called *Colatura di Alici*, which is used to dress spaghetti.

If you want to do this at home, ensure that you use the freshest fish—either anchovies or sprats work well, but don't choose the smallest specimens, which won't stand up to the pressure in the container. Ideally fish should be salted within 12 hours of being caught.

makes 2¼lbs

a large, sterilized container to hold the fish (either a glass jar or a ceramic pot with a lid)
2¼lbs anchovies (approx. 50 fish)
coarse sea salt

Snap the head off the fish just behind the eyes and pull out the adjoining intestines—if some remain it doesn't matter. Rinse the anchovies briefly and gently in cold water, and then dry them carefully in between layers of paper towels.

Sprinkle some salt in the base of your container and cover with a layer of anchovies. Scatter a thin layer of salt on top and then layer up the rest of the anchovies with the salt in the same way until the container is almost full. Put a weight on top, such as another jar with a flat bottom or a small saucer with a weight on top.

Cover the container with plastic wrap, or a lid if using a ceramic pot, and set aside in the fridge or a cold place (below 41°F) for 6–8 weeks to mature; cooler temperatures will slow down the process. During this time, the salt will draw out the moisture from the fish. The weight on top should ensure that the fish stay submerged in the brine, however if necessary you can top up the jar with a strong brine to keep them covered at all times (see page 86). Once cured, the fish will take on a flattened, brown appearance. If cured correctly, they will last up to a year in the salty brine.

To use, remove however many you need from the brine and rinse them carefully in cold water. Pat the anchovies dry on paper towels and dress with extra virgin olive oil, finely chopped chile or onion, lemon juice and parsley. Use on pizzas or in pasta sauces, or in the *Bagnetto* recipe on page 185. Alternatively see Marinated Anchovies on page 28.

GRAVLAX

Fishermen have made this Nordic dish since the Middle Ages, traditionally salting and burying the salmon in the sand above the high-tide line. *Grav* means "grave" and *lax* means "salmon," hence the term *gravlax* meaning "buried salmon."

CURED SALMON WITH DILL, MUSTARD, AND HONEY SAUCE

I like *gravlax* quite sweet, so I include more sugar than salt in my curing mixture, however you can use less sugar if you wish and reduce the amount of honey in the sauce. If you run out of dill for the sauce, as I did, simply rinse out the dill from the cure and reuse this for the sauce. My first experiments left the salmon too salty, particularly by the tail where the flesh is thinner. To prevent this, put less salt on the tail area. If you do find the fish tastes too salty, soak it for an hour in cold water after curing to get rid of some of the saltiness.

serves 10 as a starter
3⅓–4½lbs salmon, filleted

For the cure
⅓ cup coarse sea salt
¾ cup sugar
good grind of black pepper
¼ cup vodka
2oz fresh dill, finely chopped

For the sauce
3 tablespoons finely chopped dill
3 tablespoons mild honey
2 tablespoons Dijon mustard
2 tablespoons apple cider vinegar
2 tablespoons vegetable oil
salt, to taste

Mix up the ingredients for the cure, reserving 1oz dill. Sprinkle 1–2 tablespoons of the cure in a large lasagna dish and put in one of the fillets, skin-side down. Sprinkle the rest of the cure on top, reserving 1–2 tablespoons. Place the remaining fillet of salmon on top, skin-side up, to make a sandwich and sprinkle over the remaining cure. Cover the dish with plastic wrap and rest some weights on top—I use cartons of orange juice. Transfer the fish to the fridge for 24 hours. Drain off any liquid in the container every 12 hours and turn the fish sandwich over.

After 24 hours, taste a small piece of the salmon. Note that the thinner tail end will be saltier than the center, so taste a piece from the middle. If it tastes too salty, soak the fish in cold water for an hour. If you are happy with the saltiness, rinse the fish briefly in cold water and pat dry with paper towels.

Scatter the reserved dill over the flesh of the fish and sandwich it back together again. Put the salmon into a clean container and cover with plastic wrap. Store in the fridge until you are ready to eat it; it will stay good for approx. 10 days. *Gravlax* can also be frozen.

To serve, cut the salmon into thin slices on the diagonal with a long, just sharpened knife, starting at the tail end. To make the sauce, combine the ingredients in a bowl and season to taste with salt. Accompany with rye bread and lemon wedges.

PORK

Pork is surely the greatest meat to salt, as there is so much you can do with it and it is possible to achieve so many different results. Jasper Aykroyd, who makes his living from producing and selling bacon, spent time with me in my kitchen, guiding me through the various processes. He believes that salt curing is alchemy: part science and part magic. It is extraordinary to experience, hands on, the way that time transforms a pig's leg, for example, into a soft, sweet *prosciutto*, which can be cut into ultra-thin layers that melt in your mouth, delivering the unique tang of umami.

Japanese scientist, Dr. Kikunae Ikeda, first identified the so-called fifth taste in 1908 and called it "umami" after the Japanese word for deliciousness. However, umami wasn't formally recognised until the 1980s. Umami accounts for many of the flavors we love in cured food, which had previously just been considered savory and delicious. During the processes of curing, drying, and aging, enzymes break down proteins into peptides and an amino acid called glutamate, which has this savory or umami flavor. Incidentally, Dr. Ikeda realized the power of this natural flavor and invented MSG, monosodium glutamate, a processed version of it, which is now used all over the world as a flavor enhancer.

In Europe, the annual killing of the pig traditionally took place in November, using the cold months of the year as a natural fridge. Nothing from the pig was ever wasted—and we have tried to honor this by including some recipes to use up the valuable offal and some of the unfashionable cuts.

buying your pork

Where possible, choose free-range pigs that have been fed on as much natural produce as possible, as this will result in a better end product. The old breeds have a much better fat content, which makes them ideal for charcuterie. A young pig is better for sausages and bacon, while an older pig is better for charcuterie as it will have more flavor. A baconer pig is usually about 180–200lbs dead weight; a charcuterie pig is about 270–360lbs dead weight.

Make sure your butcher knows what you want to do with any cuts you ask for. We have ordered a leg of ham before for making *prosciutto*, only to find the skin had been scored.

BACON

There is nothing quite like bacon and now we make our own and enjoy it all the more.

You should use middle bacon made from the loin and the belly; it is also known as whole bacon or long back. When separated, they make back bacon (also called Canadian bacon) and bacon.

Marc Frederic, the British charcutier, recommends that you leave the ribs on when curing bacon, and then butcher it afterward. The ribs deliver flavor and help the shape of the bacon. These "bacon ribs" can then be used to flavor stocks or stews, or boiled up and served with mushy peas.

OLD ENGLISH BACON

This traditional Elizabethan recipe by Maynard Davies, famous for his wonderful books on his life as the last apprentice bacon curer, is not usually smoked although the choice is yours.

makes approx. 2lbs
2¼lbs pork loin or belly
2 tablespoons curing salts: EITHER
 ½ tablespoon Quickcure and
 1½ tablespoons salt OR ½ level
 teaspoon Prague Powder No. 2 and
 2 tablespoons salt OR 2 tablespoons
 salt with no cure
6 teaspoons soft brown sugar
2 teaspoons caraway seeds, lightly
 crushed
2 teaspoons ground ginger powder

Follow the instructions for Streaky bacon on page 96. If using pork loin instead of belly of pork, increase the curing timing: allow 7 days for every 1in to the center of the meat via the shortest route. This bacon can be cold smoked if you wish

over mild apple wood smoke, however it already has a subtle flavor so go easy (see page 103).

BACON

This is an easy recipe to start with, as it can all be done in a plastic bag and stored in the fridge. It is how we make our bacon on a regular basis at home now and I nearly always smoke it afterward. I find that 1¾–2¼lbs pork belly is a good amount to last a couple of weeks for a family of 4–6.

We have given three measures for salt, depending on whether you use Quickcure, Prague Powder, or plain salt with no cure (see page 81). Note that if you use plain salt with no cure your bacon will only last up to 5 days and it will be a brownish-gray color—that of natural roast pork. Note: Quickcure recommends a ratio of 1½oz curing salt to 2¼lbs meat, but I find this a bit salty so I've cut it down to 1⅓oz.

Bacon made with curing salts will last up to 2 weeks, stored in the fridge. However, all bacon can be frozen. This bacon can be eaten "green," which means unsmoked, or smoked (see page 163).

Expect 5 percent weight loss during the curing stage and a further 5–10 percent during hanging.

makes approx. 2lbs
2¼lbs pork belly, approx. 1½in thick
2 tablespoons curing salts: EITHER ½ tablespoon Quickcure and 1½ tablespoons salt OR ½ level teaspoon Prague Powder No. 2 and 2 tablespoons salt OR 2 tablespoons salt with no cure
2 teaspoons crushed black pepper
1 teaspoon demerara sugar

Combine the salt, pepper, and sugar for the cure and rub into the meat, allowing approx. 90 percent for the flesh side and 10 percent for the skin. Put the belly

into a freezer or vacuum bag, taking care not to let the cure touch the seal if using a freezer bag. Seal the bag, expelling as much air as you can or use a vacuum machine. Leave the bacon in the fridge for 5 days**, turning daily to distribute the juices evenly around the bag.

Remove the meat from the bag and pat dry with paper towels; do not rinse. Place the bacon on a wire rack to allow air to circulate and set aside in the fridge, or hang in a curing chamber, to dry for 1–5 days. The longer it is left the more concentrated the flavor; also the texture will become firmer and drier. The bacon is ready when it feels firm to the touch and not jellylike. If cured correctly, it should have lost 10–15 percent of its initial weight. If you would like it smoked, see page 163.

To store, wrap the bacon in parchment paper and keep in the fridge for up to 2 weeks. Bacon can also be frozen.

** If the belly is thicker than 1½in, increase the curing timing: allow 7 days for every 1in to the center of the meat via the shortest route.

BEER AND CHILE DRY-CURE BACON

This is Jasper Aykroyd, The Bacon Wizard's recipe for spicy bacon. In his own words: "it could not be simpler." Curing salts, dried malt extract and hops are widely available from any homebrew shop, high street or online, and won't break the bank or perish quickly. Soft, light-brown sugar will work as a replacement for the malt, but it's much more fun to make a dry-beer mix! This can be done with belly or loin of pork.

This makes a wicked and delicious bacon sandwich washed down with a pint of your favorite tipple.

makes approx. 2lbs
2¼lbs pork belly (approx. 1½in thick) or loin

For the cure
1⅓oz curing salts: EITHER ⅓oz Quickcure and 1oz salt OR ½ level teaspoon ¹⁄₁₆oz) Prague Powder No. 2 and 1¼oz salt OR 1⅓ oz salt with no cure
1⅓oz dried malt extract
½oz dried hops (any will do, but you may have a favorite—Jasper prefers 'Saaz' or 'Cascade')
¼oz red pepper flakes (optional)
¼oz bay leaf, crushed

Mix all of the ingredients together for the cure and apply liberally to your pork, allowing 90 percent for the flesh side and 10 percent for the skin. Massage the cure really well into the meat, leaving no part uncovered. Transfer the pork to a bag or a container with a lid. In this particular recipe, because you want the meat to really absorb the flavors from the cure, it's quite all right to leave it wrapped in a bag or sitting in its juices in a tightly fitting tub. However, if you are a purist, you can elevate the pork in the tub by raising it up on chopsticks or similar and pour off the juices periodically. Allow 5 days in the fridge for (belly) bacon or 7 days for back or Canadian (loin).

Once the bacon has finished curing, quickly rinse it under cold water to wash off the salt and pat dry with paper towels. Transfer the bacon to a wire rack or similar with a baking sheet underneath to catch the juices. Dry the bacon for 2 hours at room temperature and then transfer to the fridge overnight (uncovered is best to allow the air to circulate and finish off the curing process, but only do this if you have nothing else in the fridge that could taint it like onions or garlic).

To store, wrap the bacon in parchment paper and store in the fridge for up to 2 weeks.

DRY-CURED PANCETTA

Pancetta (air-dried pork belly) is used to flavor dishes such as pasta sauces, soups, and stews, and it is one product we couldn't do without in our restaurants. The wonderful flavor of *pancetta* comes from the concentration of herbs and spices used in the dry-cure mixture.

makes 1lb 10oz
2¼lbs pork belly (approx. 2⅓in thick)
2 tablespoons curing salts: EITHER
  ½ tablespoon Quickcure and
  1½ tablespoons salt OR ½ level
  teaspoon Prague Powder No. 2 and
  2 tablespoons salt OR 2 tablespoons
salt with no cure 2 teaspoons
crushed black peppercorns
1 teaspoon demerara sugar
8in sprig of rosemary, needles
removed

To cure the pork belly, follow the method for bacon on page 96, adding the rosemary needles with the curing salts. After the bacon has finished curing for 5–7 days in the fridge, remove it from the bag and pat dry on paper towels. Hang in a curing chamber at 53–61°F for at least a month and up to 2 months (see page 141). It can be hung for longer, but it will become harder and saltier.

To serve, slice thinly and wrap around chicken breasts or scallops or cut into small lardons and use as a flavoring in soups, sauces, or *ragùs*. *Pancetta* can also be ground and included in meatballs. Always remove the skin before cooking, as it is too tough to break down during cooking.

Variation
To make *guanciale*, cured pork cheek, follow the recipe for *pancetta* but cover the surface with finely ground black pepper before hanging—this was traditionally done to keep the flies away.

PETIT SALÉ

The French equivalent of bacon, *petit salé* is also made with belly of pork. Once cured, the salted pork is traditionally boiled and the broth used for cooking pulses such as lentils. *Petit salé aux lentilles* is one of my favorite French dishes. It is usually served on top of the lentils along with boiled *saucisson sec* and ham hock, sometimes with *sauerkraut* too.

METHOD Follow the method for bacon on page 96, curing for a week in a bag in the fridge; use curing salts if you wish to preserve the pink color or plain salt for a natural pork color. Remove from the bag, rinse briefly, and pat dry with paper towels. To cook, put the *Petit salé* (if you wish with a ham hock and a *saucisson sec* or two) into a large stock pot two-thirds full with cold water. Bring the water slowly to a boil. Taste the water and if it is too salty for a stock discard it and start again. From boiling point it should take between 40 minutes–1 hour to cook the pork through. The internal temperature of the belly should be 171°F. Remove from the heat. Gently fry a little roughly chopped carrot, celery, and onion in a saucepan until soft. Add the lentils, a couple of bay leaves and a sprig of thyme and stir through, pour over enough ham stock to cover them. Cook until tender, drain, and serve topped with sliced belly, sausage and flaked ham hock. Cool and freeze any leftover stock for another day.

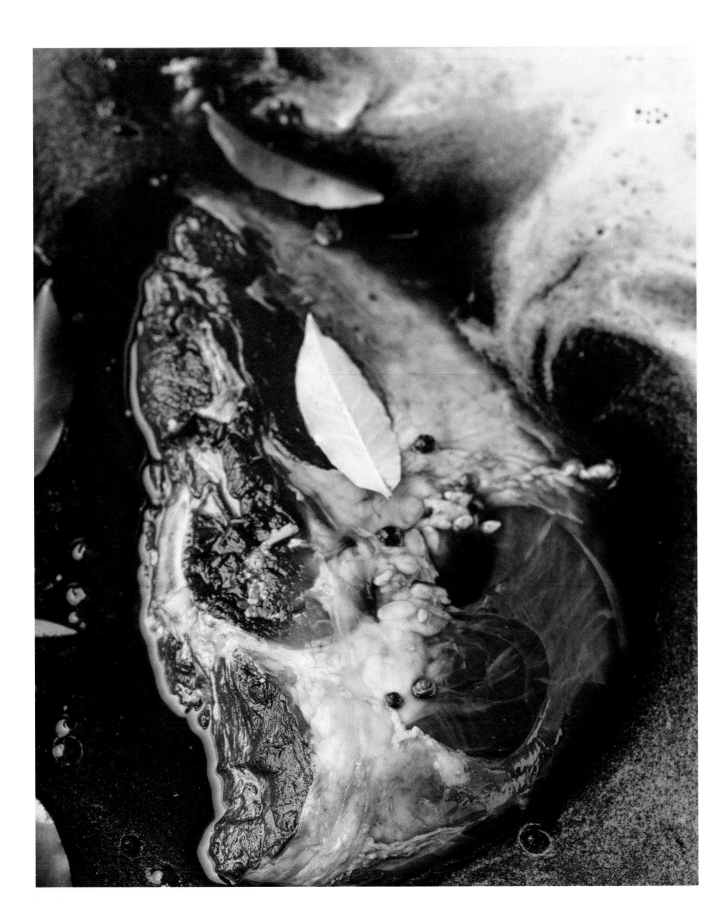

HAMS

There are two main methods of turning a slab of pork into sweet, pink alluring ham: dry-curing and wet-curing (or brining). Dry-curing involves rubbing the pork with salt and sometimes sugar or molasses; wet-curing involves soaking the pork in a sweet bath of flavored brine—lucky ham! Both methods can be made with or without curing salts, but without you will not have the traditional pink color we associate with ham and you won't have the same protection curing salts give against decay and contamination.

During our first experiments, it was easy to see where the cure hadn't penetrated to the inside because when we cut the ham open the center displayed a circle of gray meat while the surrounding area was pink. This can be corrected when wet-brining by injecting the brine into the center of the cut with a brine pump. This speeds up the process because the brine enters the meat from the outside and the center, ensuring all of the meat is evenly cured. Alternatively, you can leave the ham for longer in the brine.

After curing, large hams will always be very salty on the outside and the middle much less so. This is why hams are traditionally hung for at least a month afterward to equalize the saltiness throughout. Alternatively, they can be soaked overnight in cold water to remove excess salt or boiled in several changes of water.

For dry-curing, allow 3½oz curing salts per 2¼lbs of meat: EITHER ½oz Quickcure and 3⅓oz salt OR ½ level teaspoon (¹⁄₁₆oz) Prague Powder No. 2 and 3½oz salt. For wet-brining, allow 3½oz curing salts per 2¼lbs of curable ingredients—i.e. water and meat combined.

Once the ham has been cured, it can either be left unsmoked or smoked. At home, we smoke our Christmas ham, air-dry *prosciutto* and smoke and air-dry *speck*.

BRADENHAM-STYLE HAM

This traditional British ham is dry-cured to begin with and then given a sweet bath of wet-brine flavored with dark beer, stout, or porter. The original recipe is protected, but this is a good alternative. The first stage is to make a cured ham—i.e. one that has been treated with curing salts—this will help to preserve it, give it the pink color, and offer protection against bacteria.

serves 18–20
9lbs boned leg of pork

For the dry-cure
1⅓ cups curing salts: EITHER 2½ tablespoons Quickcure and 1¼ cups salt OR 1 tablespoon Prague Powder No. 2 and 1⅓ cups fine salt

For the brine
4 quarts Guinness (use in equal weight to the amount of cured meat and make sure it is fully submerged—you can use half Guinness and half water but there will be a weaker flavor to the end result)
1¼ cups molasses
4 bay leaves
2 teaspoons juniper berries
4 teaspoons coriander seeds
4 teaspoons black pepper

To cook
2 teaspoons mustard seeds
3 bay leaves
1 teaspoon allspice berries
honey and demerara sugar, for the glaze

Mix the curing salts with the salt and divide this mixture in half. You will need half now and the rest in 2 weeks; the remaining half can be kept in a plastic bag in a dark place. Rub the mixture into the pork, applying 90 percent of the mixture to the exposed meat and fat and 10 percent to the skin. Place the pork in a container, preferably raised up on a nonmetal rack to allow the water that will leach out of the meat to drain off. Alternatively, slope the container so you can drain off the water easily. Cover and store in the fridge or in a cold place (below 41°F) for 2 weeks. Turn daily and pour off the brine periodically.

Remove the pork from the container and rub the reserved cure mixture into the meat. Rinse out the container, put the pork inside and return it to a cold place to cure for a further 2 weeks.

Rinse the cured ham under cold running water and pat dry with paper towels; wash the container. Put the ham on a wire rack at room temperature to dry overnight.

Meanwhile, make up the brine by heating the Guinness with the molasses and flavorings; set aside to cool completely.

Place the ham in the container and pour over the brine. Weigh the meat down if necessary to keep it submerged. Set aside in a fridge or a cool place (below 41°F) for 14 days, turning every 2 days.

Remove the ham from the container and discard the soaking liquor. Dry the meat with paper towels and hang in a curing chamber at 54–61°F for 1 month (see page 141).

Before cooking, soak the ham for 24 hours in cold water. To cook the ham, place it in a pan of fresh water with the spices and bring to a boil. Put on a lid and simmer for 25 minutes per 1lb or until the internal temperature is 167°F. Once cooked, remove from the heat and allow the ham to cool down and relax in the juices for 30 minutes. It can either be eaten like this or glazed and roasted in a hot oven to finish.

To glaze and roast the ham, remove the ham from the pan, cut off the skin and discard. Smother the fat side in honey and press on a coating of demerara sugar. Cook in a hot oven, 350°F, for 30–45 minutes until the glaze has deepened to a rich golden brown. Remove from the oven and allow the ham to rest for 30 minutes before eating. Eat immediately or allow it to cool and store in the fridge for up to 5 days.

CHRISTMAS HAM

Christmas wouldn't be the same without a ham bubbling away on Christmas Eve waiting for its skin to be scored into diamonds and stuffed with cloves. I rub ours with homemade marmalade, and this year I decided to cure and smoke it myself. After a few trial runs during the year before the big day, I am happy to say the flavor was wonderful from the start and I will be doing it every year.

serves approx. 18
9lbs boned leg of pork leg

Brine for weeks 1–2
2lbs curing salts: EITHER 3oz
 Quickcure and 1lb 13oz salt OR
 1oz Prague Powder No. 2 and
 1lb 15oz fine salt
5 quarts cold water
2¼ cups dark brown sugar

Brine for weeks 3–4
2lbs curing salts: EITHER 3oz
 Quickcure and 1lb 13oz salt OR
 1oz Prague Powder No. 2 and
 1lb 15oz fine salt
5 quarts cold water
2¼ cups dark brown sugar

Mix together the first batch of curing salts with the water and sugar to make the brine for the first 2 weeks. Stab the pork a few times with a skewer to help the brine to penetrate and put it into a large plastic box or nonreactive metal container just bigger than the cut. Pour over the brine and weigh down the meat to keep it submerged—I use a full carton of juice inside a freezer bag as a weight. Cover the container with a lid or plastic wrap and set aside in the fridge or in a cold garage to cure for 2 weeks. Turn the meat daily and ensure it is completely submerged in the brine for the whole time.

After 2 weeks, discard the brine and give the ham a quick rinse under cold running water; clean out the container. Put the ham back into the container and mix up the next batch of brine; pour this over the ham. Transfer the ham, covered, to a cool place for 2 weeks, as before, turning daily.

After the ham has finished curing, remove it from the brine and pat dry with paper towels. Put it on a wire rack to allow air to circulate and transfer it to a cool place (such as a fridge) to dry overnight or for up to 2 days before smoking it.

To smoke the ham, follow the instructions for cold smoking on pages 164–165.

If you decide not to smoke the ham, hang it for at least a month in a meat safe in a cool room or in a curing chamber; air-drying improves the flavor and equalizes the saltiness.

After smoking, allow the ham to come slowly down to room temperature before hanging as above. For best results hang the ham to allow the smoke flavor to equalize within the ham. Hanging time can be a bit shorter if smoked, 2–3 weeks is fine. After hanging, scrub the ham with a brush and soak overnight before cooking in several changes of water.

To cook the ham, follow the instructions on page 164–165. Once cooked, the ham will keep for up to 5 days in the fridge.

Variation
If you wish, you can flavor the brine with juniper berries, rosemary, or bay leaves.

SMALL PROSCIUTTO

Giancarlo and I have enjoyed so much wonderful *prosciutto* from San Daniele in Friuli, the north of Italy, and from Parma in Emilia-Romagna in the center of Italy, that anything we have been able to produce here in the UK with our climate just doesn't match up. After countless legs of pork being wasted, not to mention time and money, we have come to the conclusion that it is better to leave this product where it belongs in Italy. Instead we have taken great pride in making successful small *prosciutto* that are quicker and easier to prepare and take up less space.

Small (2¼–4½lbs) pieces of pork are a wonderful way to test your curing abilities. With these you will be able to practice larding and wrapping and discover how salty you like your meat. On these smaller pieces you are looking for 30 percent weight loss before the meat is ready to eat. This will depend upon your environment, but you should be able to make a small *prosciutto* such as this within 2 months. It is really important to weigh the ham at the beginning to calculate the weight loss.

In particularly dry environments, such as Parma and San Daniele in Italy, curing salts are not always used. The combination of salting, rising acidity in the meat (where particular bacteria thrive and cause fermentation), and drying makes an environment where it would be difficult for bad bacteria to grow. However, we do not have such a climate in the UK, and hence there is little tradition of this kind. So when recreating these recipes, we always include the curing salts for safety's sake.

makes approx. 3lbs

4½lbs lean pork with part skin (taken from the leg cut)

⅔ cup curing salts per 2¼lbs of meat: EITHER 1 tablespoon Quickcure and ⅔ cup salt OR 1 teaspoon Prague Powder No. 2 and ⅔ cup salt

½ cup demerara or light brown sugar

Remove the skin with a sharp knife, leaving a layer of white fat on the meat. Combine the curing salts with the sugar in a bowl. Rub the curing mixture into the meat all over, with more on the flesh side and less on the fatty side, making sure it is well covered and you haven't missed any crevices. Put into a nonmetal container on a plastic rack (or put the container on a slope). Cover and store in the fridge or in a cold place (below 41°F) for 3 days. Turn the meat every day and drain off any water in the container.

After 3 days, wipe off the cure with paper towels and weigh your meat. Rinse under cold running water and wash down with apple cider vinegar or white wine vinegar. Wrap the *prosciutto* in two layers of cheesecloth and fasten with string. Hang on a butcher's hook in your curing chamber at 54–61°F until the prosciutto has lost 25 percent of its weight; this will take approx. 5–6 weeks depending on the size of the meat.

At this stage, the *prosciutto* should be unwrapped and larded (see page 102) to equalize the cure. Return the larded ham to the curing chamber for a further few weeks until it has lost at least 30 percent of its original weight, ideally 35 percent for optimum texture and flavor. When the *prosciutto* is ready it should feel firm to the touch.

Now for the exciting part… cleaning off an area of ham and slicing off the first sliver. Slice another and taste it. We were really pleased with ours, our very own small *prosciutto*—it wasn't San Daniele or Iberico, but gosh it was sweet, salty, and made our mouths water for more! Once you have cut into your ham, either wrap it in plastic wrap and consume within a couple of weeks, storing it in the fridge, or re-lard it and hang it back in your curing chamber. The longer you leave it the harder it will become so I recommend you use it up within the month.

COPPA

Coppa is made from the nape of the pig, at the top of the shoulder where it joins the loin. The nape usually measures approx. 10in in length and 5in across from an average pig. If you split a boned-out shoulder, you can use the nape for *coppa* and the rest of the shoulder for *speck*. *Coppa* is a relatively easy and quick ham to make and we think it works well in most climates.

This recipe is for a 3⅓lbs nape of pork. For smaller or larger cuts, allow 2oz curing salts per 2¼lbs of meat (EITHER ½oz Quickcure and 1½oz salt per 2¼lbs OR ⅛oz Prague Powder No. 2 and 2oz salt).

makes approx. 2¼lbs

3⅓ lbs nape of pork, trimmed

5 tablespoons curing salts: EITHER 1 tablespoon Quickcure and 4 tablespoons salt OR ⅔ teaspoon Prague Powder No. 2 and 4⅓ tablespoons salt

Trim and tidy the cut to get rid of any shaggy pieces hanging off the nape. Rub the curing salts into the pork. Transfer the pork onto a rack inside a plastic container with a lid. Set aside to cure in the fridge for approx. 7 days. (If your

pork is larger than this, allow 7 days per 1in to the center of the pork via the shortest route.) Pour the water off daily.

Rinse the cured *coppa* quickly under cold running water (but don't soak it) and pat dry with paper towels. Wrap the pork in two layers of cheesecloth and fasten with string. Weigh the *coppa* and hang in your curing chamber at 54–61°F until it loses 35 percent of its weight, checking regularly. In our experience, it took 3 weeks to achieve this. We found it wasn't ready below 25 percent and it had dried out above 45 percent.

Serve finely sliced, preferably cut on a slicing machine or with a very sharp knife. After opening, wrap in plastic wrap and keep in the fridge. Consume within a couple of weeks.

Variations
CHILE, LEMON, AND ROSEMARY COPPA
This is a wonderful, slightly spicy version.

Follow the method for curing the *Coppa* (see page 101), adding the following flavorings with the curing salts: finely grated zest of 1 lemon, finely chopped needles of 2 sprigs of rosemary, and ½oz red pepper flakes. After curing, pat dry on paper towels and rub the flesh with 2 teaspoons of red pepper flakes. Wrap the *coppa* in cheesecloth and air-dry in your curing chamber as before.

VANILLA COPPA
Marc Frederic's favorite way to make *coppa* is using vanilla salt, which he makes by infusing some vanilla pods in his curing salt for a few weeks before using.

LOIN OF PORK
Loins can be cured in the same way as *coppa*. Loin of pork is a great meat cut to start with because it doesn't take long to cure. For maximum flavor, try covering it with smoked paprika or black pepper before drying in your curing chamber.

SPECK

Speck is a method rather than a cut that comes from the Austro-Italian border. *Speck* can be made either using the shoulder or leg of pork. According to the Italians, it must not be smoked with resinous woods such as pine—however, the Germans and Austrians say it should be!

Traditionally *speck* is not larded, but we have found this useful (see below). For speed, we chose to cure a small shoulder rather than a large leg. Often curing salts are not used, but we prefer to use them for safety.

makes approx. 4½lbs
2 bay leaves
5 teaspoons juniper berries
1–2 teaspoons freshly ground black pepper
8½ tablespoons curing salt: EITHER
  1½ tablespoons Quickcure and
  7 tablespoons salt OR 1 tablespoon Prague Powder No. 2 and
  7½ tablespoons salt
2 garlic cloves, finely chopped
6¾lbs boned pork shoulder, neatly trimmed

Whizz the herbs and spices in a spice grinder or crush in a mortar and pestle; mix with the curing salt and garlic. Rub the mixture over the meat and place, skin-side down, in a plastic container. (It doesn't need to be on a rack, as the mixture will form a pickle that the meat sits in.) Put on a lid and set aside to cure in the fridge for about 10 days. As a rule of thumb, allow 7 days per 1in to the center of the meat via the shortest route.

Remove the cured pork from the container and rinse it quickly under the tap. Pat dry on paper towels and place on a wire rack to dry at room temperature for an hour or two (provided it isn't a hot summer's day).

Cold smoke the *speck* over beech wood—this will take 7 days over gentle smoke in an open smoker or 3 hours in a Bradley smoker, where the smoke is more concentrated.

After smoking, weigh your *speck* and hang in a curing chamber at 54–61°F for approx. 5–6 weeks until it has lost 25 percent of its weight. After this, the *speck* should be larded (see right) and rehung for a further 6 months.

At this point, you can try a slice from one end just in from the outer edge and see if it is ready to eat. If it seems soft or not tasty enough, re-lard that end and rehang for a further month. Serve cut into wafer thin slices with pickled gherkins and sourdough rye bread.

LARDING

Larding really improves the texture and flavor of your meat, and smoothes out any hard areas of flesh. It should be carried out after the initial drying process (once the meat has lost 25 percent of its original weight).

METHOD Mix together lard and flour in equal quantities, depending on the size of your cut. We start with 7oz flour and 7oz lard and make up more if necessary (any leftover lard can be stored in the fridge in a covered container). Slather the mixture over your meat—this is very therapeutic—and return it to the curing chamber until the meat has lost 30–40 percent of its original weight.

Right (clockwise): *Coppa*, small *prosciutto, pancetta.*

SAUSAGES

Sausage-making is a giggle, at least the first time—it causes an infernal amount of teenage innuendo but it really is fun to do. Sausages are really not that difficult to make and can be cooked and eaten right away or allowed to dry—I know that if you cook and eat them immediately this isn't strictly food preservation, but if you have all the equipment why not make use of it? Sausagemeat can be made into patties or meatballs if you cannot find casings or a sausage machine.

We alter the stuffings frequently as you can see from some of our favorite recipes on the following pages.

EQUIPMENT

grinder with approx. ¼in holes—
  or buy coarsely ground meat
  from your butcher
sausage-making machine—this
  is essential if you are making
  more than a few sausages
  (although you could try filling
  the casings with a plastic
  funnel). Some food mixers,
  such as Kenwood, come with a
  sausage-making attachment.
sausage pricker, corn-on-the-cob
  skewer, or thick pin
butcher's string
probe thermometer to check
  the internal temperature of
  cooked foods
butcher's hooks

which casings?

There are a variety of natural casings available. The standard ones for sausage-making are hog casings made from pig intestines. Small sausages, such as *merguez*, are frequently made with lamb intestines, and these are useful if you are not a pork eater, however these are more delicate and can tear easily. Large skins made from beef middles are used for salami-making; these should be removed before eating. Extra-large casings made from beef, known as ox bungs, are used for huge sausages like *mortadella*. Natural casings are kept in salt in bags or they can be frozen. They don't smell great and should be washed before use. Avoid using discolored or gray casings, and throw them away if they smell really bad or break easily.

Collagen casings, made from animal hide, are not as pleasant to eat as those made from intestines. However, they are convenient because most of them don't require soaking before use (check the manufacturer's instructions) and they are usually sold ready to transfer straight from the spool onto the machine spout.

making sausages

All natural casings should be soaked in water with a little vinegar for 1 hour (up to overnight) in the fridge before use to soften them. Allow time to unravel the lengths. To help them open, so that they glide easily onto the machine, pour a little cold water into the open end to lubricate it from the inside. A good tip is to thread them onto the spout of a faucet and let the water run through; cut the end off where it came into contact with the faucet for cleanliness. This will push the impurities out and show any holes.

SAUSAGE-MAKING TIPS

HYGIENE Keep everything super clean and fridge cold. Work in a cold environment. When we worked with the butchers in Lazio, I have never been so cold in my life! Your hands might hurt when mixing cold meat, but it will help keep the bacteria from growing.

SALT As a rule of thumb, allow ⅔–¾oz salt per 2¼lbs of meat for regular sausages and 1oz per 2¼lbs for cured sausages that will hang, such as salami.

MIXING Mix the ingredients together really well with your hands until thoroughly mixed. Remove any glands and bloody parts you see.

TASTING YOUR MIXTURE Take a little of the mixture out and fry it in a pan to check the seasoning before filling the casings.

FILLING THE CASINGS Keep the skins wet while on the nozzle, dabbing them with cold water frequently. Ease them off with one hand while guiding the sausage with the other. Prick the skins immediately if you see an air bubble. Sausages don't need to be pricked unless you see a lot of air bubbles.

Twisting or tying? For fresh sausages, twist the sausages a few times at the desired lengths after you have finished filling the casings. For cured sausages, such as salami, don't twist in the normal way (or the air won't be able to circulate properly around them during hanging). Instead, fasten them at intervals with butcher's string. For best results, hang like a garland in the chamber so that they don't rest against each other.

HANGING For cured sausages, wipe the finished sausages with vinegar to make them shiny and attractive. This should deter insects if you are hanging them, but don't rely on this.

RESTING IN THE FRIDGE Allow fresh sausages to rest in the fridge overnight before cooking them. This helps meld the flavors together.

COOKING Cook fresh sausages over low heat in a frying pan or in the oven at 350°F, turning frequently in the pan or twice in the oven. Make sure they are cooked through to the center; a temperature probe is ideal for this. They should have an internal temperature of at least 162°F.

Combine the ingredients for the filling in a stainless-steel, plastic, or glass bowl until they are thoroughly mixed. It is important to include a minimum of 20 percent back fat to stop the mixture from drying out; I prefer 30 percent as a general rule for better flavor and texture. We prefer to cut the fat by hand as we find it softens and creams in the grinder. Always taste some of the filling by cooking it in a pan before filling your casings to check for seasoning. Go easy on the garlic; we have learned from experience that a little goes a long way.

TRADITIONAL PORK AND LEEK SAUSAGE

After much experimentation, we LOVE these sausages. The addition of leeks just gives them a lick of sweetness, which marries so well with the pork. We used pork belly mixed with shoulder meat, as between them there is a good mixture of fat and lean meat. We regularly make a batch and eat some immediately (even though they are better after a day resting in the fridge). The rest we freeze in fives, the number in our family, tightly wrapped in plastic wrap in two layers.

makes approx. 20 sausages, 5in long
approx. 13 feet hog casings
5½lbs mixed belly and shoulder of
** pork with fat and lean bits**
7oz leeks, finely chopped
2 tablespoons extra virgin olive oil
3½ cups stale white breadcrumbs
7 teaspoons fine salt
1 teaspoon ground white pepper
1 teaspoon grated nutmeg
1 small garlic clove, peeled and grated

Prepare the casings as on page 105.

Meanwhile put the meat through a coarse grinder or ask your butcher to grind it for you. Set aside in the fridge to cool. Cook the leeks in the oil over medium heat until soft but not brown. Set aside to cool completely.

To make the filling, mix all of the ingredients together really well in a large bowl. Cover with plastic wrap and transfer to the fridge while you clean up and set up the sausage stuffer.

Fill the canister of the sausage-maker with the prepared meat mix. Put a length of hog casing onto the nozzle and tie a knot in the end. Turn the handle to start filling the sausages. Filling is easier when there are two of you, so that one person is turning the handle at the correct speed while the other helps guide the casings off the end of the nozzle, watching out for air bubbles and pricking them when they appear. Finish a length either when the casings run out or when the meat does. Link or tie the sausages as necessary (see page 105) and set aside in a container in the fridge to rest for 24 hours. Either eat immediately or "open" freeze on trays in your freezer and pack into ziplock or vacuum bags once frozen. Frozen sausages should be consumed within 3 months.

ITALIAN FENNEL SEED SAUSAGE

These taste really authentic and Tuscan. When we first made them, they brought tears to Giancarlo's eyes as he remembered home!

makes approx. 18 sausages, 5in long
approx. 10–13 feet hog casings
3 garlic cloves, peeled
⅓ cup white wine
5½lbs pork (⅓ back fat and ⅔ lean
** meat), coarsely ground**
4 tablespoons salt
1 teaspoon whole fennel seeds,
** very lightly crushed**
1 teaspoon ground white pepper

Prepare the casings as on page 105.

Grind the garlic with the wine in a food processor to form a paste and mix with the remaining ingredients. To fill the casings, follow the instructions for pork and leek sausage (see left).

Variation
Substitute 18oz of the pork with 18oz ground pork liver and leave out the fennel seeds. We saw this done in Lazio, where the sausages were called *Salsicce neri* or black sausages, since they become dark from the livers. I am not an offal fan, but I thought the flavor was outstanding—rich, more meaty, and slightly softer in texture. This recipe is a great way to use up the liver. You can include the heart and spleen too, but I felt it would make the sausages too strong in flavor.

SMALL "COTECHINO" STYLE SAUSAGE

Cotechino is usually a large salami-style Italian sausage, but we saw individual ones on a recent trip to Turin and decided to make our own. Often the large ones are sold ready-cooked as this can take hours. *Cotechino* is often served on lentils with *fonduta*—a pecorino cheese sauce.

This recipe makes great use of the scraps of pork, such as the skin, ears, and tougher cuts, which are left behind after the main pieces have been removed for making *prosciutto* or salami. The long, 1½-hour boiling time softens the texture, resulting in a tender, savory sausage that melts in your mouth.

makes 24 sausages, approx. 5in long
approx. 13–16½ feet hog casings
4½lbs pork (35 percent back fat; the
** rest should be made up of lean meat**
** and scraps, see above), finely ground**
12 teaspoons curing salts: EITHER
** 3½ teaspoons Quickcure and**
** 7 teaspoons salt OR 1 teaspoon**
** Prague Powder No. 2 and**
** 11 teaspoons fine salt**
1 teaspoon freshly ground black
** pepper**
1 teaspoon freshly grated nutmeg
½ teaspoon ground cloves

To make the sausages, follow the method for Traditional pork and leek sausage (see left). Do not prick them, as they will be boiled. To cook the sausages, put them into a saucepan of cold water and bring to a boil; reduce the heat immediately to a simmer and cook for 1½ hours.

FRENCH SAUCISSON

This recipe is a mixture of the *Saucisson de Ménage* (or *de Campagne*) and the *Saucisson à l'Ail* from Jane Grigson's wonderful book, *Charcuterie and French Pork Cookery*. It is a really versatile sausage with a lovely garlicky flavor that just gets better with time. Eat them after a day boiled or fried, or hang them in a curing chamber for up to a month to dry them out (see page 141) and enjoy dried like salami. They are also great smoked (see page 163). Boiling them gives a great stock, which you can use for cooking lentils in or making into soup. Jane Grigson uses the typical mixture of *quatre épices*, which is a pre-mixed blend of four spices chosen from allspice, cloves, cinnamon, ginger, and white pepper.

makes approx. 12-15 sausages, 6in long

10–13 feet hog casings
4½lbs pork (⅓ fat and ⅔ lean meat)
4 garlic cloves, pounded in a mortar and pestle
9 teaspoons curing salts: EITHER
  3 teaspoons Quickcure and
  6 teaspoons fine salt OR 1 teaspoon Prague Powder No. 2 and
  8 teaspoons fine salt
2½ teaspoons ground black pepper
1½ teaspoons *quatre épices*, made up from a pinch each of allspice, cloves, cinnamon, and white pepper
4 teaspoons sugar

To make the sausages, follow the method for Traditional pork and leek sausage on page 107. If eating fresh, rather than curing, twist the sausages at the desired length and store in the fridge overnight before cooking.

For cured sausages, *Saucissons sec*, fasten the sausages at intervals with butcher's string and hang in the curing chamber at 54–61°F for 1 month (see page 141). Eat as salami, slicing them thinly. Store cured sausages in the fridge, wrapped in plastic wrap, and consume within a couple of weeks as they will continue to dry out.

For smoked sausages, fasten the sausages at intervals with butcher's string and hang in your fridge (or curing chamber at 54–61°F) for 24 hours to form a pellicle. Cold smoke over oak or apple wood for 2–3 hours (see page 163). Either eat immediately or hang in the curing chamber at 54–61°F to dry for a further month (see page 141). The sausages can be frozen at any stage, but should be consumed within 3 months.

SOBRASADA-STYLE SPREADING SAUSAGE

The traditional *sobrasada de Mallorca* has a protected name, meaning that it cannot be called that if it is produced outside Mallorca (where it is made from the local pigs). *Sobrasada* has been made for centuries, its first mention being in the 17th century. It is the same size as salami and also made from pork with paprika, salt, and spices as flavorings. It is cured but not hardened, meaning it can be cut open and spread on hot toast—usually topped with a slice of Manchego cheese—or stirred into pasta sauces or casseroles. Our version is small to give a faster curing time. In the dry climate of Mallorca these sausages do not traditionally contain curing salts, but we have added them and suggest you do as a precaution against bad bacteria forming during the short hanging time.

makes approx. 20 sausages, approx. 5in long

3lbs belly pork
¾ cup plus 2 tablespoons paprika
approx. 10–13 feet hog casings
1½lbs lean pork meat
9 teaspoons curing salts: EITHER
  3 teaspoons Quickcure and
  6 teaspoons fine salt OR 1 teaspoon Prague Powder No. 2 and
  8 teaspoons fine salt
1 teaspoon ground black pepper
1 teaspoon dried thyme
1 teaspoon dried oregano

Grind the meat through a grinder using a 0.1–0.2in diameter grinder disk. To make the sausages, follow the method for Traditional pork and leek sausage on page 107. Tie the individual sausages at intervals with butcher's string instead of twisting.

Hang the sausages in a warm room overnight (64–75°F) to kickstart fermentation. Then transfer to the curing chamber at 54–61°F for an additional 2 weeks (see page 141). Eat immediately or wrap in parchment paper or plastic wrap and store in the fridge for up to 2 weeks where they will continue to harden.

chorizo

According to Spanish chef, José Pizarro, every town in Spain has its own recipe for *chorizo*—and that is just the ingredients. Some *chorizos* are spreadable in consistency, some are firm, some are for cooking, others for slicing for tapas, some are fresh, others are air-dried and some are smoked or made with smoked paprika. In the following recipes we used a mixture of sweet paprika (*pimentón dulce*) and hot paprika (*pimentón picante*) to give just the right degree of pungency. Paprika is made from ground dried red peppers (see page 127 for how to make it yourself).

SPANISH FRESH CHORIZO

This recipe, and the following one for dried *chorizo*, comes from chef and writer Nick Sandler. Nick likes to use a 2-year-old pig for *chorizo*, preferably a Black-Footed Pig; this has a good amount of shoulder and back fat as well as a good flavor. This fresh *chorizo* is great crumbled into rice dishes, put onto pizza or simply fried and served with eggs.

makes 30–35 sausages, 5–6in long
approx. 20–23 feet hog casings
9lbs belly pork, ground through an
   ⅓in-gauge grinder
5 tablespoons fine sea salt
14 cloves garlic, peeled and pounded
   to a paste
4½oz Spanish paprika (3oz *pimentón
   dulce* and 1½oz *pimentón picante*)

Prepare the casings as on page 105.
   Put gloves on (or the mixture will dye your hands) and combine the ingredients really well in a bowl for 5 minutes. To fill the casings, follow the method for Traditional pork and leek sausage (see page 107); store in the fridge for 24 hours. Either use immediately, store in the fridge for up to a week or freeze for up to 3 months.

SPANISH DRIED CHORIZO

This dried version will last longer than the fresh *chorizo* (left) because it contains curing salts. Over time it will become firm enough to slice. Nick prefers to mix the meat with the curing salts and flavorings the night before making the sausages to kickstart the curing process. He then chills the mixture overnight in the fridge so that it is properly chilled before it goes in the casings.

makes 12 sausages, approx. 12in long
approx. 13–16½ feet hog casings
4½lbs back and belly fat
9lbs lean pork, ground through an
   ⅓in-gauge grinder
9 tablespoon curing salts: EITHER
   3 tablespoons Quickcure and 6
   tablespoons fine sea salt OR 1½
   tablespoons Prague Powder No. 2
   and 7½ tablespoons fine salt
6oz Spanish paprika (3oz *pimentón
   dulce* and 3oz *pimentón picante*)
14 cloves ground garlic, pounded in
   a mortar and pestle

Prepare the casings as on page 105.
   Cut the fat into ½–¾in cubes with a sharp knife. Put gloves on (or the paprika will dye your hands) and combine the fat with the remaining ingredients in a large bowl. Cover the bowl with plastic wrap and transfer to the fridge overnight.
   Make the sausages following the method for Traditional pork and leek sausage on page 107, tying them at 12in intervals with butcher's string. Weigh your sausages. (If you wish to smoke the *chorizo*, see pages 146–147.)

Hang the sausages in a curing chamber at 54–61°F until they have achieved 30 percent weight loss; ours took approx. 28 days. Make sure that the air can circulate freely and that none of them are touching. Check on the sausages daily and wipe off any molds that aren't white with strong alcohol—we use Grappa.
   Once dried, the *chorizo* can be stored in the fridge for up to a month or frozen for up to 3 months.

NORTH AFRICAN MERGUEZ

These spicy sausages are usually made with lamb and/or beef. They are stuffed into sheep intestines, which are smaller than typical hog casings and are very delicate to work with. If your casings split, don't despair: keep the good ones and either put the stuffing through again from any that have broken or shape into balls and fry like meatballs—they will taste just as good! *Merguez* are spiced with harissa paste, a fiery paste made from chile. They are wonderful grilled and eaten with couscous or in a tagine.

makes approx. 12–15 sausages, approx. 5in long
10–13 feet sheep casings
1lb 10oz finely ground lamb
9oz finely ground beef
18oz beef or lamb fat, finely ground
7 teaspoons salt
⅓ cup harissa or rose harissa paste
   (see page 187)

Prepare the casings as on page 105.
   Combine the ground meat in a bowl with the rest of the ingredients and mix really well with your hands. Make the sausages following the method for Traditional pork and leek sausage on page 107. Cook immediately or rest overnight in the fridge.

Serve with citrus couscous: combine some couscous with lots of olive oil, plenty of salt and pepper, and loads of mixed citrus juice (lime, orange, and lemon), stir in some dried fruits and raw onion and pour over enough water to cover. Leave overnight to fluff up and serve with the *merguez* and some fried chicken.

SOUTH AFRICAN BOEREWORS

These are often cooked on a South African *braai*, a barbecue, accompanied by fried onions and sweet chutney and, of course, a Southern African beer or two. They are filling and spicy and great in a soft bun. Try them with one of our chutneys on pages 32–41.

makes 20 Boerewors, approx. 6in long

13–16½ feet hog casings
8 teaspoons coriander seeds
1 teaspoon cloves
2¼lbs fatty pork (this could be from really fatty belly or neck and/or cheek), coarsely ground
4½lbs coarsely ground beef
2 teaspoons ground allspice
¼ nutmeg, grated
½ cup apple cider vinegar
3 teaspoons honey
¼ cup fine sea salt
3 teaspoons freshly ground or crushed black pepper

Prepare the casings as on page 105.

Toast the coriander seeds and cloves in a dry frying pan to release their fragrance and grind until smooth in a mortar and pestle or spice grinder. Combine with the remaining ingredients. Mix really well with cold, clean hands—it will hurt as your fingers get cold, but try to keep going for at least 5 minutes to ensure the meat is really well blended with the flavorings. To make the sausages, follow the method for Traditional pork and leek sausage on page 107. Store in the fridge and consume within 5 days or freeze and consume within 3 months.

ITALIAN SOPRESSATA

This reminds me of British haslet, in that the meat is pressed. It is a great way to use up non-prime cuts of meat, including the skin of pork—this releases gelatin during the cooking process, which helps to hold the shape of the *sopressata* together.

makes approx. 4½–6¾lbs

11¼lbs pork trimmings, such as skin, bones with flesh on, etc.—one-third of this should be lean meat
½ teaspoon ground nutmeg per 2¼lbs of cooked meat
1 teaspoon ground black pepper per 2¼lbs of cooked meat
1 teaspoon crushed fennel seeds per 2¼lbs of cooked meat
½ teaspoon ground cinnamon per 2¼lbs of cooked meat
3 teaspoons salt per 2¼lbs of cooked meat

Put the meat and bones in a large saucepan. Cover with cold water and simmer for 2 hours or until the skin is tender. Drain through a colander, discarding the stock, and set aside to cool slightly.

Once the pork is cool enough to handle, pick the flesh from the bones and set aside with any pieces of boiled skin. Discard the bones. Chop the cooked flesh and skin into ¾in pieces and place in a large bowl; you should be left with approx. 4½–6¾lbs edible meat and skin. Weigh the contents and calculate the salt and spices. Add these to the bowl and mix well. Put the mixture into a double layer of cheesecloth and squeeze tight. Tie with string at both ends to form a very large fat sausage shape. Hang in the fridge or curing chamber overnight. The next day it will have set so that it is firm enough to slice. To serve, unwrap the sausage and cut into thin slices. Enjoy with other cured meats as antipasti or with salad, or serve with pickles and warm bread.

SALAMI

Salami is a cured sausage that is fermented and air-dried. The word "salami" comes from the Italian *salare*, meaning "to salt." Roman soldiers were often paid with salt, hence the term "salary," and they used this to preserve meat such as salami to offer a valuable source of protein in times when fresh meat was unavailable.

RICCARDO'S SALAMI

Giancarlo remembers making salami as a child. When Riccardo Cappelli, a visiting chef from Castello Banfi in Tuscany, came to our restaurant they had a wonderful time creating this Tuscan salami and recreating a little of Giancarlo's past.

makes 6 salami, approx. 10-11in long

6–9 feet ox casings
6¾lbs lean pork shoulder, coarsely ground
10½oz white back fat, cut into ⅓in cubes
2 fat garlic cloves, green stems removed, peeled and crushed to a smooth paste
14 teaspoons curing salts: EITHER 5 teaspoons Quickcure and 9 teaspoons salt OR 1 teaspoon Prague Powder No. 2 and 13 teaspoon salt
½ teaspoon ground cinnamon
½ teaspoon ground nutmeg
1 tablespoon whole black peppercorns
½ cup red wine

Wash the casings with water and vinegar and leave to soak while you prepare the mixture. Keep the meat in the fridge until you are ready to use it.

Combine the ground pork with the fat in a bowl. Add the garlic, curing salts, spices, and red wine and mix thoroughly by hand for 10 minutes— it will change color from pinky-red to brown.

Fill each sausage to 10in and then fasten with butcher's string. Make sure the meat really fills the casings; there should be no air holes and the filling should be really compact inside. Continue filling the rest of the casings with sausagemeat, tying at intervals with string. (If you tear a skin, squeeze out the mix and put it through again into a new skin.)

Use a pricker (or corn-on-the-cob holder) to prick the sausages all over, and then massage them smooth with your hand to release any air bubbles trapped inside.

Hang the sausages in your curing chamber at 75°F for 2 days, and then move them to a cooler place (at 54–61°F) to finish curing. Curing will take 2–3 months. For more information on salami-making, see box right.

The salami will continue to harden if left in the curing chamber so don't leave them too long before eating. Once cut wrap the cut end tightly in parchment paper or plastic wrap and store in the fridge for up to 6 weeks.

Variation
FENNEL SALAMI
Omit the black peppercorns and replace with the same amount of fennel seeds.

SALAMI-MAKING TIPS

MEAT Choose shoulder meat and back fat for salami-making. Avoid using white fat from belly of pork as it will smear; back fat is firmer and holds its shape better.

CURING TEMPERATURE Monitor the temperature in your curing chamber regularly with a thermometer.

For fermented meats, such as *prosciutto* and salami, it is necessary to introduce slight warmth (up to 75°F) during the first couple of days of air-drying to encourage fermentation. This provides a friendly climate for good, salt-tolerant bacteria, such as *Lactobacillus* and *Leuconostoc*, to flourish. In turn, these produce lactic and acetic acids that lower the pH value of the salami from 6 to 4.5; this is too acidic for most harmful bacteria to survive.

After a couple of days in the warmth, the salami should be transferred to a cooler temperature to finish curing (54–61°F is fine).

INTRODUCING GOOD BACTERIA
To encourage friendly bacteria and molds to grow, it is a good idea to place a previously made salami in the curing chamber with your homemade salamis.

HUMIDITY Monitor the humidity in your curing chamber regularly with a hygrometer and check your salami daily for unwanted mold and any stickiness. If patches of slight tackiness are found, you may have a humidity problem. Wipe off the stickiness with vinegar and paper towels and re-hang before this becomes a problem. Real stickiness is a bad sign and it is best to discard your salami.

PRECAUTIONS The harmless white mold found on the outside of salami helps the fermentation process and is nothing to worry about. However, any other colored mold is trouble; if you catch it very early on you can wipe it off with paper towels dipped in vinegar.

CURING TIMES Allow 2–3 months in the curing chamber. Some people cure their salami for longer to acquire a stronger flavor and firmer meat; others prefer it softer and milder. In a professional environment, the temperature can be kept low to allow a controlled and slow-maturing process, however at home this is rarely possible and you have to follow the ebb and flow of temperatures; this often results in a speedier process than 3 months.

OTHER MEATS

RHUBARB-CURED HAUNCH OF VENISON BY PAUL BURTON

The story of this cure is that a culled hind was given to Paul just as forced rhubarb was coming into season. Seeing the two in his kitchen, he decided to marry them together. The high acidity of the rhubarb, and its enzymes, have a preservative and tenderizing effect on the meat.

makes approx. 1lb 10oz

**18oz (4–6 ribs) forced rhubarb
   (unforced is more bitter so add
   a teaspoon more sugar)
1 teaspoon juniper berries
½ teaspoon cloves
1 teaspoon black peppercorns
1 teaspoon allspice berries
2 teaspoons demerara sugar
14 teaspoons curing salts: EITHER
   5 teaspoons Quickcure and
   9 teaspoons salt OR 1 teaspoon
   Prague Powder No. 2 and
   13 teaspoons salt
2¼lbs trimmed loin of venison**

**For the rub
2 teaspoons juniper berries (optional)
4 teaspoons black peppercorns
2 tablespoons gin**

Roughly chop and crush the rhubarb either in a food processor or using a meat mallet on a chopping board. Grind the spices, sugar, and curing salts in a spice grinder. Combine the rhubarb with the spice mixture in a plastic container and add the venison. Rub the rhubarb/spice mixture all over the venison to coat it well and then put a lid on the container. Transfer the venison to the fridge or a cold room at 36–41°F to marinate for 5 days, turning every other day.

Rinse the cured venison under the tap and pat dry on paper towels. Put on a wire rack, resting on a baking sheet and set aside in a warm room at 75°F to start the fermentation process.

The following day, make up the rub: grind the spices in a spice grinder and combine them with the gin in a small bowl. Sprinkle the mixture over the venison and press down to coat it on all sides. Return the meat to the rack for a further 24 hours before smoking.

Smoking flavors the venison and allows the natural enzymes and lactic beasties (Paul's words, not mine) to do their work. We also find it disguises the metallic tang that can sometimes be detected in less well aged examples. If you don't have a smoker, go to the next step. To smoke the venison, place it over fruit wood such as apple for 24 hours in gentle smoke; we did ours in the barbecue smoker. For more information on Smoking, see pages 146–147.

After smoking, wrap the venison in cheesecloth and hang in a curing chamber for 2 weeks at 54–61°F. Serve thinly sliced with bread and sliced pears. To store, wrap tightly in parchment paper or plastic wrap and keep in the fridge for up to 1 month.

CURED DUCK AND GOOSE BREASTS

Cured duck and goose breasts have an intense gamey flavor after hanging. They are delicious cut into thin slices and eaten at room temperature as part of an antipasti platter. If the game is wild, freeze it first to kill any parasites.

**2¼lbs duck or goose breasts
8 teaspoons curing salts: EITHER
   1 teaspoon Quickcure and
   7 teaspoons fine salt OR
   ½ teaspoon Prague Powder No. 2
   and 7½ teaspoons fine salt**

Rub the curing salts into the duck or goose breasts, rubbing it more generously over the thicker areas and using less on the thinner areas and skin. Put onto a rack or a couple of chopsticks inside a plastic container so that the juices can leach out. Transfer to the fridge to cure for 1–3 days. A small duck breast will only need a day but a large, fat goose breast could need the full 36 hours.

Rinse the breasts briefly under cold running water and pat dry on paper towels. Leave them to dry on a rack at room temperature for a couple of hours.

Hang the duck breasts in a curing chamber at 54–61°F to dry for a further 10 days to lose weight and concentrate the flavor. Eat immediately or wrap in plastic wrap and keep in the fridge for up to 6 weeks.

DUCK BREASTS CURED WITH KUMQUATS

For this recipe, we cured the duck breasts in the citrus brine from the Salted kumquats on pages 88–89. The duck flavor is intensified by the salting and drying process and the orange flavor is subtle but delicious.

serves 4

**2 teaspoons Quickcure and 21
   teaspoons brine from the Salted
   kumquats (see pages 88–89) OR
   ½ level teaspoon Prague Powder No.
   2 and 24 teaspoons of brine from the
   Salted kumquats (see pages 88–89)
2¼lbs duck breasts**

Combine the curing salts with the kumquat brine. Pour a little of the salty brine into the bottom of a small plastic container. Put in the duck breasts, skin-side up, and cover with the rest of the salty liquid. Put on a lid and set aside to cure in the fridge for 36 hours.

Remove the duck breasts, discarding the cure. Rinse them briefly under cold running water and dry with paper towels. Hang in a curing chamber at 54–61°F to dry for 10 days, or put on a wire rack, uncovered, in the fridge. Serve thinly sliced. Accompany with a few thinly sliced pieces of salted kumquat, arugula leaves, and warm bread and butter.

DRY-CURED BRESAOLA

Bresaola is made in the north of Italy and is usually dry cured. It is full of iron and low in fat. We serve it as part of our antipasti boards in our restaurants, but I like it at home as a canapé rolled with arugula and shaved Parmesan inside.

3⅓lbs beef silverside or top rump (it could be in 2–3 pieces)

For the cure
4in sprig of rosemary, needles
  removed
1 teaspoon juniper berries
1 teaspoon cloves
1 teaspoon black peppercorns
2 bay leaves
7 teaspoons curing salts: EITHER
  2½ teaspoons Quickcure and
  4½ teaspoons fine salt OR
  1 teaspoon Prague Powder No. 2
  and 6 teaspoons fine salt
6 teaspoons sugar
1 level teaspoon orange peel powder
  (optional, see page 133)

First make the cure. Whizz the herbs and spices in a spice grinder or crush in a mortar and pestle. Combine with the curing salts, sugar, and orange peel powder in a bowl. Rub half of the cure into the meat; the rest should be stored in a plastic bag in a dark place. Put the meat into a freezer bag or vacuum bag and set aside to cure in the fridge for 7 days, turning daily.

Remove the meat from the bag and rinse quickly under water. Dry carefully on paper towels and rub in the remainder of the cure. Put the meat in a clean freezer bag or vacuum bag and return to the fridge for a further 7 days, turning daily.

Remove the meat from the bag and wipe off the cure with paper towels. Weigh the meat. Wrap the meat in two layers of cheesecloth and hang in a curing chamber at 54–61°F until it has lost 30–35 percent of its weight; this will take approx. 5–6 months. Check on the meat every week and wipe off any spots of mold that are not white using paper towels dipped in vinegar. Once fully cured, the meat should feel firm to the touch with a slight give on the inside.

Once the beef has lost one-third of its weight it is ready to taste. Remove a small piece of meat, bearing in mind that the outside will be very strong, and see if you like the flavor. If necessary, you can rewrap and hang the meat until it is dried to your liking.

After air-drying, wipe down the meat with vinegar and store in clean cheesecloth in the fridge. Use within a few weeks; it will keep on hardening, so don't leave it too long.

Below: *Bresaola.*

SALT BEEF

This recipe makes the most of a cheap cut of beef. Brisket has plenty of connective tissue and a covering of fat, both of which will offer flavor and break down during cooking. You can make this without curing salts if you wish, but it will lose the bright red color you associate with salt beef.

makes approx. 6¾lbs
6¾lbs beef brisket

For the cure
4 quarts water
1 cup curing salts: EITHER ⅓ cup Quickcure and ⅔ cup fine salt OR 1 tablespoon Prague Powder No. 2 and 14 tablespoons fine salt
1 cup soft brown sugar
2 medium dried chiles
1 teaspoon crushed juniper berries
1 teaspoon whole allspice

For the stock
1 fat carrot, cut in half lengthwise
1 medium onion, cut in half
1 bay leaf
1 sprig of rosemary
1 sprig of thyme
2 celery sticks, including leaves
4 garlic cloves, crushed with the flat of a knife
10 black peppercorns

CURING INSTRUCTIONS Combine the water, curing salts, and sugar in a large saucepan and bring slowly to a boil. Skim off the scum and add the spices. Simmer for 4 minutes, stirring to dissolve the sugar; remove the pan from the heat and set aside to cool to room temperature.

Pour the curing liquid into a plastic container with a lid and chill in the fridge. Once cold, add the meat and weigh it down with weights—I use a carton or two of juice inside a freezer bag; cover with a lid. Transfer the container to the fridge for 7–10 days, turning the meat twice during this time.

COOKING INSTRUCTIONS After the beef has finished curing, remove it from the container, discarding the curing liquid. Rinse briefly under cold water and put into a large saucepan. Cover with fresh water and add the carrot, onion, bay leaf, rosemary, thyme, celery, garlic, and peppercorns. Bring to a boil, cover with a lid and then reduce the heat to low. Simmer for approx. 2–3 hours or until the meat is very tender when prodded with a skewer. Serve hot (or reheated in its broth). Alternatively, set aside to cool and serve sliced with pickled gherkins, rye or sourdough bread, *sauerkraut*, and mustard. Store any leftovers in the fridge, wrapped in plastic wrap, for up to a week.

PASTRAMI

Pastrami was introduced to the United States by Eastern-European immigrants and was adopted by the Jewish community. It can be made from lamb or venison, however beef brisket is the most well known version. Don't think pastrami is relegated to the typical sandwich with pickles and mustard. It is also great on an antipasti platter and makes a low-fat snack rolled around a whole small gherkin. Ask your butcher for a trimmed brisket with a very thin layer of fat to make pastrami.

serves 20
6¾lbs beef brisket, mainly trimmed but with a thin covering of fat

For the rub
1 tablespoon black peppercorns
1 tablespoon pink peppercorns
1 tablespoon coriander seeds
1 tablespoon paprika
2 tablespoons soft brown sugar
3 fat garlic cloves, peeled and crushed

To cure the brisket, follow the curing instructions only for Salt beef (see left).

Rinse the cured beef quickly under cold running water and pat dry on paper towels. Crush the spices for the rub in a mortar and pestle or spice grinder and mix with sugar in a bowl. Massage the crushed garlic all over the meat, and then coat with the spice mixture. Transfer the meat to a large plastic bag, seal the top of the bag and suck out as much air as possible using a straw. Set aside to marinate in the fridge for 24 hours, turning it a couple of times. After this time, remove it from the bag and discard the juices. Allow the meat to dry for a few hours in the fridge before smoking.

Hot smoke over oak until the internal temperature reaches 158°F— as a guide ours takes 4–5 hours at 221°F in a Bradley smoker (for more information on smoking, see pages 146–147). Remove from the smoker and eat immediately or leave to cool. To store, wrap in plastic wrap and keep in the fridge for up to a week. Serve thick or very thinly sliced in sandwiches or on an antipasti platter.

Right: Pastrami.

air

If we dry any food, so that it loses two-thirds of its original weight, we can halt bacterial growth. Without water, microorganisms that cause decay are unable to survive. We can remove the water using a number of processes—from leaving the food out in the hot sun to dry to using a dehydrator, a machine especially designed to dry food.

Preserving food by dehydration has been carried out in almost all cultures since the dawn of man. Probably the first dried foods were discovered by accident—perhaps dates fallen from the tree, or meat hung in thorn bushes to keep it safe from animals, only to be discovered much later dried and edible. We know that ancient Egyptians dried fish and poultry in the hot sun as far back as 12,000 BCE and ancient Japanese made pots to gather shellfish for drying in 10,000 BCE. Much later, Native Americans mixed dried meat with fat and dried fruit to make a high-energy food known as *pemmican*. This had a long shelf-life and contained virtually all the nutrients needed for survival, making it perfect for taking with them on their travels.

Today, of course, we don't rely on this method of preserving food for our survival, but it is still a good way of improving the flavor of certain foods and introducing an appealing texture. Many foods that are preserved by drying take on an intense, concentrated and complex flavor—think of the difference between biting into a crisp, slightly tart fresh apple and chewing on a sweet, dried apple ring or the contrast between a fresh tomato and a chewy, intensely flavored sun-dried tomato, or raw beef and jerky. Through drying, we can play with the layers of flavor and alter the way the food feels in the mouth.

For those who follow a raw food or living food diet, drying is treated as a necessity. Dehydrators provide a way of preserving and changing food without compromising the goodness it holds, since enzymes, vitamins, and nutrients are kept intact; these can be destroyed at the high temperatures used to cook food in the traditional manner.

SUN-DRYING

Sun-drying must be one of the earliest ways of preserving food known to man. In its simplest form it involves leaving the food outside in the hot sun to dry—for example think of sun-dried tomatoes from hot, sunny Italy. When I went porcini picking in Italy, I noticed that the locals used a thorny bush to dry their mushrooms. The mushrooms were picked early in the morning, pierced onto the branches of the bush and left to dry in the hot sun during the day.

Since our ancestors had no choice they would sun-dry all foods from meat for jerky, fruit for *pemmican* and fish for use another day. I have successfully used the sun (when we see it) to dry all types of food and it is free. However you do need a warm day, no sign of rain, protection against insects and no animals around, which can limit you.

METHOD In hot, dry weather, scatter your fruit or vegetables on a rack, cover with a fine mesh to keep off insects and place outside in direct sunlight. At the first sight of rain,

or at night, you should bring the rack inside. Drying should take 2–3 days, depending on temperature and humidity. To speed up the process, place your fruit or vegetables behind a pane of glass or inside a warm greenhouse. In wet weather, bring your produce indoors and leave to dry on a sunny windowsill—if necessary, move the food around the house to maximize the heat from the sunshine.

SOLAR-DRYING FRAMES If you enjoy drying your own produce, it is well worth constructing a purpose-built frame. This should be enclosed with fine mesh on all sides, to keep out insects, and fitted with a tilted pane of glass or plastic on top to speed up the drying process. Make sure the frame is large enough to accommodate a baking sheet—that way, you can finish off the drying process in the oven afterward (see below) if the weather deteriorates.

OVEN-DRYING

An oven can be used for all types of food but it is the most costly method and takes the longest amount of time. Part of the reason for this is that there is not much air blowing across the food despite the fan in the oven. If you think of fish drying in the sun in a hot country such as Sri Lanka the sun is accompanied by a strong sea breeze or hams drying in San Daniele in Italy, which are in a building that catches the light mountain and sea winds through vents in the narrow windows. For this reason I prefer to use the oven for drying foods that don't need long, such as leathers or apple rings. Forget plums into prunes and dried fish, it just takes too long. Check your produce frequently and move trays around as ovens can have hot spots.

METHOD Preheat your oven to a low setting, 130–150°F is ideal. A convection oven is perfect; if using a conventional oven, leave the oven door slightly ajar. Arrange your loose fruit or vegetables on a wire rack to allow air to circulate or, if making fruit leathers, spread on a baking sheet (see pages 133–135). For temperatures and drying times, see indivdual recipes.

DEHYDRATORS

An electric dehydrator is a sensible investment if you plan to do a lot of drying. Not only does it dry the food in half the time compared to a conventional oven, but is more energy efficient and produces more consistent results. Most models come with a thermostat to control the temperature and a timer, as well as silicone mats suitable for drying liquids such as fruit purées. We also use our dehydrator for rising bread if we are in a hurry and incubating yogurt and cheese.

I first heard about dehydrators a few years ago when a friend built one when he was on a raw food diet. I thought dried food sounded horrible and couldn't understand why you would want to dehydrate fresh food. Three years later we own a dehydrator and we love using it—sometimes it's good to be proven wrong! We lent our dehydrator out recently and one of our sons demanded it back saying he missed the rolls of sweet fruit leather.

There are plenty of foods that can be preserved in a dehydrator—from fruit leathers (see pages 133–135) and herbs to kale chips and pungent, earthy dried mushrooms. We find the process so addictive we are constantly experimenting with new ideas. On the following pages are just a few ways to dry our favorite foods but there are so many more possibilities and ideas.

drying food in a dehydrator

Only use produce in good condition and pick over it checking for insects. Wash the food well and dry in a salad spinner or on clean dish towels. Remove any tough stalks that would take much longer to dry than the attached leaves for example and cut produce into even-sized pieces so that all of it has roughly the same drying time.

As a general guide you should dehydrate herbs at 95°F, vegetables at 125°F, fruits at 135°F, and meat and fish at 155°F.

drying times and storage

These vary considerably depending on what you are drying. As a general guide the safe maximum percentage of water left after drying is 10 percent for vegetables, 20 percent for fruit, and no more than 20 percent for meat. Weight loss can be measured by digital scales but I must admit we don't do that as the amounts we make are so small. The point of measuring is to make sure your produce has lost enough water to last a long time but if you are going to consume it relatively quickly weight loss is not an issue.

It is down to personal choice as to whether you dry foods to a crisp or semi-dry them to a leathery stage. Crisp foods such as the hard, brittle banana chips that you can buy in health food stores, will have almost no moisture left inside them so can be stored for up to a year and maybe longer. Personally we prefer them dried to a semi-dried or leathery state even if they will only last a matter of weeks. You can tell when the produce has dried enough by allowing it to cool and cutting through the center. There should be no visible

sign of moisture. If it is darker inside, or obviously wet, you need to dry it more. You can test fruit by squeezing it: if no moisture comes out it is ready. Fruit leather is not called that for nothing; it should feel leathery when done.

Vacuum-packed foods where there is very little air inside the package will last longer than those in an airtight can where there is still some air inside. Vacuum-packed foods can be frozen to last longer still. All foods should be inspected regularly for signs of moisture and mold. Trust your eyes and nose and if you are suspicious throw it away.

HUMIDITY

Humidity will affect your drying time enormously i.e. on very damp days it will take longer to dry your food than on dry days. If you want to measure it you will need a hygrometer. However for simple fruit drying you just need to be aware that drying times will differ day to day and throughout the seasons.

EQUIPMENT

For general drying of fruit and vegetables no special equipment is necessary unless you want to invest in a dehydrator. For drying outside you will need mesh food covers to stop insects landing while drying. Most dried foods can be stored in airtight jars or vacuum bags. For drying meat for charcuterie these are some of the things you may need:

A hygrometer: a device for measuring humidity
Thermometer
A small fan
Racks or homemade devices such as chopsticks over a dish to dry food

DRYING FOOD— A BASIC GUIDE

fruit

Always choose good quality fruit that is fresh but not soft or overripe. All fruits that can be sliced thinly—such as apples, bananas, mangoes, coconuts, apricots, figs, strawberries, pears, and peaches can be successfully dried (see below for individual fruits). All of these make delicious snacks. They can also be used in cooking; the strawberries add great flavor and texture to cookies and chopped dried apple is great in granola. There are some fruits that have such a large water content, and cannot be sliced easily, that take far too long in my opinion to be worth drying whole, such as grapes. Raspberries and blackberries should be carefully broken into pieces by hand. Alternatively you can purée the fruit to make fruit leathers (see page 135 for recipes). Crisply dried fruit can last up to a year.

Note: Drying times for individual fruits vary according to the water content of the fruit and the humidity on the day, so don't rely on your previous experiences. Approximate drying times are given below and right; these are a guide only, check your dehydrator or oven regularly to see when your fruit is ready to your liking.

APPLES AND PEARS Core the fruit and cut into rings or slices 1¼in thick; it's up to you whether you leave the skin on or off. Brush or dip in lemon juice or citric acid to prevent discoloration if you wish. I skip this step because I don't mind my fruit discolored, and anyway dried fruit never lasts long in our house—not because of any bacterial growth, just because it is so delicious! Arrange the fruit on a rack and dry at 135°F for 5–7 hours in a dehydrator or 150°F in an oven for 6–12 hours or until pliable. Pack into airtight containers or vacuum bags and store in a cool, dark place for up to a year.

PLUMS For fruit with tough skins such as plums, blanch in boiling water or steam for 3 minutes beforehand. This process will help to crack the skins so that water can be lost more easily. After blanching, plunge into ice-cold water to cool quickly and then pat dry on paper towels. Cut the fruit into halves and remove the stones. Arrange the fruit on a rack in the dehydrator and dry at 135°F for up to 24 hours or until pliable and leathery. Pack into airtight containers or vacuum bags and store in a cool, dark place for up to a year. Use in any recipe that calls for prunes such as the Spiced red onion marmalade on pages 38–40.

BANANAS, PEACHES, AND MANGOES Cut into uniform slices, approx. ¼in thick. Arrange on a rack in the dehydrator and dry at 135°F for approx. 4–6 hours or use an oven at 150°F and dry for about 6–8 hours until leathery. Pack into airtight containers or freezer bags and store in a cool, dark place for up to a year.

STRAWBERRIES Cut into slices approx. ¼in thick—you can make them thinner or thicker if you wish, but in my experience wafer-thin slices tend to stick to the mats. Arrange on a rack in the dehydrator and dry at 135°F for 5–7 hours or use an oven at 150°F and dry for about 7–9 hours until leathery and crisp. Store in freezer bags in a cool, dark place for up to a year.

FIGS AND APRICOTS Cut figs into quarters and apricots in half removing the pits. Flatten and arrange on a rack in a dehydrator at 135°F and dry for up to 30 hours until pliable. Dried figs are delicious soaked in brandy and then dipped in chocolate, Calabrian style, or included in cake and cookie recipes, see the *Pan de higo* recipe on page 132.

Right: Bananas and strawberries, coconut, mango, apples, and strawberries.

vegetables

ONIONS AND GARLIC Peel and finely slice the onion and peel and roughly chop the garlic. Scatter onto the racks or mats in a dehydrator and dry at 130°F for 5–6 hours. Alternatively dry on a baking sheet in the oven at 150°F for 6–7 hours or until crisp. Pack into airtight containers or freezer bags and store in a cool dark place for up to 6 months. Dried onion pieces are great in homemade bread or for dressing a Thai curry.

To make onion or garlic powder, grind the dried onion/garlic pieces in a spice grinder; store in an airtight container. Onion and garlic powder make ideal flavorings for chips, potato

Left to right: Garlic; onions drying; dried crimini mushrooms.

wedges, fried chicken, jerky, batters, and rubs for meat and chicken.

MUSHROOMS This method is suitable for drying all sorts of mushrooms. At home we collect fresh porcinis and dry them to really concentrate the flavor.

Cut into slices ¼in thick and dry on a rack in a dehydrator at 135°F for 3 hours. Alternatively spread on a wire rack in the oven and dry at 150°F for 5 hours or until crisp. Store in an airtight container or vacuum bag in a cool dark place for up to a year.

To make mushroom powder, grind the dried mushroom pieces in a spice grinder. Store in an airtight jar in a cool, dark place for up to 3 months. This gives an earthy, umami punch to cooking. Rub into steak with sea salt and extra virgin olive oil, stir into gravy or stock, scatter through roast vegetables before cooking, mix into bread dough, and savory biscuits.

To rehydrate dried mushrooms, soak in warm water for up to 30 minutes until soft. Reserve the soaking liquid

for flavoring sauces etc., however make sure you strain it carefully to remove any grit. Rehydrated mushrooms are great for the Mushroom ketchup on page 43.

KALE Dehydrated kale leaves make great chips when dried and lightly salted. To make kale chips, cut away the leaves (cut into quarters if leaves are huge), discarding the core, sprinkle lightly with salt, chili powder, or onion/garlic powder, and toss gently with your fingers. Spread on wire racks and dry in an oven or dehydrator until crisp. This is one method of drying where the oven is quicker. Cavolo nero or curly kale will take 1–2 hours in an oven at 150°F or 3–4 hours in a dehydrator at 135°F. Store in an airtight container in a cool, dark place for up to a year.

To make kale chips in a hurry, sprinkle the finely shredded kale with sea salt and drizzle with extra virgin olive oil. Spread on a wire rack in the oven at 400°F and bake for 5 minutes or until crisp. These make a great snack

with drinks before a meal, especially if you have the oven on anyway. Eat immediately.

TOMATOES, ZUCCHINI, PEPPERS, AND CHILES It might be a romantic thought but I do think the natural combination of drying in the sun and air gives a better flavor to these fruits and vegetables than drying in an oven with a fan.

Lay halved cherry tomatoes or quartered large tomatoes onto racks and scatter over a generous pinch of fine sea salt, sugar, and a little thyme (fresh or dried). Lay ¼in zucchini slices, finger-width slices of peppers, and halved chiles onto racks. Dry in the sun covered with mosquito netting for up to several days, bringing the food inside in the evenings when humidity rises and the temperature drops.

Alternatively you can dry tomatoes on a rack in a dehydrator at 135°F for approx. 5–8 hours or in the oven at 150°F for 6–9 hours depending on the size of the fruit. Either store in airtight containers or under oil (see page 183). Zucchini and chiles can be dried in a dehydrator at 130°F for 2–3 hours or in the oven at 150°F for 3–4 hours. Zucchini and chiles should not be stored under oil as they have little or no acidity. Instead store in airtight containers or vacuum bags for up to a year.

We dry halved chiles and small hot peppers in a basket in our kitchen or outdoors in the sunshine and sometimes smoke them afterward (see pages 152–153). Once dried, they can be ground for dried chili powder, or smoked and then ground for paprika. Chiles are best ground in a spice grinder as the dust particles can affect your eyes if you use a mortar and pestle.

Zucchini can be rehydrated or used in a semi-dried state and fried briefly, scattered with salt, and dried mint and served as chips. Or use them in the *Zucchini alla Poverella* on pages 182–183.

beans

BEANS AND PEAS These can be dried on the plant and then stored in jars. However, beware, dried beans can be susceptible to bean weevil, which means you could find adults emerging in your stored beans! To break the life cycle of the weevil, either freeze the dried beans for 5 days or keep in the fridge for a minimum of 7 days. After that they can be stored in a cool, dark pantry until needed for up to a year. They should be rehydrated before use. Beans can be kept in sealed glass jars or vacuum bags.

POPCORN Hang whole corn cobs in a sunny, drafty place until well-dried.

Left to right: Fresh chiles; zucchini blossom; tomatoes; dried chiles.

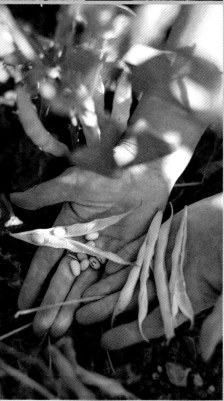

Remove the kernels with a sharp knife and store in airtight containers or vacuum bags in a cool, dark place for up to a year. Use for making popcorn.

seeds and flowers

Many growers dry seeds from their favorite plants to sow the following year. However, any spare seeds taken from plants such as sunflower, pumpkin, fennel, or cilantro are great to use in cooking. To dry them, simply scatter them over a sheet of parchment paper and put in a warm place to dry.

MUSTARD SEED Tie bunches with string and hang upside down inside a large paper bag to catch the tiny seeds. Do this in a warm, well-ventilated room to encourage the seed pods to open. If the plant is not already dry, you should make a few holes in the bag around the top to allow air to circulate.

FLOWERS AND LEAVES FOR TEA Chamomile and certain types of jasmine flowers (if not from a plant treated with pesticides) can be preserved for tea. Pick the flowers early in the morning and dry as soon as possible. Dry the flowers on a sunny windowsill, or put in a dehydrator at 110°F for 6–8 hours; alternatively microwave on high for 30-second bursts. Young blackberry leaves can be dried slowly in a paper bag. Give them a shake daily before use.

PUMPKIN AND SUNFLOWER SEEDS Dry in a dehydrator or oven at 122°F until brittle. Use in breads and cakes.

POPPY SEEDS The best seed to cultivate is the breadseed poppy, *Papaver somniferum*, whose seeds do not open to disperse, making them easier to harvest. I pick poppies from my garden and simply shake the seeds from the

dried pods into bread and cakes, or use them as a garnish.

herbs

Although we love fresh herbs there are some that are just as good, if not better, dried. Oregano is usually sold dried in bunches in Italy. The flavor is more intense and so a little goes a long way. It makes a huge difference to our pizza sauce when we use our own home-dried oregano rather than a bought dried version or fresh leaves. Dried oregano and thyme are wonderful rubbed into meat or chicken before cooking, with a little olive oil and salt. Dried mint is perfect for Harissa paste (see page 187).

OREGANO, MINT, AND THYME On a warm day these herbs can be left to dry naturally on a wire cake rack on the kitchen windowsill. Alternatively you can hang them in bunches upside down. Once dried put the herbs into a clean bag and rub them to loosen the leaves. Discard the stems and store in airtight jars in a cool, dark place.

Soft-leaved herbs such as basil and mint can be dried efficiently in a microwave. Lay individual leaves between sheets of paper towels and put into the microwave on high for 30-second bursts until crisp and dry. Once dried store in airtight jars in a cool, dark place for up to a year.

storage of dried foods

Containers should be thoroughly cleaned and have secure lids to keep out moisture and insects. Glass jars with lids or Mason-style jars are ideal, as are vacuum or freezer bags. Always store dried foods in a cool (50–60°F), dark place away from moisture.

PEPPER AND ALMOND CRACKERS

These terracotta-colored crackers are deliciously sweet and salty. They are a great way of using up a surplus of red peppers, which I love in almost any form. This recipe is based on one from the *Preserve it Naturally* cookbook that normally comes with an Excalibur dehydrator. It is a fascinating book to read, especially if you are interested in raw and living food diets.

These crackers take a long time to make, so it is worth drying other items in the dehydrator at the same time. They are delicious topped with hummus, guacamole or cream cheese and Debi's tomato, chile and ginger jam (see page 37). I have only given the method for making these in a dehydrator, as I think they would take forever in the oven.

serves 4-6 as a snack
2 tablespoons raisins
⅓ cup warm water
1 red pepper, destalked and seeded, cut into quarters
⅔ cup whole or ground almonds
pinch of dried thyme
pinch of salt
pinch of ground chile (optional)

Soak the raisins in the water for 30 minutes; drain, reserving the water. Put all the ingredients into a food processor with 2 tablespoons of the raisin water and blitz until smooth; if you prefer a chunky texture, leave slightly coarse. Mix to a spreadable paste with a little more of the raisin water, if necessary. Taste and adjust the seasoning.

Spread the mixture onto a silicone sheet and dry in a dehydrator at 125°F for 4 hours. Once dry enough to handle, peel off the paste and place upside down on a plastic or metal rack to dry out the other side. Reduce the temperature of the dehydrator to 105°F and bake until crisp, approx. 4–6 hours. Once the cracker is brittle and dry all the way through, break it into pieces and eat straight away or store in an airtight container for up 5 days.

TARHANA—TURKISH HOMEMADE INSTANT VEGETABLE SOUP

Tarhana is said to be the first instant soup, invented by the Turks of Central Asia. Apparently this soup was served to the Sultan when he was a guest at a poor peasant's house, hence the name *tarhana*, deriving from the Turkish *dar hane*, meaning "poor house." *Tarhana* was traditionally prepared by the women of the village in summer using the surplus of seasonal vegetables and stored throughout winter to make into soup. There are many variations of this dried soup including a Cypriot version made with yogurt, wheat, and mint. Feel free to experiment with your own flavorings: powdered cumin, coriander, or paprika all work well.

makes approx. 2¼lbs/each 3½oz serves 4
5½oz tomatoes, peeled
5½oz red pepper, seeded
5½oz onions, peeled
5½oz cooked chickpeas, mashed
5½oz thick Turkish or Greek yogurt
2¼ teaspoons instant yeast
5⅔ cups all purpose flour
a handful of parsley, finely chopped
1 tablespoon dried or finely chopped fresh mint leaves
3 tablespoons olive oil
1 tablespoon dried oregano
1–2 teaspoons salt

Use a food processor to finely chop the tomatoes, red peppers, and onions, or do this by hand. Combine the chopped vegetables in a bowl with the rest of the ingredients and mix to a firm paste with a little water. Bring together in a ball and turn out onto a clean work surface, scraping the bowl clean. Knead until the mixture is smooth and soft, and then return to the bowl. Cover with plastic wrap or foil and set aside to ferment in a cool place such as a fridge for at least a day (up to 10 days). The length of time you leave the dough to ferment is up to you; the longer you leave it the stronger the fermented flavor. We prefer it after just 3 days. Knead the dough every day for a few minutes and return to the bowl.

Once the dough has fermented to your liking, flatten it onto sheets and set aside to dry at room temperature or in the oven at 140°F or a dehydrator at 135°F until the outside is dry and the inside is still slightly moist, approx. 6–8 hours. Turn the flat breads every few hours so that they dry evenly on both sides. Crack them into pieces to help the air to circulate.

Once dry, grate the flatbreads into crumbs on the coarse side of a grater or push through a sieve onto a clean dish towel. Collect up the crumbs and spread them out on a baking sheet to dry. Transfer to a warm place (not outside or in a dehydrator or they will blow away!), moving the crumbs around from time to time to ensure they dry uniformly.

You now have your instant soup granules, your tarhana. Traditionally they are kept in cotton bags, but you could store them in glass jars. They will last up to a year, stored in a cool, dry place.

To rehydrate your soup
Put 3½oz tarhana granules in a bowl with 2 cups water and set aside until

the grains have swelled and there are no hard lumps, approx. 30 minutes. Tip into a large saucepan, stir in 1 quart chicken, meat, or vegetable stock (or water) and bring to a boil. Season to taste with salt and stir in a tablespoon of tomato purée if you wish. Ladle the soup into bowls, crumble some halloumi cheese or cooked roasted red peppers over the top, and garnish with shredded mint leaves. Finish with a swirl of extra virgin olive oil.

Below: Cracked *Tarhana* drying; **Right:** *Tarhana* soup.

PAN DE HIGO— FIG AND NUT CAKES

This dense and gooey fig and nut cake is traditionally served in Spain with Manchego cheese and honey. It can either be made as a whole cake, served sliced, or made into balls, and either wrapped in vine leaves or rolled in sesame seeds. *Pan de higo* is a good use of your dried fruits and stores well.

makes 18-20 balls

18oz dried figs
3½oz dried apricots
1⅓ cups walnuts or almonds
½ teaspoon ground nutmeg
½ teaspoon ground cinnamon
½ teaspoon ground cloves
2 tablespoons honey
2–4 tablespoons sweet wine or brandy
⅔ cup sesame seeds, for coating

Remove any stems left on the fruits. Put them in a food processor with the nuts and spices and pulse to a coarse paste; alternatively finely chop everything by hand. Scoop the mixture into a bowl, adding the honey and enough wine to bring the mixture together in a ball. It should be firm but malleable. Break the mixture into golf-ball-sized pieces and shape into individual balls. Scatter the sesame seeds onto a plate and roll the balls in the seeds to coat them. Arrange on a wire rack and set aside at room temperature to harden for a day or two. Eat immediately or once hard, store in a container with a lid in a dark, cool place for up to 3 months.

Right: Raspberry fruit leather.

citrus powder

Instead of throwing away peel from oranges, limes, and lemons you can turn it into citrus powder. Our patisserie chef Dawid scatters a little citrus powder over a dessert plate before presenting a slice of cake or tart. He also uses it on ice creams and I use it to flavor Almond cookies such as the ones in Cold, page 270.

METHOD Peel the colored zest only away from the fruit, leaving the white pith behind. Either leave in finger-width pieces if you are going to grind it later or use a zester to get long thin strips that will dry more quickly. Dry until crisp—either outside in the sun or in a dehydrator at 135°F for 2–4 hours, or in a low oven. I often put mine in the oven overnight if I have been cooking; the residual heat cooks the peel for no extra energy. Grind the brittle strips into powder using a spice grinder or mortar and pestle.

To make a zingy lemon salt for grinding over fish or into casseroles, zest a lemon onto a thin bed of coarse sea salt. The essential oils will spray onto the salt. Dry as above and then crush with a mortar and pestle, a salt grinder or your fingers for use.

fruit leathers

These shiny, sweet strips of fruit make your mouth water and pucker with flavor. Whenever the kids make them they are swiftly eaten within the day as they are just so delicious.

Fruit leathers can be made from most puréed fruits, provided their water content is not too high—which rules out fruits such as citrus or rhubarb on their own, although these can be mixed with other fruits such as apple or banana. Ideal fruits are apples, berries, grapes, pears, peaches, plums, tomatoes, mango, pineapple, and more. Always choose fruit in a good condition that is not bruised or overripe. Sweeten with sugar or honey to taste, although this isn't always necessary because the drying process concentrates the natural sugars anyway. Flavorings can be added such as vanilla to banana, chile to pineapple, and cinnamon to apple. Adding nuts or oats gives an interesting texture and ultimately makes the leather more filling for snacks. Tear or cut into strips in a pasta machine.

FRUIT LEATHER RECIPES

makes 1 leather approx. 14in square

MANGO LEATHER

1 large mango

RASPBERRY AND BANANA LEATHER

2 bananas
7oz raspberries
juice of ½ lemon

APPLE LEATHER

4 apples
juice of ½ lemon

Cut the fruit with or without the peel into chunks and purée in a food processor or blender. Pour the purée onto silicone mats or plastic wrap-lined sheets. Make sure the pool of purée doesn't go over the edge of the sheets; smooth out by shaking and tilting the sheet to make it spread out. The purée should be no thicker than ¼in.

Dry in the dehydrator at 135°F for 4–6 hours, or in the oven at 140°F for 6–8 hours. Fruit leathers are ready when they are not sticky to the touch, but can be peeled easily from the mat or plastic wrap. Lift the edge, which will adhere lightly to the surface, and peel it back. If it peels back easily, it is ready.

RHUBARB AND STRAWBERRY LEATHER

2 long rhubarb stalks, roughly chopped
4 tablespoons sugar
8 strawberries

Cook the fruit with the sugar until it is soft and pulpy. Push through a sieve to remove the seeds and tough fibers, and then dry following the method left.

CARRIE'S RASPBERRY AND ALMOND LEATHER

My friend Carrie has a garden where she grows a whole host of vegetables and fruit. She picks her raspberries, makes them into leather, and then enjoys it as a snack while she works.

10½oz raspberries
1½ tablespoons light corn syrup
¼ cup sliced almonds
¼ cup oats

Cook the raspberries and syrup together until soft and push through a sieve. Mix with the almonds and oats and pour onto silicone mats or plastic wrap-lined sheets and dry as left.

STORING YOUR FRUIT LEATHER
Either eat immediately or cover the dried leather in a layer of parchment paper and roll up, or cut into 2in wide strips and roll up. Store in an airtight jar in a cool, dark place for up to 6 weeks, but do check regularly for any signs of mold. Alternatively pack into vacuum bags and store in the freezer for up to 3 months. Leathers made with oats or nuts will become rancid if left for longer than a month, however they can be frozen.

FLAVIO'S CHICKEN FAJITA RUB

Once a week we eat fajitas with our sons, Flavio and Giorgio. I was cautious about buying packages of pre-mixed rubs and salsa so we started to make our own. After a lot of fun experimenting this is the version we liked most. Use as a marinade for chicken and serve with tortillas and Giorgio's salsa (see page 254).

makes approx. 4 portions
(each portion is enough rub for 6)
6 tablespoons coriander seeds
6 teaspoons cumin seeds
1 tablespoon dried oregano
  (see page 128)
1 teaspoon saffron (not the terribly
  expensive kind as this is more
  for color)
1 dried red chile
2 teaspoons salt
¼ teaspoon ground nutmeg
2½in cinnamon stick
1 heaping teaspoon pink peppercorns

Heat the coriander and cumin seeds in a dry frying pan until they just start to pop; remove from the heat and cool. Put into a spice grinder with the remaining ingredients, in two batches if there isn't room, and grind until you have a powder. Store in a small glass jar for up to 3 months. It will keep for longer but the intensity of the spices fades with time. To use, coat diced chicken in the powder and leave for 30 minutes or up to 2 hours to marinate in a bowl in the fridge. As a guide 1 tablespoon of powder will coat two diced chicken breasts. Fry the chicken in a little cooking oil until cooked through and use to fill soft warm tortillas with Giorgio's salsa on page 254.

FISH

Only the freshest fish should be dried and, if it has not been salted first, the quicker it is done the better before it starts to go bad. Fish are 80 percent water. If they are dried to hold only 25 percent water, bacterial growth is halted. If they are dried to under 15 percent water, molds cannot grow.

In Sri Lanka we saw stalls selling all types of dried seafood—from tiny shrimp to slabs of tuna. The hot sun and sea breezes quickly dry the fish, after gutting first, while it is still on the boats. Dried fish is used to enhance complex flavors in many dishes.

As a general rule lean fish such as cod and shellfish dry better than oily fish, since the fats in these can oxidize and become rancid.

Stockfish—usually cod—was traditionally freeze-dried in the cool, windy climate along the Norwegian, Swedish, and Icelandic coastline, but it is now produced in factories. It has a strong, pronounced flavor of umami (see page 94), which I love but Giancarlo dislikes in fish. Stockfish should be soaked for a few days in several changes of water to prevent bacterial growth as it rehydrates. It can then be pounded to a creamy paste or poached in portions and cooked like fresh cod only with more flavor. *Baccalà* is similar but it is salted before drying.

AIR-DRIED MACKEREL FILLET

This delicious Japanese method of drying fish was shown to me by Rieko Hara, who teaches Asian cooking. Air-dried mackerel has a rich, sweet taste with a hint of saltiness. Herring and sardines can also be dried in this way.

serves 4

4 mackerel fillets
fine sea salt
¼ cup mirin
¼ cup sake
½–⅔ cup Japanese soy sauce
¼ cup sugar
2 tablespoons white sesame seeds
thinly sliced cucumber and radish
  dressed in sweet vinegar, to garnish

Sprinkle the mackerel fillets with salt. Cover with plastic wrap and set aside in the fridge for an hour.

Meanwhile make the marinade. Place the mirin and sake in a saucepan and bring to a boil to burn off the alcohol. Add the soy sauce and sugar and stir well over low heat to dissolve the sugar, taking care not burn. Set aside to cool to room temperature.

Rinse the mackerel fillets in cold water and pat dry with paper towels. Pour the marinade into a large shallow container and add the fish, making sure the fillets don't overlap. Cover the container with plastic wrap and set aside to marinate in the fridge overnight.

The following day, lift out the fillets and dry carefully on paper towels. Sprinkle the sesame seeds over the flesh side of the fillets to coat them evenly. Arrange the fillets on a wire rack, sesame-side up, and set aside to dry in a cool place such as a north-facing room or garage, taking precautions to keep flies away, for 5–6 hours or until the surface is firm and no longer sticky. Either cook straight away (see below) or pack into freezer bags and store in the freezer for up to 3 months.

To serve, grill the mackerel fillets for 3–4 minutes on each side until slightly brown and the sesame seeds are toasted. Serve with a cucumber and radish salad.

Right: Mackerel at the beginning of the salting process.

MEAT

beef jerky

Jerky, as it is called today, originates from Peru, where *ch'arki*, as it was known in the Inca language, was traditionally made using leftover meat from a hunt. It was originally created from wild game, however as farming methods grew it was made more and more from beef. Its popularity spread into North America, where jerky became the survival food for the pioneers as it could be taken on long journeys to provide vital nutrition.

Jerky should be made from lean, if tough, cuts of meat as fatty cuts are more susceptible to rancidity. Beef, lamb, venison, or wild boar are all good. Jerky is high in protein and so it makes a nutritious and filling snack.

BEEF JERKY

Our son Giorgio loves jerky but it is expensive to buy so we make our own; this is his recipe. One of the joys of making jerky is experimenting with different flavors. However, do write down your experiments to repeat or avoid them next time. We recommend the following flavorings: spices such as coriander, curry powder, or chile; powders such as garlic and onion (see page 126), or sauces such as soy sauce, teriyaki, Worcestershire, or Mushroom ketchup (see page 43). If you wish you can finish your jerky in a smoker after drying.

makes 18oz
2¼lbs beef, such as rump, flank, or top round

For the marinade
2 cups soy sauce

1 tablespoon crushed coriander seeds
1 tablespoon dark brown sugar
2 garlic cloves, peeled and finely chopped
1 teaspoon red pepper flakes
½ teaspoon freshly ground black pepper
2 heaping teaspoons grated fresh ginger

If your meat is tough, put it in the freezer and partially freeze it; this makes it easier to cut.

Cut the beef into ¼in slices, cutting with the grain if the meat is tender or against the grain if it is not. If necessary, put the slices between sheets of plastic wrap and bash with a meat mallet to tenderize them and make them all the same thickness. Cut any large pieces in half so they are all a similar size. Very roughly 5–6in in length and 1½in in width is ideal.

Mix together the ingredients for the marinade and pour into a large lasagna dish or similar. Add the beef strips, turning them so they are evenly coated in the marinade. Cover the dish with plastic wrap and set aside to marinate in the fridge for at least 6 hours (preferably overnight).

The following day, take out the meat strips and pat dry on paper towels. Arrange the meat on racks and dry at 155°F in a dehydrator for 4–8 hours or in the oven at 140°F for up to 8–10 hours. The jerky is ready when it feels dry and leathery; you should be able to bend it without snapping. Store in an airtight container or vacuum bags in a cool, dark place for up to a month or in the fridge for up to 6 months. It can be also frozen in vacuum bags and kept for up to 6 months.

Variation
Follow the instructions above with fresh salmon for salmon jerky but there is no need to bash out the pieces.

Right: Beef and salmon jerky.

biltong

South African biltong and chile pork loin strips can be made in a dehydrator, oven, or purpose-built biltong box. The Bantu men of Africa originally taught the skill of drying meat to the Boers. Salt and air preserved the meats, which were hung out to dry; coriander seed was used as a flavoring or possibly as an insect deterrent. Eventually when the Boers settled they added saltpeter to the mix, which preserved the red color of the meat and enabled it to be stored for longer. This recipe was given to me by Grant Fletcher, who now lives in the UK. He misses his biltong so much that he has resorted to making it himself in his own purpose-built biltong box.

makes approx. 18oz

2¼lbs beef—a roasting cut, such as top rump or a similar cut of venison
rock salt
2 cups apple cider vinegar
approx. 2 teaspoons freshly ground black pepper
approx. 2 teaspoons ground or crushed coriander seeds

Cut the beef into steaks, approx. ¾in thick and the same length as the cut of meat. Put a scattering of rock salt into the base of a dish. Layer up the steaks, placing a sprinkling of salt in between each layer and covering with more salt on top. Set aside for 20–30 minutes, during which time the meat will sweat as the salt starts to draw out the moisture.

Pour the apple cider vinegar into a bowl and mix the spices into it. Grant's tip (or confession!) is that he never measures the spices—he says he just throws them in for good measure!

After 30 minutes, remove the steaks from the dish and scrape off as much salt as possible from each one using the back of a knife. Dip the steaks in the vinegar and spice mixture, coating them on each side; this should wash off the salt and give them a nice coating.

Hang the steaks in a biltong drier (see below right) for 3 days or in a dehydrator at 155°F for about 6 hours. To check it is fully dry, and ensure that it has lost enough water to preserve it, you can weigh the bundle. If dried correctly, the biltong should have lost half its original weight and the strips should snap when you bend them.

BILTONG BOX This is designed to mimic the African climate where biltong is traditionally made. You can make a drier yourself from a small cabinet or cupboard fitted with rails at the top from which you hang your biltong to dry (see photo below right). Biltong driers are usually fitted with a light inside to drive off humidity and provide a little warmth, and a fan at the bottom. Two light bulbs and a computer fan are ideal for this job.

chile pork strips

Although these are made in a similar way to biltong, it is important to use special curing salts because pork is potentially more dangerous than beef.

makes approx. 18oz
2¼lbs lean pork (leg meat is good)
7 teaspoons curing salts: EITHER
  2½ teaspoons Quickcure and
  4½ teaspoons coarse salt OR
  1 teaspoon Prague Powder No 2
  and 6 teaspoons coarse salt
1 cup apple cider vinegar
2 level teaspoons chili powder
½–1 teaspoon red pepper flakes
1–2 teaspoons fennel seeds, lightly
  crushed

Follow instructions for the biltong, using curing salts and coarse salt instead of rock salt and chili powder instead of the pepper and cilantro. After dipping the meat in the vinegar, scatter with red pepper flakes and fennel seeds (sparingly), pressing them into the surface of the meat. Dry as before.

Left: Chile pork strips and Beef and venison biltong; **Below:** Our homemade biltong box.

HAMS, SALAMI, AND SAUSAGES

Most dried pork products, particularly hams, are salted first before being air-dried. In regions such as Parma and San Daniele in Italy, drying is traditionally done using the gentle local breezes.

where to cure

After curing sausages and meat with salt the next stage is to dry them so that they slowly lose moisture. This reduction in water content combined with the increased salt levels this creates will prolong the shelf-life of the product and improve the flavor.

Although fermented charcuterie such as cured sausages need a little warmth to kick-start fermentation, after that they need to be moved somewhere cool. Similarly hams and any other cured meats need to be stored where the temperature does not exceed 60°F.

Before refrigeration, meat was cured in the coldest months of the year and hung in the coolest areas of people's houses. This might have been in a pantry against a north-facing wall, with a small window for ventilation (but not a direct draft) and this is still viable today if you are lucky enough to have one. We have also had success with a curing box. By this I mean an old kitchen cupboard that has had a new door fitted onto it with a window and mosquito netting attached. This stands in our garage where the badly fitted garage doors allow air to circulate. The box keeps the meat away from direct draughts and the mosquito netting stops the insects. The temperature and relative humidity (see right) is fairly stable in our garage during the winter months and can be monitored from the warmth of our kitchen with a remote sensor.

However, conditions including temperature, humidity, and air flow should always be monitored and controlled and this is hard to do in a large space like a garage. For this reason it makes life easier to create a small environment where this can be done easily, where you are in control. At home I have successfully cured bacon, salami, and small hams in my wine fridge, which has a fan to circulate air, racks for hanging, and a built-in temperature control. A small portable weather station will tell you the temperature and humidity. The humidity can then be altered by not hanging too much in the space and by the saturated water (see Altering the humidity levels right).

Alternatively an old fridge can be adapted for this purpose. To increase air circulation a computer fan can be put inside. It needs to have a small, thin wire to ensure the door shuts properly and the door seal is not disrupted. You can buy gadgets that control temperature and humidity and a humidifier can be employed to adjust this. There are plenty of plans and more detailed ideas of how to do this online.

Make sure wherever you choose to dry your charcuterie it is scrupulously clean and has no traces of mold. You only want to encourage certain molds for your meat. Hanging is better than putting meat on a rack as air can distribute easily and there are no marks or imprints left on the food.

humidity

Humidity is measured with a hygrometer. If you are going to start curing and drying, this is an essential gadget to have. We have a digital one that was not expensive and measures temperature as well as relative humidity (known as RH). It also has a remote sensor that I use in my garage or play house when cold smoking.

The ideal humidity for curing meats is RH 75 percent, however anywhere between RH 65–80 percent is acceptable; in fact you will always have some variance during the day unless you are using a fridge. At the beginning of the curing period, RH80 percent is fine to encourage fermentation to take place and to kick-start the nitrates.

ALTERING THE HUMIDITY LEVELS

The humidity in an enclosed space such as a fridge can be altered using saturated salt in a container. Pour an amount of water, say 4 quarts, into a large saucepan and set it on the stove to boil. Add salt a little at a time and stir to dissolve. At some point you will not be able to add any more—you will see that it won't dissolve—this is when the solution is saturated. Allow the solution to cool and place in the curing chamber. Some crystals of salt will develop on the bottom of the bowl but don't worry about these. The solution has the ability to raise and lower the humidity as needed.

Note: If your chosen area is too dry or drafty your meat may develop "case hardening"—this is when the outside of the sausage hardens. If this is allowed to form, the sausage will not cure properly on the inside and will remain soft. If this happens the sausage should be discarded.

temperature

Curing is historically done in the winter when the foods, equipment and storage areas are naturally cold. By curing foods at lower temperatures we slow down the growth of bacteria extending the shelf-life. The temperature surrounding the curing meat should be monitored at all times using a thermometer.

For fermented meats such as *prosciutto* and salami, etc. slight warmth (up to 75°F) for the first couple of days at the beginning encourages fermentation. However, this should always be followed by a long period in cooler conditions (54–61°F is fine). It is perfectly fine to cure bacon in a normal fridge at a temperature of around 39°F. All meats should be kept in the dark while they are curing.

fermentation cultures

Fermentation happens at the beginning of making cured salami and sausages when the temperature is often a little higher to encourage it. All meat contains lactose, a type of sugar; bacteria eat this and make lactic acid. It is this enzyme activity that creates amino acids, which give us the unique flavor we enjoy in cured sausages. In a way it is a form of controlled rotting, which sounds unpleasant, but is in fact the natural breakdown of meat; this is why we like 28-day-hung steak rather than fresh.

molds—good and bad

Most white, dry, powdery molds are good and help starve out other molds; they form either as small white spots or as a fur. To prevent white molds from completely swamping your meat, wipe them off regularly with vinegar or a strong spirit such as Grappa on a piece of paper towel. Before eating, it is advisable to clean off any molds with a nail or toothbrush; keep the brush only for this task.

Most green molds are bad and if these form you are better to err on the side of caution and discard the meat. However, a spot or two of green or blue mold can be cleaned away with vinegar and the meat re-hung.

Slimy gray or black, yellow, orange, and red molds definitely mean throw the meat away.

Many suppliers, such as Weschenfelder, sell fermentation kits with existing cultures in them to be included in sausage and salami mixtures. Some curers hang a sausage from a previous batch in with the new batch to introduce the right molds.

Left: Rhubarb cured venison;
Below: A horse bone used to test the smell of curing meats. Bad molds such as these mean you should discard the meat immediately.

smoke

It is good to know that you can create some really stunning smoked food with very basic equipment. At its simplest, food is smoked by putting it into a contained space with a smoky fire lit near it. Our ancestors have been doing this since man first learned to light a fire, without the use of any gadgetry such as internal temperature gauges, timers, and briquettes.

What is fascinating is that there is something called "the smoke line"—which neither Giancarlo nor I had heard of until we went to Friuli in Italy to research curing and smoking ham. It was explained to us that Friuli, which is situated just below the Alps, is on the border of this latitude that extends around the world. Areas above this latitude traditionally smoke their foods, while areas below it generally air-dry. This is due to the humidity in the atmosphere that makes food difficult to dry in regions above this smoke line—instead food is traditionally smoked as well in order to ensure it is properly preserved. Fascinating! It just demonstrates how humans all over the world have learned to adapt to their environment in order to make food last, using whichever method works best with the natural conditions.

I suggest you start with some very simple techniques such as smoking a piece of cheese (see page 154) to get the feel of what you are doing, and then you can progress to things like cold smoking bacon and hot smoking fish. Once you get confident—and hooked—you can begin to tweak the basic methods and experiment with different woods, etc.

Just one word of caution: research suggests that smoked foods should be eaten in moderation since they can damage your health in large quantities. However, whereas smoke used to be applied in a much more heavy-handed way, to ensure foods would last, nowadays foods tend to be smoked for flavor, more than as a preservative, so a lighter approach can be adopted.

how smoking preserves food

Wood smoke contains compounds that inhibit the growth of microorganisms, slow down the rancidity of fats, and provide a flavor that most of us find really delicious. Smoking also deters insects. As smoking only tends to penetrate the surface of the food, most foods are salted first and dried as a further preservative (see Salt and Air chapters for more information). Drying forms a "pellicle," which is a slightly tacky film on the surface of the food. If you press your finger against the surface it will "snap" as your finger is removed. This slight stickiness will help the smoke stick or cling to the food. And, of course, foods that are salted, dried, and then smoked have a wonderful flavor, since drying helps to concentrate the flavor of the food and salt enhances it: think of smoked bacon, smoked salmon, or peppered mackerel.

hot and cold smoking

There are two types of smoking: hot and cold. Cold smoking is a gentle process, which takes place at a low temperature. Cold smoking dries out the food, preserves it, and gives it a smoky flavor, without cooking it. Hot smoking takes the temperature much higher, and so it does actually cook the food. Strictly speaking, hot smoking in itself does not preserve food for long. However, if the food has been salted first it will keep for longer—Peppered mackerel (page 168) and Hot smoked chicken (page 173), for example, can be enjoyed for days longer than their fresh counterparts. Also, hot smoked food tends to be eaten hot from the smoker, or fairly soon afterward. Hot smoking originally gave shelf-life to fish

that spoiled quickly, such as herrings that were turned into kippers. With refrigeration, this is now unnecessary so some smokers prefer to cold smoke only as it gives a gentler flavor; the food can then be cooked afterward. In cold weather most foods can be cold smoked as long as they have been salted first.

wood choices

A variety of woods are available from specialty suppliers in the form of dust, chips, or logs, all of which are ideal for smoking. Hard woods, such as oak and beech, should always be used since the sap in soft woods is not good for us—although certain recipes, such as German *speck*, are bizarrely

smoked over pine (however, we don't recommend this).

Ideally you want to keep the temperature down and the humidity levels high. Larger pieces of wood should be green—that is, not completely wet and just cut, but not dried out either. Logs cut and left for approx. 6–9 months are ideal. This way, the wood will smolder well. However, you can soak older logs and wood chips first to slow the burning time and make smoke, not fire. Sawdust can be sprayed with a water spray to do the same.

For cold smoking, milder flavors such as apple, cherry, oak, and beech are often used, whereas for hot smoking a quick blast of a strong flavor such as hickory or mesquite is more effective over a short time.

CHOICE OF WOOD

This is a rough guide to the various woods and the suggested foods they should be married with.

Alder A light, versatile, slightly sweet flavor—good with fish, seafood, poultry, and game birds.

Apple Mild and fruity, slightly sweet —good with cheese, bacon, poultry, and pork.

Beech A good all-rounder—ideal for fish, bacon, and poultry.

Birch Medium strength, similar to maple—good with fish, poultry, and pork.

Cherry Mild and fruity, versatile— good all-rounder with fish, poultry, pork, and beef.

Citrus Light and fruity—good all-rounder.

Hickory Strong—good with beef and lamb.

Juniper Spicy branches of juniper add flavor to Eastern European sausages.

Maple Fruity and sweet—good with pork, poultry, vegetables, and cheese.

Mesquite Strong flavor, good for hot smoking.

Oak A good all-rounder.

Pear Light and sweet—good with poultry and pork.

Walnut Heavy flavor—good with game and beef.

Enthusiasts such as David at hotsmoked.co.uk agree that smoking should be about the food not about the smoke, so it is important to enhance the flavor of food, not disguise it. That being said, certain woods do complement particular foods—for example, beech and salmon, or cheese and apple wood.

Native Americans cooked salmon over thin planks of wood soaked in water. This gives a subtle flavor. The food sits on top and as the wood steams the flavor is forced through the food. Planks are produced commercially for smoking or you can make your own—just ensure that the wood hasn't been treated with any chemicals.

Peat has been used for centuries for smoking to give a unique flavor. Traditionally, peat was popular in areas where there was little firewood. Environmentally, many people are against using peat as it is not sustainable.

cold days and high humidity

Smoking has long been a tradition in mountainous areas where the high altitude and low humidity has created the perfect conditions for this form of food preservation. The outside temperature, humidity and breeze all influence smoking. It is better not to cold smoke in warm or humid weather, as you could inadvertently create the ideal environment for bacteria to breed. For cold smoking, the temperature inside your smoke chamber should be 50–86°F, with the ideal being 72–79°F; humidity should be no more than 85 percent. Fish starts to cook above 86°F, so you need to keep the temperature well below this for safety. To be absolutely safe, I always do my cold smoking in cold weather and I enjoy the fact it has become a seasonal activity. If it is very cold outside you can heat the smoking chamber in an electric smoker such as a Bradley to about 77°F. I know from experience trying to cold smoke salmon for Christmas dinner in the snow that it took longer than normal to get the smoke to adhere to the fish.

Humidity is good when hot smoking to prevent the foods from drying out; often water, or in some cases beer or wine, are introduced into the drip tray of the smoker to increase humidity. In the case of hot smoked Arbroath smokies, humidity is increased by splashing water onto the fire in the barrel before the fish are suspended over it. Wet sackcloth seals the top of the barrel so that, effectively, the fish are steamed in smoke—which creates a wonderfully moist result.

HOW AND WHERE TO SMOKE?

There are many, many ways to smoke food, using containers such as cardboard boxes, old fridges, or barrels to professional smoke chambers, and purpose-built smoke houses, some of which develop a wonderful layer of black tar on the inside over time to enhance the flavor. The smoky flavor of food is affected by many factors, including the density of smoke it is exposed to, the external and internal temperature of the smoking space and the fire temperature generated by the heat source.

We now have five different methods of smoking in and around our house and we use them all, depending on what and how much we want to smoke. Each method has its own pros and cons, however you really don't need five—just pick one or two that suit your surroundings and lifestyle.

COLD SMOKERS

the external fire source

Enthusiasts usually prefer to have an external fire source, which means you don't get smoked yourself while tending to your fire, and there is no chance of the flames and the heat being too close to your food. DIY fanatics often make their own using a length of ducting to channel the smoke from the fire source to the smoking chamber. My nephew Jamie has made his own, low-cost cold smoker, which he loves and tends to like a child. As far as he is concerned, it is all part of the joy of smoking to wake up in the middle of the night and relight the fire! If you fancy going down the DIY route, there are all kinds of forums, websites, and books devoted to building your own model: take your pick!

multi-purpose smokers—the bradley smoker

For not a lot of money, and a lot less time spent scratching your head over calculations and drawings, you can simply buy a Bradley smoker, which plugs in and uses purpose-made bisquettes. We have one of these and it is great for both cold and hot smoking, as it has an element inside to control the heat. The beauty of a Bradley smoker is that it also has a timer and an oven control so it will keep going for hours without any fuss. The downside is that you have to buy the bisquettes, which makes it the most costly method of the five we recommend—although you might choose the ease of using it over the effort required for other methods. Our tip would be to learn to use the air vent (called the "damper") on the top of the smoker effectively, since it is important to control the flow of smoke around the food because a high density of smoke will result in a very strong flavor. To get the most out of the cost of the fuel it is worth smoking as much as you can at the same time.

Heat the chamber up to temperature first when hot smoking. Use the drip tray not only to collect fat and juices falling from the food but also to induce some humidity where necessary. Often wine, beer, juice, or water is poured into it. See the instruction manual with your Bradley for more information or their website (see page 290).

the old grill

Our grill broke years ago and was waiting for a trip to the dump. However, it now has a new lease of life as a cold smoker. Where once there was charcoal, we now have a ProQ Cold Smoke Generator in it. This is a maze made of wire mesh that contains enough fine sawdust to let out small wafts of smoke for 10 hours, so it produces slow, gentle cold smoke to give a subtle flavor. It is also available as an economical and eco-friendly smoking chamber consisting of a cardboard box fitted with a generator, shelves and drip trays. We have had wonderful results with our old grill, using it for smoking whole sides of salmon, cheese, tomatoes, and more—it is absolutely my preferred method for cold smoking salmon and bacon. I can buy all sorts of dust easily, so I can have fun experimenting with flavor, and the whole process is inexpensive.

the playhouse—garden smokehouse

The kids have lost interest in the playhouse, so now it has a greater purpose in life: a smokehouse for cold smoking. Any outhouse or shed will also suit this purpose, it doesn't have to be completely airtight as a gentle flow of air through the building is ideal. If there aren't already gaps you can drill holes low down in the door, for example, to allow air in and more holes opposite and high up for the smoke to exit. This has the advantage of carrying the smoke up and through the food.

A garden smokehouse has the big advantage of being low tech, inexpensive, and offers space for smoking plenty of food. The flavor of the food is greatly influenced by the density of the smoke it is exposed to; therefore this method of smoking using logs gives a mellow and perhaps less acrid taste to the food than other techniques. A small garden shed (approx. 6 x 3½ft) is ideal.

In one corner we light a small fire from kindling and logs in a fire bowl—a purpose-made, heavy-duty metal bowl for outdoor use—which sits on paving slabs to prevent the spread of heat onto the wooden floor. If you don't have a fire bowl, a metal box or disused wood burner is ideal. Over the fire is a metal sheet, which limits the air supply to the fire to keep down the flames and heat. The food to be smoked is in another corner, high up on a rack resting on poles. While the fire smolders gently and eventually burns out, we monitor the temperature and humidity from inside our kitchen using a remote sensor fitted on the rack. I occasionally use the smoke generator part of a Bradley in here to give more gentle smoke in a large area, especially when smoking lots of produce.

Left and Above: Giancarlo smoking ribs in the Bradley smoker; Below: the playhouse smoker (left) and salmon smoking above the ProQ Cold Smoke Generator in our old grill (right).

HOT SMOKERS

the trashcan

Cheap, simple, unsophisticated and it works! This is our version of the barrels used to make Arbroath smokies. We light a fire, using kindling and birch logs in a small grate in the bottom of a galvanized trashcan, and wait until it has subsided to embers. We spray these with a water-spray and then put a rack over the top on which the food sits, then we put the trashcan lid on. A wet towel over the top helps trap the smoke inside.

Iain Spink, a fourth-generation smoker from the Scottish coastline, demonstrated the traditional process of hanging Arbroath smokies over the fire, which is done in a particular way so that they do not fall into the embers. After numerous attempts to reproduce this system at home, I decided on the rack idea instead and we can now hot smoke mackerel, haddock and lean, smaller cuts of chicken in this way. This method should not be used to hot smoke fatty cuts of meat over a long period of time, since dripping fat could re-ignite the flames underneath. I love this method: it is cheap to construct and I can move my trashcan around wherever I want it—although I make sure it stands on a paving slab or some tiles, so it doesn't burn the lawn or decking. The process doesn't take long and is simple and not difficult to get right. You just have to lift the lid to see if the food is done.

the wok

Many people smoke in a wok lined with foil but we have never been pleased with the results and ruined a wok in the process!

the cameron stovetop

A favorite with our kids, this is small and portable so we can use it indoors on the stove under the extraction fan, or outdoors with the burner to take on picnics. It is also economical, as a spoonful of dust is all it takes to create enough smoke to flavor foods such as salmon or mackerel.

HOW LONG TO SMOKE FOR?

As with so many of the processes in this book, this is probably the toughest question to answer. Invariably the experts I talked to would all begin with: "Well, that depends!" As I have mentioned, density of smoke, outside temperature, humidity, and draft all affect the smoke and so does the freshness and size of the food to be smoked. You have to be the judge of when it is done and how smoky you want it to be.

Commercial smokers, who need consistent results, will take a more mathematical approach and measure weight loss. However, for home smoking the best way to tell is to use your senses:

MOVE the product away from the smoke and give it a few minutes, then smell it for the strength of aroma.

TOUCH it to feel the firmness and the loss of weight. Bill and Sukie Barber run courses in the Scottish Borders on smoking and other subjects and shared their knowledge with us. Bill explained that properly smoked food should feel like a block of firm gelatin: firm with a very slight give; it becomes quite translucent too.

LOOK AT THE COLOR—often smoked foods will take on a golden appearance, particularly for eggs or mozzarella, where it shows up against the milky white of the food. However, dark meats do not show the color change at all.

CUT A SMALL PIECE AND TASTE IT— either raw for salmon or cheese or cooked for chicken or pork. The outside of the food will be most affected by the smoke, so taste a second slice further in.

ALWAYS use a probe thermometer for checking the internal temperature of hot smoked meats.

The timings we give are just a guide, as humidity, temperature, and wind will alter the smoking to an extent. Over time you will build up a feeling and an instinct for when your food is done. I found this happened quite quickly, particularly when you repeat the same process with the same food. We love our smoked salmon and it wasn't long before I felt confident to produce great results each time. I think it is like bread-making, how do you know when your loaf is done? After a while you just know; trust your instincts.

captain's log

Like the good old Captain Jim on Starship Enterprise, make a log. Note your smoking times, wood choice, humidity, outside temperature, and results so that next time you are not guessing what to do. Experiment with small amounts of food and time them in the smoker for, say, 20 minutes, 30 minutes, and so on—preferably on the same day so the external conditions are the same. This way you will have a record of previous smoking times so you can improve or repeat the success! Don't forget, though, that outside conditions will affect your results.

what happens when the fire goes out?

Often food is actually drying in the smoker, as well as smoking, so it doesn't matter if the fire goes out while you are cold smoking; you are still helping concentrate the flavor of the food at the same time. This is a good reason why you should always make sure the weather is cold when you are smoking, since in warm weather it could be dangerous to leave the food in the smoker for too long. For hot smoking, it is important to have a constant and reliable heat source.

brining and salting

Before smoking food should be "cured" with salt. This can be in the form of dry salt or salt and water sometimes mixed with sugar known as wet brining. The food is cured to extend its life, harden the flesh making it better for handling during smoking and for flavor. For more information on this see the Salt chapter.

drying before smoking

As I mentioned at the beginning of this chapter, foods are often dried before smoking but this is a matter of individual choice: some people prefer very dry and heavily smoked food while others prefer it hardly dried at all, so it is still juicy and succulent with just a gentle hint of smoke. Many smokers will dry the food only briefly and allow it to drip-dry as it smokes—this also creates moisture in the air. This is often the case with fish such as Arbroath smokies. Size and oiliness matters: salmon can be left to dry for up to 24 hours, while a thin duck breast may only need a couple of hours; trout and eel are best not dried at all as they are already dry.

where to dry the food before smoking

In the days before refrigeration food was hung to dry in a breeze in a cool spot or in a pantry before being smoked. This might still be appropriate in high altitude where there are no flies and fresh mountain air can circulate around your food. However, for many of us insects and higher humidity are a problem so drying is better carried out in a fridge, pantry, or curing chamber.

Initially some foods made with curing salts such as Christmas ham (see page 100), bacon, venison, and beef benefit from being hung at a higher temperature (up to 75°F) so that good bacteria can flourish and a degree of fermentation can begin. At most this would be overnight and the curing salts will help protect the food. Salami is further protected by its skin. If you can do this in an area of low humidity and be sure insects cannot get to the food you may well achieve a better result but for safety's sake we recommend drying in the contained environment of a fridge, pantry, or curing chamber.

COLD SMOKING RECIPES

The timings below are approximate and only given as a guideline based on timings taken in our garden in England on a cool, calm day. With a little trial and error you will soon be the judge of when your food is ready. Begin with some easy produce such as nuts, cheese, and eggs or a small piece of fish. All should be rested on metal racks unless specified in the recipe.

All the products below should be cold smoked on a cold day when the temperature is low—70–88°F is ideal—so that it does not warm the produce. Very low temperatures may extend the smoking time—in snowy weather or strong cold winds I have smoked salmon for two days—so always be prepared for external conditions to affect timings.

COLD SMOKED NUTS

Shelled almonds and walnuts are delicious smoked and these are good, small things to put in while you are smoking something else so as not to waste space. After smoking they can be salted or tossed in maple syrup, butter, and sugar or spice rub and baked in a conventional oven for 15 minutes at 350°F.

Olives and coarse sea salt can also be smoked in this way.

PREPARATION Place the nuts on foil, which has had a few holes perforated into it with a skewer to let the smoke through, or a fine mesh tray.
WOOD CHOICE Alder, beech, oak.
TIMING Cold smoke for 4–8 hours in a grill or garden smokehouse; 2 hours in a Bradley smoker.
STORAGE Eat immediately or store in an airtight container up to 2 weeks.

COLD SMOKED EGGS

Vary the smoking time according to the size of your egg.

PREPARATION Hard-boil the eggs and shell them. If you wish you can brine them before smoking for a salty flavor: soak for 15–30 minutes depending on their size in medium brine (see page 86).
WOOD CHOICE Oak or beech.
TIMING Cold smoke for 2–3 hours for quail eggs or 4–5 hours for hen eggs in a grill or garden smokehouse; 1–2 hours for quail eggs or 3–4 hours for hen eggs in a Bradley smoker. The eggs should take on a light golden hue when ready.
SERVING SUGGESTION Smoked quail's eggs are delicious served with a small pile of celery salt to dip them in.
STORAGE Wrap in plastic wrap in the fridge and consume within 48 hours.

COLD SMOKED BUTTER

Smoked butter is really delicious in mashed potatoes, baked potatoes, or hot toast. For extra satisfaction, use your own homemade sea salt butter (see page 197 for a recipe).

PREPARATION Cut a 9oz block of butter into four pieces. Put onto foil, which has had a few holes perforated into it with a skewer to let the smoke through, or a fine mesh tray.
WOOD CHOICE Beech or fruit wood.
TIMING Cold smoke for 10 hours in a grill or garden smokehouse; 3–4 hours in a Bradley smoker.
STORAGE Wrap in plastic wrap or parchment paper and store in the fridge. Consume within a couple of weeks.

COLD SMOKED CHEESE

Cheese is a good indicator of temperature: if it is too hot inside the smoker the cheese will melt. This method is suitable for most cheeses, including hard cheese such as Cheddar and soft cheese such as mozzarella; the smaller the piece of cheese the quicker the smoke will penetrate, so you can chop a block of cheese into quarters if you prefer as this will increase the surface area for the smoke. If smoking Cheddar, it is best to smoke a large piece approx. 10½–18oz in weight and store it in the fridge after smoking for several weeks before sampling to allow the smoky flavor to really penetrate the cheese.

PREPARATION If smoking mozzarella, pat dry on paper towels before smoking.
WOOD CHOICE Fruit wood such as apple or oak.
TIMING Cold smoke for 2–3 hours in a Bradley smoker for Cheddar, depending on size, and 1 hour for mozzarella. Cheddar will become a deeper yellow when done; mozzarella should become slightly golden.
SERVING SUGGESTION Smoked mozzarella is gorgeous on pizza or cubed and stirred through hot pasta.
STORAGE Smoking will increase the shelf-life of most cheese by approx. 3 days. Store hard cheeses such as Cheddar in a plastic bag—a vacuum bag is ideal—for at least 3 weeks before sampling. Store smoked mozzarella wrapped in plastic wrap in the fridge for up to 4 days.

COLD SMOKED TOMATOES

Cherry tomatoes are a real treat when smoked.

PREPARATION Cut the tomatoes in half around the equator (rather than pole to pole) and lay them on a wire rack. Scatter over a little salt and white sugar and dry them in a low oven at approx. 122°F for about 4 hours until shrivelled but still holding some moisture.
WOOD CHOICE Alder, beech, birch, oak.
TIMING Cold smoke for 10 hours in a grill or garden smokehouse; 4 hours in a Bradley smoker.
STORAGE Once smoked, put the tomatoes into a sealed container as they are, or put under extra virgin olive oil and keep in the fridge for up to 10 days. For best results, allow them to come to room temperature before serving.
SERVING SUGGESTION Serve with cheese and crusty bread or stir them through hot pasta.

COLD SMOKED RED PEPPERS AND CHILES

Use cold smoked peppers and chiles anywhere you would use unsmoked ones to enhance the finished dish. To intensify the flavor blacken in a hot oven and peel before cooking.

WOOD CHOICE Alder, beech, oak, maple.
TIMING Cold smoke for 10 hours in a grill or garden smokehouse; 4 hours in a Bradley smoker.
STORAGE Put the peppers and chiles in a bag or container and store in the fridge up to 4 days.
USES Make your own smoked paprika by drying the peppers and chiles after smoking and grinding them in a spice mill.

COLD SMOKED FISH AND SHELLFISH

general advice

Most fish can be cold smoked and then cooked later, like kippers, so don't worry if you only have a cold smoker. Oily fish such as mackerel, salmon, and herring are ideal, however other firm fish such as tuna (although in short supply so best avoided), haddock, and trout also work well.

As I mentioned on page 150, as far as I am concerned, hanging fish inside your smoking area is for the professionals. However, if you want to have a try bear in mind that the fish might drop as they smoke. I think it is far easier to smoke delicate foods such as fish on a rack. Whichever system you choose make sure the fish are gutted. If you smoke them unfilleted, prop open their bellies with a toothpick so the smoke can circulate easily.

Note: It is important to use produce that is as fresh as possible for smoking. Wild fish should be frozen first to kill any parasites.

COLD SMOKED SALMON

You will need a pin-boned side of salmon; avoid trimming the fat off the edges.

PREPARATION Wash the fillet carefully in cold water and remove any blood; pat dry on paper towels. Sprinkle some salt over a sheet and lay the fillet on top, skin-side down. Scatter the surface of the fish with more salt, very lightly on the tail and more on the thicker parts. You can either use large grain or fine salt. Absorption of salt on the skin is minimal—it is the skin that stops the salt water becoming a brine to the fish and sucking water out of it at sea—so apply just 10 percent of the salt to the bottom of your sheet and more to the top. Set aside to to cure for 8–10 hours in the fridge, sloping the tray so that the brine can run off freely. The length of time the fish takes to cure will depend on the thickness and freshness of the fish, and the amount of salt.

Remove the fillet and rinse briefly under cold water, discarding the brine. Pat dry on paper towels and place, skin-side down, on a wire rack to dry for up to a day to form a pellicle. This could be in the fridge or in a pantry protected from insects.
WOOD CHOICE Oak or beech.
TIMING Cold smoke for 14–17 hours in a grill; at least 24 hours in a garden smokehouse; 4–8 hours in a Bradley smoker with the vent ("damper") wide open. Note: I normally smoke fish overnight over a cold smoke generator in our grill. If after 10 hours, the length of time it takes for the maze to burn through, the fire has gone out—or I am not happy with the smell and feel of the fish—I will set it to smoke for longer. I normally allow 14–15 hours for a medium fillet of salmon.

Note: If the salmon tastes too salty or too smoky after this time, you can always soak the fish in cold water for a few hours afterward, changing the water once. It won't be great smoked salmon, but you could always flake it up for pâté or add it to pasta dishes.
STORAGE Wrap in plastic wrap and set aside in the fridge for a day before eating. It will last up to 2 weeks in the fridge.
SERVING SUGGESTION Cut into thin slices, starting from the tail. Serve with wedges of lemon and wheat bread and butter.

COLD SMOKED TROUT

Bill Barber, a smoker and teacher in the Scotttish Borders, showed us how he cold smokes trout fillets.

PREPARATION Scatter some fine sea salt over the base of a lasagna dish or similar. Arrange the trout fillets, skin-side down, on top and sprinkle over a light covering of salt. Set aside in the fridge to cure for up to 20–30 minutes or until the fish feels firm to the touch. Rinse briefly afterward and smoke immediately. Pat dry on paper towels. There is no need to air-dry trout after curing, as with other fish, because it is already a dryish fish.
WOOD CHOICE Alder or oak.
TIMING Cold smoke for 6 hours in a grill or garden smokehouse; 2 hours in a Bradley smoker.
COOKING INSTRUCTIONS Poach in gently simmering water for 5–7 minutes, depending on their size. Once cooked they can be made into the Smoked trout pâté on page 193.
STORAGE Wrap the cooled cooked or uncooked fish in plastic wrap and store in the fridge for up to 10 days or freeze and use within 3 months.

KIPPERS

Smoked herrings are called kippers. To "kipper" something used to mean to smoke it. As this was frequently done to the herring, the words became interchangeable. Kippers are traditionally butterflied before smoking to expose the maximum area to the smoke. They are usually eaten at breakfast time with wheat toast and a poached egg. "Bloaters" are whole herrings; "red" herrings are those that have been smoked for a long time or been dyed.

Choose your fish carefully, making sure they are plump and fresh—this will depend upon their reproductive cycle as after spawning the fat content drops greatly—there is no point in going to the effort of smoking them if there is nothing but bones to eat!

PREPARATION Make up a strong 70 percent brine (see page 86) and set aside to cool.

Butterfly the herring or ask your fishmonger to do this for you. To do it yourself, cut the fish open along the belly from tail to head. It should be open from the top to the bottom on one side so that it opens out fully. Discard the guts and gently rinse the fish inside and out under the tap, being careful not to break the skin. Leave the backbone and head in place. Remove the gills and guts and wash well under cold running water, scraping away any blood.

Brine the fish for approx. 15–20 minutes, depending on the size of the herring (I have had tiny fillets of herring that were delicious but only needed 7 minutes in the brine.) Pat dry on paper towels and hang or leave on a rack to dry in the fridge or a cool room for a few hours to form a pellicle.
WOOD CHOICE Beech or oak.
TIMING Cold smoke for 8 hours in a grill or garden smokehouse; 2–4 hours in a Bradley smoker (with the damper open wide).
STORAGE Wrap in plastic wrap or pack in vacuum bags or sealed containers. Store in the fridge for up to 10 days or in the freezer for up to 3 months.

COLD SMOKED ANCHOVIES AND OTHER SMALL FISH

Smoking even small fish will extend their shelf-life for a few days. As fillets of tiny fish such as anchovies or sprats tend to be delicate, it is better to dry-cure them whole—without gutting them—before smoking.

PREPARATION Scatter some fine salt over a sheet and lay the whole fish on top. Sprinkle the surface with a fine layer of salt and set aside to cure in the fridge or in a cold room for up to 15 minutes or until the fish are the same texture as hard gelatin. Rinse under cold running water and pat dry on paper towels. Arrange the fish on a wire rack and set aside in the fridge or a cool breeze for 30 minutes to form a pellicle.
WOOD CHOICE Alder, beech, birch, oak.
TIMING Cold smoke for 1 hour in a grill or garden smokehouse; 30 minutes in a Bradley smoker.
STORAGE Smoked anchovies can be stored under oil in a sealed container in the fridge up to 2 weeks. Serve as a mouth-watering appetiser.

COLD SMOKED MUSSELS

I was hesitant about the idea of smoked shellfish but actually I couldn't have been more wrong. Mussels look stunning when you remove them from the smoker—all plump and orange sitting in their slate gray half shells.

PREPARATION Make up a weak brine solution using a ratio of 3 tablespoons salt per quart of water; set aside to cool to approx. 37°F. To speed things up, we use a little boiling water to dissolve the salt and make up to the full amount with cold water.

Open the shells and throw one half away, leaving each mussel in a half shell. Layer up the mussels in a lasagna dish and pour over the cold brine. Cover with plastic wrap and set aside in the fridge or a cool place for 10 minutes. Remove the mussels from the brining liquid, shake off any excess

brine and arrange in a single layer on the rack inside your smoker.

WOOD CHOICE Oak, birch, or beech.

TIMING Cold smoke for 2 hours in a grill or garden smokehouse; 15–30 minutes in a Bradley smoker.

STORAGE Remove the mussels from their shells and transfer them to a sealed container with a lid. Store in the fridge for up to 24 hours.

SERVING SUGGESTION Enjoy as they are as part of a shellfish antipasti, or make into Sukie Barber's delicious pasta dish (right).

TAGLIATELLE WITH CREAMY SMOKED MUSSELS

serves 6

4½lbs cold smoked mussels (see pages 158–159)
⅔ cup heavy cream
18oz pasta, such as tagliatelle or spaghetti
a small handful of fresh chives and their flowers
freshly ground black pepper
juice of 1 lemon
fine salt (optional)
2 zucchini (optional)

Heat the smoked mussels in the heavy cream and leave in a warm place for 30 minutes for the smokiness to flavor the cream. Put the pasta into a saucepan full of lightly salted boiling water. While the pasta is cooking reheat the creamy mussels and at the last moment add the chives. Season with freshly ground black pepper and lemon juice. It probably won't need any salt as the smoked mussels will have a hint of salt but taste to make sure.

Thinly slice a zucchini lengthwise using a mandolin or a potato peeler, then cut each piece down the middle to create tagliatelle-shaped pieces with a green edge down one side. Add these to the pasta water just before it is cooked for about 30 seconds. Drain the pasta and add to the pan with the sauce. Toss together and serve straight away scattered with a few chives and their flowers.

COLD SMOKED SHRIMP

Eating shrimp with your hands straight from the shell with a squeeze of lemon, some crusty bread, and a smoky glass of Pouilly Fumé is my idea of heaven. It doesn't happen often enough in my life, but I savor moments like this and I would encourage you to do the same. We first ate smoked shrimp at Cley Smokehouse in Norfolk, England. They were so delicious we went back for more and enquired how they made them. To get around the problem of overcooking them, we were told to use cooked frozen shrimp instead of fresh ones.

I would only do these in a Bradley smoker or similar that has strong smoke—so the frozen shrimp smoke quickly—since you don't want to have the shrimp sitting around too long.

PREPARATION You will need frozen jumbo or tiger shrimp in their shells for this. Lay the frozen shrimp on the rack inside your smoker, spacing them apart so that the smoke can swirl around them.

WOOD CHOICE Oak or beech.

TIMING Cold smoke for approx. 3 hours in a Bradley smoker, depending on the size of the shrimp. In cool weather they will just defrost in that time and take on the flavor and yellowish color from the smoke.

STORAGE Store in the fridge and eat within 24 hours.

SERVING SUGGESTION Serve with crusty bread and wedges of lemon. In my opinion, keep it simple and don't be tempted to disguise the wonderful flavor with sauces.

ANDREW FAIRLIE'S COLD SMOKED LOBSTER

This is Michelin starred Andrew Fairlie's signature dish at his restaurant in Gleneagles, Scotland. I had heard that Andrew was keen on smoking and curing, so we took a trip to his kitchen to find out more. He was keen to use local Scottish lobster, which is tender and sweet, on his menu and had seen smoked lobster before in France. To smoke a whole lobster would spoil the tenderness of the flesh, so he and his Head Chef, Stephen McLaughlin, came up with this method after much experimentation. In this way the shells only are smoked. I am not exaggerating when I say this is one of the most delicious foods I have ever tasted. There is no wonder he won *The Times* UK Best Restaurant of the Year 2012.

serves 4

4 lobster, weighing approx. 2lbs
juice of ½ lemon
juice of ½ lime
2 tablespoons heavy cream
9oz unsalted butter

good pinch of salt
freshly ground black pepper
2 tablespoons finely chopped mixed fresh herbs, such as chives, tarragon and parsley

Cook the live lobsters in boiling water for 8 minutes or until the shells are pink. Remove them from the water and cut the shells along the belly with kitchen scissors or a knife. Carefully remove the flesh as neatly as you can without tearing it. Split the shells and put them on the rack of a Bradley smoker. Cold smoke for 40 minutes over oak or beech wood. Remove them from the smoker and set aside to cool. Store in the fridge until needed.

To make the sauce, pour the citrus juice into a small saucepan and bubble away over low heat until it has almost disappeared. Add the cream and shake the pan to amalgamate. Cut the butter into ¾in lumps and add to the sauce, one lump at a time, stirring constantly to amalgamate each lump before you add the next. This will take approx. 15 minutes; don't rush it. Season with salt and black pepper to taste.

Arrange the lobster meat in the smoked shells. Put the meat from the knuckle in the head and the claw meat on top to raise it up. Trim away the messy end from the tail and slice the meat on the diagonal. Put this into the tail. It is sliced to stop it twisting as it heats and to ensure the heat penetrates quickly to stop it from drying out. The meat should be tightly packed inside the shells. Spoon 3 tablespoons of the sauce over each lobster so that it goes into the crevasses. Transfer the lobsters to the fridge, covered, until you are ready to eat.

To serve, transfer each lobster into an individual roasting sheet, adding 2 tablespoons of water under the shells. Wrap the sheets very tightly in foil, "drum-skin tight," as Steve told me in his Scottish accent. Place over high heat on the stove so that the water boils quickly to produce puffs of steam—these will penetrate the smoky flavor of the shell and transfer the smokiness into the flesh. Once the foil puffs up, after approx. 1 minute, take the lobsters off the heat and set aside to rest for 3 minutes while you finish the sauce.

Put the sauce over low heat to reheat and stir in the cooking juices from the baking sheets along with the chopped herbs. Transfer the lobsters to a plate and dress with the butter and herb sauce. Serve immediately.

COLD SMOKED MEAT

COLD SMOKED SAUSAGES

Smoked sausages are popular in many regions of the world, especially in areas above the "smoke line" (see page 145). Some people mimic the flavor of smoking with smoked paprika or smoke extract, but we think the real thing is sublime. Use a strong flavored sausage made with curing salts such as the French *saucisson* on page 108 or the Spanish dried *chorizo* on page 111.

Straight after making the sausages hang them in a garland to dry at room temperature overnight (or for 8 hours) so that the air can circulate around them. The sausages are then ready to smoke.

After smoking they can be eaten immediately or hung to cure longer in a curing chamber at 54–61°F until they have achieved up to 30 percent weight loss; ours took approx. 28 days. Make sure that the air can circulate freely and that none of them are touching. Check on the sausages daily and wipe off any molds that aren't white with strong alcohol—we use Grappa.

WOOD CHOICE Oak or apple wood.
TIMING Cold smoke for 6–8 hours in a grill or garden smokehouse; 2–3 hours in a Bradley smoker.
STORAGE Once dried, the sausages can be stored, wrapped in plastic wrap in the fridge for up to a month or frozen for up to 3 months.

COLD SMOKED BACON

We have given three recipes for cured bacon in the Salt chapter, see pages 94–96, and all of these are suitable for smoking. Note that smoking is always carried out after curing. It is important to hang the bacon for at least a day before smoking to form a pellicle.

PREPARATION Follow the recipes on pages 94–96 for curing the bacon. Rinse off the cure under cold running water and pat dry on paper towels. Set aside to dry for 24 hours on a rack at room temperature under mosquito netting, in the fridge, or a cool room before smoking. After smoking eat immediately or for a firmer texture hang in a curing chamber to dry for 1–5 days. The longer it is left the more concentrated the flavor; also the texture will become firmer and drier. The bacon is ready when it feels firm to the touch and not jellylike. If cured correctly, it should have lost 10–15 percent of its initial weight.
WOOD CHOICE Beech, apple, or maple.
TIMING Cold smoke for 8–10 hours in a grill or garden smokehouse; 4 hours in a Bradley smoker.
STORAGE To store, wrap the bacon in parchment paper and keep in the fridge for up to 2 weeks. Bacon can also be frozen.

COLD SMOKED GOOSE AND DUCK BREAST

We used to buy smoked goose breast for our restaurants for the antipasti platters of cured meats. Now we make our own. A wet brine with curing salts is good for inducing a little moisture into the breasts before smoking. Be prepared to experiment within the timings given below with the curing and smoking of the breasts. Write down your results so you can repeat the process. We actually forgot our cured and smoked duck breasts in the fridge while we went on vacation. We tasted them when we came home and the extra time had made all the difference! Ideally we should have left them in the curing chamber as they became case hardened in the fridge but still the flavor was there. It took us quite a few trials at this as there are various stages to the finished process, but the result is wonderfully soft meat with layers of flavor that melts in your mouth and impresses your guests. The flavor of the salt, the smoke, and the meat should be equal with neither dominating. If you are doing this for the first time it is a good idea to cut a little of the flesh off the breast and cook it briefly to taste for saltiness. The outside will be saltier than the inside so bear that in mind. If it is really salty soak the breast in water for a few hours, pat dry on paper towels and then dry as before. The same applies if the breasts are too smoky.

PREPARATION For 2¼lbs of either duck or goose breasts make up a medium 40 percent brine solution using ½ cup curing salts (either 1 tablespoon Quickcure and 3 teaspoons salt or 1 teaspoon Prague Powder No. 2 and 4½ cups salt) to 1 quart of boiling water. If you wish, you can flavor the brine with up to ⅔ cup sugar per quart of red wine—substituting it for part or all of the water and a few sprigs of herbs or a tablespoon of crushed juniper berries per quart of water. Set aside to cool then chill in the fridge.

Put the breasts into the cold brine and set aside to cure in the fridge for approx. 8 hours for duck and goose. You may need to weigh them down so that they are fully submerged. Take out the breasts and pat dry on paper towels.

Place the breasts on a wire rack and transfer them to the fridge to dry a little and form a pellicle, up to 24 hours for the duck and goose (alternatively you can leave them in a cool place such as a pantry, covered with netting).

WOOD CHOICE Cherry, apple, maple.
TIMING Cold smoke in the grill overnight (approx. 14 hours); or for 2–4 hours in a Bradley smoker, depending on the size of the breasts.
STORAGE Wrap in plastic wrap to stop them from drying further and keep in the fridge, eat within 3 days.
SERVING SUGGESTION Eat as soon as they are smoked or leave on a rack or hang in a curing chamber to lose weight. Ours were at their best after 10–12 days but I have heard of an artisan Italian curer who leaves his goose breasts for 60 days. Serve raw, cut into thin slices with Pickled nectarines (see page 24) or Peach, grape, and vanilla chutney (see page 234).

COLD SMOKED HAM, BEEF, AND VENISON

Large cuts of meat require a lot more time for the smoke to penetrate. If you research the traditional methods for smoking meats you will discover they were often smoked for a matter of days or weeks. This wouldn't necessarily be over a continuous fire but one that went out and was lit again, maybe hours later, or the next day. During this time the meat would also be drying out in the smoky atmosphere—which could be up a chimney or in an external smokehouse where it was also cold. Most meats would have been salted first. To preserve a piece of bacon, for example, all four methods of preservation would have been used —salting, drying, smoking, and chilling— and this is what saved the meat from becoming bad.

As a general rule of thumb when brining and smoking your own meat at home, allow for an overall weight loss of 15 percent (with 10 percent lost during brining and 5 percent during smoking). We have successfully smoked Christmas ham, venison, and beef in our playhouse during cold weather over 3 days. For reasons of self-preservation, (avoiding food poisoning), I would recommend using curing salts for large cuts. This will safely carry them through the curing, smoking, and drying stages.

COLD SMOKED VENISON CARPACCIO

We love this recipe. It is easy and relatively quick to do as the loin is lean and slim so absorbs the brine and smoke quickly. We haven't suggested using curing salts for this recipe as the timing in the smoker is short and the meat is frozen after rather than hung. The result is soft, juicy slices of raw smoked venison that melt in your mouth and have a much more interesting flavor than regular carpaccio. We make this using a 18oz venison loin, but you could use the same method for smoking a beef tenderloin.

PREPARATION Make up a 20 percent brine (see page 86) and submerge the loin in it overnight, weighing it down if necessary. Remove from the brine, pat dry with paper towels and set on a rack to dry in a fridge or in a cool larder covered with mosquito netting for a day to form a pellicle.
WOOD CHOICE Alder, beech, birch, oak, juniper, and any fruit wood.
TIMING Cold smoke smaller cuts (under 3⅓lbs) in a Bradley smoker for 4 hours.
STORAGE Remove the meat from the smoker and wrap it in plastic wrap. Transfer it to the freezer for a day to equalize the flavor of the smoke throughout the meat and make it easier to cut. If the venison is wild, freezing will also kill any parasites.
SERVING SUGGESTION Lean, smoky venison makes a sumptuous carpaccio served with arugula salad dressed with lemon and olive oil (see photo right).

For carpaccio it is easier to cut the meat into really thin slices while it is still frozen. Alternatively, cut into thicker slices and fry briefly for fantastic steaks.

HAM HOCKS AND TROTTERS

Pork trotters or hocks are small, inexpensive cuts of meat to experiment with before you tackle larger projects, such as smoking your own hams. Ready-cured hocks are readily available from butchers or you can cure your own.

PREPARATION Remove the skin from the hocks and discard. Place the hocks in a plastic tub and cover them with a layer of fine salt. Set aside to cure for approx. 1 hour. Remove the hocks, rinse briefly under cold running water and pat dry on paper towels. Set aside on a wire rack to dry for 2–3 hours until a pellicle is formed. This can either be done in the fridge or in a cool pantry, covered with netting.
WOOD CHOICE Alder, beech, birch, oak, maple, and any fruit wood.
TIMING Cold smoke for 3 hours in a Bradley smoker.
COOKING INSTRUCTIONS After smoking, boil the hocks until cooked through and the meat is falling from the bone. Change the water at least once to get rid of the initial smoky taste. The cooking water can then be used as a stock.

CHRISTMAS HAM

The timings here are suitable for a 9lb cured leg of ham. You can either follow the recipe on page 100 for curing the ham or buy one that has already been cured for you (also known as a "green" ham).
PREPARATION To cure the ham, follow the recipe for Christmas ham on page 100. Remove the ham from the brine and dry

on paper towels. Place it on a wire rack in the fridge or a cool pantry covered in mosquito netting to dry overnight or up to 1 day to form a pellicle.

WOOD CHOICE Oak, beech, maple.

TIMING Cold smoke in intense smoke in a Bradley for 4-6 hours; over gentle smoke in a grill for approx. 10 hours; or for 2–3 days in a garden smokehouse. The longer the process the more the ham will dry out, concentrating the flavor. If you are concerned it is over-smoked it can be scrubbed and soaked before cooking.

COOKING INSTRUCTIONS To cook the ham, place it in a saucepan of cold water and bring to a boil. Taste the water to see if it is overly salty and replace with fresh cold water if necessary. Bring to a boil and simmer for 25 minutes per 1lb or until the internal temperature is 162°F. You can add flavorings such as carrots, bay leaves, and an onion to the water if you wish. Remove the ham from the pan, cut off the skin and discard.

Preheat the oven to 350°F. Using a sharp knife, dipped in hot water, make diagonal cuts in the outside fat and poke a clove into each diamond. Put the ham on a baking sheet, slather on the contents of a 12oz jar of marmalade and bake in the hot oven for 30–45 minutes until the glaze has deepened to a rich golden brown. Remove from the oven and rest for 30 minutes before eating.

STORAGE The cooked ham will keep, wrapped in plastic wrap or in a covered container, for up to 5 days in the fridge.

SPECK

Speck is often served in Italy as part of antipasti, or with pickled gherkins and sourdough rye bread for those north of the Austro-Italian border.

PREPARATION To cure the pork, follow the instructions for *Speck* on page 102. After curing, rinse the meat under cold running water and pat dry on paper towels. Hang up to dry at room temperature (providing it isn't a warm day) for 1–2 hours.

WOOD CHOICE Alder, oak, beech, birch.

TIMING Cold smoke for 7 days over gentle smoke in a playhouse or grill. Alternatively use a Bradley smoker where the smoke is more concentrated for about 3 hours.

CURING INSTRUCTIONS After smoking, hang the pork in a curing chamber at 54–61°F for 5–6 weeks until it has lost 25 percent of its weight. Remove the *speck* from the chamber and follow the instructions for larding on page 102. Return the larded *speck* to the curing chamber for a further 6 months.

At this point, you can sample a slice from one end—just in from the outer edge—to see if it is ready. If it seems soft or not tasty enough, re-lard that end and rehang for a further month.

SERVING SUGGESTION Serve cut into wafer thin slices with pickled gherkins and sourdough rye bread.

STORAGE Once the *speck* is cut into, wrap that end in plastic wrap tightly and store in the fridge. It will keep for weeks if not months more but will continue to dry out and harden.

HOT SMOKING RECIPES

Hot smoking involves cooking the food at the same time as it smokes. Smoking dries out the meat, so by introducing water into the smoker you end up partly steaming the food as well as heating it, resulting in juicy, savory, finger-licking good food.

There are several ways of introducing humidity into your smoker. If it has a drip tray, this can be filled with water (or beer); if you are smoking over an open fire, this can be dampened down with wet cloths or water sprays. If your hot smoker has a vent, this can be closed or partially closed to keep humidity inside. Another trick is to brush food such as fish with vegetable oil during smoking to help prevent it from drying out.

Hot smoking should be continuous and temperatures monitored carefully. A probe thermometer is essential so that you can safely tell when your food is done. Some probes can be left in the product and read from outside the smoking chamber—a good investment, we think, so that you don't have to keep opening the door and losing valuable heat and steam. There are also gadgets available that will read the internal temperature of the food in the smoker and inform you on your phone when you have reached the target. Amazing when you are in the pub and waiting for your pulled pork to be done (see suppliers on page 290 for where to buy one).

The Big Green Egg and Weber grills are both excellent for hot smoking. All of the following recipes will work in them but follow the manufacturer's instructions for temperature and timings.

HOT SMOKED EGGPLANT

Hot smoking the eggplant gives a wonderful smoky flavor that you just don't get by roasting it in the oven or scorching it over a flame. Smoked eggplant is delicious puréed and made into Baba Ghanoush also known as Moutabal, a Middle Eastern dip (see right). Alternatively, cut the smoked eggplant open and serve warm as a side dish with lemon juice, salt, and pepper.

WOOD CHOICE Alder, oak, beech, maple.

TIMING Hot smoke halved or sliced eggplant for 30–40 minutes in a Cameron smoker; whole eggplant should be smoked for 1–2 hours in a Bradley smoker at the maximum temperature.

TO MAKE MOUTABAL Allow the smoked eggplant to cool and scrape out the flesh; chop finely or blitz in a food processor. Combine with 2 tablespoons of tahini, 2 tablespoons of natural or Greek yogurt, 1 tablespoon of lemon juice and a good pinch of salt. Serve as a dip, sprinkled with paprika, and toasted chopped walnuts, with pita bread for dipping.

HOT SMOKED TOMATO AND RED PEPPER SOUP

Hot smoking tomatoes, peppers, and chiles is easy to do and gives really impressive results in little time. The tomatoes become soft quickly and get a deep, smoky flavor that is wonderful on toast or with an English breakfast. Peppers and chiles take longer but offer a typically Spanish flavor of spicy smoked paprika to stews and salads. Use either the Cameron stovetop smoker or a Bradley hot smoker. If you don't have round tomatoes, cherry tomatoes are fine too. It is a great way to use up slightly soft tomatoes and if left thick makes a sublime and intense sauce for pasta or gnocchi.

serves 6-8

2 red bell peppers, roughly chopped
1 red chile, cut in half lengthwise, seeded
2¼lbs round tomatoes, cut in half
sea salt and freshly ground black pepper
1 teaspoon sugar
4 tablespoons extra virgin olive oil
2 medium red onions, finely chopped
2 garlic cloves, peeled and lightly crushed
2 medium potatoes (approx. 14oz), peeled and diced into ½in cubes
2 tablespoons tomato paste
2 quarts vegetable or chicken stock
basil leaves, to serve

Smoke the peppers and chile first for 10 minutes before adding the tomatoes, cut-side upward. Scatter a little salt and the sugar over them before replacing the lid on the smoker. Continue to smoke for a further 20–30 minutes or until the tomatoes and chile are all soft. Remove from the heat and set aside to cool.

Meanwhile, heat the oil in a heavy-bottomed saucepan and fry the onion and garlic cloves for about 10 minutes or until translucent. Take care not to burn them. Add the potatoes and stir through. Continue to fry for a couple of minutes so that the cubes of potato become coated with oil.

Cut the chile roughly and taste it for heat. Add some or all of it to the pan, depending on the heat, followed by the tomatoes, and peppers. Stir through and add the tomato paste. Now add 1½ quarts of stock and bring to a boil. Reduce the heat to simmer slowly. Cook the soup, partially covered, for about an hour, stirring frequently.

Put the soup through a sieve or food mill or blitz with an immersion blender to get rid of the skins. Pour into another pan to warm. Taste and add salt and pepper as necessary. Add the rest of the stock as necessary until you are happy with the consistency. Serve bubbling hot in warm bowls with basil leaves, a swirl of extra virgin olive oil and a twist of black pepper.

PEPPERED MACKEREL

I had no idea these were so easy. Mackerel is inexpensive and good for you, and so I have eaten a lot of it over the years. In light of its recent change in sustainability, it is best to look for line-caught mackerel. Our favorite method of hot smoking them is using our trashcan smoker. It looks fun and is quick and effective.

PREPARATION You will need mackerel fillets for this. Put the mackerel fillets in a dish and sprinkle over a thin layer of fine sea salt. Cover with plastic wrap and set aside in the fridge to cure for 15–30 minutes, depending on the size and freshness of the fish, or until they are firm to the touch. Rinse off the salt and pat dry on paper towels. Arrange the mackerel on a wire rack and set aside to dry either in a cool breeze, covered with netting, or in the fridge for 1 hour to form a pellicle. Now is an ideal time to build the fire. Scatter the flesh side only with crushed black peppercorns and press down well with your palm.

WOOD CHOICE Oak or beech.

TIMING Hot smoke medium-sized fillets over a medium fire for approx. 30–40 minutes in a trashcan smoker; or over low heat for approx. 20–30 minutes in a Cameron smoker. To tell if they are cooked through, press down on the fish with your index finger; they should feel firm to the touch.

SERVING SUGGESTION Serve hot in a roll with lemon juice and parsley, or cold with brown bread and homemade Horseradish sauce (see page 25).

STORAGE To keep, allow the mackerel to cool and wrap in plastic wrap. Store in the fridge and eat within 5 days or freeze and consume within 3 months.

ARBROATH SMOKIES

This method involves steaming whole gutted haddock in smoke, which is what makes Arbroath smokies so succulent. Iain Spink is one of the few smokers left to smoke haddock in the traditional way in old whisky barrels in the small fishing town of Arbroath on the west coast of Scotland. He is a fifth-generation smoker and we went to meet him to see how he smokes these famous fish. He told us that traditionally it was the fishwives who would clean, gut, and smoke the fish while the fishermen were out at sea. As I mentioned earlier, our trashcan smoker is ideal for making these because it is based on the barrel method of smoking.

If you want to try Iain's method, tie similar sized whole gutted haddock together by the tails with string, making sure that it is neither too tight or too loose—Iain explained that if the string is too tight it goes through the bone and if not tight enough the fish will fall into the fire. He wasn't kidding; we tried this several times at home and each time they fell. Now we lay the fish on a rack and use large fillets rather than whole fish.

This is how Iain Spink smokes his Arbroath smokies: he makes a fire in the bottom of a barrel that has been buried in the earth or on the pebble beach. When the fire is hot, after approx. 20 minutes, he sprays it down with water and then suspends his fish over the top to cook for approx. 40 minutes–1 hour. The belly of each fish is held open with a small stick so that the heat and smoke can permeate throughout. Iain places wet burlap sacks over the top of the barrel to introduce humidity and also starve the fire of oxygen so that it cannot take hold again. After they are cooked, he squeezes the fish from side to side and the fish pops off the bone.

Down the road at Gleneagles, the chefs told us of their visit to Arbroath. They thought that this hot smoked fish, fresh from the barrel, was just outstanding. Iain had some ready as we arrived with our children. On a chilly October morning we devoured hot, salty, smoky fish with our fingers. The chefs were right; it is one of life's experiences not to be missed.

PREPARATION To follow our method, you will need small (approx. 18oz) haddock. Buy them ready filleted or do it yourself. Gut the fish and remove the heads; split them in half leaving the backbone in one side. Remove the black membrane that runs along the backbone of the fish, if it is still there. Sprinkle some fine sea salt over a large lasagna dish or similar and arrange the fish on top in a single layer. Cover with a thin layer of salt and repeat this process to give more layers of fish and salt. Set aside in the fridge to cure for 2–10 hours, depending on the freshness and size of the fish—we allow approx. 30 minutes–2 hours as they are fillets rather than whole fish. They will be firm to the touch when done.

Rinse off the salt briefly under cold running water, pat dry on paper towels, and allow the fish to dry for 1 hour to form a pellicle. Iain ties them in pairs by their tails and hangs them over sticks to dry in the open air, but you could lay them on a wire rack in a cool breeze covered in mosquito netting. After drying, they can be smoked.

I struggled with Iain's traditional method of hanging the fish in pairs over triangular lengths of wood in the smoker and now prefer to lay them side by side on a rack inside our trashcan smoker instead.

WOOD CHOICE Oak or beech.

TIMING Hot smoke medium haddock fillets for 30–40 minutes over a medium fire in a trashcan smoker; or for 2–4 hours in a Bradley smoker at 320°F with the damper just open.

SERVING SUGGESTION I am not going to write a "serve with…" because you just shouldn't! At most they need wheat bread and butter and maybe a squeeze of lemon. After they are cold, you can use the smoked haddock in fish pies, Scottish Cullen skink soup, or pâté.

STORAGE Keep wrapped in plastic wrap or in a covered container in the fridge and consume within 7 days or freeze for up to 3 months.

HOT SMOKED SALMON

I still remember the first time I ate this at Billingsgate market in London, it was around 6am and the fishmonger broke a piece up for us to try. The flavor was so sweet, salty, and smoky; I licked the oil from my fingers not wanting to waste a drop. We have also seen it being prepared in Arbroath: we watched a smoker start a fire in a large, well-tarred box. When it was really burning fiercely, he splashed water over it to take the fire down to smoldering embers and introduce steam. He quickly laid trays of salmon portions on racks inside and closed the lid. After 1½ hours he lifted the lids and the most incredible rich aroma flowed out of the box. The salmon was ready; hot and juicy, it flaked apart easily as we ate it straight away with our hands.

I still don't see hot smoked salmon enough in the shops and therefore feel it hasn't had all the glory it deserves. This is one of the easiest recipes to make.

PREPARATION You will need salmon fillets for this. The size doesn't matter—thicker pieces will take longer than thin. Sprinkle a thin layer of fine sea salt over the base of a lasagna dish or similar and arrange the salmon fillets, skin-side down, on top. Sprinkle some more salt over the surface of the fish, cover the dish with plasic wrap, and set aside to cure in the fridge for approx. 1 hour.

Rinse the fillets briefly under water

and pat dry on paper towels. Arrange on a wire rack in the fridge or a cool room to dry for approx. 30 minutes or so to form a pellicle.

WOOD CHOICE Alder, maple, beech, or oak.

TIMING Hot smoke for approx. 20 minutes in a Cameron or trashcan smoker; 45 minutes–1 hour in a Bradley smoker at 220°F. Once the fish is cooked it should feel firm to the touch.

SERVING SUGGESTION Enjoy hot, straight from the smoker. Alternatively, cool it down and have it with watercress salad and crème fraîche dressing (see page 223). Also see Pasta with hot smoked salmon, cream, and chile vodka (below).

STORAGE Keep wrapped in plastic wrap or in a covered container in the fridge and consume within 7 days.

Variation

HOT SMOKED SPICY SALMON

After salting, rub the flesh side of each portion with ½ teaspoon finely chopped chile and garlic. Smoke as before.

PASTA WITH HOT SMOKED SALMON, CREAM, AND CHILE VODKA

There is a well-known recipe in Italy that combines smoked salmon with penne and vodka bound together with cream. I am not sure of its origin, as neither salmon nor vodka is found traditionally in Italy. However it is a wonderful combination whatever the origin and even better when made with your own produce. I love to serve each person with a shot glass of chile vodka to drink with their pasta—it adds a real kick and a giggle to the meal.

serves 8–10

1¼lbs rigatoni or penne pasta
1 white onion, finely chopped
2 garlic cloves, peeled, lightly crushed but left whole
2 tablespoons extra virgin olive oil
salt and freshly ground black pepper
3 tablespoons chile vodka (see page 210)
10½oz hot smoked salmon (see pages 171–172)
2 cups heavy cream
roughly chopped fresh parsley, to serve

Put the pasta to cook in a large saucepan filled with boiling salted water. Meanwhile, cook the onion and garlic in the olive oil in a large frying pan over medium heat until soft but not colored, approx. 5 minutes. Add a pinch of salt, bearing in mind that the salmon will be salty already, and a generous pinch of black pepper. Pour in the chile vodka and ignite if you wish (stand back) or simply leave for a couple of minutes to burn off the alcohol. Flake the salmon into the pan and pour in the cream. Cook over low heat until the sauce has thickened and the pasta is al dente. Drain the pasta through a colander and add to the pan with the salmon and cream. Toss through gently so as not to break up the salmon any more and serve with a sprinkling of fresh parsley.

RUBS FOR HOT SMOKING

A good way of introducing extra flavor to your smoked foods is to rub them with spices before smoking. This is a great way to introduce complex flavors to mingle in with the smoke.

PASTRAMI

See page 118.

CHINESE HOT SMOKED DUCK BREASTS

Our children love stir-fried noodles and Chinese Peking duck with plum sauce and pancakes. This recipe for hot smoked duck has all the lovely spiciness you would expect from Peking duck but the flesh is soft and juicy.

serves 2
2 duck breasts, each weighing approx. 1lb
1 tablespoon fine salt
2 tablespoons dark brown sugar
3 teaspoons Chinese five spice powder
1 teaspoon ground Szechuan pepper

For the glaze
3 teaspoons honey
3 teaspoons soy sauce
3 teaspoons rice or white wine vinegar

PREPARATION Put the duck breasts in a bowl. Mix together the salt, sugar, five spice powder, and Szechuan pepper and rub well in to the duck flesh. Cover the bowl with plasic wrap and set aside to marinate in the fridge overnight.

The following day, wipe off the cure with paper towels. Combine the honey, soy sauce, and vinegar in a small bowl and brush half of the mixture over the duck breasts.

WOOD Oak, beech, birch, fruit woods, walnut.

TIMING Hot smoke for 30–40 minutes in a Cameron smoker; 40 minutes–1 hour in a Bradley smoker—or until the internal temperature reaches 130°F for medium rare.

SERVING SUGGESTION Serve sliced on the diagonal in a noodle stir-fry with the Chinese plum sauce on page 43. Alternatively, cut into strips and serve in pancakes with hoisin sauce, cucumber batons, and scallions.

STORAGE 3–4 days in the fridge.

HOT SMOKED PHEASANT BREAST

This is an excellent way to cook pheasant when in season and plentiful.

PREPARATION Make up enough medium 40 percent brine to cover the breasts and set aside to cool. Transfer to the fridge to chill. Put the pheasant breasts into the cure for 1 hour. Remove from the brine, pat dry on paper towels, and set aside on a rack to dry in the fridge or in a cool room temperature for 2 hours to form a pellicle.

WOOD CHOICE Alder, Oak, beech, birch, fruit woods.

TIMING Hot smoke for 20–30 minutes in a Cameron smoker; approx. 30–45 minutes at 320°F in a Bradley smoker.

SERVING SUGGESTION Lovely hot served with bread sauce and buttery cabbage, these can also be served cold and sliced in a sandwich with mayonnaise, lemon juice, and black pepper.

STORAGE Keep in the fridge and consume within 3 days. Freeze wrapped in plastic wrap and consume within 3 months.

HOT SMOKED CHICKEN

This is one of those dishes that you need to eat with your fingers. There are all sorts of rubs you can try, but really if you buy a good free-range chicken that has seen about 6 months of life it will reward you with enough flavor naked.

A whole chicken wouldn't fit in the Cameron stovetop smoker or the dustbin smoker so we hot smoked ours in the Bradley.

PREPARATION You will need a 3½lb free-range chicken. Make up a weak 20 percent brine allowing ⅔ cup fine salt to 2 quarts of water, and set aside to cool (see page 86). Immerse the whole bird in the cold brine and transfer to the fridge for 8 hours.

Remove the chicken from the brine, pat dry on paper towels, and place on a wire rack to dry for 8 hours in the fridge to form a pellicle.

WOOD CHOICE Oak, beech, alder, mesquite, hickory, or cherry.

TIMING Hot smoke in a Bradley smoker at 250°F for 3–4 hours or until the internal temperature reaches 185°F.

SERVING SUGGESTION Serve with bread and salad. If you want to serve some sauce on the side, try it with Southern sweet mustard sauce (see page 178) or a dash of Debi's tomato, chile, and ginger jam (see page 37).

STORAGE 3–4 days in the fridge.

HOT SMOKED CURRIED LAMB

I love to do this when entertaining. It means I can prepare all the side dishes in advance, except the rice, and then have the lamb cooking slowly outside to bring in when we are ready, with the aroma circling around the kitchen. I like the addition of the extra spices, but this is equally delicious smoked plain.

We hot smoke ours in the Bradley due to the size of the lamb, filling the drip tray with water to introduce some steam into the smoke chamber.

serves 4–6

4lbs butterflied leg of lamb
1 portion of Manjula Samarasinghe's Sri-Lankan spice paste for meat and chicken curries (see page 282)

PREPARATION Rub the lamb with the spice rub and set aside in the fridge, covered, to marinate overnight. The following day, take the lamb out of the fridge, and allow it to come to room temperature.
WOOD CHOICE Alder, oak, beech, birch, or fruit wood.
TIMING Hot smoke for 4–5 hours at 250°F in a Bradley smoker or until the internal temperature is 140°F. Set aside to rest, covered with foil, for 20–30 minutes before serving. It will be juicy, tender, and full of flavor.
SERVING SUGGESTION Serve with rice, Green bean curry (see page 263), Mango chutney (see pages 35–36), and yogurt and mint raita.
STORAGE Store any leftover meat in the fridge, covered, for up to 4 days.

BOSTON BUTT BARBECUE

Our friends Margaret and Mike, from Georgia, make this Boston Butt twice a year for family and friends at holiday time. Although the cut of pork used is known as a Boston butt, it is actually the shoulder—and sometimes the shoulder, hand, and spring—that is used. A large shoulder can be cut into two pieces, one known as the Boston butt and the other as the "picnic" ham.

This is definitely not a meal in a hurry, as it can take up to 17 hours of slow cooking to achieve the meltingly soft

strands of meat. However, this quantity makes a large amount of pulled pork once complete, which is wonderful for feeding a huge crowd. And as it can be eaten hot, cold or reheated (or frozen for later use), the waiting time is well worth it. Many people like to eat the pork inside a huge bun, however Margaret loves hers in a toasted baguette sandwich, while Mike likes his with coleslaw and potato salad.

Variations

There are an infinite amount of recipes for this dish as every Southern region and every family puts their own twist on it. Recipes for the sauce also vary with many different names such as "Kick Ass" or "Slap Yo Mama"; Mike's own version is "Wild and Wicked" according to him! In North Carolina they often make a vinegary "mop sauce" to inject into the pork before cooking and then regularly use a small mop to moisten it further during the cooking, but personally I think there is enough going on with the rub and barbecue sauce without giving yourself any further work.

Boston butt has now become a family favorite of ours. This is our tried and tested version based on Margaret and Mike's recipe. Feel free to experiment with your own flavorings—just remember to write down the quantities you used for next time. Additions you might consider are yellow mustard smeared all over the pork before you add the rub. I quite like this, despite my loathing of ready-prepared sauces, as I like the sweetness it gives.

My chile powder is hot, so I have limited it to 2 teaspoons and it still has enough kick—but, again, it is up to you

serves 12–14

6¾lbs shoulder of pork on or off the bone

For the rub
⅓ cup soft brown muscovado sugar
3 tablespoons paprika
1 teaspoon coarsely ground black pepper
1 tablespoon fine salt
2 teaspoons chile powder
2 teaspoons mustard powder
3 fat garlic cloves, peeled, and finely chopped

PREPARATION Mix the ingredients together for the rub and massage it into the pork. Put the pork into a large plastic bag and marinate in the fridge for 24 hours. Remove the meat from the fridge and allow it to come up to room temperature.

For a large cut of meat such as this I would recommend using a Bradley smoker, Big Green Egg, or a Weber grill, however many people successfully smoke their pork butts in customized grills. Light the smoker and bring up the heat in the chamber to 212°F. Remove the marinated pork from the bag and set it on the rack in the smoker.
WOOD CHOICE Hickory, maple, mesquite.
TIMING If I have people coming for Sunday lunch or early dinner I marinate the shoulder from Friday night through to Saturday night. I then get the smoker ready and smoke overnight and through Sunday until around lunchtime. The pork will then need to be rested for an hour before eating. It shreds better after resting for an hour and, if necessary, can be reheated in a covered dish in the oven.

Leaving the bone in adds flavor to the meat, but removing it speeds up the cooking time: the "choice is yours," as my friends say whenever I try to pin them down on recipes and cooking methods.

The butt will need approx. 2 hours per 18oz in the smoker at 212°F; I would allow approx. 12–17 hours for a joint such as this, as sometimes you can encounter "the stall." This is when a large cut of meat, such as this, stops rising in temperature. It is thought that this is due to the evaporating moisture from the meat cooling down the chamber temperature. To stop this happening, when the internal temperature reaches approx. 150°F, wrap the meat in foil, adding a couple of spoons of apple juice, cider, or water to the parcel, and put it back in the smoker. The temperature should start to climb slowly after this time until it reaches 167°F, which is when the meat is safe and ready to eat. Another way to get over the stall, if it happens, is to whack up the temperature of the smoker. Alternatively, you can remove the pork and transfer it to a hot oven (350°F) to finish cooking. Always use a temperature probe to check the internal temperature; the pork is cooked when it reaches 167°F.

At this point, remove the foil (if you have used it) and transfer the pork to a conventional oven at 350°F for approx. 30 minutes to crisp up the "bark." This is the crisp outside of the meat, which should become really black in color, and lined with deep crevasses. It is fantastically tasty and regularly causes fights in our family, as we can't wait to pull pieces off as soon as it is out of the oven. To make the bark even more delicious, glaze with some of the wild and wicked barbecue sauce (see right) before putting it in the oven.

SOUTHERN SWEET MUSTARD SAUCE

Serve this with the pork at the table.

serves 8

⅓ cup salted butter
5 tablespoons extra virgin olive oil
3 large white onions, finely chopped
salt and freshly ground black pepper
4 tablespoons Dijon mustard (smooth or seedy)
4 tablespoons brown muscovado sugar
4 tablespoons apple cider vinegar

Heat the butter and oil in a medium saucepan. Add the onion and cook over medium heat until really soft and translucent, approx. 10–15 minutes. Add the remaining ingredients and stir through, allowing them to splutter. Simmer gently for 5 minutes. If the sauce is very thick, thin with a little water and heat through until you have the consistency you like. Taste for seasoning and serve warm with the pork.

WILD AND WICKED BARBECUE SAUCE

serves 20

1½ cups Tomato ketchup (see page 44)
2 tablespoons black strap molasses
3 tablespoons Worcestershire sauce
3 tablespoons apple cider vinegar
few drops of Tabasco sauce
generous pinch of salt and freshly ground black pepper

Mix the ingredients together in a small saucepan and bring to a boil, then turn the heat down and simmer gently for approx. 10 minutes. Taste and adjust the seasoning if necessary.

We use half of the sauce as a glaze (see left) and the rest as an accompaniment. If you have any left over, you can store it sterilized glass jars in the fridge and use within 2 months.

oil, fat & butter

Walk into any delicatessen or food hall and you will see trays of tempting roasted peppers, sun-dried tomatoes, green asparagus, and garlicky mushrooms coated in oil. Oil prevents the oxidization of food by stopping it from coming into contact with air. This protects it from natural decay, airborne bacteria, and molds.

Preserving food in oil is most popular in Mediterranean countries where olive trees grow. Olive oil is the preferred oil for the task because it takes on the flavor of the food and can be used as a dressing afterward. Extra virgin olive oil is a delicious, if costly, way to preserve and is suitable for a variety of foods including peppers, artichokes, eggplant, tomatoes, onions, asparagus, mushrooms, fish, lemons, and shellfish, to name a few.

Sometimes a layer of oil, butter, or fat is added on the surface of a product to protect the food underneath from oxidizing. This method is used for Fermented tomatoes (pages 234–235) and Sun-dried tomato pesto (page 185), as well as *Bagnetto* (page 185) and Smoked potted chicken (page 191). In the case of confit, animal fat is used both to cook and store the food, which is completely encapsulated by the fat and so protected from the air.

While oil and fat are good at preserving foods, they cannot be relied on to do the job on their own. This is because bacteria such as *Clostridium botulinum* can exist without oxygen. Foods with low acidity in particular, such as artichokes or eggplant, require an additional measure to protect them from decay—usually another preservative in the form of an acid like vinegar or lemon juice. This acidity, combined with the oil, creates an inhospitable environment where bacteria cannot survive. How can this be, I hear you ask, when sun-dried tomatoes are preserved in oil and they don't taste of vinegar? Tomatoes are usually high in acid, and if dried their acidity is increased so that the pH of the tomatoes goes from 4.6 to 4 (a level at which bacteria cannot survive), so there is no need for the vinegar.

pH value and pH testing strips

The pH value of a product is a measure of its acidity. Foods with a pH below 4.6 are generally too acidic for bacteria to breed; these foods don't usually require the addition of any extra acid to make them safe to preserve. Foods that need to be treated with caution are low-acid foods such as eggplant, zucchini, and peppers. These foods should always be supplemented with vinegar, citric acid, or vitamin C before bottling to maintain the right levels of acidity and prevent the growth of harmful bacteria.

If you follow the recipes in this chapter, you shouldn't encounter any problems—especially if you stick to the quantities of vinegar listed and follow the instructions carefully regarding waterbathing. However, if you start playing around with your own flavors, it is always safest to test the acidity levels of your product before bottling. pH testing strips are straightforward to use and are available online (see page 290 for suppliers).

garlic in oil warning

Garlic is a low-acid vegetable that, since it is grown in the ground, could contain traces of *Clostridium botulinum*, the bacteria that causes botulism, a potentially fatal form of food poisoning. When exposed to oxygen, the spores of the bacteria cannot develop, but when put under oil they are in the perfect environment for reproduction. It is with this in mind that recipes for storing low-acid vegetables under oil are better made without garlic. However, it is perfectly safe to add a little finely chopped garlic to any of these recipes just before eating.

PRESERVING VEGETABLES UNDER OIL

Marinated vegetables look very pretty, taste fantastic, and make great antipasti in a hurry served with mozzarella and fresh basil. For years Italians have bottled their vegetables in oil, but this is no longer deemed safe since some bacteria can survive under oil. I know we are going to upset the groups of people who have been doing this for years without harming anyone but we prefer to err on the side of safety and recommend you make these in small batches and keep them for less time in the fridge. Originally, preserves under oil would have been kept in a *cantina* or cellar, which was dark and cool all year. Today our homes are warmer, and the cool conditions necessary for these products are not available. There are recipes that use large amounts of vinegar to ensure the vegetables are safe to eat because high-acid environments make it impossible for these bacteria to survive. These have to be waterbathed and can then be kept out of the fridge, but actually I don't enjoy the flavor when that much vinegar is present. So here is our version of these typical antipasti favorites to be made in small quantities, kept in the fridge and easily on hand when you need them. Alternatively these recipes can be frozen for up to 3 months. Defrost in the fridge overnight and consume within a week.

sun-dried and smoked tomatoes under oil

I like the flavor of tomatoes without any vinegar and am happy to prepare them in small amounts to eat up fairly quickly. To keep semi-dried or Cold smoked tomatoes (see page 156), submerge them in oil in sterile containers and store in the fridge; consume within 10 days. The flavored oil is delicious and can be used for cooking and dressing foods.

ZUCCHINI ALLA POVERELLA SOTT'OLIO

We grow zucchini in our garden and always end up with loads of them in summer. I picked up this idea from our niece Pierangela, from Puglia, southern Italy. The flavors of the mint, vinegar, and oil are evocative of summer, and the semi-drying stops the zucchini from becoming soggy and helps them last longer.

makes approx. 1¾lbs
2½lbs zucchini, washed and sliced thinly
sunflower oil, for frying
fine sea salt, to taste
1¼–1⅔ cups extra virgin olive oil
2 tablespoons red or white wine vinegar
a handful of mint leaves, roughly chopped

Dry the zucchini according to the instructions on page 127 to the point at which they have lost some of their water, are dry to the touch, but are still flexible. They should not be crisp. This can be speeded up if dried on racks in the oven at 200°F for an hour; because they will be cooked, it is not essential to dry them slowly.

A deep-fryer is perfect for cooking the zucchini but if you don't have one, use a large frying pan instead with ⅓ cup of sunflower oil. Heat the oil until a piece of bread sizzles when lowered in. Fry the zucchini briefly until lightly browned. Remove from the oil with a slotted spoon and drain on layers of paper towels. Sprinkle them with salt to taste and layer them with the olive oil, vinegar, and mint leaves in a container with a lid. Eat after a day and store in the fridge for up to 10 days making sure the surface is covered with a layer of oil.

Variation
EGGPLANT UNDER OIL
Follow the method for *Zucchini alla poverella sott'olio* (see left) but be prepared to use more sunflower oil for frying because eggplant are more absorbent than zucchini.

ROASTED RED PEPPERS WITH THYME

This is an Italian way of preserving these bright red beauties under oil. Our friend Livia makes them regularly during summer. She uses her homegrown peppers and her husband Nello's olive oil. For this recipe, we bought all of the ingredients from our local supermarket and were very pleased with the result. Serve with steamed fish, cold meats or cheese, stirred into hot pasta with a dash of cream, or as an ingredient in stir-fries, sauces, or casseroles.

makes approx. 1¾lbs
8 red peppers
3 tablespoons lemon juice
fine sea salt
4 sprigs of thyme
2 bay leaves, torn into two
approx. 1 cup extra virgin olive oil

Preheat the oven to 400°F. Roast the peppers whole on a baking sheet until black, approx. 30–40 minutes. Using tongs, transfer the peppers to a plastic bag and set aside to cool. The peppers will sweat inside the bag,

loosening the skins. When cool enough to handle, peel off the skins, discard the seeds, and rinse the flesh briefly under cold running water to remove any black bits. Pat dry on paper towels.

Pack the peppers into a container or jar with a lid, interspersing each layer with the lemon juice, salt, and herbs. Top up with the olive oil, making sure that the peppers are fully submerged before putting on the lid.

Store in the fridge for up to 3 weeks. If you don't want to eat them all at once, remove the amount you need and make sure the rest are covered in oil. Serve at room temperature.

SALVO'S ARTICHOKES UNDER OIL

Salvatore has a garden where he grows small, violet artichokes. This is his way of preserving them. His method is to prepare the artichokes and then cook them in one-third vinegar to two-thirds salted water.

makes approx. 2¼lbs
3⅓lbs artichokes
2 lemons
white wine vinegar, salt and water
  for the poaching liquid (see above)
a few black peppercorns
a few sprigs of dried thyme
extra virgin olive oil, to cover

Trim the hard leaves and tough stems from the artichokes and remove the fluffy chokes with a small teaspoon. Cut them into quarters and rub with a cut lemon to stop them from turning black. Put into cold water as you cut them, along with the used lemons. Boil the artichokes until tender in the correct proportions of vinegar to water ratio (see above). Drain with stems pointing upwards on a clean towel for several hours or overnight.

GENERAL GUIDELINES FOR PRESERVING VEGETABLES UNDER OIL

Oil
Use extra virgin olive oil of a medium quality; don't waste your favorite single estate stuff.

After opening
If you remove some of the vegetables, always top up the container with more oil so the vegetables are submerged in oil at all times.

Don't throw away the precious oil after you have eaten your vegetables. Use it for cooking or for drizzling over salads, etc. It will have a wonderful flavor.

Troubleshooting
Bulging lids: If the lid on a container of food preserved in oil is bulging, or oil is leaking from it, your food has probably become contaminated. Don't attempt to eat it; throw it away immediately.

Mold: If you discover mold growing on your food, throw it away; likewise, if it is starting to fizz. Always trust your nose—if the food smells bad, discard it.

Sometimes garlic turns green or blue in the jar. This is due to the acidity of the product and is nothing to worry about.

Sterilize the jars and lids according to page 12. Heat the oil with the peppercorns and thyme over medium heat. Pack the artichokes into the jars and cover with warm oil, dividing the flavorings between them. Seal, and when cooled to room temperature, put them into the fridge or a cool, dark place. They will keep for up to 3 months like this, but once opened use within 10 days keep the surface is covered with oil. Serve at room temperature with mozzarella, use on pizza or grill until hot and drizzle with balsamic vinegar.

ASPARAGUS UNDER OIL

For a while after the asparagus season is over you can enjoy these tender spears with a poached egg, salad, chopped into pasta, or warmed on their own.

makes approx. 1-quart jar
1lb asparagus
1¼ cups white wine vinegar
1 cup water
a few sprigs of thyme
a few black peppercorns
2 cups extra virgin olive oil

Trim away any woody ends of the asparagus and cut into lengths to fit inside your jar with enough headroom that they can easily be covered in oil. Cook them in the vinegar and water until just tender, then drain until dry on paper towels. Grill, if you like, to add a roasted flavor and black lines. Warm the oil with the flavorings and sterilize the jar(s). Pack the spears into warm sterilized jar(s) and cover with the warm oil. Add the flavorings and seal. When cool transfer to the fridge and store for up to a month. Once opened make sure the asparagus spears are always covered with oil.

CYRUS TODIWALA'S LIME PICKLE—LIMBU MARCHA NU ACHAAR

This simple chile and lime pickle is certainly very popular with Cyrus's customers in his restaurants Café Spice Namasté and Mr Todiwala's Kitchen. Cyrus was keen to point out that there is no point making miniscule quantities of pickle and chutney as they need time to mature for the flavors to develop fully. They should always be made when the fruit or vegetable is abundant and in season. Pickles made well should last a long time, providing you ensure that the pickle is submerged beneath the oil. Wipe down the sides of the jar with paper towels each time you remove some.

This simple recipe is very versatile and can be made with lemons, zucchini, rhubarb, or asparagus. My advice is don't panic at the quantity and strength of the chiles at the beginning. Wait. After just a week, even though I was supposed to leave it longer, the flavors really mellow. This pickle is delicious served with curry or alongside grilled white fish. I am so glad Cyrus told me to make loads of it.

makes 3 x 2-cup jars
1lb large green chiles (or red chiles in season)
10 limes
2–2½ cups extra virgin canola oil
15–20 garlic cloves, peeled
5 heaping tablespoons mustard powder, like Colman's
3 tablespoons salt
1 heaping teaspoon turmeric
1 teaspoon asafoetida

Wash the chiles and dry. Remove the stems and cut the chiles into approx. ½-in pieces. Wash the limes, trim off the ends, and dice into ½-in pieces, skins and all. Place the chiles and limes together in a large bowl. Meanwhile,

heat the canola oil in a pan to smoking point; set aside to cool to room temperature.

In a blender, purée half the oil with the garlic, mustard, salt, turmeric, and asafoetida. Scoop the purée into the bowl with the chiles and limes and mix well with a large spoon so everything is well coated. Reheat the remaining oil until hot, and then pour over the mixture in the bowl. Stir well for 1–2 minutes, and then wipe down the sides of the bowl with paper towels. Push down any chiles or limes that float to the surface; you might need to heat up some more oil if necessary to cover them completely. Cover the bowl with a cloth and set aside in a warm place for a couple of days to ferment, checking regularly to make sure everything stays submerged to protect it from the air.

Spoon the pickle into sterilized jars and top up if necessary with more oil. Cover the tops of the jars with a small circle of cheesecloth, fastened with string or a rubber band, and then transfer them to a sunny windowsill. Leave the pickle to mature for 2 weeks before tasting. (If it is not sunny, leave it for up to a month.) During this time it will undergo lacto-fermentation (see Fermentation for more details on this, page 234). Expect to see a few bubbles, but wait for them to stop before you bottle. After that time the jars can be sealed with nonreactive lids and stored in a cool, dark place. The pickle will keep for up to a year.

PASTES AND PESTO

We believe the best way to preserve the flavor of fresh basil is in frozen Pesto cubes (page 273). However, here are some alternative pastes, and a tomato pesto sauce, that keep well in the fridge under oil.

SUN-DRIED TOMATO PESTO

This is a spicy little number that keeps well in the fridge for about a month. It is a great paste to spread onto hot crostini and top with goat cheese. Alternatively, stir it into hot pasta and grate on your favorite hard cheese. You can also try it stirred into couscous with some of the Roasted red peppers on page 183. For maximum flavor, use your own homemade dried or semi-dried tomatoes.

makes approx. 1 x 1¼-cup jar

4oz sun-dried or semi-dried tomatoes (see page 127)
1 garlic clove, peeled
¼ cup whole almonds, toasted until golden in a hot oven for a few minutes
½ teaspoon salt
½–1 whole dried red chile, to taste
1 tablespoon lemon juice
⅔ cup extra virgin olive oil, plus extra to top up your jar with at the end

Mix all the ingredients together with a stick blender or in a small food processor until you have a paste. I like to stop before it becomes completely smooth because I prefer a coarse texture. Taste and adjust the salt and chile accordingly. Spoon into a sterilized jar, top up with some extra virgin olive oil, and put on the lid. Store in the fridge for up to a month, keeping the top covered with a layer of olive oil at all times to stop oxidisation.

BAGNETTO— PIEMONTESE SAVORY SAUCE FOR FISH AND CHICKEN

Imagine looking in an Italian mamma's fridge in Piemonte, northern Italy. There you are bound to discover a little jar of sauce that doesn't look or taste like anything you have experienced before, but you love it. It is umami—salty and savory and full of things that you can't quite place, but you know you want more. It is so well balanced that not one flavor dominates and the result is something you want to spread on hot toast, drizzle onto pan-fried fish, or scoop from your plate onto roast or poached chicken. This recipe was given to me by such an Italian mamma, Giorgina Vogliolo, who stills cooks with a passion at the age of 89.

I am eternally grateful to her and I am sure I will be making *bagnetto* into my eighties if I am so lucky.

In Italy they eat this with *bollito misto*, the famous dish of boiled meats that is pushed around on a cart in old-fashioned restaurants by waiters in white jackets and black bowties. Giorgina's daughter, Luisa, is a friend of ours and told us the reason it is so good is that you have to make it with care. Her mother only uses salted capers, which she wipes free of salt with paper towels first, and she only uses anchovies under salt. Apparently she even keeps a special little spoon to serve it with so that it never takes on any other flavors.

makes 4oz

2 tablespoons capers
2 tablespoons chopped Salted anchovies (see pages 90–91)
6 tablespoons finely chopped parsley
2 tablespoons tomato paste
2 tablespoon Dijon mustard
6 tablespoons extra virgin olive oil, plus extra to top up your jar with at the end
1 tablespoon red wine vinegar
½–1 teaspoon freshly ground black pepper
½ teaspoon red pepper flakes
1 teaspoon sugar, to taste

Chop the capers and anchovies finely by hand with a mezzaluna (a half-moon-shaped knife), or a large cook's knife, grouping them into a pile on a large wooden chopping board. Transfer to a bowl with the remaining ingredients and mix well. Alternatively, put all the ingredients into a food processor and blend until smooth. Taste and adjust the seasoning as necessary. Spoon into a small jar and top up with extra virgin olive oil. Store in the fridge and consume within 2 weeks.

HARISSA PASTE

This recipe is from Moroccan chef Ghalid Assyb. Harissa is strong, powerful stuff usually made with a mixture of chiles in different strengths—some dried and some fresh. Ghalid uses a mix of jalapeño, Scotch bonnet, bird's eye, and Serrano. I have my own long red chiles that I dry (see page 127) and so used a mixture of those and some fresh red chiles to make up the amount to 4 ounces. Ghalid told me harissa should have a smokiness about it, so he blackens not only the peppers but also the fresh chiles and garlic, too. We eat this on roast chicken, stir it into couscous, or just use it as a condiment when we want a bit of spice.

makes approx. 9oz

4 ounces mixed chiles (see above) consisting of ¼ dried and ¾ fresh
2 red peppers
2 fat garlic cloves, still in their skins
½ teaspoon cumin seeds
½ teaspoon coriander seeds
½ teaspoon caraway seeds
3 tablespoons lemon juice
¼ cup extra virgin olive oil, plus extra for topping up the jar at the end
1 tablespoon tomato paste
fine sea salt, to taste

Preheat the oven to 400°F. Soak the dried chiles in cold water for about 30 minutes. Place the peppers on a baking sheet in a hot oven for 20 minutes, and then add the fresh chiles and garlic cloves and return to the oven for another 10–15 minutes until the peppers and chiles start to blacken. Using tongs, transfer the roasted vegetables to a plastic bag and set aside to sweat. Meanwhile, toast the spices in a dry frying pan until they release their fragrance; set aside to cool and then grind to a powder in a spice grinder or mortar and pestle.

Once the peppers and chiles are cool enough to handle, peel away any blackened areas of skin. It is a good idea to do this wearing thin gloves because the heat can stay on your fingers for a while afterward and it can burn your eyes.

Drain the dried chiles through a fine sieve, discarding the liquid. Squeeze the garlic cloves from their papery skins and place them in a blender or food processor. Add the chiles and peppers along with the remaining ingredients and blend to a smooth paste.

Spoon the paste into a sterilized jar and cover with a layer of olive oil. The harissa will keep in the fridge for up to a month.

Variation
To make the wonderfully scented Rose Harissa, add a large handful of fresh edible or dried edible rose petals to the paste, adding a little more extra virgin olive oil to make a paste. Make sure the petals have never been sprayed with pesticide and have a good natural perfume.

FISH UNDER OIL

MARINATED SALTED ANCHOVIES

These are made using the Salted anchovies on pages 90–91.

makes approx. 10oz (serves 8–10 as a canapé or appetizer)
7oz Salted anchovies (see pages 90–91)
juice of 1 lemon
1 cup white wine vinegar
1 cup extra virgin olive oil

To serve
1 red onion, finely chopped
1 garlic clove, finely sliced
½ chile, finely sliced
juice of 1 lemon
3 tablespoons extra virgin olive oil
1 tablespoon roughly chopped parsley

Remove the anchovies from the salt and wash them in cold water. Place them in a plastic container, squeeze in the lemon juice, and pour in the vinegar. Set aside to soak for 30 minutes.

Wash the anchovies again and squeeze them gently between paper towels to remove any excess moisture. Put them into a small container, such as a sterilized jar or small plastic box, and cover with the oil. Put on a lid and store in the fridge for up to 2 weeks.

To serve, lay the anchovy fillets on a serving dish and dress with the onion, garlic, chile, lemon juice, oil, and parsley. Eat with toasted bread.

CONFIT

The term confit comes from the French word *confire*, meaning "to produce, make or prepare." Confit was originally used to describe fruits that had been cooked slowly in sugar or honey, hence the French word *confiture*, meaning jam, and the English word "confection" for sweet treats. Today the term is used to describe any food that had been prepared for preservation by immersing in a liquid and by being cooked slowly.

Confit making, as we know it today, began during the 18th century in south-west France, where fattened geese and ducks were salted and then cooked very slowly in their own fat, which rendered down during the cooking process. This method was designed to preserve meat throughout the winter.

Traditionally salt or saltpeter was used in the recipe to keep the meat pink and help to protect it from bacteria. However, this isn't necessary today if you keep the confit in the fridge, since the long, slow cooking process tenderizes the meat and kills off any unwanted bacteria.

The process of confit works so well because over time the collagen in the meat, usually the tough legs of goose and duck, is broken down. In his book *Cooking for Geeks*, Jeff Potter writes about tests that have been done to show that it is this length of time that softens the meat, not the fat, so actually you could cook the meat in olive oil to save the cost of the duck fat. The duck-flavored olive oil can also be used up afterward and has a lot more uses than the expensive duck fat.

If done properly, this process is a simple and effective way of preserving meat. To reheat the meat, simply pull out the duck legs from the jar and cook until crisp. The flesh should be meltingly tender, while the fat can be used for flavorful roast potatoes.

CHRIS TERRY'S DUCK CONFIT

Crispy skin and soft, melting meat that falls from the bone—this is how confit of duck should be. Before writing this book I had never attempted this dish, thinking it was too complicated. However, our photographer, Chris Terry, had perfected the recipe and showed us how easy it was. Now it has become a staple dish we make at home for entertaining. We can prepare it in advance and cook it in the oven when the guests are present, knowing we are going to get a fantastic result. We serve it with roast potatoes cooked in the fat or oil from the duck and a jar of Peas in sweet brine (see page 259). The fat or oil can be used two or three times for another confit; after that it becomes too salty.

This recipe is also just right for using in the Cassoulet recipe in Heat, page 261.

serves 4

1 head of garlic, broken into cloves and peeled
1 tablespoon juniper berries
1 tablespoon crushed black peppercorns
1 tablespoon fresh thyme leaves, plus a couple of sprigs
¾ cup coarse sea salt
1 tablespoon bay leaves, roughly chopped with scissors
4 duck legs
4 cups duck fat or goose fat or 4–6 cups extra virgin olive oil

Lightly crush three garlic cloves, the juniper berries, peppercorns, and thyme leaves in a mortar and pestle. Add this mixture to the salt and cut bay leaves. Lay the duck skin-side down in a ceramic or plastic container, preferably raised off the bottom so it doesn't sit in the brine. You could use a plastic rack for this or a few chopsticks laid down will do. Layer the duck legs with the salt and the flavorings between them. Put the lid on the container and transfer to the fridge or a cool place below 40°F for 12 hours or overnight.

Preheat the oven to 200°F. Brush most of the salt off the duck and then give it a really brief rinse under running water to remove the rest. Thoroughly pat dry with paper towels. Warm the duck fat or olive oil in a heavy ovenproof casserole then add the fresh thyme and the remaining garlic cloves, which should be lightly crushed.

Lay the duck skin-side up in the fat or oil, making sure it is submerged, and put the casserole into the oven. Cook for 4 hours or until a skewer slides into the meat with little or no resistance then remove from oven. During this time it is a good idea to measure the temperature with a digital probe, as it should never go above 200°F in the fat or oil. Although small bubbles will appear in the oil or fat, it should never boil. Although the oven is set at 200°F, the temperature in the casserole rarely gets to around 195°F.

The duck can be eaten right away, but to preserve it, it should be stored in the fat. To do this, put the legs into a heatproof container and carefully pour in the fat or oil, but not the liquid at the bottom. (This will make duck jelly when set, which is excellent as a base for a stock or gravy.) The meat should be completely submerged in the fat or oil. The duck will keep for up to a month in the fridge like this. If you eat only one or two duck legs at a time make sure the remaining legs are covered in fat to protect them from oxidization.

To reheat the duck legs preheat the oven to 350°F. Lay the duck legs onto an ovenproof dish skin-side up and roast for 30–40 minutes, turning halfway through. This gives a delicious crispy result to the skin.

BOTTLING TIPS Jane Grigson recommends putting two sterilized sticks (one-third of a chopstick will do) in the bottom of each jar so that the meat is completely encircled by the fat. Other recipes suggest a scattering of salt at the bottom of the jar. Jane also recommends that you put a little circle of foil on top of the fat, pressing it down well on the surface, so it cannot become contaminated by air.

ANTONIO'S CONFIT OF TOMATOES

Antonio Sanzone, Head Chef at our restaurant Caffè Caldesi, taught me this recipe. During the summer my family had arranged to come for lunch. It was a beautiful sunny day and, although I had made some fresh bread, I spent the morning lazing around in the garden, letting time slip away. When my family suddenly appeared, I realized I had to think fast and prepare something to eat. I remembered Antonio's tomato confit in the pantry. This is just what the idea of preserving is all about, I thought— rustling up a quick meal from your pantry. I roughly tore up some mozzarella and put it onto a serving dish. Then I cut up the tomatoes from the jars, and placed these over the cheese, followed by most of the oil from the jar and some fresh basil. The result was delicious, and so simple served with warm bread, and none of my family realized I hadn't spent all morning preparing it!

Do use very flavorful tomatoes for the best result. Tomatoes grown out of season in greenhouses just won't hit the spot.

makes 2 x 2-cup jars

2 cups extra virgin olive oil
1 banana shallot or 3 small shallots, thinly sliced
½ teaspoon fine sea salt
12 medium round, flavorful tomatoes
2 sprigs of rosemary
2 sprigs of marjoram
4 sprigs of mint
2 sprigs of thyme
2 leafy stems of basil
20 fennel seeds
2 star anise
10 black peppercorns
4 tablespoons lemon juice

Heat a couple of tablespoons of the oil in a frying pan and soften the shallots, sprinkled with the salt, over low heat for a few minutes. Meanwhile, peel the tomatoes: make a cross in the bottom of each one and cut out the core; drop into a pan of boiling water for 12–15 seconds (30–40 for San Marzano since the skins are tougher), and then plunge into ice-cold water; peel off the skins.

Make sure your sterilized jars are completely dry. Divide the herbs and spices between the jars, placing them in a layer at the bottom. Some tomatoes have a visible ridge on them running from stem to bottom. If this is the case, cut the tomatoes along this line, so that the seeds are trapped inside. Each tomato should be cut into quarters. Transfer the tomatoes to a large bowl and put in the softened shallots, along with the oil and lemon juice. Toss everything together gently with clean hands, and then spoon the shallots and tomatoes into sterilized jars. Top up the jars with oil so the tomatoes are completely submerged. Cut out two disks from parchment paper to fit inside the jars and press down well to form a seal. Put on the lids, and process the jars for 45 minutes using the waterbathing technique on page 252. If waterbathed correctly, the tomatoes should keep in a cool, dark place for up to a year.

POTTED PÂTÉS AND TERRINES

In medieval times, chopped meat and fat was pressed and cooked either inside an earthenware pot with a pastry lid or was completely encased in pastry. This is where the French term *pâte*, meaning pastry, comes from. Over time the French did away with the pastry, and pâté as we know it today was born.

A terrine is a coarser version of a pâté, although both were traditionally made using raw meat that was pressed and cooked slowly in a waterbath. They were often weighted down to make them even more compact and expel the air.

In England, potted meats, shrimps, and salmon are usually made with cooked meat and fish—making them an excellent way of using up leftovers—and they are traditionally preserved under a layer of clarified butter.

Today these historic terms for preserved meat have become interchangeable. Ingredients range from chicken and trout to game or rabbit—but they always contain a high percentage of fat. Flavorings are as exotic as foie gras and truffle, but can be as simple as leeks and rosemary. Terrines can be made in elegant layers that are visible only when sliced or blended until smooth and scooped out with a spoon. Either way, hot toast is essential, as is a selection of pickles. Try them with the Swedish pickled cucumbers on page 21.

POTTED SMOKED CHICKEN

Potted meats were traditionally made using leftovers to create another meal. This recipe can be made with other cooked meats such as ham, beef, pork, rabbit, or other game. It has a lovely flavor from the smoking, although it isn't essential to use smoked chicken if you are looking for a way to use up leftover roast meat. Feel free to experiment with the flavorings—try tarragon or lemon zest with unsmoked chicken, sage with pork, or add a little chile or mustard seed with beef. In the past, we have used the leftover wing and leg meat from a roast chicken for this (after eating up all the breast meat first). Go easy with the thyme; it can easily overpower the flavor of the chicken.

serves 6 as an appetizer
8 tablespoons (1 stick) salted butter
1 medium onion, finely chopped
2 cups chopped smoked cooked chicken or plain roast chicken
½ teaspoon chopped thyme leaves
1 tablespoon finely chopped fresh parsley
½ cup chicken or vegetable stock or hot water
fine sea salt and freshly ground black pepper, to taste
7 tablespoons clarified butter

Melt the salted butter in a frying pan over low heat and gently cook the onion until soft and translucent. Roughly chop the chicken either in a food processor using the pulse button or with a large kitchen knife. Add the chicken to the pan, add the herbs and stock (or water), and cook for 5 minutes until heated through. Season with salt and pepper to taste. Divide the mixture among six ramekins and set aside to cool to room temperature; don't let them sit out any longer than an hour. Heat the clarified butter and pour some over each pot to form a thick protective layer. Transfer the ramekins to the fridge to set. They will keep for up to a week in the fridge.

Variation
POTTED SALMON
This recipe can also be made with leftover cooked salmon instead of chicken. Omit the thyme and instead add the juice of half a lemon and some lemon zest to taste.

POTTED CHEESE

You can use any kind of cheese for this. I learned this recipe in Italy from our chef friend Gino Borella, who made it with pecorino and Parmesan, but I have since tried it with a mixture of leftover cheeses, including some blue cheese from my fridge, and it worked brilliantly. Either enjoy it plain or introduce your own flavorings such as a pinch of chile powder or grated nutmeg, some dried herbs, or lemon rind. This is lovely spread onto hot crostini, stirred into pasta, or served on a cheese board with chutney.

makes 8oz (enough for 10-12 crostini)
5–6oz mixed cheeses of your choice
3 tablespoons extra virgin olive oil, plus extra to cover
4 tablespoons white wine

Grate the cheeses either by hand or using the grater attachment in a food processor. Combine with the remaining ingredients in a bowl and beat until smooth. Either use right away or spoon into a standard-sized jar and press down well. Cover the surface with a layer of oil and store in the fridge for up to a month.

DIANA'S CHICKEN LIVER PÂTÉ

Diana Bethwaite has been making this pâté for years. Her children love it and demand it at every family occasion. They favor a *pâté de campagne* texture, which is quite rough, and the crust is their favorite part. Pig's liver can be used for a stronger flavor. I really like the flavor of this version and pair it with Mrs. Wishdish's plum and ginger chutney (see page 32), the Chrain on page 26, or the Swedish pickled cucumbers on page 21.

makes 1 x 1lb loaf

1 cup lard
1lb chicken livers, cut into strips with the sinewy bits removed
2 medium onions, finely chopped
7oz unsmoked bacon, cut into small pieces
2 garlic cloves, peeled and finely chopped
1⅓ cups dry white bread crumbs
1 teaspoon chopped mixed herbs, such as rosemary, thyme, and oregano
1 teaspoon ground mace
2 level teaspoons salt
1 level teaspoon freshly ground black pepper
2 eggs
3 anchovy fillets, finely chopped
4 tablespoons brandy
a little oil, for brushing

Line a 1lb loaf pan with parchment paper. Preheat the oven to 325°F. Melt the lard in a large frying pan and add the livers, onion, and bacon. Cook over medium heat until the livers are just cooked through and the onion is soft. Add the garlic and cook for another 2 minutes. Remove the pan from the heat and set aside to cool.

Tip the cooled mixture into a blender or food processor and process to a rough or smooth texture as you wish. Spoon the mixture into a bowl and stir in the rest of the ingredients. Transfer the mixture into the prepared loaf pan and smooth the top. Brush with a little oil and cover with a small piece of foil to stop the top from burning. Sit the loaf pan inside a roasting pan half filled with hot water and transfer to the oven to bake for 2 hours. After an hour, remove the foil from the top to form the crust. Once cooked, carefully remove the pan from the water and place on a wire rack to cool. Turn out once cold and wrap in wax paper until needed. The pâté will keep in the fridge for up to a week.

Variation
Add a handful of fresh cranberries to the mixture with the rest of the ingredients. For pork pâté, replace the chicken livers with pig's livers and use sherry instead of brandy.

SMOKED TROUT PÂTÉ

This is Tim Lobb's recipe from Brookleas fish farm. Tim breeds trout, smokes them, and sells them at local farmers' markets. Brookleas is a beautiful farm on the site of an old mill on the river. We love taking the children there because we can fish for trout and hot-smoke it afterward on our little Cameron smoker. With a bottle of chilled Sauvignon nestling in the picnic basket and happy children, it's a perfect day out! The pâté can be made with any smoked fish—in particular, it is a good way of using up broken or overcooked pieces of fish left over while learning to smoke your own fish.

serves 6

10oz smoked trout (approx. 2 trout, filleted)
⅓ cup low-fat yogurt, heavy cream, or crème fraîche
juice of ½ lemon
freshly ground black pepper
½ teaspoon paprika
a few drops of Tabasco, to taste
pinch of fine sea salt, to taste
clarified butter, to seal

Put all the ingredients apart from the butter into a food processor and blend until you have the consistency you like. Giancarlo prefers his pâté smooth, but I like mine chunky and a bit rough, so stop blending as you wish. Season to taste and serve right away or store in the fridge in one or individual containers sealed with clarified butter as in the recipe for Potted smoked chicken (see page 191) for up to 5 days.

RILLETTES

My family used to take vacations in Normandy, France, every year, and I remember my mother buying rillettes to slather onto warm baguettes. Since we were a large family, we always had picnics and traveled with all the necessary items including freshly ground black pepper and sharp knives. Rillettes were eaten with delicious ripe tomatoes and black pepper. This is the French version of British potted meat, using shredded rather than chopped meat.

This recipe is based on one shown to us by Marc Frederic, who has been inspirational in getting us into charcuterie. Rillettes can also be made with rabbit and pork fat or duck and goose with their own fat. Poultry fat melts at a lower temperature than pork fat so the end result is more spreadable. Always serve rillettes at room temperature like a good wine or cheese.

makes 4 x 12-oz jars

1lb pork back fat, cut into small pieces
2lbs pork from the shoulder or belly
½ cup white wine
2 garlic cloves, peeled and finely chopped
½ teaspoon ground nutmeg
1 teaspoon freshly ground black pepper
1–2 teaspoons salt

Put the fat into a heavy-bottomed saucepan or a slow cooker over low heat to melt. Meanwhile, cut the pork into 2-in cubes. Add the pork to the warm melted fat and pour in the wine. Add the garlic, nutmeg, and black pepper. Bring to a boil, cover, and cook over very low heat for 3–4 hours, until the meat is tender and falling apart.

Strain the meat through a sieve over a heatproof bowl to collect the fat. Transfer the meat to a cutting board and shred it finely between two forks. Place the shredded meat in a clean bowl and gradually pour in some of the

warm fat, little by little, until it reaches the consistency, according to Marc, of a peat bog—if you press down on the shredded meat, the juices should rise to the top—not that I've ever been to a peat bog, but I think he means it should be really, really thick with the juices just visible with pressure! Season with salt to taste.

Spoon the mixture into sterilized jars or ramekins and set aside to cool. To seal your jars, melt some of the remaining fat in the pan and pour a thick layer on the top of each jar to cover the surface completely. Put on the lids and store in the fridge for up to 2 weeks. Serve with hot toast or bread, Swedish pickled cucumbers (see page 21) and ripe juicy tomatoes.

WILD GARLIC PESTO

To me, the sight and smell of wild garlic growing in our local woods heralds the first sign of spring. I love making this wild garlic pesto, which is delicious stirred into hot pasta or spread over fish before grilling.

serves 4-6

2oz young wild garlic leaves
⅓ cup pine nuts, almonds or cashews, toasted in a hot oven for 3–5 minutes
freshly ground black pepper
½ cup extra virgin olive oil, plus extra to cover
¼ cup finely grated Parmesan or Grana Padano cheese
pinch of salt, to taste

Rinse the garlic leaves in cold water and pat dry on paper towels. Blend to a paste with the nuts and pepper in a food processor or a mortar and pestle. I like my pesto fairly coarse, but keep grinding if you prefer it smooth. Pour in the oil and pulse quickly to blend. Transfer the pesto to a bowl and stir in

the cheese. Season to taste with salt if necessary. Spoon the pesto into clean jars with lids, top up with extra virgin olive oil to cover, and store in the fridge for up to 2 weeks.

WILD GARLIC WRAPPED CHEESE

Another great way to use these delicately scented leaves, known as ramsons.

makes 1 x 2-cup jar

approx. 50 young wild garlic leaves
8oz soft cheese, such as the *Labneh* (page 222)
1 dried red chile, sliced
extra virgin olive oil, to cover

Rinse the garlic leaves and pat dry on paper towels. Dot a teaspoonful of the soft cheese at the fat end of each leaf. Roll up the leaves individually and pop into a sterilized jar. Sprinkle each layer with some of the chile and drizzle with some olive oil. Continue until the jar is nearly full, allowing an inch of headroom. Push out any bubbles with a chopstick. Top up with olive oil, making sure that none of the leaves protrude above the surface. Close the lid and put into the fridge. Store for up to 1 week. Serve with hot crusty bread.

BUTTER

If you have ever overwhipped cream, you will know how easy it is to make butter. By churning cream, we can separate the fat in the form of butter grains from the water-based part of the cream, called buttermilk.

Traditionally butter producers use the evening milk, which is 4 percent higher in fat than morning milk, because it is produced over a shorter period so it is more concentrated. Butter can be made out of fresh or fermented milk or cream. The color of butter varies depending on the cow's feed; manufactured varieties often contain colorings such as carotene.

to make butter

This can be done very simply in a glass jar with a tight-fitting lid. Pour heavy cream into a jar and add a couple of ice cubes. Shake the jar vigorously until the fat has separated into a ball that floats in the buttermilk. To speed up the process, churning can also be done in a food processor with a tight-fitting lid. Whip the cream until it becomes very thick. Eventually it will separate into lumps of butter and buttermilk.

After churning, whether you have used a jar or a food processor, it is essential that you wash the lumps of butter in a sieve under very cold water to get rid of any buttermilk, which will make it spoil. Break up the lumps with your hands to remove any traces of buttermilk that could cause spoilage. Once the water runs clear, the butter can be pressed together. This is traditionally done with butter paddles, which have ridges on them to leave a pattern and also to encourage the water to run away. Failing that, you could press the butter with your hands or

roll it into a sausage shape in a piece of parchment paper.

After pressing, you can flavor the butter if you wish with fine or coarse sea salt, chile, or herbs. Shape into logs, wrap in parchment paper, and keep chilled until ready to use. Butter will keep for a couple of weeks in the fridge.

to make cultured butter

In small dairies, milk was traditionally collected over several days before being made into cream or butter, and by this time it had started to ferment. During fermentation, cream naturally sours as bacteria convert milk sugars into lactic acid. This fermentation is what gives the resulting "cultured" butter its strong flavor, and today cultured butter is attracting lots of attention from chefs and the public alike. Nowadays, cultured butter is usually made on a large scale from pasteurized cream, which has been fermented with the addition of bacteria cultures such as *Lactococcus* and *Leuconostoc*. However, it is possible to make cultured butter at home.

METHOD First you need to ferment the cream. Put a couple of tablespoons of live yogurt into 2 cups heavy cream and set aside, covered, in a warm place for 24 hours. Alternatively, mix in a pinch of mesophilic starter (bought online from cheese-making suppliers, see page 290) and set aside in a warm place for 12 hours.

To turn your fermented cream into butter, follow the method for making butter (left) using 3 parts heavy cream to 1 part fermented cream. As before, it is essential that you rinse the butter really well in plenty of cold water before seasoning it with salt. Store as for fresh butter.

FLAVORED BUTTERS

These versatile little pastes make wonderful toppings for baked potatoes, hot steak, or burgers, or they can be stirred into pasta or melted onto hot sourdough toast, chicken, or fish—I told you they were versatile!

Bring 4 sticks of butter to room temperature. Put the softened butter in a bowl and use a fork to mash in your chosen flavorings (see right); season with salt and pepper. Spoon the butter onto a piece of parchment paper and roll up into a log shape. Put the flavored butter in the fridge to harden and then cut into slices if you wish, wrapping them individually in parchment paper or plastic wrap. Store in the freezer for up to 3 months or keep in the fridge for up to a week.

flavorings

WILD GARLIC Add 6 tablespoons of finely chopped wild garlic leaves. Use on steak or in baked potatoes.

TRUFFLE Add a generous grating of fresh truffle or half a teaspoon of truffle oil. Melt over hot pasta.

TARRAGON Add ⅓ cup of finely chopped fresh tarragon. Melt over hot roast chicken or stuff under the skin before cooking. Alternatively add a cube to hot steamed carrots before serving.

PORCINI Soak a small handful of dried porcini mushrooms in hot water to rehydrate them, and then drain well. Pat dry on paper towels and finely chop. Cook briefly in extra virgin olive oil with a finely chopped garlic clove. Drain from the oil and allow to cool. Mix into the butter. Melt over hot pasta, steak, or stir into mashed potato.

CHILE AND GARLIC Add 2–3 teaspoons of finely chopped fresh red chile or red pepper flakes and 5 teaspoons of finely chopped garlic. Stir into rice, melt over chicken, or spread on hot thick toast for garlic bread.

FLAVORED OILS

Oils flavored with fresh herbs and spices do not have a long shelflife. There is also a small risk of inviting unwanted bacteria into your oil with the additional flavorings—there have been a few cases of botulism coming from garlic preserved in oil. We prefer to make Spice Cubes for cooking, see page 273 in Cold, or we make small amounts of flavored oil and keep them refrigerated for use within 3 days.

CHILE OIL

Pour ¾ cup of extra virgin olive oil into a clean bottle and stir in 2 teaspoons of red pepper flakes. (To make these yourself see Air, page 127.) Cover and store in the fridge and consume within 3 days. Chile oil is delicious drizzled over pizza or stir-fries when you want a dash of heat and others don't.

Variations
HERB OIL

Mix the oil with 1 teaspoon of dried thyme, 1 teaspoon of dried oregano, and 2 chopped bay leaves as above. Pour this over steak, grilled chicken, or lamb.

BASIL OIL

This is a great way to use up the dried leaves of basil that appear on a plant when it has been in the sun. Put a handful into the oil as above and store in the fridge overnight. Strain and use as a dip for hot bread. Store in the fridge and consume within 3 days.

ZHUG

This cilantro and chile paste originates from Yemen and Yemenite Jews introduced it to Israel. *Zhug* is now popular all over Israel on falafel stalls. Green *zhug* is made from green chiles, and red *zhug* is made from red ones. *Zhug* looks like a Middle-Eastern version of pesto, since it also contains plenty of fresh herbs blended with oil. I love Middle-Eastern cooking and so use it quite frequently with couscous, harissa, North African merguez sausages (page 111) or over halved hard-boiled eggs and roasted vegetables. It is really versatile, and you can alter the strength of the heat by adding or subtracting chiles as you like.

makes 6oz
1 cup fresh cilantro
⅔ cup parsley
2 green chiles
3 garlic cloves, peeled
2 tablespoons lemon juice
4 tablespoons extra virgin olive oil, plus extra to cover
1 teaspoon coriander seeds
½ teaspoon cumin seeds
½ teaspoon cardamom pods
4 cloves
½ teaspoon fine sea salt

Wash the herbs and pat dry on paper towels. Discard any large tough stems from the cilantro and parsley (you can freeze the parsley stems for use in stocks). Place the herbs, chiles, garlic, and lemon juice into a food processor with the olive oil and process to a paste. Grind the spices and salt to a powder in a mortar and pestle or spice grinder, discarding the cardamom husks once they have released their seeds. Add the spices to the food processor and process again—it doesn't have to be completely smooth, I prefer mine a little chunky. Use right away or spoon into a sterilized jar and top up with olive oil. Store in the fridge for up to a week but the flavor is better before 5 days. Alternatively freeze cubes of *zhug* in an ice-cube tray for up to 3 months.

FETA IN OIL

Look out for good-quality feta that is sold in a tub of brine from a deli. The flavor and acidity will be superior to the plastic-wrapped variety. This is a great way to use your dried herbs (see page 128). Don't add garlic cloves if you wish to keep the cheese for more than a week.

makes 1 x 2-cup jar (serves approx. 6)
10oz feta
1 teaspoon dried thyme
1 teaspoon dried oregano
1 teaspoon red pepper flakes
1 strip of lemon zest (optional)
1 cup extra virgin olive oil

Cut the feta into 1-in dice and put into a clean jar, interspersed with the herbs, red pepper flakes, and lemon zest (if using), leaving an inch of headroom. Pour in the oil, moving the cheese around gently with a chopstick to ensure that there are no air bubbles left and that the cubes are completely submerged in oil.

Wait a day before eating to let the flavors infuse. If you remove some cheese, make sure the remainder is completely covered in oil. It will keep for up to 2 weeks in the fridge. Make a Greek salad from your marinated feta with large cubes of tomato, cucumber, and olives, using the oil as the dressing. Alternatively toss with slices of roast eggplant or mix with cubes of watermelon, fresh mint, the oil from the jar, and a splash of balsamic vinegar.

alcohol

Bottling in alcohol is one of the oldest, simplest, and definitely most pleasurable ways of preserving fruit. Boozy fruits, as my mother used to call them, make wonderfully sweet, yet citric, desserts. And then, of course, there are plenty of spirits you can enhance with the addition of fruits, such as blackberries.

We are a family of foragers who have been picking sloes from our thorny bushes for years now to make sloe gin. However, since writing this book, summer lunches in the garden have been brightened by peaches in rosé wine, and chilly winter nights have been warmed by shots of plum whisky—my new favorite nightcap—and blackberry gin.

Many of these recipes double up as boozy fruit or fruity booze. We lift out the fruits and serve them with crème fraîche or whipped cream, and then drink the liquor that is left afterward—either on its own over crushed ice, as a base for cocktails, or in a champagne flute topped with Prosecco or Champagne. Boozy fruits are incredibly versatile—you can add them to apple or pear crumbles or pies, or spoon them on oatmeal or muesli —or you can use both the fruit and the liquor together in trifles, or purée them together to make a sauce for meat, add to gravy, or pour them over ice cream.

The only downside to the recipes in this chapter is that you need to wait 2 weeks for the quickest result, and up to a year for the slowest—but it is worth having patience!

which alcohol and what flavors?

As long as the alcohol is strong—i.e. above 37.5 percent proof, such as gin, vodka, rum, etc.—you can mix and match to suit your preference. However, don't be tempted to economize and use poor-quality spirits, because you will definitely taste the difference in the end result.

You can add extra flavorings such as cinnamon sticks, allspice berries, vanilla pods, and star anise, but remember the flavors will increase in strength over time so don't go overboard.

sterilizing bottles and jars

Wash bottles and jars in the dishwasher or with hot soapy water and rinse well so that there is no inherent smell or taste. Put in the oven at 285°F for 30 minutes to sterilize. If you are filling them with hot liquid, leave them in the oven until the last minute so that you are pouring hot into hot to avoid cracking. If you are filling with cold liquid, cool the jar or bottle upside down on a rack after sterilizing. Make sure you use nonreactive lids, which should be sterilized before use by boiling them separately for a few minutes; leave in the water until you need them.

filling your bottles

Sterilized funnels should be used to fill bottles. The fruit should be completely covered with alcohol to stop spoilage.

storage

Unless you are using dark-colored jars or bottles, store your fruity booze in a cool, dark place away from the light.

a note about sweetening

The usual way to make sloe gin and similar drinks is to put the fruit, sugar, and alcohol together in the bottle, and then gently shake it every other day for the first week until the sugar dissolves. The advantage of this method is that the job is done all at once and all you have to do is sit back and wait for it to be ready. However, the only problem with this method is sometimes the resulting drink turns out to be sweeter than you would like—since much depends on the sweetness of your fruit, which can vary from one season to the next. Now, thanks to Jared Brown of the artisan distillers Sipsmith, I have discovered a better method, which allows you to control the sweetness. Jared recommends that you sweeten your drink after it has matured using simple syrup, which you can add to the bottle little by little until you have the sweetness you like. If you are concerned about diluting your spirit, you can always make a more concentrated version using two-thirds sugar to one-third water—however, add it cautiously because it will be really sweet.

SUMMER FRUITS IN BRANDY

This method is suitable for preserving all sorts of summer fruits, including berries, plums, and apricots. The boozy fruit should be ready to eat within 2 weeks, but you can leave it to mature for longer if you wish—we make this using late summer fruits to give as Christmas presents.

Our favorite way of serving the boozy fruits is with ice cream, yogurt, or cake. The fruity brandy is delicious served hot in shot glasses, or mixed with red wine for a variation on mulled wine. Alternatively, purée the fruits with their liquor and use as a sauce for desserts or with game dishes.

makes approx. 4 x 12-oz jars
2¼lbs summer berries or fruits
2 cups sugar
4 cups brandy

Wash the fruit and pat dry on paper towels. Pit and halve the fruits. Divide the fruit and sugar among the sterilized jars and top up with brandy. Seal and set aside in a cool, dark place for at least 2 weeks, turning the jars upside down every day until the sugar dissolves. Store for 3 months before sampling, although it can be matured for up to a year in a cool, dark place.

PEACHES IN ROSÉ

This drink is just delightful on a sunny day. Instead of drinking plain rosé wine, I like this at lunchtime as an aperitif. The wine only requires a couple of weeks to take on the flavor of the peaches, so this is a great one to make in the summer—although it will keep into winter for when you want a reminder of the sun. The peaches are delicious served with vanilla ice cream or crème fraîche—we fish them out after 2 weeks, leaving a quart of enriched wine to drink later.

make approx. 2 x 1-quart jars
4 ripe peaches
1 cup sugar
3 cups rosé wine
½ cup grappa, eau de vie, or vodka
2 small bay leaves

Put the jars into the oven to sterilize, see page 202. Make two small crosses in the top and bottom of each peach. Drop them into boiling water for two minutes. Remove and immediately put into iced water to cool them down quickly. Peel the peach and cut into quarters, discarding the skin and pit.

Divide the peaches and the remaining ingredients among the sterilized jars and screw on the lids tightly. Store in a cool, dark place and gently shake the jars every day until the sugar dissolves.

After 2 weeks, fish out the peaches from the liquid and eat. You can either serve the wine at the same time—we like it chilled as an aperitif—or leave it to mature for up to a year in a cool, dark place, by which time you will be ready to make some more!

CARAMELIZED ORANGES IN BRANDY

These remind me of when I first met Giancarlo. He had an ancient, slightly squeaky dessert cart in his restaurant that would wobble as it was pushed around, loaded with typical Italian desserts. The sticky, bittersweet oranges in brandy were in a big glass bowl at the bottom and were always my favorite. As dessert carts went out of fashion and customers began eating fewer desserts, we stopped making them—until I started writing this book. Now that I have been reminded of how much I love them, I have a jar permanently on standby ready to serve with whipped cream and toasted almonds, whenever friends arrive, or, if time allows, I can pour them over some cake and top with homemade custard to make a trifle.

makes 2 x 1-quart jars
12 small oranges (1½lbs without peel and pith)
2 x approx. 2-inch cinnamon sticks
2 teaspoons allspice berries
3⅓ cups cold water
1½ cups sugar
1 cup brandy

Preheat the oven to 285°F. Sterilize your jars, see page 202. Prepare a waterbath, see pages 253.

Using a peeler, cut away the zest from two of the oranges in long pieces (try not to get any of the white pith) and set aside. Cut the peel and pith from all the oranges and set them aside. Discard the pith. Put the zest into a large saucepan with the cinnamon, allspice, and water and bring to a boil. Reduce to a simmer.

Put the sugar into a large saucepan over medium heat. Without stirring, let the sugar caramelize until it is golden brown. At arm's length, slowly pour this molten sugar into the water with the peel. It will splash so be careful.

Stir and then add the oranges and cook for 10 minutes. Remove the pan from the heat.

Use a slotted spoon to remove the zest and the oranges from the syrup and put into the jars. Add the brandy to the syrup and stir. Pour into the hot jars, dividing the cinnamon sticks and allspice berries between them. Screw on the lid and process in a waterbath following the hot-pack method for 30 minutes (see page 253). Allow to cool for 5 minutes, remove from the water with jar lifters, and cool to room temperature. Label and store in a cool, dark place for at least a month and up to a year.

RUMTOPF

I can remember my mother making this wonderful German concoction in an old crock. I love the fact that there is no set recipe and you can keep adding to the layers of fruit throughout the season, starting with the first strawberries of the year and continuing until the last blackberry is plucked from the brambles.

The key is to pick only perfect, just ripe fruit. However, some fruits work better than others. I would go for strawberries, raspberries, blackberries, blueberries, grapes, pears, peaches, nectarines, apricots, and cherries. Of the others I have tried, I found plums and apples become rubbery, bananas are too sweet, and melon is too watery.

METHOD You need approx. 2½ cups of sugar for every 2½lbs of fruit. Wash all the fruit gently and dry on a clean towel. Sterilize a large glass jar or ceramic casserole dish and put in the first layer of fruit—either a single variety or a mixture. Cover with a layer of sugar and pour in enough dark rum to cover the fruit by at least an inch, so none of it is sticking out. Put a lid on and set aside in a cool, dark place. As different fruits come into season, you can build up additional layers of fruit, sugar, and rum until your jar is full. Sample after 6 weeks or leave to mature for up to a year.

Once matured, the boozy fruit can be eaten as a potent dessert with cream, or you can drop individual berries into glasses and top them up with Prosecco for a Berry fizz. Alternatively mix into crumbles or pies. The flavored rum can be served in shot glasses or mixed with sparkling wine as an aperitif.

RUM PLUM COMPOTE

This idea was given to us by our friend, and home-brewing expert, Debi King. The compote doubles as a delicious sweet drink, best served in shot glasses, or a rich sauce to pour over ice cream. It could also be made with brandy or kirsch instead of the rum.

makes 6 x 1-cup jars
3½lbs plums
1¾ cups brown sugar
1¼ cups Amaretto
1¼ cups rum

Halve and pit the plums and put them in a large saucepan with the sugar. Set over low heat, stirring frequently to dissolve the sugar, and cook until the fruit is soft and pulpy, approx. 20 minutes. Push through a sieve into a clean bowl, discarding the skins. Put the puree into a saucepan and bring to a boil, stirring constantly. When bubbling, remove from the heat and add the alcohol. Stir and pour into hot sterilized jars. Put on the lids and process in a waterbath following the hot-pack method for 10 minutes (see page 253). Store in a cool, dark place for up to a year.

SLOE GIN

My favorite gin and tonic has now been supplanted by sloe gin and tonic, which has a pretty pink glow.

Sloes are the berries of the blackthorn tree, which have a bluish hue to them, making them look like small dark grapes. These grow commonly in the UK, but you can buy plants for your garden in the US, too, or you can buy berries at some farmers' markets. If you pick your own, watch out for the slender thorns on the tree, and never take all you can see—leave some for the birds. This year I got advice from Jared Brown from the artisan distillers Sipsmith, who makes excellent sloe gin. This is what he suggests.

Ideally pick the berries after the first frost, because this freezing tenderizes the skins. However, don't pick them before they are ripe. You can tell when they are ripe by gently squashing them between your fingers. If they are rock hard, leave them on the tree. If they ripen before the frost, pick them and put them into the freezer overnight. There is no need to prick the berries provided they have been frozen—either by the frost or in your freezer. A lightly crushed almond added to the bottle with the sloes gives a subtle marzipan flavor. Add the simple syrup to taste just before you want to drink the gin. This allows the natural flavors of the fruit to be extracted and developed by the alcohol alone, and will prevent the finished drink from becoming too sweet.

makes 2 x 1-quart bottles
1⅓lbs ripe sloes
1 quart gin
2 almonds, lightly crushed (optional)

For the simple syrup
1 cup sugar
1 cup water

Wash the fruit and dry between two clean towels. Unless the berries were picked after the first frost (see left), put them in a plastic bag in the freezer overnight.

The following day, take the fruit out of the freezer and let it defrost. Divide the berries between your sterilized jars and top up with the gin. Drop an almond into each jar (if using). Put on the lids and transfer the jars to a cool, dark place. Shake the bottles gently every other day for the first week, and then leave them alone for at least 3 months to mature.

After a year, you can strain out the sloes and discard them. You can then return the liquor to the same bottle to mature for several years before sampling; it will mellow with time.

Once you are ready to start drinking your sloe gin, prepare the simple syrup. Dissolve the sugar in the water in a saucepan over medium heat, then set aside to cool. Add the concentrated simple syrup to the bottle, little by little, stirring thoroughly and tasting regularly until you are happy with the sweetness—you may not need it all. Store in a cool, dark place for up to a year.

Variations
PLUM GIN

What a lovely tipple. On a freezing cold night in January, my father and I decided to sample all the liqueurs I had made. This was my favorite, and we both found it warming and welcome. It had so much flavor I didn't like to dilute it with tonic and ice, so instead I would recommend serving it in shot glasses.

METHOD Follow the recipe for Sloe gin, substituting plums for the sloes. Ignore the note about freezing the fruit.

BLACKBERRY GIN

This adds not only color, but also sweetness and a wonderful berry flavor to the gin.

METHOD Follow the recipe for Sloe gin (see left), substituting 10oz blackberries for the sloes and using 2 cups gin. Ignore the note about freezing the fruit. Make the simple syrup with ¾ cup sugar and ⅔ cup water.

SERVING SUGGESTION This is great for making a version of the cocktail called Bramble, which is usually made with blackberry liqueur. Just muddle some of the blackberries from the finished gin in a glass with a dash of lemon juice, add a large shot of the blackberry gin, a teaspoon of sugar, and some crushed ice. Garnish with a mint leaf and enjoy!

PLUM WHISKY

Chris Terry, our photographer on this book, gave this idea to me. During our big tasting nights, my father decided this was his favorite. He loved the strength of the whisky (I did use a single malt!), followed by the sweetness given by the sugar and plums—so we renamed it Papa's Medicine!

Top left: Blackberry gin; **Top right:** Plum whisky; **Bottom:** Sloe gin.

METHOD Follow the recipe for Sloe gin (see page 206), substituting 10oz plums and using 2 cups whisky (preferably single malt) instead of the gin. Ignore the note about freezing the fruit. Make the simple syrup with ¾ cup sugar and ⅔ cup water.

VIN D'ORANGE

Choose a dry white wine that you like to drink for this—don't be tempted to use a really cheap one or the result won't be as good.

makes approx. 2¼ quarts
4 oranges
2 bottles of white wine
2 cups vodka, eau de vie, or grappa
1 cinnamon stick
1⅔ cups confectioner's sugar

Wash the oranges well and cut into quarters, leaving the peel on. Put into a large, sterilized container or divide into several jars and pour over the wine. Add the remaining ingredients and stir to dissolve the sugar. Put a weight on top of the oranges to keep them under the level of the wine. Put on the lid(s) and leave in a cool, dark place for 2 weeks, stirring every other day.

Strain the liquor from the container and discard the oranges. Taste and add a little more sugar if you prefer it sweeter. Pour through a funnel into sterilized bottles and fit a cork into each. Store in the fridge for up to 6 months.

PINEAPPLE VODKA OR RUM

This can be used in cocktails or served with dessert. Serve pineapple vodka neat over crushed ice; pineapple rum makes a great cocktail mixed with simple syrup and coconut milk.

makes 2 x 1-quart jars
1 medium ripe pineapple (approx. 3lb)
1 quart vodka or white rum

Cut the pineapple into triangles, discarding the skin and core along with any black areas. Divide the pineapple pieces between the sterilized jars and pour in the vodka or white rum to cover. Put on the lids and set aside in a cool, dark place for a week.

Pour the contents of the jars into a blender and purée until smooth. Sweeten to taste with simple syrup, using a ratio of equal parts sugar to water (see Sloe gin, page 206). If you wish it to be clear, you can strain it through cheesecloth. Pour the sweetened purée into a cold sterilized bottle and store in the fridge until needed. It will keep for up to 3 weeks. Serve chilled in martini glasses.

Variations
WATERMELON VODKA

METHOD Remove the seeds and skin from a small watermelon and cut the flesh into chunks. Put the chunks into a large sterilized jar and top up with vodka. Put on a lid and set aside in a cool, dark place for 5 days.

After 5 days, strain through a fine sieve lined with cheesecloth, squeezing the juice from the melon chunks as you do so. Serve over crushed ice in martini glasses or use as a base for cocktails.

VODKA WATERMELON

Not exactly preserving, but this is good fun.

METHOD Make a hole in your watermelon the same size as a cork and pour in the contents of a bottle of vodka, little by little each day over a period of 5 days, blocking up the hole with a cork. To serve, either cut the boozy watermelon into wedges and enjoy as it is, or purée and strain the watermelon through a sieve lined with cheesecloth to collect the juices and serve as a drink over crushed ice.

CHILE VODKA

Surely the easiest recipe in the whole book. I love the herbiness and heat the chiles bring to the vodka, and we have had such fun drinking it. Our favorite way of serving it is in Pasta with hot smoked salmon, cream, and chile vodka (see page 172)—and to cut through the fat, we serve a shot of chile vodka on the side. It's a real ice-breaker, try it! Chile vodka also makes a wicked Bloody Mary.

METHOD Open a 2oz bottle of vodka, put in a whole red chile, screw on the lid and wait at least 6 weeks. Over time the chile will lose its color.

Right: Chile vodka and Pineapple rum.

fermenting

Fermentation is a really exciting area in the world of food. It has been practiced all over the world throughout history and has formed a valuable, if not essential, part of our diet for centuries. Georgians are reputed to have produced wine for up to 8,000 years, Babylonians have made fermented drinks since 5,000 BC and Egyptians started fermenting in 3,150 BC. In Japan, miso apparently existed during the Neolithic Age, and it has been used as a preservative and flavoring for generations. Miso is made by fermenting soybeans, rice, barley, or a mixture of soy and one of the other grains with the yeast mold known as *koji* and salt. We know that Roman soldiers existed on a diet of slowly fermented sourdough and apparently Inuits traditionally wrapped whole orks (seabirds) in sealskins and buried them underground. Months later they dug them up to eat the delicacy that was fermented bird... yum! We also know that early settlers carried sourdough starters across America, and Captain Cook's sailors took *sauerkraut* to sea to provide a vital source of vitamin C on long voyages.

You might think that we don't need these fermented foods any more, since we have refrigeration and greenhouses to provide us with fruit and vegetables all year round—and anyway, we have vitamin pills. And it is true that since industrialization, fermented foods have been on the decline. This is partly due to the fact that fermentation gives variable results and it is hard to produce fermented foods on a large scale. In order to make food safe and increase shelflife, it has become far easier for manufacturers to turn to other methods of food preservation such as pasteurization, canning, or using large amounts of vinegar and salt as a preservative. Today you can't just grab a jar of *sauerkraut* off the supermarket shelf and assume you are eating something really nutritious; it will most likely contain vinegar to get the typically acidic flavor and will have been pasteurized. If you really want to benefit from the health giving proportion of fermented foods, you will have to make them yourself.

Fermentation is exciting because it not only appears to have incredible health benefits, but also by fermenting everyday food we can bring really interesting flavors and textures into our diet.

how fermentation works

Fermentation works by encouraging certain good bacteria and fungi (including yeasts and molds) to flourish, outcompeting the bad ones that would normally cause spoilage. While all the other chapters in this book deal with killing or halting the development of microorganisms, this one sees us positively encouraging them. Food that has been fermented not only lasts longer, but this method also preserves most of the beneficial vitamins and enzymes.

For food to be fermented, it must contain carbohydrate or have it added in the form of sugar—say for Kombucha (see page 245). Micro-organisms such as yeasts, bacteria, and mold eat this carbohydrate and produce either lactic, ethyl, or acetic acid. These microorganisms could be in the form of an added culture, such as a small quantity of live yogurt being added to milk to make more yogurt, or they could be bacteria already present in the food or in the air around the food to kick off fermentation. The latter is known as wild fermentation, and this is the method used to make sauerkraut and sourdough starters.

health benefits of fermentation

We need certain bacteria to stay alive—in fact, we are made up of more bacteria than human cells—and most of these are found in our intestines. We know that these natural flora are easily upset by changes to our diet, illness, antibiotics, stress, and other factors. However, it is believed that certain fermented foods containing "good" bacteria can help with digestive recovery—and if our gut is healthy, it has a better chance of absorbing the nutrients in the foods we eat.

In recent years, nutritionists have identified that fermented foods have a beneficial effect on the bowel and can help treat "leaky gut syndrome," also known as intestinal hyperpermeability, a much hypothesized condition. Although science is lagging behind, it is believed that a whole raft of other illnesses, including autism, celiac disease, irritable bowel syndrome, and multiple sclerosis may be linked to damage to the gut lining. Probiotic foods such as kefir are thought to help repair this damage, allowing beneficial nutrients to be absorbed into the body.

Today, in the United States, fermentation is a buzzword that is sweeping the country like a fashion craze. According to American writer and "fermentation fetishist" Sandor Ellix Katz, author of *The Art of Fermentation*, almost every culture in the world originally had a fermented product in their diet that promoted good gut health. "In the normal scheme of things," he writes, "we'd never have to think twice about replenishing the bacteria that allow us to digest food. But since we're living with antibiotic drugs and chlorinated water and antibacterial soap and all these factors in our contemporary lives that I'd group together as a 'war on bacteria,' if we fail to replenish [good bacteria], we won't effectively get nutrients out of the food we're eating."

While most of us consume cheese, sauerkraut, and pickles, we usually eat pasteurized versions—or bastardized ones that use vinegar rather than the naturally occurring living solution produced by the foods themselves. The drawback of modern processing methods is they end up destroying the "live" content of our foods, which is why we end up having to substitute our diets with little bottles of probiotics containing strains of lactic-acid bacteria to counteract the imbalance. This shouldn't be necessary, as they should be present naturally in our diet.

While many people shy away from eating unpasteurized or fermented foods, they shouldn't be something to be scared of unless you are pregnant or suffering from ill health.

kefir

This fermented probiotic, enzyme-rich food is filled with friendly micro-organisms that promote gut health by feeding it good bacteria such as *Lactobacillus acidophilus.* These friendly bacteria inhibit the growth of harmful bacteria in the gut and, more specifically, they are thought to help with yeast infections, the poor health suffered after a course of antibiotics, and peptic ulcers.

Kefir is simple and inexpensive to make at home. The grains are thought to originate from the Caucasus Mountains—kefir is a popular drink throughout the Middle East and Russia—and you can buy them from some health food stores or online (see page 290). At home, we drink milk kefir on its own in small glasses or mix it with fruit such as mango in smoothies. I have given two recipes: water kefir and milk kefir; water kefir is made from small, transparent water kefir grains fermented in sweetened water, and milk kefir is made from milk kefir grains, which are cream-color and resemble cauliflower florets, fermented in milk.

A note of caution: do not let your kefir grains come into contact with reactive metals such as copper, brass, zinc, iron, or aluminum since they are acidic and can react with certain metals. To be on the safe side, use a plastic sieve and plastic utensils for making kefir.

WATER KEFIR

When I had my first glass of sparkling water kefir (see left), served over ice with a slice of lemon, my mind and body felt completely refreshed. I now have a pitcher fizzing quietly in the corner of my kitchen for when I feel exhausted or just need a little awakening.

Water kefir is a lightly sparkling probiotic drink that is refreshing, good for you, and economical to make. It is made with water kefir grains, a culture of bacteria and yeast, in sugary water. The basic recipe can be flavored with different herbs or fruit to produce different flavors (see Variations, below).

makes approx. 1 quart

Equipment
1 quart (or larger) glass jar with a lid
wooden or plastic spoon
plastic sieve
sterilized bottles for storage

Ingredients
⅓ cup sugar**
4 cups filtered, nonchlorinated water (leave boiled water to stand overnight to remove chlorine)
approx. 3oz water kefir grains (available online or from health food stores)
3 tablespoons organic raisins or other unsulfured dried fruit
juice of ½ organic lemon
1 thin slice of fresh ginger, peeled

** Do not use honey in place of sugar; honey has antimicrobial properties that will damage the water kefir grains or delay their proliferation.

Stir the sugar into the water in a clean glass jar using a nonmetal spoon. Add the kefir grains, raisins, lemon juice, and ginger and stir to combine.

Cover the jar loosely with a cloth or lid (don't tighten it at this stage) and set aside to ferment at room temperature for 24–72 hours, depending on the strength you prefer and the temperature of your home. The warmer your home, the faster the water kefir will brew. As the kefir ferments, it will take on a distinct and pleasant aroma that becomes more vinegary the longer you leave it. In time you will know what

it should smell like when it is ready for you. I don't like it too strong, so a couple of days is usually enough for me.

Strain the liquid through a sieve lined with cheesecloth and bottle into smaller containers. Save the grains for another batch, but discard the added fruit. Put on the lids, but don't tighten them at this stage, and set aside at room temperature for another 24–48 hours to complete the fermentation and produce natural carbonation. After this time, you can tighten the lids.

Store the kefir water in the fridge, where it will keep for up to 1 week. Serve cold with ice and a slice of lemon or lime, or add flavorings such as lemon juice, fruit juice, cucumber or mint.

Variations
Some people replace the ginger with fresh mint, star anise, or cardamom, while others substitute figs, mango, prunes, strawberries or dried cherries for the raisins for a lovely rosy-hued water kefir. Dried fruit can be left to

REUSING YOUR WATER KEFIR GRAINS

Once you have strained the grains, don't throw them away. Simply put them back into a clean jar and repeat the process. They can be used indefinitely.

If you need a break from tending to your grains—for example, if you are going on vacation—store in a small amount of the sugar/water mixture in the fridge for up to several weeks. Strain them when you come back to make a new batch of kefir.

infuse for a week, but fresh fruit should be changed daily. For best results, keep the fruit pieces large or put them into a cheesecloth bag so they are easy to remove and don't become tangled in the kefir grains.

milk kefir

Milk kefir is made with live kefir grains (available online or from health food stores—see page 290 for suppliers). It is more nutritious than yogurt and supplies protein, essential minerals, and valuable B vitamins. As a source of nourishment, it is good for all of us but particularly those with compromised immunity and bad gut health. It can be drunk on its own or mixed with fruit, such as mango or dates, and vanilla seeds for rich and delicious smoothies. Milk kefir can be used for any recipe that calls for yogurt; it is excellent in salad dressings, cucumber and mint raita, or frozen yogurt desserts.

Fellow fermentation enthusiast Sarah Moore gave my milk kefir grains to me. We transferred a small jar of these amazing grains from handbag to handbag over lunch. As soon as I was home, I put them into a clean jar and added milk—within days I was enjoying fresh kefir at home.

When you first receive your grains in their milk solution they will be hard to see, but they are there! After the first brew they will have grown in size and quantity. If cared for correctly, you will have a lifetime supply of kefir grains. A little goes a long way!

METHOD Put approx. 1 heaping tablespoon of live or dried milk kefir grains into a clean glass jar (a 2-cup or 1-quart jar is best). The quantity of grains doesn't matter—it will just take longer to ferment the milk with less. Fill the container with milk until it is two-thirds full. Cover the jar with a clean towel and put it in a closet at room temperature and out of direct sunlight. Set aside to stand for at least 24 hours (sometimes it can take 48–72 hours) or until it has separated and reached the desired sourness. Occasional rocking/stirring is helpful as it helps the grains absorb all the nutrients from the milk. As with many forms of fermentation, making kefir is not a precise science; many people find the kefir a little too sour once separation has occurred and prefer to bottle their kefir much faster. We use ours after just a day in the warmth of our kitchen.

To serve, strain the kefir through a nylon sieve into a clean jar and transfer it to the fridge to chill. (You can reuse the grains for another batch, see right.) If you want to make your kefir fizzy, place the strained liquor in a sealed bottle and set aside at room temperature for 1–2 days. This will make very sour, fizzy kefir.

REUSING YOUR MILK KEFIR GRAINS

Once you have strained the grains, don't throw them away. Simply put them back into a clean jar and repeat the process. They can be used indefinitely.

If you need a break from tending to your grains—for example, if you are going on vacation—put the grains in a jar with milk (as you would to make kefir), cover with a tight-fitting lid, and store in the fridge; the low temperature will slow down the fermentation process of the grains, causing them to go into a semi-dormant state. Every week or two, change the milk and drink the kefir that you have made in your fridge. Your grains may survive longer than this, so if you do neglect them for a time it's always worth trying to rejuvenate them before deciding you have killed them completely. Make a batch or two of kefir and see how they do.

YOGURT AND STRAINED YOGURT

We worked with cheesemaker Christine Ashby, who has been making yogurt and cheese for many years and teaches her passion to others. Making your own dairy produce is very rewarding because you are in control of its contents and you can tailor the recipes to the flavor and texture that you enjoy.

yogurt

Yogurt is derived from the Turkish word *yoğurt*, meaning coagulated milk. Pliny the elder, writing in Roman times, described how "barbarous nations" knew how to thicken milk into a substance of "agreeable acidity." The lactic acid produced by lactic bacteria in heated milk is what gives its tangy, slightly sour flavor. These same cultures give you the healthy dose of "live" probiotic bacteria known to balance the intestines.

Yogurt is versatile, usually low in fat, high in protein and calcium, and rich in vitamins B6 and B12. It is also inexpensive and easy to make. We know you can buy good yogurt easily, but somehow it tastes better made at home. Use the type of milk you like: cow, goat, or sheep milk work equally well.

CHRISTINE'S TOP TIPS FOR YOGURT-MAKING

Hygiene is critical; milk will support the growth of undesirable microorganisms. Make sure your surrounding area is clean and any equipment coming into contact with your yogurt or is sterilized. Put cheesecloth through the washing machine and dry properly; just before use, pour boiling water through the cloths in a sieve.

Milk We always prefer to use organic milk if available.

Temperature The area you work in must be warm, ideally above 70°F.

Heating the milk should be slow and involve indirect heat, if possible, e.g. using a double boiler, since excessive heating will damage the milk proteins. Giancarlo and I don't have a double boiler, but we do have very heavy-bottomed pans and an induction burner, both of which conduct the heat well.

The temperature of the milk is critical so it is worthwhile investing in a probe thermometer.

where to incubate your yogurt

Incubation of the yogurt can be done in a host of ways, and you don't need to rely on specialist equipment to keep it warm. For example, you could put covered jars of yogurt around a warm pot overnight, you could wrap the bowl in blankets, sit it in a low oven or inside an insulated cooler, or use a wide-mouthed thermos or electric blanket. My kitchen is pretty warm after an evening's cooking and although the temperature drops below 95°F, it does set the yogurt, albeit slowly.

THICK, CREAMY YOGURT

Traditional Greek or Turkish yogurt is made with sheep milk and it is strained afterward to thicken it. It has a strong flavor, which is great in cooking, but I prefer a version made with cow milk. Instead of straining it, you can add cream beforehand as we have done. To get ours started we used a starter culture bought from an online supplier, but you could add a previously made or store-bought live Greek yogurt. If you wish you could leave out the milk powder and make it with milk and cream alone, but it won't be as thick and creamy.

makes approx. 5lbs
2 quarts whole milk
⅔ cup heavy cream
¾ cup powdered skim milk
starter culture (available from cheese-making suppliers, see page 290)—follow the manufacturer's instructions for how much you need or 3 tablespoons live yogurt

Sterilize all your equipment either in an oven, see page 12, or with sterilizing liquid, following the instructions. Warm the milk and cream to 86°F in a large, heavy-bottomed saucepan, stirring constantly so that the mixture doesn't catch on the bottom. Remove from the heat and add the milk powder. Whisk thoroughly until well blended.

Return the pan to the burner and heat to 195°F, using a probe thermometer for accuracy. Stirring constantly, keep it at this temperature for 5 minutes. Remove the pan from the heat and cool to 110°F. The best way to do this is to put your pan in a sink of cool water and stir it constantly until the temperature drops. Add the starter culture and whisk for 5 minutes. Transfer the mixture to a sterilized bowl and cover with plastic wrap. Wrap the bowl up in a blanket and set aside in a warm place (ideally at 95°F) overnight. See the ideas, above left, on where to incubate your yogurt.

The following morning, the yogurt should be set and taste pleasantly sour. If it is still runny and not strong enough in flavor, set it aside for a bit longer. I often leave mine for another few hours to obtain a flavor that we enjoy. When you are happy with the set and the flavor, whisk the yogurt well to blend out any lumps. It should be smooth and glossy. At this point you can spoon it into small, clean plastic or glass containers or jars and transfer them to the fridge. You can also flavor the yogurt with fruit and sugar if you wish. We like to put fruit compote such as the Rhubarb and ginger jam (see page 57) at the bottom of a jar and top it up with yogurt. You can use a jam jar lid to seal it before storing in the fridge.

Our yogurt lasts for up to 3 weeks— if we haven't eaten it by then—but trust your nose and if it smells or tastes

YOGURT-MAKING EQUIPMENT

You don't need any specialist equipment to make yogurt; just make sure everything is scrupulously clean. Here is what you need:

thermometer, preferably a probe thermometer
saucepan
glass, plastic, or china bowl
some sort of warming devices (see opposite)
cloths to keep it warm or a large tea cozy
Sterilizing fluid to clean your equipment beforehand

unpleasant or has a fizzy sensation throw it away. Also discard it if any mold or fuzz appears on the surface. Only good yogurt should be used to start a new batch.

Variation

NATURAL YOGURT

This yogurt is lower in fat because there is no added cream. It is not as thick because there is no added skim milk powder. To make natural yogurt, follow the instructions above, omitting the cream and powdered milk.

Right: Strained yogurt—*labneh*— with chives and chive flowers.

STRAINED YOGURT— LABNEH

In the Middle East, yogurt is often strained to separate the curds from the whey, and the resulting yogurt is known as *labneh*. Depending on how long it is strained for and how much whey comes out it, *labneh* can be very thick but soft and creamy, or firmer like cream cheese. This is Anissa Helou's recipe for *Labneh bil-Zeyt*, a delicious way of preserving

strained yogurt under oil. You can enliven the taste of the *labneh* balls by flavoring the oil with red pepper flakes and/or sprigs of dried thyme. It is important that you mix in enough salt with the strained yogurt before shaping it into balls to preserve it.

Note: This recipe is made with store-bought yogurt, but you could use your own homemade yogurt (see page 220) made using cow, sheep, or goat milk.

makes 12-14 balls, approx. 1in in diameter

16oz container goat, sheep or cow milk yogurt (this will give approx. 5oz strained yogurt and approx. 5oz whey)
1 teaspoon fine sea salt
fresh or dried herbs
1 dried red chile (optional)
extra virgin olive oil

Place a clean cheesecloth in a sieve and pour boiling water over it to sterilize it. Lay the cheesecloth in a double layer over a sieve or colander and pour the yogurt into it. Gather the edges to make a pouch and tie with string. Hang the filled pouch over the sink, or anywhere else, over a receptacle to receive the draining liquid (whey); set aside to drain overnight (see photo on page 212).

The following day, scoop the strained yogurt into a bowl and beat in the salt—don't stint on the salt as you need it to preserve the yogurt. The whey can be used in place of water when making a sourdough starter (see page 225) or for fermented fruits (see page 234), or for making scones.

You can either eat the *labneh* as it is, mixed with some fresh herbs such as chives or thyme (leaves and flowers), or shape it into balls and store them under oil.

To make *labneh* balls, spread out a clean towel on a tray. Pinch off little pieces of strained yogurt and shape into balls the size of a small walnut. Arrange the balls on the cloth and set aside to dry at room temperature for 24–48 hours or until firm to the touch. Cover them with a fly net or drape some cheesecloth over the top, propped up on a few cans to allow the air to circulate underneath.

Once the balls are set, carefully pack them into a 1 quart sterilized glass jar and top up with extra virgin olive oil. Flavor the oil with a dried chile and

some sprigs of dried thyme if you wish, and seal the jar. Store in the fridge and eat after 3 days and before 1 month, making sure the balls are always covered with oil.

Variations

Mix the strained yogurt with salt and pepper, wrap the balls in wild garlic leaves and store in extra virgin olive oil, as before (see page 194).

Mix the strained yogurt with salt and crushed red pepper flakes before shaping into balls. Roll in sesame seeds and dry for a day in a warm room or until firm to the touch. Store in olive oil in the fridge for up to 3 weeks. To serve, crush gently and mix into lettuce or couscous salad.

CRÈME FRAÎCHE

This is absolutely delicious, better than anything you can buy from a supermarket and totally irresistible. I love crème fraîche with compotes or with a dollop of low-sugar jam. It is also creamy and luscious with chicken and a scattering of fresh tarragon.

Crème fraîche is produced in a similar manner to sour cream, although the end result has a higher fat content and is less sour in flavor. Made with cream and culture, crème fraîche remains stable when heated, which makes it ideal for adding to soups and sauces. This recipe is from our Scottish cheesemaker friend Katy Rodgers, whose beautiful old dairy we visited. She uses the farm's own milk to make this product, which is used in her popular café and tearoom in Stirlingshire, Scotland.

makes approx. 2¾lbs

1 cup whole milk
5 cups heavy cream
4 tablespoons powdered skim milk
1 heaping tablespoon live yogurt,
or the tip of a teaspoon of
crème fraîche starter culture,
or 3 tablespoons crème fraîche
from a previous batch

First sterilize all your equipment. Mix the milk with the cream and heat to 98°F in a large bowl set over a saucepan of gently simmering water—this way you can control the temperature more easily. Stir in the powdered milk to dissolve. Once the powder has dissolved, bring the mixture up to 175°F. Now place the bowl in a sink of cold water and cool it back down to 85°F. Whisk in the yogurt or starter culture (or some crème fraîche from a previous batch).

Pour the mixture into sterilized plastic or glass jars and transfer them to an incubator, low oven, or warm room for approx. 12 hours, or until the cream has set; the ideal temperature is 85°F, but as long as the temperature is between 65–85°F it will work. Find the warmest room in your house, or somewhere with underfloor heating. If the crème fraîche is not firm enough for your liking, it can be whipped thicker with an electric mixer. Put on the lids, cover and transfer the jars to the fridge for another 24 hours before use. Store in the fridge for up to 5 days.

To make a simple dressing, mix the crème fraîche with lemon juice or tarragon vinegar, a pinch of salt and sugar, and some chopped chives. The acidity cuts through oily fish such as salmon beautifully, see Hot smoked salmon on pages 171–172.

WHAT TO DO WITH YOUR YOGURT

Turn it into thicker-style yogurt by straining it; if it is really thick it can be rolled and flavored, and then preserved in oil and spices (see *Labneh*, left).

Mix it with the Tikka masala curry paste on pages 282–283 and use as a marinade for chicken.

Use it in smoothies (see page 286).

Enjoy as an accompaniment to smoked eggplant purée (see Moutabal, page 166).

Layer it up with sliced banana and raspberry jam as a dessert.

Mix it with chopped cucumber, a little sugar, finely chopped mint leaves, salt, and crushed toasted cumin seeds to form a raita to serve alongside Asian or Middle-Eastern dishes.

Blend it with fruit to form fruit yogurt: sweeten the fruit first with confectioner's sugar, and then push it through a sieve to form a purée before mixing in the yogurt. Alternatively, cook the fruit briefly in a saucepan on the stove or in a bowl in the microwave until the fruit has softened and the sugar has dissolved. Wait until it is cool before stirring in the yogurt. I like to leave mine not completely stirred in so you end up with bursts of sweet fruit mixed with tangy, creamy yogurt. For 4 cups yogurt, allow 7oz fruit and ¼ cup confectioner's sugar.

SOURDOUGH

I can't think of a single food that has more care and attention paid to it in its preservation than a natural yeast starter. You feed it, give it water, keep it warm, or help it cool, and generally cater to its every need, all to maintain it in peak condition for making loaves of sweet-smelling bread.

Immigrants to foreign countries were known to take their sourdough starters with them among their treasured possessions, so fearful were they of losing part of their heritage and way of life. Sourdough has a big following in the US, and there are known to be sourdough starters as old as 170 years. A starter is also known as a "mother," or *madre* in Italy.

We have given the recipe for a white, rye, or buckwheat starter. We use the rye and white versions regularly for making bread, but sourdough starters can also be used successfully in anything that requires baker's yeast, including pancakes and pizza bases. Our pancake recipe on page 228 is for Sri Lankan hoppers, but the starter also works well in ordinary pancake batter. If you leave the batter to ferment overnight, your pancakes will result in bubbling light versions with a pleasant acidity.

There are three stages to making sourdough bread: developing the starter, making the sponge, and finally making the dough.

flours

There are so many brands of flour—from mass-industrial suppliers to small artisan mills. I would stick to an organic one, particularly for the starter. I would also stick more or less to the same brand, especially at the beginning, since different brands give different results.

Once you are confident with the basic technique, you can start experimenting with new ingredients.

FIRST STAGE—MAKING THE STARTER

To make the starter, choose either white, rye, or buckwheat flour. In my experience, a rye or buckwheat flour starter is easier to make—and you can always feed a rye or buckwheat starter with white flour once it is started. Bear in mind that if you use a rye starter for white bread, you will end up with some flecks of dark flour in your loaf. Make sure your flour is organic so that the yeasts can grow easily, uninhibited by any chemicals.

Note that rye and buckwheat flours are more absorbent than white flour, so you may need more water than is stated. Whey can be added to help to get the fermentation going, but it is not essential.

For the starter
makes approx. 11oz
2¼ cups organic white flour, rye flour, or buckwheat flour
tepid water
2 teaspoons whey (optional)

STAGE ONE Combine ¾ cup flour and ¼ cup warm water in a bowl with the whey, using your hands and shape into a ball. Transfer to a medium (2-cup) jar. Close the lid and set aside in a warm place, out of direct sunlight, for up to 2 days. When the starter begins to crack on the surface and bubble underneath, which you will be able to see through the sides of the jar, move on to stage two.

Note: Fermenting times vary considerably depending on the weather. In warm weather your starter will begin to bubble within a day; in cold weather fermentation will be slower and could take a couple of days.

STAGE TWO Add ¾ cup flour and ⅓ cup water and stir through. Close the lid and set aside in a warm place, out of direct sunlight, for up to 2 days. When the starter is bubbling and approaching the top of the jar, go to the next stage.

STAGE THREE Discard half the mixture. Feed the remaining mixture with ¾ cup flour and ⅓–½ cup water (the higher amount is for rye or buckwheat starters). If you wish to turn a whole-wheat starter into a white one, this is a good time to do this, as the starter has become established. Close the lid and set aside in a warm place, out of direct sunlight, for up to 2 days.

STAGE FOUR By now your starter should be active, lively and bubbling, and the consistency should be that of a very thick batter. (A little more flour or water can be added to adjust this.) At this point, your starter can be transferred to the fridge in the closed jar to slow down fermentation until you are ready to use it. Note: if storing in the fridge, you will need to refresh your starter regularly (see page 226) to keep it alive.

A NOTE ON TEMPERATURE, TIMING, AND HUMIDITY

In warm weather your dough will rise more quickly, perhaps too quickly to develop the sour flavor we seek from sourdough. Therefore, in warm weather we recommend you put the dough in the fridge to rise more slowly. This also helps if you are getting tired and it's getting late as you can continue in the morning.

SECOND STAGE— MAKING THE SPONGE

The sponge is the next stage in making a sourdough loaf. This stage is best done in the evening before you go to bed so that it is ready in the morning. A Friday night works well for me. I bake on a Saturday late afternoon and have wonderful sourdough for that evening and the rest of the weekend, and then I freeze one loaf to enjoy midweek—that way, I am baking just once a week.

CARING FOR YOUR STARTER

You can keep your starter alive and kicking in the fridge indefinitely, or put it to sleep in the freezer for up to a year. If you make bread regularly (I bake once a week), it makes most sense to store your starter in the fridge. I always keep at least 10oz starter on standby in my fridge—this way I have 5oz for the sponge (see above) and some to keep going for another day. Even if you are not using it, you must keep feeding your starter with more flour and water at least once a week (preferably every 3–4 days) to keep it going. (I feed my starter a couple of days before baking so it is fresh and bubbling by the time I need it.)

Note that after your dough has been refreshed a couple of times in the fridge, its strength will increase. A young starter will often lack strength and structure to begin with, but after it has had time to mature it will take on a distinctive flavor.

5oz starter (see page 225)
1¼ cups white or whole-wheat flour
⅔ cup warm water

Place the ingredients in a large bowl and stir together with a spoon until well blended. Cover with plastic wrap and set aside overnight in a warm, draft-free place. After this time, your sponge should have doubled in size and the surface should be covered in bubbles—if it hasn't, give it longer. It should smell sweet but beery and slightly acidic.

Method to feed your starter

Assuming you have approx.10oz starter in your fridge, weigh out half of it and discard the other half (or use or freeze or give it to a friend). Mix in ¾ cup of flour and around ⅓ cup of water to give the consistency of a very thick batter.

What if you go on vacation?

If you go away, either feed your starter as above and store in the fridge for up to 2 weeks or transfer it to the freezer—I have frozen mine successfully before (for 2 years!) and once defrosted it smelled as sweet as the day I froze it. Alternatively, and this is perhaps the safest option, divide your starter into two and freeze half and store the other half in the fridge. You can then use some, discard some, and feed it again on your return home. If you find the starter collects a pool of gray water on the surface, pour this away and feed it regularly to refresh it. A strong alcoholic smell will dissipate with regular feeding, but if the starter has gone moldy it is best to throw it away and start again.

THIRD STAGE—MAKING THE BREAD

makes 2 loaves
For white dough
1lb sponge (see left)
4¾ cups organic white flour
1 heaping tablespoon fine salt
1½–1⅔ cups tepid water

For rye or whole-wheat dough
1lb sponge (see left)
4¾ cups flour, made from ⅔ organic whole-wheat and ⅓ rye flour
1 heaping tablespoon fine salt
1¾–2 cups tepid water

To make the dough, put the sponge, flour, and salt into a bowl, and pour in the water a little at a time. Mix to a soft, malleable (but not floppy) consistency using a plastic dough scraper. Turn out the dough onto a floured worksurface and knead for 7–10 minutes or until the dough bounces back to the touch. Transfer the dough to a plastic or glass bowl, cover with oiled plastic wrap or a towel, and set aside in a warm, draft-free place to rise for 2–4 hours or until doubled in size.

Meanwhile, prepare two proofing bowls or baskets. These should be approx. 5in high, 5in at the base and 9in across the top; it doesn't matter whether they are round or long but they should be suitable for a 1lb loaf. They could either be floured cane bread baskets, closely woven wicker baskets, linen-lined baskets, or ordinary mixing bowls or bread baskets lined with clean towels and dusted heavily with flour.

Turn out the dough onto a floured worksurface and knead again for a couple of minutes. Cut the dough in half and shape into two loaves, folding the edges into the center until you have a ball. Put them into your proofing baskets, smoothest side down and

scatter more flour over the surface. Cover with a towel and set aside in a warm, draft-free place until the loaves have doubled in size, have a rounded shape, and bubbles can be seen under the surface of the dough. In a warm house, this should take 2–6 hours. The timing is vague because making sourdough is never a precise science—brands of flour vary, and temperatures and humidity levels change constantly depending on the time of year—therefore, you will have to be the judge and decide when to bake your loaf. As a rule of thumb, if you press your finger lightly into the dough, it should return slowly and not spring back when it is ready. It takes a while to get this timing correct, but practice makes perfect, so be patient. If you run out of time and bake your bread too soon, don't worry; the flavor won't be as acidic, the characteristic holes won't be as large, and the texture won't be as moist as perfect sourdough, but it will taste fine. On the other hand, your sourdough will overrise if it is left too long in a warm house; the texture will become soft and lacking in structure.

Preheat the oven to 475°F. Turn an baking sheet upside down and put it in the middle of the oven—this will give you a smooth surface to slide your loaf onto. Place a second sheet the normal way up underneath it. Have half a kettle of hot water on standby. Five minutes before you are ready to bake, pour the hot water from the kettle into the bottom baking sheet and shut the door. (This will create the all-important steam that is needed for the perfect crust.) Carefully turn out your loaf from the basket upside down onto a floured wooden board. It might deflate very slightly at first, but it will soon bounce back when it goes in the oven. If the top is not fully covered in flour from the basket, sprinkle over some more. Slash the top of the loaf cleanly a couple

of times with a sharp serrated knife. This will allow the dough to expand easily. Repeat with the second loaf.

To bake your loaves, open the oven door and quickly transfer each loaf onto the hot baking sheet. If there is not room for two, just cook one at a time. Spray the oven and the loaf with water from a spray bottle and close the door quickly to keep in the heat. After 10 minutes, turn the oven down to 425°F and bake for another 30–35 minutes or until the crust is dark brown. Remove your loaves from the oven—they should feel light, not dense, when you pick them up. Set aside to cool on a wire rack so they don't sweat underneath.

Variations
PINK SOURDOUGH AND PIZZA
Sourdough specialist Emmanuel Hajiandreou bakes deep pink loaves, by adding grated raw beets to the dough at the third stage (roughly 1½ cups to 1 loaf of dough—double if you're making two loaves). The same can be done with parsnip and celeriac. You can also use some of your dried produce to flavor your bread, such as oregano, rosemary, onions, porcini mushrooms, apples or dill, nigella, and poppy seeds. The dough can also be used for wonderfully flavored pizza bases. Use half "00" at the third stage. Each 7oz of dough will make one pizza. Use your favorite toppings and bake at your oven's hottest temperature for 7–10 minutes.

SOURDOUGH HOPPERS

Hoppers are Sri Lankan pancakes known locally as *appa*. They are made from a fermented batter of rice flour, coconut milk, and a little yeast. The yeast helps to ferment them and gives them their characteristic slightly sour flavor. We make our hoppers using the sourdough

starter on page 225 (although you could use baker's yeast). Hoppers are traditionally made in a small domed pan (see page 290 for suppliers). However, I have tried the same mixture in my crêpe pan with great success.

makes 16–20
3 cups rice flour
2 teaspoons palm or white sugar
4oz sourdough starter or a pinch of baker's yeast (approx. ½oz)
2½ cups tepid water
approx. ¾ cup coconut milk
1 teaspoon salt
a few teaspoons of sunflower oil, for frying
eggs (optional)
salt and pepper (optional)

Combine the flour, sugar, starter (or yeast), and water in a large bowl. Pour in the coconut milk a little at a time and whisk to a loose pancake batter. Cover the bowl with a towel and set aside to ferment at room temperature for 6–8 hours. When the surface is covered with bubbles and the mixture has almost doubled in size, it is ready to use. Add the salt and stir well to combine.

Heat a little oil in a pan and wipe it over with paper towels to achieve just a thin film. The pan should be hot but not smoking hot when you pour in the batter or it will cook too quickly and not move around in the pan. Drop a ladleful of batter into the pan and swirl it around to cover halfway up the sides. (If you would like an egg in it, crack it in now followed by a little salt and pepper.) Keep the pan over medium heat and put the lid on. Cook for just a few minutes or until the pancake is golden brown around the edges and cooked through in the center. Slide it out with the help of a spatula onto a plate and serve immediately or set aside while you cook the rest.

LACTO-FERMENTED VEGETABLES

There is a dispute as to which came first, kimchi or sauerkraut, but in fact the earliest recorded details of fermented cabbage exist in China. It is thought that the workers were given kimchi to eat during the construction of the Great Wall. Kimchi is regarded so highly in Korea that employers give out a grant to their employees to make their own supply. It preserves tradition and keeps their workforce healthy. Fermentation pits for preserving tropical fruit have been used in Fiji for centuries and traditionally a prospective husband's pits would be inspected by the bride's parents before the couple were allowed to marry.

Vegetables and fruit mixed and left with salt will begin a process called lacto-fermentation (see Salted kumquats and lemons on pages 88–89). Sauerkraut and kimchi are traditionally made from cabbage, but this method of fermentation is suitable for preserving almost any vegetable or fruit. Salt physically draws out water from the produce to make a brine. This brine is so concentrated that harmful bacteria cannot survive in it, but many beneficial bacteria thrive in these conditions—which is why sauerkraut and kimchi are so good for you. Lacto-fermented foods are higher in vitamin C than their unfermented counterparts.

containers

Our German friends kindly brought us a huge sauerkraut vat on their last visit. The smooth, straight, shiny insides make it easy to push the weights that came with it down onto the food to keep it submerged in the brine. It has a cleverly designed lid to allow a small amount of gas to come out and a rim that is filled with water to stop insects from getting in. If you aren't lucky enough to own such a vat, you could use a large glass jar with a rubber seal or a nonreactive lid.

Note: Avoid using metal containers or utensils because the acids produced by the fermentation process could react with them. Cover your containers with vinegar-proofed lids since ordinary lids will corrode.

cleaning and preparation

As with all methods of preservation, hygiene is important. I wash my jars and vats in the dishwasher or with very hot soapy water, rinse them thoroughly with water to dispel any soapy aromas and then allow them to cool and dry upside down on a clean rack. Avoid using chemical sterilizers that might leave traces in the jars, as you don't want to destroy all the good bacteria you are actively trying to encourage.

weights

These are essential to keep your vegetables fully submerged in the brine solution, or molds will be able to grow and your kraut will rot. A plastic bag filled with brine works—the reason I suggest filling it with brine, rather than water, is in case the bag leaks. Alternatively, a small sterilized rock works well. You can collect various sizes on a trip to the beach, scrub them well with hot soapy water, then boil them for 30 minutes in a saucepan of water and dry them out before use. An upturned plastic lid (with holes bored into it) or a glass jar smaller than the diameter of the opening of your jar will also help to keep the vegetables or fruits submerged and not trap air underneath. Boil it in hot water for 10 minutes then cool before use.

troubleshooting

SCUM A thin white scum of mold can sometimes appear on the surface of your fermenting fruit or vegetables. If it has only just appeared, and it is very thin, you can simply stir it back in. However, if there is fuzzy or colored mold on the surface, you should discard the batch and start again.

AROMA Lacto-fermented foods should have a clean, slightly sour smell. Discard any that are cloudy or smell "off" and unpleasant. Trust your nose.

GAS Be aware that gases can build up during the fermentation process and these need to be released from time to time. Ferments are living things that cannot be ignored!

BRINE Your produce should be fully submerged in brine at all times. If necessary, top it up with fresh brine to keep it undercover. It is especially important to keep an eye on the brine in cold weather when the vegetables will produce less juice.

WHEN TO EAT This is up to you. Many people really enjoy the fizziness of fermented fruit and vegetables, while others prefer to put the ferments into the fridge after a few days to limit this occurring.

SAUERKRAUT

Roman writer Pliny the Elder wrote about sauerkraut, and apparently Julius Caesar was fond of pickles. Popular in Germany and most of Eastern Europe, sauerkraut can be made from white cabbage alone or red and white cabbage, carrots, and garlic. Traditionally many people eat sauerkraut with hot dogs, sausages and corned beef, but it is also lovely mixed into a salad with grated carrot, olive oil, and walnuts, in coleslaw, stir-fries, combined with batter to make into pancakes, or used to fill spring rolls or Polish dumplings.

makes 1 quart
2lbs organic white or red (or mixed) hard cabbage
1 heaping tablespoon fine salt

For the brine
4 tablespoons salt dissolved in 4 cups filtered water

Discard the outer cabbage leaves if they are very damaged. Cut the cabbage into quarters from tip to root, and cut out and discard the hard core in the center. Shred the cabbage either using the grating disk on a food processor or by hand. Place the cabbage and salt in a large bowl and mix together thoroughly with your hands. Squeeze the cabbage quite hard as you mix to encourage it to start weeping; keep going until all of it has been squeezed.

Transfer the cabbage into a vat or clean jar and pour in the juices from the bowl. Push the cabbage down well with another smaller jar or a potato masher to expel most of the air inside. Add a weight on top so that the vegetables are completely submerged in the liquid. If they aren't fully covered, top up the jar with some of the fresh brine, making sure you leave an inch of headroom to allow the cabbage to expand as it ferments. Close the lid and set aside at room temperature for a week. Check on your sauerkraut daily: skim off any scum that forms on the surface and push down the vegetables so they remain below the line of the brine.

You will notice some bubbling occurring as the fermentation gets underway. When this has died down,

after a few days, your sauerkraut is ready to eat. You can either enjoy it young, fresh, and crisp after about 5 days or leave it to mature for longer, when it will become more sour in flavor and softer in texture. Store in a cool, dark place (under 60°F is ideal). For maximum health benefits, do not heat the sauerkraut but enjoy it raw.

Variations
Mix in some grated onion, carrot, garlic, or celeriac, or flavor with a teaspoon of caraway, cumin, or fennel seeds or some juniper berries. Probably my favorite way to serve sauerkraut is mixed with apple pieces and seasoned with freshly ground black pepper.

CUCUMBERS IN BRINE

One of the easiest and most satisfying of the fermented vegetables has to be pickled cucumbers. Vinegary versions are available everywhere and you can make them as described on page 21, but they won't have the fermentation health benefits of this recipe. Here they are made from cucumbers, salt, and water. If you want a little more acidity and a vinegary taste you can add 2 tablespoons of cider vinegar but no more as it will halt the process of the lactic-acid producing bacteria that you are trying to encourage.

How to keep the crisp snap of a pickled cucumber is a subject of endless debate among pickling enthusiasts. Some use leaves, others believe the addition of a few carrot sticks helps, and others swear by blanching the cucumbers briefly first. I believe mine are better if small, left whole, and moved to the fridge as soon as fermentation has started.

Typical flavorings such as dill, garlic, chile, or pickling spices such as mustard seeds and caraway can be added as you wish. Depending on the size of your cucumbers, you can choose your container accordingly. Little cucumbers fit into short, squat, tubby jars, and long ones fit into tall jars. I use a 6-cup jar for five cucumbers measuring around 7in. Water for fermenting should not be chlorinated so leave tap water to stand overnight for the chlorine to evaporate. Alternatively use bottled or filtered water.

makes 6 cups
approx. 1½lbs small cucumbers
2 tablespoons fine sea salt
4 cups cold, non-chlorinated water
a small handful of dill
1 tablespoon pickling spice
2 garlic cloves
1 horseradish or grape leaf or a few
  oak leaves (optional)

Wash the cucumbers in cold water, being careful not to bruise them. Remove any blossoms from the end but try not to pierce the skin. Make up the brine by stirring the salt into the water. Put the cucumbers into your very clean container and pour in the brine, followed by the flavorings and leaves if using. Put a weight over the cucumbers to keep them submerged under the brine. Fasten the lid, making sure the rubber seal is present, and leave at room temperature for up to 7 days. Sunlight, if you are lucky enough to have any, helps keep the mold at bay through the ultraviolet rays. Release the pressure by opening the lid at least once a day. When you are happy with the taste and texture of the cucumbers move them to the fridge or a cool room below 60°F and consume within a few months.

Variation
PICKLED CARROTS WITH CARDAMOM

Most vegetables can be fermented in this way with varying results. Do the same with carrot sticks and flavor them with crushed cardamom pods.

KIMCHI

This hot and spicy delight is usually served with Korean, and more recently Vietnamese, meals. That doesn't mean it is only good served alongside spicy food. We love it with barbecues, roast pork, or grilled chicken and fish. The juice can be poured out and used in place of hot sauce, such as Tabasco, on oysters or to spice up a Bloody Mary.

makes approx. 4lbs

8 cups cold water
½ cup fine salt
4½lbs mixed vegetables, such as carrots, bok choy, scallions, green beans, cabbages, peppers, daikon, snow peas
3 garlic cloves, peeled and roughly chopped
3 tablespoons chopped fresh ginger
1½oz Korean red pepper powder (available from Asian shops)
2 teaspoons sugar (optional)

Make up the brine by mixing the water with the salt. Wash, peel if necessary, and cut all of the vegetables into bite-sized pieces. Put them into a bowl with the garlic and brine solution and mix thoroughly with clean hands. Weigh the vegetables down with a clean plate, so they are fully submerged in the brine solution, and cover with a cloth. Set aside at room temperature for at least 6 hours or overnight if possible.

Drain the vegetables through a colander, reserving the brine, and taste. If they taste too salty, rinse them in very cold, nonchlorinated water; if they taste to your liking there is no need to rinse them. If they are not salty enough, mix in a little more salt (up to a couple of teaspoons should be sufficient).

Combine the ginger, red pepper powder, and sugar (if using) in a bowl. Add a little of the brine and mix to a smooth paste. Combine this mixture with the vegetables and mix thoroughly with clean hands.

Pack the vegetables into large jars and press down thoroughly with a wooden rolling pin. If there is still space at the top of the jar, add some more vegetables and squeeze down again. Top up the jars with some of the reserved brine so that the vegetables are fully submerged, leaving an inch of headroom to allow for expansion. Put on the lids and store in your kitchen for a few days and up to a week. Taste the kimchi every day and push the vegetables back down with clean fingers so they are totally submerged in the brine; if necessary, weigh the vegetables down. Once the kimchi has stopped fizzing, and if you are happy with the flavor, move it to the fridge or a cool room below 60°F where it will keep for several months. Traditionally kimchi is stored buried in the ground to keep it cool or in a cellar to last throughout the winter.

HAKUSAI NO TSUKEMONO, OR JAPANESE PICKLED CABBAGE

This is similar to the sauerkraut and kimchi recipes in that cabbage, in this case Chinese long cabbage, is the main vegetable of choice. Kombu is dried seaweed, which gives a particular flavor to the cabbage, but if you can't find it, leave it out. A yuzu is a citrus-scented fruit, like an intense limy lemon. Use a lemon if you can't find them in Asian shops. *Tsukemono* are good to eat on their own, as a side dish to fried foods or with rice and spicy dishes.

makes 1 pickled cabbage

1 Chinese Napa cabbage
1 tablespoon fine sea salt
4 scallions, roughly chopped
juice of one yuzu or a lemon
1 tablespoon fermented soy sauce
8in dried kombu, cut into finger widths (optional)
1 teaspoon red pepper flakes

Pull away the outer leaves of the cabbage and reserve for later. Cut away the hard core from the end and then slice the cabbage lengthwise into quarters. Now put the cabbage onto a baking sheet and put into sunlight or the warmest part of your house. Leave for about 5 hours in sunshine or overnight if no sun. This will concentrate the flavor of the cabbage and make it sweeter.

Meanwhile find a container that will hold the cabbage; I use a rectangular plastic container with a lid. I can fit a smaller one inside it that I fill with water to act as a weight. The Japanese have pickling pots called *tsukemonoki* with screw-down lids that are perfect for this.

Sprinkle the cabbage quarters with the salt over the container so that any surplus drops inside. Layer the cabbage with the remaining ingredients and then put the weight on top. Cover the container and leave at room temperature for up to a week. When the juices run from the cabbage, push the weight down to make sure that they are submerged. If there is not enough juice, add brine (using the Kimchi recipe left) to cover them. Turn the cabbages a couple of times to make sure the flavorings and salty brine are equally distributed. When you are happy with the flavor, transfer to the fridge and consume within a month.

LACTO-FERMENTED FRUITS

This is a new and exciting world for us. Before writing this book and reading about fermented foods, I would have instantly thrown away fizzy or bubbly foods. Yet having read books by Sandor Ellix Katz and Sally Fellon and fermenting bloggers' experiments I have understood this whole neglected world so much more. Over recent months I have begun to ferment peaches, apples, and grapes and have loved the results. Fruit ferments quickly, as we know from leaving fruit bowls untouched for days. By adding a small amount of salt to chopped fruit, you can encourage the good bacteria to do their job of breaking down the fruit and offering us a store of *Lactobacillus acidophilus* to consume, not to mention new flavors and textures to enjoy. For a midmorning snack, I now open my jar of fermented peaches with grapes and vanilla and enjoy a few tablespoons of it with natural live yogurt. It is filling and satisfying and a healthy alternative to the wheat-based snacks that I would normally turn to.

PEACH, GRAPE, AND VANILLA CHUTNEY

This is a naturally sweet and delightful mixture of fruits that are fermented to make a healthy chutney that can be kept in the fridge. The fermentation can be hastened by the addition of a small quantity of whey (see page 222). Depending on the sweetness of the fruit and your taste, the added sugar is optional. However, don't be tempted to add honey instead as its antibacterial qualities are not what we need in this case. The salt encourages the healthy bacteria—you can use fine sea salt or the citrus salt from Salted kumquats or lemons (see pages 88–89). Once made, this recipe makes a quick dessert or breakfast with yogurt, or it can be used as a chutney to enjoy with cold meats, cheeses and bread.

makes around 2lbs, you will need a 2-lb Kilner jar

- 1½lbs soft fruit such as peaches, plums, nectarines
- 4oz seedless grapes, or raisins or golden raisins (optional)
- 1 tablespoon light brown sugar (optional)
- 2in cinnamon stick
- 1 vanilla pod, split lengthwise in two, or ½ teaspoon of organic vanilla extract
- ¼ cup whey (optional)
- finely grated rind and juice of 1 lemon or 2 limes
- 1 level teaspoon fine salt or 1 heaping teaspoon finely chopped Salted kumquats or lemons (see pages 88–89)

Wash and prepare the fruit, discarding the pits but keeping the skins on the fruit. Chop into bite-sized pieces. Mix all the ingredients together in a bowl. Pack into a sterilized and cooled jar allowing an inch of headroom. Push the fruit down under the juice with a plastic spoon or wooden rolling pin. If the juice doesn't cover it, add a little nonchlorinated water to make sure it is submerged. Add a weight to make sure the fruit stays down. Close the lid tightly and stand in a warm place out of direct sunlight. It should start to bubble as it ferments. Leave for 2–3 days, lifting the lid daily to allow any gases to escape. When you are happy with the taste (it should be slightly sour and may have some fizziness), transfer the jar to the fridge where it will keep for up to a month. It will keep slowly fermenting and continue to soften in the fridge and may become fizzy and smell of alcohol. All of these effects are fine—simply eat it how you like it.

FERMENTED TOMATOES

This is a very simple way of preserving the wonderful sweet tomatoes we get at the end of summer. In this way they hold their texture and flavor for up to a year. You need to be brave and persevere through the initial aroma and fizziness but it is really interesting to watch the transformation they undergo. They can be used in cooking for tomato sauce, soups, and casseroles, or to preserve their goodness, use them raw in salsa.

makes approx. 5½lbs

- 5½lbs organic, flavorful tomatoes (can be a mix of round and cherry)
- 2 level tablespoons salt
- 1–2 cups nonchlorinated or filtered water
- extra virgin olive oil

Wash the tomatoes and cut roughly into bite-sized pieces, discarding any hard cores and the part where they were attached to the stems. Put them into a clean jar or large nonreactive bowl. Mix the salt with 1 cup of water and pour this over the tomatoes, using clean hands to combine. Push the tomatoes down, releasing their juice and making sure they are covered with water. Top up with more water if necessary. Cover the jar with a clean towel or cheesecloth so that the tomatoes can breathe but insects can't join them.

Leave in a warm place out of direct sunlight for a few days. The tomatoes might begin to smell awful, yes, awful! (This doesn't always happen; some batches ferment quickly in warmer

weather and don't go through this.)
However, you must stir them through
at least twice a day, preferably three
or four times. There should be small
bubbles as the fermentation takes
place. Watch for a surface film of white
mold—this should be stirred in if very
thin or removed if thick. If you see
green or black mold, discard the batch
and start again.

After two or three days, the aroma
will change to a really pleasant fresh
smell and any bubbling will dissipate.
Wait until the good aroma has been
there a day and there are no obvious
bubbles. Be brave and taste your
tomatoes—you will be surprised how
they taste as if just picked and cut. If
they smell, taste, and look good with
no evidence of fizzing, they are ready
to bottle. The process so far should
have taken about 4–5 days depending
on the temperature around them. Ladle
the tomatoes into clean jars, leaving
an inch of headroom. Put the lids on
but do not tighten them. This way you
will stop insects getting in but let any
gases out. Leave for a couple of days
in a cool, dark place below 60°F until
you are sure the bubbling has stopped.
Now pour a layer of oil approx. ½in
thick over the surface and close the
lids. Keep an eye on the jars for the first
week, loosening the lids every so often
to allow any gases to escape, then close.
The tomatoes can be left like this for
up to a year.

ALCOHOLIC DRINKS

The pleasures of alcohol have been enjoyed since our hairy ancestors realized that eating fermented fruit from trees made them giggle. Since then almost every culture has perfected the art of fermenting fruit into alcohol. My early experiences of making wine date back to when I was a student, when I used to make it for parties from packs bought at the local pharmacy. I hadn't touched winemaking again until last year, but now I am really hooked. At home we take lots of pleasure in the "country wines" we produce—the sort you make simply from foraged or homegrown produce such as plums and raspberries. Crushing fruits with a meat tenderizer or your hands and dealing with large amounts of bubbling berries in a plastic vat is lots of fun. We love to watch the yeast become activated and the smell is incredible. Our plum wine is rich, full-bodied, and delicious. Our elderflower champagne was ready for popping at New Year, and we discovered its sweet perfume went perfectly with our rich orange trifle on New Year's Day.

What we cover in this chapter is very much at entry level into winemaking. If you like what you make, read C. J. J. Berry's brilliant book, *First Steps in Winemaking*, and Andy Hamilton's books for many other wonderful recipes. To help us on our way into winemaking, I have enjoyed the help of friend Debi King who has been making wine for years, and Doctor Maslin who is also an eager winemaker. We haven't touched on grape wines or beermaking in this chapter, as they should really go in a book by themselves because there is so much to write about and we don't grow our own grapes.

ingredients

FRUIT

Most fruits, edible flowers, and some vegetables can be used to make wine with the addition of sugar, yeast, and yeast nutrients.

YEAST

Wine is made from fruit, which is crushed and allowed to ferment with the addition of yeast. The process of fermentation converts the sugar in the fruit to alcohol. By adding a carefully chosen yeast, the winemaker can control which yeast forms. (The natural yeasts that are present on the skins of the fruit or in the air are impossible to control and don't provide a reliable method of winemaking.) Alcohol is the by-product of the yeast's reproduction, which begins to happen as soon as the yeast is put into the right conditions for it to thrive.

SUGAR

Like any other living organism, yeast needs warmth, liquid, and food to survive—so the sugary solution made by crushed grapes that are full of natural glucose is ideal. The sugar is converted approx. half into alcohol by weight and half into bubbles of carbon dioxide. Professional winemakers working with grapes are not allowed to add sugar (since there is enough in the grapes), but for country wines it is nearly always added—which is why country wines can be made from fruits that are low in sugar.

Any golden or brown sugar will affect the color and, less so, the flavor of the wine—so some people choose this to improve the appearance of their wines. Granulated, beet, or cane sugar give the same result, so the choice is yours. C. J. J. Berry recommends "when starting a wine off it is always better to use little sugar rather than too

much, because dry wine can always be sweetened, but there is little you can really do about a wine which is oversweet, other than blend it with a dry one of the same type."

Sugar is often added in stages to boost the activity of yeast when it drops. You can calculate the amount of sugar to add using a hydrometer (see right); consult specialist wine-making books and online charts to find out more. We had to add more sugar to our plum wine to get the fermentation going again after it slowed down; this was because the fruit was not sweet enough that season. This secondary dose of sugar boosted the flavor and strength.

YEAST NUTRIENT

This additive will give the yeast a much-needed boost. As we have said before, pure grape juice provides all the elements yeast needs to thrive, but when other fruits are used, a nutrient is required to provide the correct doses of nitrogen and phosphate. It also enables the yeast to work for longer so that more of the sugar is turned into alcohol, which is a great help in the production of dry wines. It is less important for fruit wines but more important for flower wines, which have less "substance" for the yeast to thrive on.

PECTIC ENZYME

This is needed for fruit and vegetables that are naturally high in pectin, such as plums and parsnips. It speeds up the breakdown of the fruit and ensures a clear wine. If using pectic enzyme add it to the fruit when it is cool, 24 hours before the yeast.

CAMPDEN TABLETS

These are used to kill off any naturally occurring yeasts on the fruit before you add the wine yeast to your brew. This way, only your chosen yeast will be the one that reproduces. Campden tablets are also used at the end, after fermentation has finished, to kill the added yeast so as to avoid unwanted secondary fermentation in the bottle. Some winemakers do not like to add them as they contain sulfites.

equipment

You will need a fermentation bucket, a probe thermometer, a wine-straining bag, a funnel, a length of plastic tubing, a long-handled plastic spoon, a wine strainer or strong large sieve, some demijohns, bungs with fermentation traps (see below), bottles, corks, and a cork fitter. You will also need a room thermometer to work out the best place to ferment your brew (see page 239). Thermometer strips are also useful for monitoring the temperature of your individual demijohns or bottles. A hydrometer isn't essential but it is helpful for determining the amount of sugar in the liquid, from which you can also discover the alcohol content. For wine-making suppliers, see page 290.

STERILIZING EQUIPMENT

Specialist sterilizers are available from home-brewing suppliers, however I have used both Campden tablets and Milton fluid with success. Make up the sterilizing solution in your fermenting bucket and put in all the equipment you will need, including the long plastic spoon and a sieve if necessary.

UNWANTED VISITORS AND FERMENTATION TRAPS

A visiting fruit or vinegar fly will more than likely cause your wine to turn to vinegar. These annoying flies appear as soon as fruit begins to overripen. This is where the name *vinaigre* comes from in French, meaning "sour wine."

To prevent unwanted visitors, always make sure your wine is covered. In the first stage this could be with a cloth or plastic lid. In the second stage you will need an airlock or fermentation trap to prevent flies and bacteria from contaminating your wine; these also control the air supply to the yeast and allow carbon dioxide to escape. Airlocks are controlled by a small amount of water filling the U-bend of the trap. A good tip is to place a piece of crushed Campden tablet into

this water so that if a fly does enter, it cannot contaminate the water, which occasionally drips into the wine when the trap is removed. Alternatively a small cotton ball stuffed into the top of the trap will prevent flies from entering.

After fitting the trap and adding the water to it, you will see and hear bubbles of carbon dioxide coming through it. It is a delightful sound and sight and will continue for some months as fermentation progresses.

fermentation

Fermentation occurs in two stages. The first, lasting up to 6 days, is aerobic (with air) and is usually frothy and obvious. The second, which can go on for months, is anaerobic (without air); it is subtle and often barely visible. As the process of fermentation continues the alcohol content rises, usually stopping approx. 15–16 percent. At this point the yeast cannot reproduce in such an environment. This means that any leftover sugar that hasn't been converted into alcohol will remain.

temperature

Temperature is crucial for the yeast to work efficiently, and at the right pace, to ensure a good flavor to the wine. At temperatures above 100°F the yeast will die; too cold and it will reproduce very slowly or not at all. Fermentation should begin within the first few days when the fruit and yeast are held at 70°F. I have found our kitchen to be the perfect environment for stage one, and it means the vat is in front of me so I remember to check on it regularly. During the second stage of fermentation, the wine should be held at about 60°F. My garage is ideal for this, providing the wine is stored off the floor and away from the draft by the door. As a rule of thumb, fermentation that takes place slowly produces better wine than wines produced in a hurry. Your finished wine should be kept at a fairly constant 50–55°F.

racking

Wines often remain cloudy in their first few months due to the yeast suspended in them. However, after time, the solids sink to the bottom to form a thick, brownish visible layer and clear wine above. This is when you are ready to rack. Racking involves siphoning off your wine from the demijohn, leaving the lees (the sediment from the yeast) behind, and putting it into new demijohns or bottles.

bottling

It is essential you use clean sterile bottles for bottling. Either buy new ones or thoroughly clean old wine bottles. Never be tempted to use bottles that have had another strong flavor inside; it will spoil the flavor of your finished wine. Some people prefer not to bottle their wine and instead leave it in the demijohns with their safety bungs in place (in case it starts to re-ferment). They can then pull it off at the last minute into a bottle or decanter, thereby avoiding the stage of sterilizing bottles, corking and labeling.

MAKING WINE FROM FRUIT AND FLOWERS

It is wise to understand a few basics before you embark on fermenting your fruit. Here is the process in a nutshell:

1) Extract the flavors by pressing, soaking, or boiling.

2) Add sugar and yeast, plus nutrients/citric acid/pectic enzyme depending on the type of fruit or flower.

3) Set aside to ferment in a bucket in a warm place (68–77ºF) for up to 10 days.

4) Strain off. Put the resulting liquid into a fermentation container with a fermentation trap (to let the carbon dioxide out and nothing else back in).

5) Set aside to ferment in a cooler place (60ºF) until bubbling ceases.

6) "Rack" several times (i.e. siphon off the wine, discarding the yeast debris, or lees). Return the wine each time to a fermenting container with a fermentation trap until fermentation is over. After this time, the wine can be safely bottled without exploding; this usually takes place after approx. 6 months.

DOCTOR MASLIN'S PLUM WINE

This recipe is based on C. J. J. Berry's recipe for plum wine from his book *First Steps in Winemaking*; he describes it as "a beautiful, satisfying wine." Doctor Maslin, a homemade wine enthusiast, advises that you taste the plums for sweetness first. The good doctor is lucky enough to have a damson plum tree in his garden, and so he can choose precisely the right moment when the fruit is ripe enough to use without having to compensate by adding lots of sugar. Our fruit was quite unripe, as the season had not been a good one, so we added sugar to the demijohns later to get the fermentation going once it had slowed down (see page 239).

makes 9 quarts

10–11lbs firm, ripe damson plums, if available, or small red or black plums (the higher amount for good body)
Campden tablets (optional, see pages 236–237)
6½–7lbs sugar, depending on the sweetness of the plums
12½ quarts boiling water
pectic enzyme (pectolase)—refer to the manufacturer's instructions for quantity needed
cooled, boiled water
burgundy or red wine yeast—refer to the manufacturer's instructions for quantity needed
yeast nutrient—refer to the manufacturer's instructions for quantity needed

Pick through the fruit, discarding any rotten plums along with the stems and leaves. Wash the fruit in cold water and put into a sterilized fermentation bucket. Add the crushed Campden tablet (if using). Using a large sterilized rolling pin, mush up the fruit with half of the sugar and the boiling water. Stir with a sterilized spoon to dissolve the sugar.

Put the lid on the bucket and set aside to cool to 95°F, testing with a sterile probe thermometer. Mix the pectic enzyme with ⅔ cup cooled, boiled water and stir into the cooled fruit. Set aside at room temperature (68–77°F) for 24 hours, stirring every few hours with a sterile plastic spoon. At this point, your house should fill with the intoxicating smell of boozy fruits.

Prepare the yeast and yeast nutrient by stirring them into a little cooled, boiled water, or refer to the manufacturer's instructions. Pour the mixture into your fruit and stir through. Set aside at room temperature (68–77°F) for 2–3 days.

Sterilize a wine-straining bag (you could use two pieces of cheesecloth but it would be much harder), funnel, another bucket and demijohns. Add the remaining sugar to the bucket and put the bag into the funnel. Strain the wine into the bucket. Discard the fruit. Stir through to dissolve the sugar. Now pour the wine through the funnel into the sterilized demijohns. Fit the bungs with fermentation traps and fix onto the demijohns. If necessary top up to within an inch of the top with cold, boiled water. Move the wine to a cooler place (60°F) until it clears. This will take a few months.

Once the wine clears, you can siphon it off into clean demijohns or bottles, leaving behind the sediment. Top the bottles up if necessary to within an inch of the top with cooled, boiled water. You can sample your wine after 6 months, but it will be better after a year.

RASPBERRY WINE

Wow, I am pleased with this. We love this dry wine full of fruit and flavor, not to mention the glowing color gleaming through the glass. What a lovely summery flavor to enjoy in the middle of winter! Either serve very chilled on its own or mix with sparkling white wine and serve as an aperitif or to have with dessert. Frozen raspberries are fine to use as they release more juice after being frozen. This means you can pick and freeze your own raspberries or those from a farm, or take advantage of sales in the supermarket, until you have enough to turn into wine.

makes 5 quarts

3½lbs raspberries
1 Campden tablet (optional)
2⅔lbs granulated sugar
4½ quarts boiling water
pectic enzyme (pectolase)—refer to the manufacturer's instructions for quantity needed
an all-purpose wine yeast or white wine yeast such as Lalvin 71B-1122—refer to the manufacturer's instructions for quantity needed
yeast nutrient—refer to the manufacturer's instructions for quantity needed

Follow the instructions for Doctor Maslin's plum wine (see left), substituting raspberries for the plums.

RHUBARB AND GINGER WINE BY DEBI KING

This is a pale pink, dry wine that has a delicate but clear flavor of rhubarb with a background kick of heat from the ginger. I love it as an aperitif or served in a shot glass as part of a dessert made with rhubarb.

Debi uses the method invented by Mrs. Suzanne Tritton in C. J. J. Berry's book *First Steps in Winemaking*, adding rhubarb for body in the wine—the taste is not strong, but she feels it makes a better ginger wine for its presence. She adds lots of sugar because she likes it quite sweet, potent and fiery, but you could reduce the sugar by 8 ounces if you wish, although the wine will be less strong. Debi told me it is best to use the rhubarb at the beginning of the year and not to get it too hot, or you can have problems with it turning to jelly.

makes 4½ quarts
10oz fresh ginger
2¾lbs rhubarb
2¾lbs sugar
1 Campden tablet (optional)
cooled, boiled water
dessert wine/high alcohol yeast—refer to the manufacturer's instructions for quantity needed
yeast nutrient—refer to the manufacturer's instructions for quantity needed

To get a good ginger flavor, you need to work at it. Peel the ginger and chop finely or process in a food processor. Wipe the rhubarb with a damp cloth, but don't peel it. Chop the rhubarb finely with a knife or in a food processor.

Put the rhubarb and ginger into a fermenting bucket and stir in the sugar. Add the Campden tablet (if using). Put on the lid and set aside at room temperature for at least 24 hours (up to 2 days) to allow the sugar to draw out the juices from the fruit.

Strain off the sugary juices into a sterile pitcher, cover and set aside. Return the fruit pulp to the bucket and pour in 2 quarts of cooled, boiled water. Stir well with a sterilized spoon and strain again to collect all the sugary juice, discarding the fruit. Place all the juice back in the fermentation bucket and make up to 4½ quarts with cooled, boiled water.

Prepare the yeast and yeast nutrient by stirring them into a little cooled, boiled water (or refer to the manufacturer's instructions). Add the yeast mixture to the bucket with the juice and set aside at room temperature (68–77°F) until fermentation slows right down (i.e. the bubbles drop to fewer than one per minute, which you can see happen through the fermentation trap).

Place a sterilized funnel in your demijohn and pour in the wine. Fit the bungs with fermentation traps and move to a cool room (60°F) until the wine clears. This will take approx. 4 months. Rack and bottle when finished (see page 239).

SPARKLING ELDERFLOWER WINE BY LUTHER DAVIES

This is an old family recipe that our friend Hannah's grandfather used to make. You can plant your own edlderberry bush, available from specialist nurseries. It is best to pick the flowers from elderberry bushes early in the morning and when they are still young. If the petals shake off easily, they are past their best. Dip any leftover flowers in a light batter and fry. Serve drizzled in honey with a little grating of lime zest.

makes approx. 5 quarts
40 fully ripe elderflower heads, ideally picked when dry
3⅓lbs sugar
4½ quarts boiling water
1 teaspoon champagne yeast
juice of 2 lemons
sugar cubes

Shake off any insects from the elderflowers but do not wash them. Dissolve the granulated sugar in the boiling water in a large saucepan over low heat. When all the crystals have dissolved, add the elderflowers immediately. Remove from the heat and leave to cool. Cover the pan with a lid and set aside at room temperature (68–77°F) for 2 days. Place cheesecloth in a sieve and pour through some boiling water from a kettle to sterilize it. Strain the elderflower juice through the cheesecloth into a fermenting bucket. Stir in the yeast and lemon juice. Put on the lid and set aside in a warm place (60°F) for 14 days until the vivacious bubbling stops.

Strain the wine through a cheesecloth again, and then bottle in used (and washed!) champagne or sparkling wine bottles. Add 1 sugar cube to each bottle. If using corks, these will need to be wired down. Alternatively, use swing-top bottles. Store the bottles vertically in a cool place for 6 months. Luther warns of unlikely explosions from the continuing fermentation in the bottle due to the build up of gas—so do make sure you store the bottles away from people! We kept ours in the garage and uncorked it for the New Year without any explosions!

APPLE CIDER

This is a wonderfully easy recipe based on one from Darina Allen's book *Forgotten Skills of Cooking*. We pick cooking apples from our local pick-your-own farm. They are enormous apples and have a wonderful crisp flavor. Not enough people use these farms, and rely instead on supermarkets, so I am on a mission to get more people to have a great, inexpensive day out. It has nothing to do with waiting in line, junk food, or expense and we come away with fresh fruit and plenty of things to do with them.

makes approx. 7½ quarts
6⅔lbs cooking apples
7½ quarts cold water
2lbs sugar
½ cup chopped ginger
3 cinnamon sticks

Grate the apples in a food processor—skin, cores, and all. Put them into a plastic fermentation bin and cover with the cold water. Stir with a sterilized spoon, leaving it in the bin. Cover and stir every day with the spoon for a week. Strain through a sieve and return to the bucket.

Stir the sugar into the juice, add the spices, and set aside to macerate for a day. Strain through clean cheesecloth. Pour into sterilized bottles and seal with screwtop lids. Store in a cold, dry place for up to 6 months. Wait 3 months before sampling.

ROSEHIP MEAD

We collected the rosehips for this as soon as they were ripe, placing them in a bag in the freezer until we had enough. This recipe is based on C. J. J. Berry's recipe in his book *First Steps in Winemaking*. Although we have called this rosehip mead, the correct term is rhodomel, because mead is traditionally made with berries. Rosehips are rich in vitamins C, D, and E and are a good source of antioxidants. During World War II, British children were paid to collect rosehips to make into syrup. This was drunk to obtain vitamin C in the fight against scurvy.

makes approx. 8 quarts
4½lbs rosehips
4 quarts hot water
4½lbs unpasteurized, organic honey
8 quarts cold water
½oz citric acid
yeast nutrient—refer to the manufacturer's instructions for quantity needed
high alcohol yeast—refer to the manufacturer's instructions for quantity needed

Wash the rosehips, discarding any large stems. Put them into a large saucepan with the hot water and bring to a boil. Cook until tender, approx. 15–20 minutes. Mash with a potato masher to break up the hips so that they release their juices. Line a sieve with cheesecloth and pour through a kettleful of boiling water to sterilize it. Strain the rosehip mixture through the cheesecloth in the sieve into a fermenting bucket with a lid. Bring up the sides of the cheesecloth to squeeze the hips so you extract as much of the juice as possible.

Add the honey, cold water, citric acid, and yeast nutrient and stir thoroughly to dissolve the honey. Allow the mixture to cool slightly, until it is lukewarm, and then stir in the yeast. Cover the bucket with a lid and set aside to ferment at room temperature (68–77°F) until the vivacious bubbling stops. Strain into demijohns and set aside in a cooler place (60°F) until fermentation ceases; this will take a few months. Rack and bottle as for Doctor Maslin's plum wine on page 240.

kombucha

Kombucha is a fermentation of sweetened tea made with a starter culture. It has been drunk in Russia, where it is called *kvass*, China and Japan for centuries. During fermentation, beneficial bacteria and yeasts present in the culture metabolize the sugar and turn it into acetic acid. When properly cared for and regularly cultured, they produce a wonderful probiotic-rich beverage and will continue to grow and reproduce indefinitely.

Like kefir (see page 217), kombucha is a refreshing and energizing drink that is thought to have health-giving properties. I prefer to drink kombucha while it is still young when it is fresh and light (after fermenting for about 4 days), but you could mature it for longer if you wish for a stronger flavor.

To make your own kombucha at home, you will need a starter culture bought from an internet supplier (see suppliers page 290). This is sometimes called a SCOBY—an acronym for Symbiotic Culture Of Bacteria and Yeast. For best results, follow the instructions from your supplier because quantities vary depending on the size of your SCOBY. Do not use metal utensils when making kombucha.

METHOD Brew some sweetened tea and let it cool. Transfer to a glass jar and float the culture on top. Cover with a towel and set aside at room temperature for 3–4 days before tasting.

When you are happy with the flavor, drain off the tea and store in the fridge to enjoy chilled. You can then make another batch, reusing the mother, which will continue to grow. Eventually you will be able to give part of that mother to a friend to make their own kombucha.

Variations

You can vary the taste by trying different teas—our favorite kombucha consists of two-thirds black tea to one-third redbush. Alternatively, flavor your tea by infusing it with fresh herbs or by adding lemon or ginger.

heat

In the early 19th century, Nicolas Appert, a French confectioner and brewer, discovered that if he sealed food in a glass container, then heated it in boiling water, the food inside would stay edible for months afterward. It was said that he made "the seasons stand still" and his invention won him a 12,000-franc prize offered by Napoleon in 1809 to find a method of preserving food so that he could efficiently feed his troops. Keeping food from the air and heating it to a high enough temperature to kill microorganisms preserves it from spoilage. Appert perhaps didn't fully understand how his idea worked, but his discovery marked the beginning of canning. His ideas spread and the Englishman Peter Durand began experimenting with heating food in metal containers and then sealing them. In 1810 King George III gave him a patent for his technique. The term "canning" came from the tin-coated iron canisters he used, which were similar to those used to store tea.

We often have the misconception that preserved food is inferior to fresh. However, the key to successful preserving is to bottle ingredients when they are in season—not only will they be at their best at this time but also they will be less expensive. Canning opens up a whole realm of possibilities too good to miss out on in this book. With the right equipment we really can make our own meals, sauces, stews and soups and store them out of the fridge and in the pantry ready to pull out, reheat, and enjoy. Putting food in jars, often called "putting up," gives you more freezer space and it doesn't cost energy for storage. We generally keep bottled goods in our garage, but you could use a shed, a dark pantry, utility room, spare room where the heating is off, cellar or *cantina*—just make sure the temperature doesn't drop below freezing or the glass could shatter.

the effect of heat

In this chapter, we look at the preserving effect heat has on food after it has been bottled or canned. There are two methods of heat processing depending on whether your food is high in acid or low in acid (see right).

WATERBATHING is safe for high-acid foods and involves heating your jars in a waterbath to 212°F for a controlled period of time (see page 252 for instructions). It will work for high- and low-sugar products so it is ideal for low-sugar jams, cordials, and fruits with or without syrup.

PRESSURE CANNING is essential for low-acid foods (see right). This method involves heating the jars in a pressure canner (not to be confused with a pressure cooker) to 240°F for a controlled period of time (see page 258 for instructions). The amount of time the jars should be processed for and the pressure needed is difficult to calculate at home, so it is better to follow the recipes here or from a reputable source.

There are two main recognized authorities on pressure canning. The US Department of Agriculture (USDA) gives clear advice on safe practice. For more information, see the book *Complete Guide to Home Canning and Preserving* or refer to the website. Another very good book is the *Blue Book Guide to Preserving*, which gives explanations of water canners and pressure canning. I recommend getting both if you want to invest in a pressure canner and start canning.

Note: Traditionally people used to heat-process in the oven, but this method is no longer recommended because it is unreliable and temperatures are difficult to maintain inside the jars in an oven over a long period.

botulism

The reason you need to process low-acid foods at a higher temperature than acidic foods is due to the greater risk of botulism—a deadly form of food poisoning caused by the bacterium *Clostridium botulinum*, which can survive in low-acid conditions even after boiling at 212°F. *Clostridium botulinum* is very resilient and can survive harmlessly in soil for many years, but if it is given the right conditions to multiply it can produce a deadly toxin. The reason we recommend pressure canning, rather than waterbathing, for low-acid foods is because the temperature inside a pressure canner is pressurized and therefore high enough to destroy *Clostridium botulinum* bacteria. Note that acid foods contain enough acid to block the growth of bacteria after waterbathing at 212°F.

acidity and pH

The first step with heat processing is to discover if your food is high in acid or low in acid. Then you can determine which method of heat processing is required: waterbathing (high acid) or pressure canning (low acid). The safest method to determine the pH value is using pH strips, which are available online. Alternatively you can refer to the box, right. Low-acid foods have pH values higher than 4.6; this group includes most vegetables, meats, sauces, stews, poultry, and seafood. Combinations of low- and high-acid foods should be treated as low acid and processed by pressure canning.

Note that the acidity levels of low-acid foods can be increased by adding lemon juice, citric acid, or vinegar.

a note on tomatoes

Although tomatoes are generally considered to be an acidic food, it is worth noting that some varieties can have pH values slightly above 4.6. For this reason, the USDA suggests that additional acid in the form of lemon juice, citric acid, or vinegar is added to processed tomatoes to guarantee acidity levels. We have followed this advice in our recipes for tomato sauce and salsa (see page 254), but I know Giancarlo's family and others in Italy have been canning jars of tomato sauce for years without any ill effects and wouldn't dream of adding lemon juice to their jars. This may be because over the years tomatoes have been selectively grown for sweetness and some acidity has been lost. Note that if you combine tomatoes with meat (a low-acid food), the resulting *ragù* should be treated as low-acid and processed by pressure canning (see page 258).

a note on jams

Foods that contain over 60 percent sugar do not need to be heat-processed, as explained in Sugar on page 52. However, if the figure drops below 60 percent—for example, for low-sugar jams and spreads—the jars should be heat-processed after bottling for the time indicated in the recipe.

fat, oil, and canning

Fats and oils should be avoided or used in minimal quantities in recipes or poured away prior to canning. This is because they can coat the food and provide an anaerobic environment where the bacteria that cause botulism can breed. If you want to can gravy or stock, it is better to remove the fat after it cools before canning. The same goes for *ragù*—simply pour off the excess oil before bottling.

pressure canners and pressure cookers

Pressure cookers are not suitable for pressure canning because the temperature is not high enough to kill the spores of the bacterium *Clostridium botulinum*. Pressure canners are larger than pressure cookers and therefore they can process food at higher temperatures. Pressure canners take longer to reach pressure and longer to cool down than pressure cookers.

Pressure cookers are useful for speeding up the cooking time of jams and stews, etc. because they heat to a higher temperature than boiling point, making them more efficient and energy saving than a normal saucepan on the stove. However, they do not reach the same temperature as pressure canners so don't confuse the two. We sometimes use a pressure cooker for waterbathing high-acid foods (see page 253 for instructions).

HIGH- AND LOW-ACID FOODS

High-acid foods
These foods are naturally acidic with a pH of 4.6 or lower. All are suitable for heat processing by waterbathing—see page 252 for instructions and refer to the individual recipes for timings. Don't get confused, however, when some of these fruits, such as apricots and peaches, appear as low-acid in the Sugar chapter. That is because their acidity is not high enough for setting jam but it is high enough for waterbathing. The exception is figs, which need additional lemon juice to bump up their acidity.

FRUIT
apples
apricots
blackberries
cherries
gooseberries
lemons
limes
peaches
pears
plums
red currants
tomatoes

OTHER FOODS
fruit coulis and compotes
high-acid fruits in syrup
low-sugar jams
pickles
sauerkraut

Low-acid foods
These foods should all be heat processed in a pressure canner—see page 258 for instructions and refer to individual recipes for timings.

VEGETABLES
asparagus
beets
carrots
green beans
mushrooms
okra
peppers
peas
beans
spinach
corn
turnips

OTHER FOODS
figs
meat sauces
poultry
seafood
stews, meatballs, and *ragùs*

GENERAL ADVICE FOR HEAT PROCESSING

jars, bottles, and lids

You cannot use ordinary glass jam jars for heat processing because they don't have thick enough glass to withstand the heat. The best jars to buy are Kilner or Le Parfait jars, which come with rubber seals and clips to allow the steam to escape. Alternatively you can buy Balls or Mason glass jars with two-part lids, which consist of a flat disk held in place by a screw band; these are ideal because the disk part forms a vacuum when it is secured correctly, meaning you can check the seal before you tighten the screw band. Check that the rubber seals are not damaged in any way before using. New metal disks for Mason jars should be used each time.

Specialist jars are available from cook shops or online. You can reuse the jars so it is worth investing in, say, twelve of three different sizes. I would recommend the 1-cup (250ml) size for apple butter and jam, 2-cup (500ml) jars for vegetable dishes, and 1 quart jars for *ragù* or bean soup. The lids are not reusable but the screw bands are.

All jars should be examined before use to make sure there are no chips or cracks in the glass. Also ensure that the new lids are not damaged in any way.

preparation for heat processing

Clean the jars and lids in hot soapy water and rinse thoroughly or put them through a dishwasher cycle. Heat the rubber seals, jars, and lids in simmering water to 180°F or just above; do not allow the lids to boil or the rubber or plastic will perish. Alternatively, put the jars in the oven at 185°F. If using the hot-pack method, store the jars in the water, dishwasher (with the door closed), or oven until you are ready to fill them as they should be hot for processing.

Note: This method does not sterilize but simply prepares them for processing as long as the processing time is longer than 10 minutes. If it is less than that, say for a small jar of pickles, the jars and lids should be sterilized; you can see how to do this in the general instructions on page 12.

filling the jars

Fill the jars with food allowing ¼in headroom for jams and jellies, ½in for fruits and tomatoes and an inch for low-acid foods to allow for expansion. Don't overfill the jars or the contents will bubble up inside the jar and overflow, ruining the seal. Remove any air bubbles that are trapped inside the jar by poking them with a sterilized plastic chopstick or narrow spatula. It is not necessary to do this for liquid foods and drinks. Clean the rim of the jars with water or a little vinegar on paper towels to ensure a good seal.

fastening the lids

Lift the lids out of the hot water with a magnetic prong or tongs and shake off the water. For Kilner-style jars, put the lids on, with rubber seals in place, and secure them with the spring clip. For two-part lids, put on the flat disk but don't fully tighten the screw band at this stage—a good technique, which I use, is to tighten the screw band fully first and then untighten it by just an inch. This is called finger tight (as opposed to using your full hand strength to tighten the lid). This will allow for expansion. If this is not done properly, the food will leak out and water will seep in; alternatively the lids will bulge and bend under the pressure because the air cannot escape.

testing for a seal

After heat processing, the jars should be allowed to stand in the water for 5 minutes to let the contents settle before removing them with tongs. Make sure you keep them upright at all times and leave them to cool completely for another 24 hours before checking the seals to see if a vacuum has formed. Note: You can't check the seals with Kilner or Le Parfait jars.

METHOD For Mason-style lids, remove the screw bands and try to lift the lids— they should feel stuck to the jars. If this is the case, the jars are suitable for long-term storage. If you can lift the lids off the jars at this stage, they haven't sealed completely and won't be suitable for long-term storage; transfer them to the fridge and eat within a couple of days. Providing a vacuum has formed, I tend to remove the screw bands from Mason or Balls-style jars before storing as I find they sometimes corrode and rust— although I do replace them for transport if I am giving the product away.

Note: If your jars haven't sealed correctly, you can repeat the heat-process again for things like jam or bottled fruit and vegetables (but not meat or fish). However, in my experience, the produce usually ends up too soft and overcooked after heat processing a second time.

storage of jars, and how long will the food last?

Clean the jars if they are sticky with juices. Label with the food type and date you processed them. Jars of food that are properly waterbathed or pressure-canned will last up to a year if stored in a cool, dark place, preferably between 50–68°F.

heat processing equipment: what to buy

To avoid unnecessary buying and storage of bulky pots and pans, it is a good idea to decide what exactly you want to can. If you plan to process low-acid foods (see page 249) you will have to buy a pressure canner, which is purposely designed for the job (see pages 248–249). If you are only bottling on an occasional basis and don't want to process low-acid foods, you can use a large, heavy-bottomed stockpot, pressure cooker, or a purpose-built boiling water canner as a waterbath (see page 253). Of course, you can waterbath in a pressure canner, and this will speed up the process because pressure canners heat up more quickly, but this isn't an essential piece of equipment. If you have bought a boiling-water canner follow the manufacturer's instructions.

additional equipment

jam lifters/tongs for lifting the jars out of boiling water
funnel for filling jars
magnetic prong for lifting the lids
digital thermometer for accurately measuring the temperature of the water

HIGH-ACID RECIPES

The following recipes are all suitable for waterbathing because they are all high in acid. However, if you decide to alter the recipes we cannot guarantee that they will suitable for long-term storage.

waterbathing

You can use any large, heavy-bottomed saucepan such as a stock pan for waterbathing provided it has a tight-fitting lid and it is deep enough to accommodate your jar(s). Make sure that you fit a wire or wooden rack in the bottom to stop the jars from coming into direct contact with the base of the saucepan or they could crack. If you don't have a rack, simply cut out a circle of cardboard and place it in the bottom of the pan or sit the jars on a folded towel. Boiling-water canners have specially fitted racks inside.

Of the two methods of waterbathing, also known as heat processing, hot-packing is generally thought to be better because more air is expelled from the food. This helps maintain flavor and color over time and the food is less likely to float.

Follow the raw-pack method if your food is cold or the hot-pack method if your food is hot.

RAW-PACK METHOD WATERBATHING (HIGH-ACID FOODS ONLY)
This method is suitable for raw or blanced high-acid fruits bottled in brine, water, or sugar syrup. This includes Bottled whole tomatoes (see right) and raw fruit in light syrup or water (see page 253).

Make sure you use specialist jars for waterbathing and lids in perfect condition (see page 250). Fill the cold, sterilized jars with your cold fruit and top up with hot liquid (brine or sugar syrup), leaving ½-in headroom to allow for expansion. Remove any air bubbles in the jar by poking them with a sterilized plastic chopstick or similar. Wipe off any splashes around the rim with paper towels to ensure a good seal. Put on the lids (see page 250); note that screw bands should not be fully tightened at this stage.

Place the filled jars upright on the rack inside the pan. Wind a towel around the jars to stop them from clattering about; this isn't necessary if you have a specialist rack designed to keep the jars apart. For best results, they should be at least ½in apart to allow the water to circulate

Fill the pan with cold water so that it covers the tops of the jars by at least 2in. Put the lid on the pan and place it over a medium heat. Increase the temperature and bring the water to a rolling boil (212°F) and then set your timer. Process for the time indicated in the recipe. The water should be visibly boiling throughout the process, although you might have to turn the heat down to stop it from spurting over your oven.

After processing, remove the pan from the heat and allow the jars to stand for 5 minutes before attempting to remove them. Remove the jars one at a time from the boiling water using tongs or a heatproof rubber glove, keeping them upright at all times. Leave to stand on a heatproof surface and test the seals after 24 hours (see page 250).

BOTTLED WHOLE TOMATOES

If you are lucky enough to be able to grow or buy fragrant, strong-tasting tomatoes, bottle them when they are at their peak and enjoy well after summer has gone.

Giancarlo's family gathered every year to do this, and jars of these bright red fruits lined the walls of their *cantina*. Over winter they would gradually be used up until the room was bare—just in time for the new crop to emerge the following summer. Bottled whole tomatoes are wonderful for tomato sauce, ketchup, casseroles, and *ragù*.

2-cup or 1-quart Kilner or
  Mason-style jars
flavorful, perfect tomatoes
lemon juice or citric acid
salt

Make a cross in a non-stem end of each tomato. Wash the tomatoes in cold water and drain. Plunge them into boiling water for a minute or until the skins start to split. The easiest way to do this is in a wire basket or sieve that fits in a large saucepan of boiling water. Drain and plunge into very cold water to stop them from cooking. Peel off the skins with your fingers and a knife. Either leave them whole or cut into halves or quarters. Cut out the cores.

To ensure enough acidity in the tomatoes, add ¼ teaspoon of citric acid or 1 tablespoon of lemon juice to each 2-cup jar and ½ teaspoon of citric acid or 2 tablespoons of lemon juice to each quart jar. Raw pack the tomatoes into the jars, following the instructions left. Pour over boiling water leaving ½in of headroom. Add ½ teaspoon of salt to each 2-cup jar and 1 teaspoon of salt to each quart jar. Release any air bubbles and wipe the rims. Seal according to the instructions on page 250. Process in a waterbath for 40 minutes for 2-cup jars and 45 minutes for quart jars.

Variation
TOMATOES IN THEIR OWN JUICE
To process tomatoes in their own juices, raw pack as left but put more tomatoes

into the jars and squash them down so that their juices come out and cover the tomatoes instead of boiling water. Waterbath 2-cup and quart jars for 1 hour 25 minutes. After processing, carefully remove the jars from the water and allow to cool. Test the seals after 24 hours. Remove the screw bands if they have been used and store jars in a cool, dark place for up to a year.

raw-packing fruit

We really only eat fruit in a very light sugar syrup, such as 2 tablespoons sugar to ⅓ cup water for 1 quart of sugar syrup. The sugar helps the fruit to keep its shape, color, and flavor but it is not needed for preserving in the case of waterbathing. The heat and vacuum does the job instead. Therefore if you wish you can cover the raw or hot-packed fruit in boiling water instead for a healthier option. Add flavorings such as cinnamon, vanilla, and ginger.

Prepare the sugar syrup by dissolving the sugar in the water or fruit juice.

Wash the fruit in cold water. Peel, pit, and cut the fruit into halves or quarters

RAW-PACK FRUIT TIMINGS

Sliced apple, rhubarb, berries, and pineapple need 15 minutes for 2-cup jars and 20 minutes for quart jars.

Apricots and plums need 20 minutes for 2-cup jars and 25 minutes for quart jars.

Cherries need 25 minutes for either 2-cup or quart jars.

as necessary. As you prepare the fruit drop it into acidulated water to stop it discoloring—4 cups water to ⅓ cup lemon juice is fine. Drain and raw-pack into jars following the instructions opposite. For the processing times follow the box below.

HOT-PACK METHOD WATERBATHING (HIGH-ACID FOODS ONLY)

This method is suitable for hot, high-acid foods such as Antonio's tomato sauce (page 254) and Giorgio's salsa (page 254), Apricot no-sugar, no-cook jam (page 56), and the cordials, coulis and elixir recipes in the Sugar chapter (see pages 71–74).

Make sure you use specialist jars for waterbathing, and lids and seals are in perfect condition (see page 250). Fill the hot, sterilized jars with your hot fruit or vegetables and top up with hot liquid (brine or sugar syrup) if necessary, allowing ½in headroom. For best results, sugar syrup should be heated to 140°F before bottling. Remove any air bubbles in the jar by poking them with a sterilized plastic chopstick or similar. Put on the lids (see page 250); note that screw bands should not be fully tightened at this stage. Wipe off any splashes around the lid with paper towels.

Place the filled jars upright on the rack inside the pan. Wind a towel around the jars to stop them from clattering about; this isn't necessary if you have a specialist rack designed to keep the jars apart. For best results, they should be at least ½in apart to allow the water to circulate around the jars.

Fill the pan with warm water (100°F) so that it covers the tops of the jars by at least 2in. Put the lid on the pan and place it over a low to medium heat. Bring slowly to 190°F—depending on the size of your pan, the water

should take approx. 30 minutes to heat. Increase the heat and bring the water to a rolling boil (212°F) before setting your timer. Process for the time allocated in the recipe. The water should be visibly boiling throughout the whole process, although you might have to reduce the heat to stop it spurting over your oven.

After processing, switch off the heat and allow the jars to stand for 5 minutes before attempting to remove them. Remove the jars one at a time from a boiling water using tongs or a heatproof rubber glove, keeping them upright at all times. Leave to stand on a heatproof surface and test the seals after 24 hours (see page 250).

using a pressure canner for waterbathing

WATERBATHING METHOD (HIGH-ACID FOODS ONLY)

Depending on the size of your pressure canner, you can use the larger models to waterbath high-acid foods as long as the jars will fit on the rack and you can cover them with 2in of water. Follow manufacturers' instructions (see suppliers on page 290).

HOT-PACK FRUIT TIMINGS

Cherries and berries need 15 minutes for 2-cup jars or 20 minutes for quart jars.

Apricots, peaches, pears and plums need 20 minutes for 2-cup jars and 25 minutes for quart jars.

GIORGIO'S SALSA FOR FAJITAS

This is a spicy, hot salsa for eating with fajitas. It is a great recipe for using up summer tomatoes and peppers. We developed it after much trial and error with our son Giorgio to avoid having to buy jars of ready-made salsa for our Mexican suppers.

makes approx. 4.5lbs—use 2-cup jars
2½lbs flavorful, firm, ripe tomatoes
4 tablespoons extra virgin olive oil
3 red onions, finely chopped
3 garlic cloves, peeled and finely chopped
3 fresh red chiles, finely chopped
1 red pepper, diced into ½-in cubes
1 green pepper, diced into ½-in cubes
3 tablespoons lime or lemon juice
3 teaspoons ground coriander
3 teaspoons ground cumin
1 teaspoon dried oregano
4 tablespoons red wine vinegar
2–4 teaspoons sugar, to taste
2 teaspoons fine sea salt
2 tablespoons tomato paste

Make a cross in the non-stem end of each tomato and plunge them into boiling water for a couple of minutes or until the skins split. Remove from the water and drench in cold water to stop them cooking. Peel off the skins and cut into ½-in dice, discarding the seeds.

Heat the oil in a large saucepan and gently cook the onions until soft. Add a little water to them if they start to stick. Add the garlic and chile and cook gently for a couple of minutes. Add the remaining ingredients, except for the tomatoes, and stir through until hot. Add the tomatoes and taste for seasoning. Bring to a boil and simmer for 10 minutes. Bottle into warm, sterilized 2-cup jars, leaving an inch of headroom, and put on the lids (see page 250). Process in a waterbath using the hot-pack method for 15 minutes (see page 253).

ANTONIO'S TOMATO SAUCE

Antonio Sanzone, our Head Chef at Caffè Caldesi, is from Puglia. As a child, his family used to buy tomatoes when they were still slightly green for making into sauce because they were cheaper like that, and then they would spread them out on trays to ripen in the sun at home. I have often seen tomatoes for sale in Italy marked *per passata*, for strained tomato sauce. They give the best flavor this way and make a very versatile sauce base. Or you can take the recipe one stage further and make it into a tomato sauce before bottling.

makes 3½ quarts (7 x 2-cup jars)
8 quarts water
½ cup salt
6½lbs San Marzano tomatoes
7 sprigs of basil
7 garlic cloves, peeled and any green centers removed
7 small fresh bay leaves, crushed
2 teaspoons sugar
citric acid or lemon juice

Put the water in a large saucepan over medium heat and add the salt. Stir to dissolve. Meanwhile wash the tomatoes. Once the water comes to a boil, drop in the tomatoes and simmer for 10–15 minutes until the skins split and the tomatoes start to soften. Use a strainer to remove the tomatoes from the pan and transfer them to a large bowl.

Place a sprig of basil into each cold, sterilized jar, along with a garlic clove, a bay leaf, ½ teaspoon of sugar, and ¼ teaspoon of citric acid or 1 tablespoon of lemon juice.

Put the tomatoes through a *passatutto* or food mill to get rid of the skins and seeds. Pour the strained tomatoes into the jars with the flavorings, leaving ½-in headroom and stir. Fasten the lids, put the jars into a waterbath and process for approx. 45 minutes using the raw-pack method (see page 252). Leave to cool in the water. Store for up to a year in a cool, dark place.

Variation
ANTONIO'S FLAVORED TOMATO SAUCE

This tomato sauce can bottled and waterbathed to extend its shelf-life in the same way as the plain tomato sauce.

makes 1 quart (2 x 2-cup jars)
2 tablespoons olive oil
1 medium red onion, finely chopped
1 carrot, finely chopped
1 celery stick, finely chopped
6 cups tomato sauce (see left)

Heat the oil in a saucepan and cook the onion, carrot, and celery until soft, approx. 5–10 minutes. Add the tomato sauce and bring to a boil. Reduce the heat to a simmer and cook for 30 minutes. Pour into warm, sterilized jars, leaving an inch of headroom and waterbath using the hot-pack method on page 253.

To serve, heat the sauce in a pan and add salt to taste. Pour drained, cooked pasta into the sauce and toss to combine.

For an *Arrabiata* sauce add a teaspoon of red pepper flakes with the onion.

BOTTLED FRUITS

Homemade bottled fruits are a marvelous shortcut for a quick dessert. Imagine Caramelized oranges in brandy (see page 204) served with luscious whipped cream, mulled pears with cinnamon ice cream, or peaches in brandy syrup. Or for a healthy breakfast or snack, cooked apples or rhubarb is a treat with yogurt and granola.

fruit bottling tips

Always choose fruit in perfect condition.

Take care when handling fruit not to bruise it.

Use a sterilized chopstick to push the fruit down in the jar so it is totally submerged in the sugar syrup.

After heat processing, allow the jars to cool for 5 minutes in the waterbath before lifting them out carefully with jar lifters; make sure you keep the jars upright and handle with care.

Store in a cool, dry, dark place.

If you have any fruit syrup left over after bottling your fruits, you can always bottle it separately in sterilized jars and waterbath as before, or keep it in the fridge for up to 2 weeks. We like to thicken the syrup slightly first by boiling rapidly for 5 minutes or until it thickens to our liking. Use it for sweetening cocktails or fruit salad.

PEARS IN SPICED RED WINE SYRUP

For a sumptuous dessert in a hurry, open a jar of these and serve with whipped cream sweetened with sugar and a dash of Amaretto liqueur.

makes 3 x 1-quart jars
4 cups red wine
2 tablespoons honey
1⅓ cups brown sugar
12–16 pears, peeled, quartered, and cored
3 x 2in cinnamon sticks
9 cloves
3 star anise (optional)
3 strips of orange zest

Put the wine, honey, and sugar into a medium saucepan and bring to a boil to dissolve the sugar. Divide and hot-pack the pears and spices in three warm, sterilized jars. Pour in the hot syrup, leaving ½-in headroom, wipe the rims, and put on the lids. Remove any air bubbles. Process in a waterbath using the hot-pack method for 25 minutes (see page 253). Allow to stand for 5 minutes in the water before removing the jars with jar lifters. Store in a cool, dark place for up to a year. Once opened keep in the fridge and consume within 5 days.

Variations
PEARS IN CINNAMON AND VANILLA SYRUP

Follow the recipe for Pears in spiced red wine syrup (above), replacing the wine, honey and sugar with 2 cups water and 1 cup sugar. Flavor each jar of pears with a split vanilla pod, 2 strips of lemon zest and a cinnamon stick. Process as before.

PEACHES IN BRANDY SYRUP

Follow the recipe for Pears in spiced red wine syrup (left), replacing the wine, honey and sugar with 2½ cups water, 2½ cups sugar and 1⅓ cups brandy or Amaretto. Blanch the peaches in boiling water and slip off the skins. Cut them in half and remove the pits. Divide the peaches among the jars, omitting the flavorings, and top up with the Amaretto sugar syrup. Process in a waterbath using the hot-pack method for 10 minutes (see page 253).

COOKED APPLE SLICES

Follow the recipe on page 284 but instead of freezing the Cooked apple, pour hot into warm, clean 2-cup or 1-quart jars, leaving ½-in headroom. Wipe the rims of the jars to ensure a good seal. Remove any air bubbles and put on the lids. Process in a waterbath using the hot-pack method for 20 minutes for either size of jar (see page 253). Allow to stand for 5 minutes in the water before removing the jars with jar lifters. Store in a cool, dark place for up to a year. Once opened keep in the fridge and consume within 5 days.

FRUIT PURÉES

Any high-acid fruit purée can be sweetened or left natural and hot-packed for 15 minutes for both 2-cup and 1 quart jars, leaving ½in headroom.

COOKED RHUBARB

I like to add only a little sugar to this and use the natural sweet flavor of vanilla to counter the acidity of the rhubarb. I eat it cold with yogurt or dress it with crumble (see page 284) and bake it until bubbling hot.

*makes approx. 1 quart jar or
2 x 2-cup jars*

2lbs rhubarb
1 vanilla pod, split, or a few drops
   of vanilla extract
up to 1¼ cups sugar, to taste

Wash and chop the rhubarb into bite-sized pieces. Put into a saucepan with the vanilla and a little sugar over low heat. Stir frequently until the water comes out of the rhubarb. Bring to a boil and taste, adjusting the sugar as necessary. Remove the vanilla pod and

bottle right away into hot, clean 2-cup or 1 quart jars, leaving ½in headroom and removing any air bubbles. Wipe the jars to ensure a good seal and put on the lids. Process in a waterbath using the hot-pack method for 15 minutes for 2-cup and quart jars (see page 253). Allow to stand for 5 minutes in the water before removing the jars with jar lifters. Store in a cool, dark place for up to a year. Once opened keep in the fridge and consume within 5 days.

Variation
Add a little grated fresh ginger or a length of orange peel to the rhubarb in place of the vanilla.

cordials

Follow the steps below to extend the shelf-life of the cordial and syrup recipes in the Sugar chapter (see pages 46–77). These instructions are based on Pam Corbin's advice in her wonderful book *Preserves*.

Sterilize the corks, swing-top lids, screw tops, and all bottles by putting them into your waterbath and bringing them to a boil. Store them in the waterbath until you are ready to use them.

Fill the bottles with cordial. Allow an inch of headroom for screw-top and swing-top bottles or a little more for cork tops.

Seal the lids: avoid tightening the lids completely on screw-top bottles to allow steam to escape; swing tops are fitted with a rubber seal that allows steam to escape so these can be closed; corks should be sealed onto the bottles with insulation tape or wires to stop them from popping off during heat processing.

Stand the bottles upright in the waterbath, placing them on a folded towel or a piece of cardboard so that

they do not come into direct contact with the base of the pan. If necessary, wrap a towel in between the jars to stop them clattering around, but make sure that the water can travel easily between them.

Fill the pan with water to within an inch from the top of the bottles. Bring to a simmer (190°F) and keep at that temperature for 20 minutes.

Remove from the heat and allow the bottles to stand for 5 minutes before carefully removing them from the water, keeping them upright. Place them on a heatproof surface to cool completely.

Fasten the lids tightly before storing. Corks should be sealed afterward by dipping them into melted paraffin or beeswax.

Store in a cool, dark place for up to a year. Once opened, keep in the fridge and consume within 3 weeks.

For fruit sauces such as Cranberry sauce (page 64), process as for the Fruit purées left.

LOW-ACID RECIPES

The recipes that follow must be heat-processed in a pressure canner for long-term storage (see pages 248–249). This is because they are low-acid recipes. Follow the instructions carefully regarding processing times. Note that if you decide to alter the recipes, we cannot guarantee that they will be suitable for long-term storage.

pressure canning

We recommend that you buy a pressure canner fitted with a weighted dial, otherwise it has to be checked every year. You can buy a tester in the US and do this yourself, see suppliers on page 290. Ours is a 23-quart pressure canner made by Presto; it has a weighted gauge and dial gauge so it does not need the annual check-up (refer to the USDA website for how to care for your pressure canner). The weighted gauge may mean you end up processing over the recommended pressure of 10–11 psi, but it is better to err on the side of caution.

We have given basic instructions for pressure canning, but always refer to the manufacturer's instructions as different brands vary slightly.

PRESSURE CANNING METHOD (LOW-ACID FOODS)

This method is suitable for processing low-acid foods (see page 249), which must be heated to 240°F to kill botulism spores. Note that no other heat processing method will achieve this temperature.

For hot food, use hot water in your pressure canner, and warm, clean jars. For cold food, use cold water in your pressure canner, and cold, clean jars.

Make sure you use specialist jars for pressure canning with two-part lids (see page 250). The disk-shaped lids should be brand new; screw bands can be reused as long as they are in perfect condition. Always follow the recipe carefully regarding jar size because different-sized jars will require different processing times.

Put the rack into the pressure canner and fill with approx. 3in cold or hot water, depending on whether you are processing cold or hot food. This is the correct amount for up to 40 minutes processing; add more water if processing for longer.

Fill the sterilized jars with food almost to the top, leaving an inch of headroom, depending on how much the food will expand, and remove any air bubbles with a sterilized chopstick (see page 250). Put on the lids (see page 250); note that screw bands should not be fully tightened at this stage. Wipe off any splashes around the lid with paper towels.

Lower the filled jars into the canner, keeping them upright at all times. Wind a towel around the jars to stop them clattering; this isn't necessary if you have a specialist rack designed to keep the jars apart. For best results, jars should be at least an inch apart to allow the water to circulate around them.

Put the lid on the canner, leaving the weight off the petlock or vent port. Place the canner over a high heat and allow the steam to vent vigorously for 10 minutes at full strength before putting on the weight. The pressure will rise, as seen on the dial gauge, and the weighted gauge will begin to jiggle. When the pressure specified in the recipe is reached (normally this is 10lb), start your timer. Process for the time indicated in the recipe. If necessary, adjust the heat to maintain the correct pressure for the full time. Note that if the pressure drops below the specified amount during processing, you will have to start the whole process again from the beginning—as before, wait until the correct pressure is achieved before starting your timer.

Once the time is up, switch off the heat and allow the canner to depressurize and cool. Don't attempt to remove the weight and lid until the dial gauge reads zero. Remove the weight first. If there is no more hissing, you can carefully open the lid—standing at arm's length to avoid any hot steam. Remove the jars from the canner with tongs, keeping them upright. Put them on a heat-resistant surface and allow them to cool completely. Check the seals after 24 hours (see page 250).

vegetable canning tips

Always choose young, tender vegetables in perfect condition.

Can vegetables as soon as possible after picking and avoid bruising.

Vegetables can be raw-packed, as in the Peas in sweet brine, or hot-packed, as in the Bottled asparagus.

If using salt, only use pure sea salt without anticaking agents and iodine.

Use a sterilized chopstick to push the vegetables down in the jar so they are totally submerged in the brine.

After heat processing, allow the jars to cool for 5 minutes in the pressure canner before lifting them out carefully with jar lifters; make sure you keep the jars upright and handle with care.

Store in a cool, dry, dark place.

PEAS IN SWEET BRINE

I have a guilty secret of really liking canned peas. These bottled peas make a great standby vegetable to serve with steak or to put into an egg frittata.

METHOD Wash the peas in cold water. Raw pack into cold sterilized jars, leaving 1½in of headroom. Add ½ teaspoon of salt and ½ teaspoon of sugar to each 2-cup jar. Pour boiling water over them, leaving an inch of headroom. Remove the air bubbles with a sterilized chopstick and put on the lids (see page 250). Process 2-cup jars at 10 pounds pressure for 40 minutes in a pressure canner (see left). Keep in a cool, dark place for up to a year.

bottled green beans

We grow runner and long beans in our garden, and both are ideal for bottling. Although I must admit I prefer to freeze them or make them into a curry, see page 263, bottling beans keeps the space at maximum in my freezer.

Raw-pack following the instructions for Peas in sweet brine, omitting the sugar and leaving an inch of headroom. Process 2-cup jars in a pressure canner for 20 minutes and quart jars for 25 minutes at 10 pounds pressure. Keep in a cool, dark place for up to a year.

bottled asparagus

Canning is the perfect way to make the most of the asparagus season. By preserving them in lightly salted water, their taste is not altered in any way. To serve, simply heat and dress with lemon and butter or toss cold into a salad.

fresh asparagus
fine salt (optional)

Wash and trim the asparagus, removing the tough ends. Wash again in cold water. Either leave whole or cut into pieces. Plunge the asparagus into boiling water for 3 minutes then, using tongs, pack into clean, hot Mason or Balls jars leaving an inch of headroom. Discard the cooking water and boil fresh water to pour over them. The spears should stand tall but not be too tightly packed so that the water can circulate around them. Pour over boiling water leaving an inch of headroom. Add ½ teaspoon of salt to 2-cup jars and 1 teaspoon to quart jars if you wish. Wipe the seals and fasten the lids, finger tight. Process for 30 minutes for 2-cup jars and 40 minutes for quart jars at 10 pounds pressure in a pressure canner. Keep in a cool, dark place for up to a year.

garden in a jar

I try to use as much homegrown produce as possible, picking and canning in the same day. The jars look pretty in the pantry and make a great standby vegetable to serve. I serve them heated straight from the jar with grilled meats and hot chicken or stir them into fried onion, adding some Whole bottled tomatoes (page 252),

a dash of red wine, a sprig of thyme, and a little tomato paste for a quick ratatouille.

Use a mixture of carrots, zucchini, peppers, lima beans, peas, onions, and tomatoes. (Even if you add tomatoes to this mixture, process in a pressure canner because you cannot be sure the amount will have enough acid to waterbath.)

Hot-pack the vegetables into 2-cup or quart jars, top up with boiling water, leaving an inch of headroom. Add ½ teaspoon of salt for 2-cup jars and 1 teaspoon for quart jars. Remove the air bubbles with a sterilized chopstick and fasten on the lids (see page 250). Process 2-cup jars at 10 pounds pressure for 1 hour 15 minutes and quart jars for 1 hour 30 minutes in a pressure canner (see page 258). Keep in a cool, dark place for up to a year.

TUSCAN RAGÙ

This is Giancarlo's staple *ragù* recipe, which we always have in the house. It is perfect for lasagne or simply eaten with hot pasta. Any leftover pasta already mixed with the sauce can be heated up the next day in the oven with cream and grated cheese for *pasta al forno*. Giancarlo's father made this *ragù* every ten days for himself until he was 84 years old. He kept his in jars in the fridge, eating a jar every lunchtime at 12 noon with hot pasta. When he ran out, it was time to make some more. Now that we are into pressure canning, Giancarlo makes a big batch every few months and stores the jars in our garage.

makes 4 x quart jars— each one serves 10

6 tablespoons olive oil
1¾lbs *soffritto* (see page 278)
2 garlic cloves, peeled but left whole
1 sprig of rosemary
2lbs ground pork
2lbs ground beef
1⅔ cups red wine
1½ quarts Antonio's tomato sauce (page 254)
salt and freshly ground black pepper

Heat the olive oil in a large, nonstick frying pan, add the *soffritto*, and cook over medium heat for approx. 15 minutes. Add the garlic and rosemary.

Increase the heat, add the pork and beef, and cook until the liquid from the meat has evaporated. Keep stirring so that the mixture does not stick to the bottom of the pan. When it feels dry, add the red wine and stir well—notice how the smell changes once the alcohol has burned off after a few minutes— then add the tomato sauce, stirring well to combine. Bring to a boil then reduce the heat and simmer, uncovered, for approx. 2 hours. Stir frequently to make sure it doesn't catch on the bottom of the pan, adding a little hot water if it looks dry. Taste and adjust the seasoning if necessary. Scoop off any excess oil with a spoon and discard.

Either use immediately or pour into warm, sterilized 2-cup or 1 quart jars, leaving an inch of headroom. Wipe the top of the jars with water or vinegar to ensure a good seal, and fasten the lids, finger tight. Process immediately while still hot. Process both jar sizes for 25 minutes at 10 pounds pressure in a pressure canner (see page 258). Store in a cool, dark place for up to a year. Once opened keep the jar in the fridge for up to 10 days.

Note: Instead of pressure canning, the *ragù* can be frozen in sealed plastic containers; use within 3 months.

ZUPPA DI FAGIOLI— BEAN SOUP

Bean soups are popular all over Italy, but particularly in Tuscany where the Tuscans are known as the *mangiafagioli*, the bean-eaters. Giancarlo grew up eating bean soup; his mother grew cannellini and borlotti beans in her garden and dried them every year so that they could provide the family with "poor man's meat," as they were known, to last throughout winter. I was even told when I was about to marry Giancarlo that I should learn to make bean soup—since every Tuscan expects it from his wife!

This is an easy soup to make with a good herby base flavor provided by the *soffritto* (see page 278). Other beans can be used for this, such as small white beans. For a thicker soup, blend one-third of the soup and add back to the rest. We often stir in cooked pasta at the end to make *pasta fagioli*. Alternatively, we add a couple of tablespoons of tomato paste to a quart of soup with some cooked sausages for a sausage casserole.

serves 12 (makes 3 x 2-cup jars)
6 tablespoons extra virgin olive oil
1⅓lbs *soffritto* (see page 278)
2 sprigs of rosemary
3 garlic cloves, peeled and lightly
  crushed with the side of a knife
1lb borlotti or cannellini beans,
  soaked overnight and drained
2½ quarts Brown chicken stock
  (see page 277) or vegetable stock
1 teaspoon baking soda

Heat the olive oil in a large, heavy-bottomed saucepan and cook the *soffritto* with the rosemary and garlic for about 5 minutes. Add the beans and stir, pour in the stock, and bring to a boil. Simmer gently for 30 minutes. (If you plan to eat some of the soup right away, you will need to cook the beans for another 1½ hours until tender.) Scoop off any excess oil with a spoon and discard.

Add the baking soda to soften the bean skins and stir well. Pour into warm, sterilized jars, leaving an inch of headroom, wipe the top of the jars with water or vinegar to ensure a good seal, and fasten the lids, finger tight. Process for 1 hour 30 minutes at 10 pounds pressure in a pressure canner (see page 258). Store in a cool, dark place for up to a year. Once opened keep in the fridge and use within 4 days.

CASSOULET

This recipe by Richard Bertinet is totally delicious. It makes a real meat feast that is great for a special occasion. We make some to eat right away and then have fun bottling the rest to enjoy another day when we know all we need to do is open the jar and reheat until piping hot.

makes approx. 4 quart jars
6 medium onions
3 cloves

1 large, thick piece of pork rind
1lb haricot beans, soaked overnight
  and drained
4 carrots, cut into ¼in dice
1 bay leaf
6 black peppercorns
8 garlic cloves
12oz pancetta, cut into small pieces
¼ cup dry white wine
1¾lbs diced leg of lamb
salt and freshly ground black pepper
6 very ripe tomatoes or 4 tablespoons
  tomato paste
8 Toulouse sausages
1 portion of duck confit (see page 189)

To serve
1¾ cups dry bread crumbs
a small bunch of parsley, roughly
  chopped
4 tablespoons butter, melted

Peel one of the onions and push the sharp pointed end of the cloves into it. Peel the other onions and dice.

Take a large, heavy-bottomed pot and line the bottom with the pork rind, skin-side down. Add the beans, diced carrot, diced onion, and whole, studded onion. Add the bay leaf and peppercorns. Keeping the skins on, crush the garlic cloves with the flat side of a knife and add to the pot with the pancetta. Pour in the wine and top up with cold water to cover. Put the pot over medium heat and bring to a boil. Reduce the heat and simmer gently, stirring occasionally.

Season the pieces of lamb. Add 4 tablespoons of the duck fat from the duck confit to a frying pan and put on high heat. Add the lamb and cook until it is browned. Add the browned meat and the cooking juices to the pot, and simmer gently, covered, for 1½ hours.

Meanwhile prepare the tomatoes (if using). Score each one with a cross, plunge into boiling water for 30 seconds and then into cold water. Peel off the skins, cut into quarters, and scoop out the seeds and juice. Chop the flesh into small dice.

Add the tomatoes (or tomato paste) to the pot with the sausages, stir through, and simmer for another 30 minutes, covered. Finally stir in the pieces of duck from the confit. Continue to cook for another 30 minutes until the beans are tender and the meat is heated through and starting to disintegrate slightly. Remove from the heat, put a lid on the pot, and set aside to cool overnight. Scoop off any excess oil with a spoon and discard. Either eat right away, keep in the fridge for up to a week, or can it in a pressure canner.

To do this, pick the meat from the bones and cut the sausages into thirds, return the meat to the casserole, and discard the bones. This is so that the sauce can pass easily between the smaller pieces of meat and the cassoulet can be thoroughly heated in the jars in the canner. Discard the pork rind and whole studded onion. Reheat the casserole so that the cassoulet is bubbling, adding a little hot water or stock to make sure there is enough liquid to cover the meat and beans, then hot-pack into hot quart jars. Process in a pressure canner for 1 hour 30 minutes at 10 pounds pressure.

To serve, discard the pork rind and the whole studded onion (if the cassoulet wasn't canned) and decant your cassoulet into an ovenproof dish. Combine the bread crumbs with the curly parsley, the melted butter, and 2 tablespoons of the duck or goose fat (from the duck confit). Scatter the breadcrumbs over the top of the cassoulet and bake in the oven at 350°F for approx. 45 minutes or until heated through.

GREEN BEAN CURRY

Manjula Samarasinghe, with whom I traveled around Sri Lanka, gave me this recipe. Here the spice paste is enriched with coconut milk to form a creamy sauce that works well with a variety of vegetables, such as green beans, potatoes, mushrooms, lentils, and okra.

makes 3 x 2-cup jars
(each jar serves 4)

1 portion of Sri Lankan spice paste for vegetable curries (pages 281–282)
2lbs green beans
2 x 14oz cans coconut milk
¾ cup water
fine sea salt, to taste
red pepper flakes, to taste

This recipe couldn't be simpler. Top and tail the beans and cut into bite-sized lengths approx. an inch. Simply spoon the paste into a large, nonstick frying pan and add the vegetables, coconut milk, and water. Cook over medium heat for approx. 5 minutes. Taste and adjust the seasoning if necessary with salt and more red pepper flakes if you like it hot. Spoon the curry into warm, sterilized 2-cup or 1 quart jars, leaving an inch of headroom, fasten the lids, and process for 30 minutes at 10 pounds pressure in a pressure canner (see page 258). Store for up to a year in a dark, cool place. Once opened, consume within 3 days and store in the fridge.

BEET CURRY

We grow beets every year, but I had never thought of putting them into a delicious curry before our visit to Sri Lanka. Their earthy sweetness works brilliantly in spicy dishes such as this. I like to serve this with the green bean curry (above) and rice.

ALTITUDE

Water boils at different temperatures according to your altitude and the barometric pressure of your location—so the higher you are, the more time it takes to process your food. We have based our recipes on locations below 1,000 feet above sea level, but if you live at a different altitude, please refer to the chart and adjust the timings accordingly.

This chart is based on one in Ball's *Blue Book Guide to Preserving*, which is a great sourcebook for those wishing to preserve a lot of produce using the heat processing method.

Waterbathing

Altitude in feet	Increase in processing time
1,001–3,000	5 minutes
3,001–6,000	10 minutes
6,001–8,000	15 minutes
8,001–10,000	20 minutes

Pressure canning

Altitude in feet	Weighted gauge	Dial gauge
0—1,000	10	11
1,001–2,000	15	11
2,001–4,000	15	12
4,001–6,000	15	13
6,001–8,000	15	14
8,001–10,000	15	15

makes 4 x 2-cup jars
(each jar serves 4)

3 shallots or 1 medium onion, finely sliced
3 tablespoons vegetable oil
2 portions of Sri Lankan spice paste for vegetable curries (pages 281–282)
2¾lbs raw beets, peeled and cut into julienne strips
3½ cups water or coconut milk or the two combined
fine sea salt, to taste
red pepper flakes, to taste

In a large, nonstick frying pan, cook the shallot in the oil over low heat until soft. Add the paste and cook for 3 minutes, stirring, until the paste darkens slightly. Add the beets and stir well to coat it in the spices. Cover with a lid and cook over low heat for 5 minutes until soft. Add the water or coconut milk. Taste and adjust the seasoning if necessary with salt and a little more red pepper flakes if you like it hot. Scoop off any excess oil with a spoon and discard. Spoon into warm, sterilized 2-cup or 1 quart jars, leaving an inch of headroom. Wipe the rims, fasten the lids and process 2-cup jars for 35 minutes and quart jars for 40 minutes at 10 pounds pressure in a pressure canner (see page 258). Store for up to a year in a dark, cool place. Once opened consume within 3 days and store in the fridge.

cold

Chilling and freezing are among the earliest and least complicated methods of preserving. When you chill food, you slow the growth of microorganisms, which means that you delay spoiling and rotting. If you take the process further to freezing point, this growth is halted completely, until the food is warmed again. Most foods are not changed by chilling or freezing, unlike other methods of preserving that transform them in some way. Color, texture, vitamins, and minerals are kept intact, and if foods are frozen as soon as possible after picking, they will actually have more nutritional value than fresh ones that have been traveling for days.

CHILLING

Before fridges became commonplace in the 1950s, families had to use the coolest part of the house to store their produce—perhaps a pantry, cellar, or outside space. Our house was built in the 1960s and sadly a pantry wasn't included in the original plan. However, I have learned to store all kinds of fruit, herbs, and vegetables very happily in securely covered boxes in the cool air of our garage. They last much longer out there and don't take up room in my fridge. A dark garage or shed is ideal for storing potatoes, preferably in paper or burlap sacks with the neck slightly open to allow excess moisture to escape; moisture and light are the enemy, so don't store them in plastic bags! Empty your bags or sacks out every now and then to check none of the potatoes are going bad, and no pests or insects have gotten in.

In Italy many people still have a *cantina*. Similar to an American root cellar, it is an area below ground or in a cool, insulated area of the house with a north-facing window and an earth or gravel floor to provide some humidity and help regulate the temperature throughout the year. The first time I saw Giancarlo's family *cantina*, it was like finding an Aladdin's cave full of gleaming jars of *ragù*, tomato sauce, peas in brine, and jams, all with their handwritten labels. Our friend Nello, a Tuscan farmer, keeps his legs of prosciutto in his *cantina*, hanging them above boxes of ripening tomatoes, drying onions and garlic, and dried corn and bread for the chickens. The produce to be kept cooler is close to the ground, whereas vinegars and wines, which need a small amount of warmth for fermentation, are kept higher up.

Our grandparents' generation wrapped apples individually in newspaper and kept them in crates or cardboard boxes in a cold place in the house; this is a great practice to revive. You just need to check your storage box regularly because if one fruit goes bad, the ethylene it gives off will hasten the ripening of the others, hence the expression "one bad apple spoils the barrel." Some people swear by storing dried elderflowers in with their apples to help them keep better—and lend their floral-pineapple taste to the apples as a bonus. You can use the same cold storage method for quinces, persimmons, and unripe tomatoes, just bringing out a few before you need them to give them a chance to ripen.

storing in sand

An alternative for root vegetables is to store them in a child's sandbox or in silver sand or sawdust in wooden or cardboard boxes, raised from the ground so they don't become damp—this way, they will keep over winter. Separate each vegetable into its own box and label it, so you don't have to do a lucky dip each time you need a carrot or parsnip!

chilling in the ground

If you grow your own vegetables, one of the simplest ways to keep them cool is just to leave them in the ground, rather than pulling them up, provided you have well-drained soil. Parsnips and carrots, potatoes, Brussels sprouts, cabbages, Jerusalem artichokes, leeks, and cauliflowers can all be treated in this way, but should be covered with fleece or straw to protect them from severe frost and snow. Some root vegetables, such as carrots and parsnips, actually become sweeter when left in the ground because the sugar content of the root increases in the cold.

clamping

Clamping, or storing harvested root vegetables outside in mounds of earth, is an effective way to keep them cool and fresh during the winter months. My grandfather, Leonard Beresford, who was Town Clerk of a small coastal town in the 1930s and '40s, used to advise people on how to grow and store vegetables in this way as one of his wartime duties. He and my father dug up their neat little lawn, much to my grandmother's disapproval, and gave it over to rows of carrots, potatoes, and parsnips, which, when harvested, could be buried in earth and straw for months. The store would be sealed up with burlap to keep the vegetables cold but above freezing point and also to keep out oxygen, frost, excess moisture, and light, all of which could encourage them to decay. In Italy Giancarlo remembers his family doing the same thing: one of his jobs was to go out

and fetch the potatoes and carrots from their clamps throughout the winter.

If you want to try clamping, only use vegetables in perfect condition and remove stems and leaves first, since these will rot. Never wash vegetables before storing them. Find an area of dry ground on which to mound up your vegetables and dig a shallow trench 6in deep almost all around it so that rainwater is able to drain away easily. (The part that is left is where you will stand to get to your store.) Next put a layer of straw down on the ground, followed by your vegetables. Cover the vegetables with a thick layer of straw, and top with a layer of soil from the trench you have dug. Some people finish with a layer of plastic to protect against heavy rain, but this is a more modern addition. If you do use plastic, make sure it doesn't tightly surround the clamp, making it completely airtight, or condensation will set in and your vegetables will rot.

FREEZING

Freezing is an efficient form of preserving that doesn't change the flavor and texture of most foods. Big in the 1950s and '60s, it has recently become associated with bags of prechopped frozen vegetables, burgers, and TV dinners, rather than being appreciated for what it really is—that is, a brilliant way to preserve all kinds of food. Now, thankfully, creative freezing is becoming fashionable again. It is a perfect method of storing everything from nuts and leftover egg whites to your own sauces and bases for curries, etc.

Clarence Birdseye may have made the biggest impact on the consumer when he perfected the art of mass-freezing, packaging, and selling frozen food to the public in 1930, but the first meat to be frozen, thanks to the force of nature, was probably that of mammoths, who have been discovered frozen intact after 15,000 years. According to the Inuit, who have been known to dip into their supply of frozen mammoth in hard times, the meat is still good enough to eat, if a little tough! The early Japanese and Koreans freeze-dried their fish, natives in Peru and Bolivia freeze-dried potatoes, while the ancient Chinese, Greeks, and Romans stored ice and mountain snow in cellars or icehouses to keep food cold.

Freezing has been practiced all over the world throughout history as a way of preserving food. In 1574 Nicolás Monardes, the Spanish physician, wrote of ice being transported to Paris all the way from Flanders, in Belgium. This allowed a whole new form of food to be developed, from chilled jellies to frosted fruits and iced sherbets. In England, James I commissioned the first brick-lined, round "ice houses" for Greenwich Park and Hampton Court Palace in the 17th century, and by the 19th century there were 3,000 ice houses in wealthy family homes throughout the UK; many of these igloo-like structures still exist. In 1819 the architect John Buonarotti Papworth wrote: "The icehouse forms an excellent larder for the preservation of every kind of food liable to be injured by heat in summer; thus fish, game, poultry, butter, etc. may be kept for a considerable time."

In the late 18th century, Alexander Dalrymple, a Scot who worked for the British East India Company, noted the way Chinese fishermen used ice to transport their fish. He brought the idea home and before long Scottish fishermen, with the help of MP George Dempster, started to use this method to transport their fish farther afield for sale. Ice revolutionized fish sales in the UK and helped the Scottish fishermen to earn a fair wage. It wasn't long after this that blocks of ice were taken to sea on boats in order to freeze the fish as soon as it was caught—the first step towards state-of-the-art freezing of fish at sea.

In the 1920s and 1930s, inventor Clarence Birdseye (who had worked as a fur trapper in Canada and seen the way fish froze quickly once caught, but tasted the same when thawed) battled against his own poverty and the public's fear of the new to develop the first method of fast freezing and packing food. His wife Eleanor had to put up with fish flipping around in her bathtub as Clarence continued his quest, but finally his determination paid off when he discovered a way of fast-freezing foods by sandwiching them between plates which were dipped into a brine of calcium chloride. In 1929 he received a $22 million pay-out for his invention and in 1930 the first quick-frozen produce was sold to the public.

if there could only be ten items in our freezer, we would choose:

Spice cubes (see page 273) to use as a shortcut for everyday cooking.

Sliced sourdough bread so we never run out of fresh bread.

Soffritto (see page 278) to use as a base for soups and *ragùs*.

Spice pastes (see pages 281–283) to use as shortcuts for dinner every week.

Beef (see page 272), chicken thighs, sausages.

Biscuit dough (see page 270).

Reduced stock (see page 273) for gravies, risottos, and soups.

Pesto cubes for Flavio's pasta suppers (see page 273).

Frozen bananas, grapes, berries, and plums for smoothies (see page 286).

Vanilla ice cream to whip into quick desserts.

NOTES ON HOME FREEZING

Temperature This should be kept between 10°F and 16°F. If you are going to freeze a big batch of food, remember to switch the freezer onto "fast freeze" a couple of hours beforehand so that your food can be frozen as quickly as possible. This keeps the ice crystals as small as possible and causes less damage to the cells of the food.

Restocking your freezer Don't cram as much fresh food as possible into your freezer all at once—it will raise the temperature of the freezer. Ideally you should freeze no more than 10 percent of the total capacity at any one time.

Vacuum bags These work really well. Not only do they reduce the chance of freezer burn (see below), but also you end up with flat bags that take up much less space in the freezer. To use, simply fill the pouches and then suck out the air using a pump. If you don't have a pump, you can use a straw to suck out the air from the bag before quickly sealing it.

Freezer burn This happens when water evaporates from the surface of the food in the freezer air. It leaves behind empty pockets that appear like white spots. Although freezer burn is not harmful, it does affect flavor and texture. To prevent freezer burn, always wrap food tightly in plastic wrap or use plastic freezer bags, taking care to eliminate as much air as possible (double-bagging is even better as it reduces ice crystals on the food). If using plastic storage containers, choose one the right size to avoid air pockets. Vacuum freezer bags also work well in this respect (see left).

Labeling It sounds pedantic, but life is much easier if you label whatever you freeze—and in the case of sauces and stocks, remind yourself of what quantity is in each portion. For example, I freeze Thai green curry paste in labeled portions that are the right size for a curry for four.

Keep a list If your freezer is big and stuffed with little containers of sauces, spice cubes, or vegetables, it is a really good idea to keep a list of what is in there. An inventory helps you see what you have and shows you what needs using up sooner rather than later. Keep the list on a tablet computer or cell phone, and add and delete items as necessary.

Safe defrosting Meat, fish, and poultry should ideally be defrosted slowly in the fridge. This way, they will never be in the "danger zone" at which bacteria start to grow (40–135°F). For speedy defrosting, put the meat in a plastic bag in a sink of cold water; if the water becomes warm, change it to cold again. Microwaving is only recommended if used on the appropriate "defrost" setting and only for small pieces that won't take too long to defrost (otherwise the meat will start to cook). Always cook food as soon as it has defrosted.

Refreezing It is perfectly safe to freeze items that you have cooked from a previously frozen piece of meat. For example, it's fine to defrost raw chicken overnight in the fridge, cook it thoroughly the next day into a curry, and re-freeze it when it is cold as a curry. What you mustn't do is defrost meat and poultry and re-freeze it again without cooking.

Liquids I expect most of us have inadvertently frozen a bottle of wine we were trying to chill in a hurry. Either the bottle has cracked or the cork has come out. This is because liquid expands by 10 percent when frozen. As a general rule, don't use glass and don't overfill containers. Make sure you leave at least an inch of headroom to allow for expansion; this will prevent lids being forced off during freezing.

WHAT TO FREEZE AND HOW?

Most foods freeze well and as a rule of thumb can be frozen for up to 3 months without harm; after this time they may start to deteriorate. Some vegetables are held in suspended animation if frozen immediately after being picked—for example, peas are arguably better transported frozen rather than fresh. Other foods, such as strawberries, retain their flavor but may lose their texture (refer to "What not to freeze" for a guide on things to avoid).

fruit and vegetables

RAW VEGETABLES Blanch in boiling water for 3 minutes before freezing; refresh under cold running water and drain really well. Blanching destroys most enzymes and bacteria and helps maintain color, texture, flavor, and vitamin C.

EGGPLANT SLICES A friend of ours, Carrie, introduced me to the joys of frozen eggplant. She slices and blanches lots of them all at once, then she portions them into vacuum packs and freezes them ready to pull out for moussaka, lasagne, or *melanzane parmigiana*. The joy of blanching them first means you don't need to cook them as well, since they are soft enough after freezing to be baked right away.

WILD BERRIES AND ROSEHIPS Gather these as you find them and "open freeze" on a baking sheet in the freezer. Once frozen, pack into freezer bags and seal.

HERBS Either finely chop and "dry freeze" on baking sheets (see page 273) or combine with olive oil and freeze in ice-cube trays (see page 273).

eggs and dairy

EGG WHITES Keep a container in the freezer for raw egg whites and add to it whenever you separate eggs for baking. To turn your egg whites into meringues, simply defrost them and whisk in double their weight of sugar.

HARD CHEESE AND BUTTER Seal in vacuum bags or wrap tightly in foil. Defrost in the fridge overnight. Grated Parmesan also stores well.

everyday basics

BREAD Cut whole loaves into slices first and pack into ziplock bags—this way, you can take out individual slices for toasting straight from the freezer (whereas whole loaves would take considerably longer to defrost and could dry out). Part-baked loaves are also ideal for freezing as the oven finishes them off well.

BREAD CRUMBS AND NUTS These are perfectly fine frozen. Just pile them into freezer bags, taking care to expel as much air as possible, label and pop in the freezer.

CRUMBLE TOPPING This freezes well and is a great shortcut when you are cooking in a hurry. A basic recipe for six is: 18 tablespoons butter, 2 cups all-purpose flour, 1¼ cups sugar, and 3 cups almond flour. Simply rub the butter into the flour to form bread crumbs (I use a food processor for this) and stir in the sugar and almonds. Pack into a sealed container and freeze until needed.

COOKIE DOUGH It is always worth doubling recipes for cookie dough and keeping a batch in the freezer ready to go. A good shortcut is to shape the dough into three log shapes and freeze wrapped in sheets of parchment paper. Then all you have to do is cut out the shapes and bake them in the oven when you need them. To make 50–60 x 1½in diameter Almond cookies: mix 9 tablespoons salted butter (or unsalted butter with a pinch of salt), ⅔ cup sugar, 1 cup all-purpose flour, 1⅓ cups almond flour, 1½ tablespoons heavy cream, seeds from a vanilla pod, and 1 teaspoon of baking powder. Roll into logs and freeze for up to 3 months. Remove from the freezer and leave for 10 minutes before cutting into circles ⅓in thick. Cook for 10 minutes at 350°F for defrosted and frozen dough.

STOCK I always keep chicken stock, seafood stock, and meat stock in my freezer (see pages 276–277), as well as bags of vegetable scraps and roast chicken carcasses to turn into stock another day when I have more time.

PASTA SHEETS To freeze pasta sheets, cook for 2 minutes in salted boiling water, put into iced water for 2 minutes, remove and dry on a clean towel. Stack layered with plastic wrap and freeze. Fresh stuffed pasta also freezes well: simply "open freeze" on baking sheets dusted with semolina, and bag up once frozen. Keep for 3 months.

PASTRY All varieties of raw pastry dough freeze well. However, choux pastry freezes well after cooking, too. To crisp up profiteroles after defrosting, pop them briefly into an oven for 5 minutes at 350°F.

PIZZA BASES I usually make a big batch of pizza dough and bake a few bases for just 2 minutes to go in the freezer. This

way the children have access to quick meals they can finish themselves. Try the sourdough recipe on pages 225–228; the dough has an amazing flavor.

meat and poultry

We often buy a beef box from a local farm. The beef is hung for 28 days, is organic, and we know the farmer. We cut out the middleman so the price is good for the amazing flavor and quality he supplies. However, we couldn't benefit from this kind of project without a freezer because we have to buy a large quantity all at once.

While meat freezes well, meat that has been previously frozen can sometimes end up having a slightly hard, rubbery texture. Put simply, as meat freezes, ice crystals burst through the cells and puncture them, and then as the meat defrosts, fluids leak out of the cells, which dehydrates the meat further. When you subsequently cook the meat, it leaks more water again, which is what gives you that rubbery texture. Cooked meat is less affected by freezing, since some of the fluid has already come out, and so the cells are not affected in the same way.

Here are a few tips to minimize the damage done to fresh meat when you freeze it. First of all, freeze it as quickly as possible. Lay it, open to the cold, on baking sheets with the freezer set to "fast freeze." As soon as the meat is frozen, wrap it up tightly in plastic wrap or vacuum bags and label. Use it in a matter of weeks rather than months, as it will continue deteriorating due to the loss of fluid from the cells.

WHAT NOT TO FREEZE?

FOODS WITH A HIGH WATER CONTENT, such as tomatoes, peppers, zucchini, cucumbers, radishes, lettuce, watercress, melons, avocados, bananas, and strawberries all turn to mush when you defrost them. That doesn't mean you can't freeze these foods—it's just you are better off cooking them after defrosting rather than eating them raw. Bananas, melons, avocados, and strawberries are fine to blend into a smoothie from frozen (see page 286). Or try dropping single frozen strawberries into a drink instead of ice cubes; by the time they defrost, you will have finished the drink and can eat the strawberry.

CUSTARDS, MAYONNAISE, EGG-BASED SAUCES, AND MILKY SAUCES, SUCH AS BÉCHAMEL These can become watery and lumpy when defrosted.

STEWS THAT CONTAIN POTATOES Frozen potato becomes mushy when it defrosts, so freeze the stew without the potatoes.

GRAVY Most gravies contain fat, which separates on defrosting. It is better to freeze stock to add to meat juices after roasting (see pages 276–277).

PREPARING FOOD FOR THE FREEZER

herbs

Herbs keep well in damp paper towels in the fridge, but most can be frozen to extend their life by up to 3 months.

DRY FREEZING This method is suitable for soft herbs such as basil, dill, cilantro, chives, tarragon, and mint. The advantage of "dry freezing" is the herbs freeze quickly, locking in flavor, although they often darken as they defrost—so don't expect to use them as a flash of bright green garnish.
METHOD Chop your herbs finely, spread them over a baking sheet, and put it in the freezer. Once frozen, gather them up and pack into freezer bags ready to use in cooking. Store for up to 3 months.

HERB OIL AND BUTTER CUBES This method is suitable for any herbs, and the advantage is the herbs keep their color better. Think cilantro in olive oil mixed into couscous, dill in butter in potato salad, tarragon in butter for hot chicken, or basil in extra virgin olive oil in tomato soup or just melted onto hot crusty bread.
METHOD Finely chop your herbs and sprinkle into ice-cube trays until half full. Top up with extra virgin olive oil (don't use sunflower oil because it doesn't freeze!) and put into the freezer. For butter cubes mix the herbs and butter together first and pack into the ice-cube tray. Once frozen, pack into sealed bags and store for up to 3 months. To use, stir into hot cooked pasta, vegetables, or couscous.

PESTO CUBES Pesto is great frozen into cubes, too—when melted it tastes as fresh as if it had just been prepared (see photo page 275). Flavio, our son, loves pesto and pasta, and it makes a great quick supper. All you need to do is pull out a cube or two of pesto from the freezer, defrost briefly in the microwave or melt in a hot pan, and stir it into the hot pasta once it is cooked.
METHOD To make pesto for six people, process 2 cups fresh basil leaves, 1 small peeled garlic clove, and with 1 cup toasted pine nuts in a food processor. Gradually pour in ½ cup extra virgin olive oil, and process to a coarse paste. Add ¼ cup grated Parmesan and process very briefly. Freeze in ice-cube trays. Once frozen, pack into sealed bags and store for up to 3 months.

ICE CUBES For fun, you can freeze whole mint leaves in ice-cubes for adding to rum-based drinks or borage flowers for gin and tonic.

spice cubes

One of my favorite ideas came from our son Giorgio, who loves steamed broccoli or spinach sautéed in extra virgin olive oil with finely chopped garlic and chile. He thought that we could simply freeze the garlic and chile, already chopped, in oil in our ice-cube trays. We tried it and have been doing it ever since (see page 274). It has to be extra virgin olive oil; others don't freeze as well and won't have the finished flavor. While the broccoli steams, I melt a spice cube in a small frying pan and then toss in the drained broccoli as soon as it is cooked—delicious! With some chopped parsley added to the mix, these also make an instant pasta sauce. Put some pasta on to cook and melt the cubes in a frying pan. When the pasta is done, drain it and combine with the spicy oil in the frying pan. A good shortcut for Asian dishes is to prepare the individual ingredients in advance and freeze them in ice-cube trays. Try individual portions of finely chopped ginger, chile, or garlic mixed with oil; they are a great timesaver.

stocks, gravy, and sauces

Like most people, I often have to cook in a hurry—but having a collection of reduced stocks in my freezer helps me make gravies and sauces quickly to accompany sausages, pork chops, steak, chicken, duck breasts, etc.

stocks

Freezing comes into its own twice over when it comes to stocks. My freezer is full of bags of scraps that might otherwise be thrown away: carcasses from roast chickens, ends of salami, fish bones, shrimp shells, vegetable peelings and onion pieces, parsley stems, etc.— all perfect for the stockpot. Once I have enough to make a big batch of stock, I boil everything up and, once cold, pour it into freezer containers or ice-cube trays ready to go in the freezer (see photo page 275). Then, when I roast some meat, I will add a few cubes to the gravy, along with a tablespoon of Apple and rosemary jelly (see page 66). Together with chef friends Brian Turner and Jasper Ackroyd, we agreed you need three essential stocks in your freezer: seafood, brown chicken, and meat (see pages 276–277 for recipes).

NOTES ON STOCK-MAKING
Giancarlo and I have been making stocks for years, and we are still experimenting with ways to perfect them. Here are some tips.

INGREDIENTS What you put into your stock tends to be dictated by the seasons and what you have on hand (although freezing vegetable, fish, and meat scraps ready to go helps). Bear in mind that certain additions will have an influence on the finished flavor, such as mushrooms, fennel, butternut squash peelings, herbs, tops and tails of scallions, and peppers. Onions, leeks, carrots, and celery are nearly always included for a base flavor. Never use cabbage or starchy vegetables such as potatoes or anything starting to spoil.

Veal is regarded as the king of stock. However, it can be heavy, and many people prefer to use chicken since it is more adaptable. Pig's feet, ears, tail, skin, nose, etc. are always a welcome addition to any stock, for body. For chicken stock, either use a leftover roast chicken carcass or the raw carcass left over from boning a bird; if you have one available, a whole broiler (an old bird that doesn't lay any more) or a capon (a castrated male bird) also give very good flavor.

SALT This is much better left out of stock, especially if you are going to reduce it before or after freezing as the process of reduction concentrates the flavor.

TO BROWN OR NOT TO BROWN? This depends on how intense you want your stock. Most of the time you will want to brown your vegetables and bones/chicken wings first, either with a little olive oil in a roasting pan in a hot oven (400°F) or in a heavy frying pan on the stove until an even chestnut color all over but definitely not burnt. This caramelization gives the stock a rich color and deepens the flavor. In darker stocks, it is nice to add some halved tomatoes when roasting your bones and vegetables.

For a light color and flavor (especially if using veal), you can opt out of the browning process. Simply put the meat into a stockpot and pour in some boiling water to scald the meat and sterilize the surface. Pour out the water before adding the remaining ingredients and topping up with fresh water.

THE GOLDEN RULE Never let your stock boil too hard or it will become cloudy and bitter. Think slow, bubbling brook not white-water rapids!

REDUCING To concentrate the flavor of your stock for use in sauces, etc., we like to strain it first then reduce the stock by letting it bubble away gently until it has reduced by a third of its original volume. It can then be cooled and frozen in the normal way; like this, it takes up less room in the freezer.

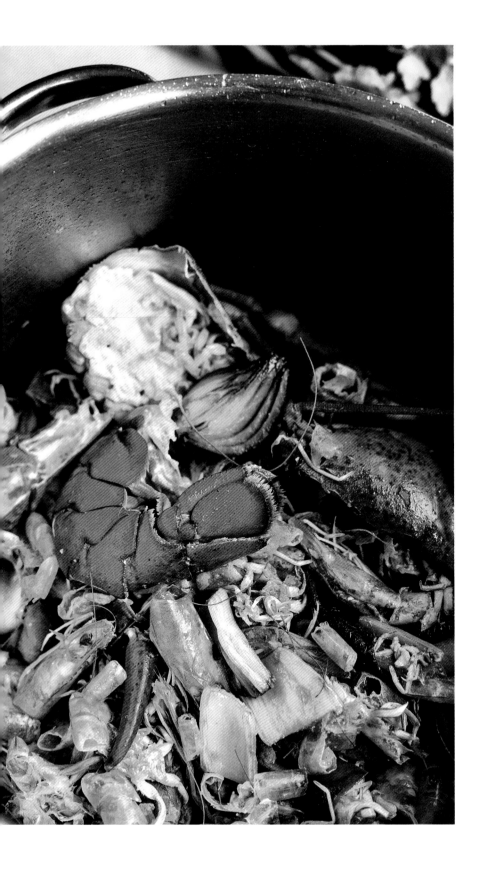

stock recipes

The following stock recipes are designed to make big batches for the freezer, and require big pans, however you can make less if you prefer. We haven't included a recipe for vegetable stock because it only takes 30 minute to make from fresh. We freeze bags of vegetable peelings for this purpose—celery tops, parsley stems, carrot peelings, onion skins, etc.—and simply boil them up when we need some vegetable stock.

ROASTED SEAFOOD STOCK

If you have ever eaten spaghetti with clams, risotto with seafood, or fish soup in a restaurant at the water's edge on vacation in Italy or France and wanted to recreate that flavor, this is how to do it. To transform a recipe from the bland to the sublime, reduce the stock to one-third of its original volume, just a few spoons, and freeze in small amounts.

makes approx. 2 quarts

2lbs mixed shellfish shells, such as those from shrimp, crayfish, lobster, and crab
⅓ cup olive oil
2 medium carrots, roughly chopped
1 large white onions, roughly chopped
2 celery ribs, roughly chopped
a large handful of parsley stems
½ cup brandy
⅓ cup tomato paste
5 quarts cold water

Preheat the oven to 350°F. Put the shellfish shells in a roasting pan and bake for 30 minutes or until they become crisp and dry.

Heat the oil in a large saucepan or stockpot and add the carrots, onions, and celery. Cook over medium to high heat for about 15 minutes until lightly browned, allowing the vegetables to catch and caramelize on the bottom of the pan. Add the shells from the oven and the parsley stems and stir through. Pour in the brandy and let the alcohol evaporate for a few minutes.

Rinse out the pan in which you roasted the shellfish shells with a little water and add the liquid to the pan. Add the tomato paste to the pan, stir through, and then add the cold water. Bring to a boil, turn down to a gentle simmer, and bubble away gently for 1½–2 hours or until the stock thickens. Strain through cheesecloth to obtain a clear stock or through a fine metal sieve for a thicker stock. If you wish, return the stock to the pan and reduce by one-third for a concentrated flavor. Cool thoroughly before freezing in vacuum bags or ice-cube trays.

BROWN CHICKEN STOCK

This is our friend Brian Turner's recipe, which works every time. This stock makes an excellent vegetable soup or a great base for risotto. If you don't have two carcasses, you can freeze one until you have another one ready.

makes approx. 2 quarts
4 tablespoons olive oil
carcasses and leftovers from
  2 roast chickens
2 medium onions, roughly chopped
2 leeks, roughly chopped
2 celery ribs, roughly chopped
2 carrots, roughly chopped
6 tomatoes, roughly chopped
2 garlic cloves, peeled and finely
  chopped
6 parsley stems
1 bay leaf
1 sprig of thyme
7 quarts cold water

Heat the oil in a large saucepan or stockpot. Pull the roast chicken bones into pieces and add to the pan along with the onions, leeks, celery, and carrots. Stir over medium to high heat for 15–20 minutes until everything is lightly browned. Put in the tomatoes, garlic, parsley stems, bay leaf, and thyme and top up with the water. Bring to a boil and skim off any scum. Now reduce the heat to a gentle simmer and bubble away gently for 2–3 hours before straining. You can either pass the stock through cheesecloth to obtain a clear stock or through a fine metal sieve for a thicker stock. If you want to concentrate the flavor more, you may wish to reduce the stock at this stage by returning it to the pan and simmering it gently until it has reduced by one-third. Cool and freeze in vacuum bags or ice-cube trays.

JASPER AYKROYD'S MEAT STOCK

This is an essential ingredient in rich gravies and sauces, especially if you reduce it well at the end so it has a really intense flavor. Jasper says he "tends" to his stock rather like a sleeping child, checking on it every now and again.

makes approx. 3 quarts
2lbs pork, veal, and beef bones,
  roughly chopped
2 large onions
¼ cup extra virgin olive oil
2 celery ribs, roughly chopped
2 carrots, roughly chopped
2 garlic cloves, halved
1 sprig of rosemary
2 bay leaves
a few parsley stems
1 teaspoon black peppercorns
2 cloves
1¼ cups red wine or brandy
6 quarts cold water

Preheat the oven to 400°F. Put the bones into a roasting pan and roast for 20 minutes. Meanwhile, peel the onions and cut each one into roughly ten pieces; set aside the ends along with the outer skins. Heat the oil in a very large stockpot and add the center parts of the onion with the celery and carrots. Cook over medium to high heat until golden brown, approx. 15–20 minutes.

Remove the roasting pan from the oven and add the reserved onion skins and ends. Return to the oven for another 20 minutes or until the onion skins start to brown. Remove the pan from the oven, pour out most of the fat (you can use this for roast potatoes or popovers), and transfer the bones and onion skins to the stockpot. Add the garlic, herbs, and spices.

Place the roasting pan on the stove over medium heat and pour in the red wine or brandy. Bring to a boil, stirring all the time, and allow the alcohol to reduce for 5 minutes. Pour the reduced liquid into the stockpot, top up with the water, and bring to a boil. Immediately reduce the heat to a gentle simmer and skim off all the scum and fat that has risen to the surface—this will taint the stock and make it cloudy. Simmer gently for 4–5 hours or until the stock has reduced by half its original volume. It will more or less take care of itself, but keep an eye on it because it will need to be skimmed from time to time. Once the stock is ready, strain it through a colander to remove the bones and again through a sieve.

If you wish, you can now reduce the stock by pouring it into a smaller saucepan or back into the stockpot and letting it bubble away gently until it has reduced by one-third. I like to reduce mine a lot to give it a really intense flavor. Freeze in ice-cube trays or plastic containers to use in gravies and sauces.

GRAVIES AND SAUCES

Frozen chicken and meat stock makes flavorful gravies and sauces. I wouldn't recommend freezing gravy because of its high fat content, which causes it to separate when you defrost it. Far better to make your gravy fresh using fresh meat juices from the roast flavored with your homemade frozen stock.

making gravy

Once your meat is cooked, remove it from the roasting pan and set aside on a plate to rest, covered with foil and a cloth to keep in the heat. (For small amounts of meat or sausages, cook until done and keep them in the pan.) Pour out any fat from the roasting pan or frying pan, but keep the all-important cooking juices. Set the pan over medium heat, add a good dash of wine—whichever color you prefer—and deglaze the pan, i.e. scrape the caramelized brown areas from the bottom (don't use any burnt bits because they will spoil the stock). Let the wine bubble away for a few minutes, and then whisk in a little cornstarch mixed with some cold water. Don't worry about lumps, if there are any, because you will strain it later. Now add the stock. You can either use frozen cubes straight from the freezer if you are making a small amount of gravy, or defrost a large amount of stock fully beforehand and add it once it is liquid again. Bring the gravy to a boil and whisk it well. Strain if necessary and season to taste with salt and pepper.

FLAVORING YOUR GRAVY You can adapt the basic gravy recipe with different flavors. For a herby gravy to serve with chicken, add some chopped rosemary or thyme; for a sweeter gravy to serve with roast lamb, add a tablespoon of red currant jelly or Apple and rosemary jelly (see page 66); for a rich onion gravy to serve with sausages or roast beef, add a spoonful of homemade Spiced red onion marmalade (see page 38).

GIANCARLO'S SOFFRITTO

A good flavorful *soffritto* forms the base of all hearty Italian stews, soups, and *ragùs*. We grow celery and carrots in our garden and make up batches of this *soffritto* when we have a lot of vegetables. The flavor is so much more intense made with our own homegrown celery and carrots, which are definitely sweeter than any vegetables from the supermarket.

makes approx. 7 ounces (enough for 1 ragù or chicken casseroles for 6 people)

⅔ **cup extra virgin olive oil**
1½ **red or white onions, very finely chopped**
2 **celery ribs, very finely chopped**
1 **medium carrot, very finely chopped**
1 **teaspoon salt and plenty of freshly ground black pepper**
2 **sprigs of fresh rosemary**
3 **bay leaves**
2 **garlic cloves, left whole and crushed with the flat side of a knife**

Heat the olive oil in a pan and add the onion, celery, carrot, and seasoning. Add the rosemary, bay leaves, and garlic and cook over low heat for 15 minutes, stirring often, until the onion is soft and sweet. Remove the rosemary and bay leaves, cool, and freeze in vacuum bags or small plastic containers.

Use in the Tuscan *ragù* recipe on page 260.

SPICE PASTES

Now we have started making and either chilling or freezing these little containers of spice paste, I wonder how we coped without them. The following recipes are for Thai, Sri Lankan, and Indian curry bases. They can be made in big batches and either used right away, or chilled in the fridge, or frozen in portions in ice-cube trays or bags.

KAY PLUNKETT-HOGGE'S GREEN CURRY PASTE

Kay was born and brought up in Thailand and speaks the language fluently. She is a cookbook writer and runs classes demonstrating Thai cooking. We persuaded her to part with her recipe for this classic Thai paste. I went shopping with Kay for the ingredients, and she reminded me that fresh ingredients make the best paste. For vegetarians and those who don't like the strong fish flavor, leave out the shrimp paste. The paste also makes a great soup if combined with lightly fried zucchini, peas, green beans, and coconut milk.

makes enough paste for 4 curries for 4 people
2–4 tablespoons roughly chopped green bird's eye chiles, depending on how hot you like your curry
4 tablespoons chopped galangal or ginger
4 lemongrass stalks, chopped
8 Thai shallots, chopped
4 teaspoons grated Kaffir lime zest
1 large bunch of fresh cilantro (stems, roots, and leaves), chopped
2 teaspoons coriander seeds
4 teaspoons white peppercorns
2 teaspoons ground cumin
4 teaspoons Thai shrimp paste (optional)
good pinch of salt

Pound the hardest ingredients first to a fine powder in a mortar and pestle than add the remaining ingredients. Grind to a smooth paste. Divide into four portions. Use right away, or store in a sealed container in the fridge up to 3 days; alternatively freeze in small vacuum bags or sealed plastic containers for up to 3 months.

KAY PLUNKETT-HOGGE'S GREEN CURRY WITH CHICKEN AND BAMBOO SHOOTS

This is Kay's recipe for a gorgeously creamy, spicy Thai green curry. We love the sweetness and, as Kay says, it sings with color and flavor. She prefers to use whole bone-in chicken thighs; she skins most of them but leaves a couple with the skins on for added oil and flavor. The meat can also be diced, which reduces the cooking time. Kay uses bamboo shoots that have been vacuum-packed in water rather than canned ones. These are available from most Asian stores in easy-to-use chunks. If you can't find them, the canned sliced ones are fine as well. You can replace the chicken with pork, beef, or shrimp.

serves 4
1 tablespoon vegetable oil
1 portion of Kay Plunkett-Hogge's green curry paste (enough for 4 people)
14oz can coconut milk
½–¾ cup water (amount depends on the thickness of your coconut milk)
1½lbs chicken thighs
2 tablespoons Thai fish sauce (*nam pla*)
1 tablespoon sugar
7oz bamboo shoots, chopped
2 Thai eggplant, quartered
4oz pea eggplant (if you can't find these add an extra 4oz Thai eggplant)
a handful of Thai sweet basil (or Italian basil if you can't find Thai basil), shredded

Heat the oil in a wok or large, heavy-bottomed frying pan and stir-fry the paste until it releases its fragrance—approx. 1 minute. Add ¾ cup of the coconut milk and bring to a boil slowly, stirring to dissolve the paste. Once the paste has dissolved, add the water and chicken. Bring to a boil, then add the rest of the coconut milk. Bring back to a boil, and then simmer for up to 45 minutes or until the chicken is cooked through. Add the fish sauce and the sugar, adjusting the seasoning if necessary. Stir in the bamboo shoots and eggplant and boil for another 3 minutes. Throw in the basil and serve accompanied with rice.

MANJULA SAMARASINGHE'S SRI LANKAN SPICE PASTE FOR VEGETABLE CURRIES

Manjula and I share a love of food. When traveling with her in Sri Lanka she introduced me to her country's cooking and we were amazed to see the variety of vegetarian curries made from mango, jackfruit, beets, green beans, mushrooms, lentils, okra, and potatoes. Now we eat Sri Lankan curry and rice twice a week at home using Manjula's spice pastes, which are really versatile (see page 263 for recipes). Sri Lankan curry paste is normally very hot, but we have made this version medium-hot to suit Western tastes. However, feel free to adjust the number of chiles to your personal taste.

makes enough paste for 4 vegetable curries for 4 people

⅓ cup coriander seeds

2 teaspoons fennel seeds

1½ teaspoons black mustard seeds

2 teaspoons cumin seeds

2in cinnamon stick

1 teaspoon turmeric

4 cardamom pods, husks discarded

10 curry leaves

10–15 fenugreek seeds

1 medium onion, roughly chopped, depending on strength

5 green chiles, finely chopped

4 teaspoons fine sea salt

⅔ cup vegetable oil

Toast all the spices in a dry frying pan for a minute or two until they release their aroma; cool and grind to a fine powder in a spice grinder or mortar and pestle. Combine the spices with the chopped onion, chiles, salt, and oil. Divide the paste into four portions. Either use right away or store in a sealed container in the fridge for up to a month; alternatively freeze in small vacuum bags or sealed plastic containers for up to 3 months.

MANJULA SAMARASINGHE'S SRI LANKAN SPICE PASTE FOR MEAT AND CHICKEN CURRIES

This paste is devised for chicken or meat curries. We make it with chicken, but you could use goat, beef or lamb instead.

makes enough paste for 4 curries for 4 people

⅔ cup coriander seeds

2 teaspoons cumin seeds

2 teaspoons fennel seeds

10–15 fenugreek seeds

1 teaspoon black mustard seeds

2 teaspoons black peppercorns

8 curry leaves

8 cloves garlic, peeled and finely chopped

4 teaspoons salt

4 tablespoons finely chopped fresh ginger

2 medium onions, finely chopped

½ cup vegetable oil

Toast all the spices in a dry frying pan over low heat until they just start to brown, about 5 minutes; cool on a plate (or a piece of paper, so you can put the spices straight into the grinder). Grind to a powder in a spice grinder or mortar and pestle.

Put the garlic, salt, ginger, and onion in a bowl. Pour in the oil and stir in the ground spices to form a paste. Divide the mixture into four portions. Either use right away or store in a sealed container in the fridge for up to a month; alternatively freeze in small vacuum bags or sealed plastic containers for up to 3 months.

MANJULA'S CHICKEN CURRY

This recipe is for a "wet" chicken curry to serve with rice or hoppers (see page 228). Manjula often adds chopped raw potatoes with the chicken to bulk up the curry. Manjula prefers to use a whole cut-up chicken rather than boneless chicken breasts because she finds it gives the sauce a better flavor, but for speed you can always use boneless chicken breasts. This recipe works equally well with raw shrimp, which require just a few minutes cooking time; if using shrimp, leave out the potatoes and use parsley at the end instead of curry leaves.

serves 4

2 tablespoons sunflower oil

1 portion of Sri-Lankan spice paste for meat and chicken curries (see left)

3 skinless, boneless chicken breasts, cut into bite-sized pieces

⅔ cup water, canned tomatoes or coconut milk

sea salt and freshly ground black pepper

a few fresh or dried curry leaves or fresh cilantro leaves, to garnish

Heat the oil and spice paste in a medium saucepan, stirring over medium heat for a few minutes until the paste darkens slightly. Add the chicken and stir through, letting it cook in the paste for 5 minutes until seared all over. Pour in the water, tomatoes, or coconut milk and simmer gently until the chicken is cooked through, approx. 15 minutes. Taste and adjust the seasoning if necessary with salt and black pepper. Serve with rice and garnish with curry leaves or cilantro.

TIKKA MASALA CURRY PASTE

This is our version of the base for this much-loved Anglo-Indian dish. The recipe is loosely based on Rupa Goolati's where the paste is mixed with yogurt and used to marinate and tenderize the chicken. I freeze our paste in four portions in vacuum bags and flatten them so that they take up little space in the freezer. The paste defrosts quickly and so makes a great midweek supper.

makes enough paste for 4 curries for 4 people

1 heaping tablespoon coriander seeds

1 teaspoon cardamom seeds, husks discarded

6 teaspoons cumin seeds

10 black peppercorns

4 cloves
½ teaspoon finely grated nutmeg
6 tablespoons lemon juice
4 medium red onions, roughly chopped
3–4 red chiles, seeds discarded,
   roughly chopped
10–12 black peppercorns
16 garlic cloves, peeled
2in piece of fresh ginger, peeled and
   roughly chopped

Grind the spices to a smooth, fine powder using a mortar and pestle or a spice grinder. Blend with the remaining ingredients in a food processor to form a paste. Divide into four portions. Use right away or keep in the fridge, covered, for a week or freeze in small vacuum bags or plastic boxes with a lid for up to 3 months.

CALDESI CHICKEN TIKKA MASALA

Although chicken is the standard way to enjoy this recipe, it works really well with salmon or shrimp. We like to use chicken thighs with the bone in for flavor, but they do take longer to cook. To cut down the cooking time take the bone out or use breast meat. If we are barbecuing, threading the chicken breast onto skewers is a great option. For a healthy alternative, stop after broiling or grilling the chicken or fish and serve with a salad, omitting the sauce.

serves 4

1 portion of Tikka masala curry paste
   (enough for 4 people)
¼ cup Greek yogurt
1¾lbs skinless chicken thighs and/or
   breasts, cut into 2in cubes
1 tablespoon ghee or salted butter
2 heaping tablespoons tomato paste
3 tablespoons heavy cream (omit this
   if you are using coconut milk)
¾ cup water or coconut milk
juice of ½ lemon

fine sea salt
2–3 teaspoons sugar
cilantro or curry leaves, to garnish

Mix one-third of the Tikka masala curry paste together with the yogurt in a bowl and add the chicken. Set aside the remaining paste in the fridge for later. Toss to combine, cover, and leave to marinate in the fridge for at least 30 minutes and up to a day. The longer the marinating time, the better the flavor.

Preheat your broiler to medium. When ready to cook the chicken, lay the pieces onto a broiler pan and pour on any remaining yogurt. Collect the juices in a tray underneath. Cook the chicken for 15–30 minutes, turning halfway through cooking, until it is cooked through and tinged dark brown around the edges. The cooking time will vary depending on the size of the pieces. They can be threaded onto a skewer to make them easier to turn.

Meanwhile, heat the ghee or butter in a large frying pan. When melted, add the remaining tikka masala paste and stir through. Cook for 5 minutes over a medium heat. Add the tomato paste, cream (if using), and water or coconut milk. Heat through and then add the lemon juice, salt, and sugar to taste. Add the chicken to the pan with the juices from the broiler pan. Stir through to combine, season to taste, adding more salt or chile, if you like, and serve scattered with torn cilantro or curry leaves. Serve with rice, Mango chutney (see pages 35–36), and Cyrus's lime pickle (see page 184).

FRUIT

As well as freezing raw fruit such as blackberries or raspberries, we like to keep a stock of homemade fruit purées in our freezer ready for turning into crumbles and pies, or serving alongside roast meats.

COOKED APPLE

Cooked apple can be turned into a filling for an apple crumble or pie, eaten as it is with yogurt and granola, served as apple sauce for roast pork, or reduced to make apple butter or cheese. I can't bear to see wonderful apples fall to the ground while we buy transported ones from afar. All we need to do it learn how to preserve our own varieties to enjoy them all year round. As blackberries and apples grow side by side, I like to use a couple of handfuls in crumbles when I have them. Quince and pears are great mixed with apple too.

makes enough for 4 crumbles for 6 people
9lbs cooking apples, peeled, cored and sliced
2 x 2in cinnamon sticks
⅔ cup raisins (optional)
1 cup soft brown sugar
4 cups cold water

Put the apple, cinnamon sticks, raisins, and sugar in a large saucepan, cover with the cold water, and bring to a boil, partially covered with a lid. Reduce the heat and simmer gently for 10–15 minutes, or until just soft, stirring occasionally to make sure the sauce cooks evenly. Once the apples are just soft, remove the pan from the heat and set aside to cool. Divide into four portions and freeze in small vacuum bags or sealed plastic containers for up to 3 months. Cooked apple could also be waterbathed in jars, see page 253.

APPLE CRUMBLE

To make up a crumble, use one portion of Cooked apple. The crumble topping can be made up in advance and will keep very well in the freezer. Open freeze on a tray and gather up into bags once frozen. Keep for 3 months in the freezer. For a variation add a handful of oats or chopped almonds to the crumble.

serves 6–8
9 tablespoons butter
1 cup all-purpose flour
⅔ cup sugar
1⅓ cups almond flour
1 portion of Cooked apple (see left)

Preheat the oven to 350°F. Rub the butter, flour, sugar, and almond flour together by hand to make the crumble mixture. Put the cooked apples in baking dish and scatter the crumble on top. Bake for 30–40 minutes or until golden. Serve with homemade Crème fraîche (see page 223).

QUINCE AND APPLE

This makes a really fruity and zingy filling for crumbles or pies, and it also doubles as a sauce to complement salty roast pork. Make as much as you can when quinces are around and freeze in portions.

makes enough for 1 crumble for 4 people (or 16 servings with roast pork)
2 quinces
juice of 1 lemon
1 vanilla pod, split into two
¾ cup cold water
2 cooking apples
½ cup sugar

Peel and core the quinces and cut into thin slices. Put these into a saucepan with the lemon juice and vanilla pod, and cover with the water. Bring to a boil and cook until just soft, approx. 20 minutes. Meanwhile, peel and core the apples and cut them into thin slices. Once the quinces are just soft, stir in the apples and sugar. Cook for another

5 minutes. Eat right away as a sauce or cool and freeze in small vacuum bags or sealed plastic containers for up to 3 months. To make into a crumble follow the recipe left.

FROZEN COCONUT SAMBAL

In Sri Lanka coconuts are grated using a machine that clamps onto a table and is turned by a handle. The sharp end is shaped like half a lemon with a series of serrated blades that grind the two halves of the coconut down from the inside. Grated coconut is primarily used to make coconut milk and oil. Coconut graters are available from some Asian shops, but a simple grater would work, too: break the coconut into pieces and grate the white part only.

Coconut sambal is delightful served with the hoppers on page 228, or as an accompaniment to either of the Sri-Lankan curries on page 263.

makes 8 ounces, enough for 8 portions

1 coconut
½ medium onion or 1 small banana shallot, finely chopped
1 garlic clove, peeled and finely chopped or grated
1–2 teaspoons fine salt, to taste
generous pinch of freshly ground black pepper
a few curry leaves (optional)
1 teaspoon cayenne powder
2–4 teaspoons lemon juice, to taste

Crack open the coconut with a hammer and grate the flesh on a fine grater. If possible, try to include some of the brown skin, which contains some of the oil and flavor. Combine the onion, garlic, salt, black pepper, and curry leaves (if using) in a mortar and pestle and pound to a smooth paste. Add the cayenne powder followed by the grated coconut. Pound again with the pestle for a couple of minutes until well blended, and then spoon the contents into a bowl. Stir in the lemon juice to taste and season if necessary with more salt or pepper. Either eat right away or divide into small containers and store in the fridge for up to 5 days or in the freezer for three months.

FREEZER PICKLED CUCUMBERS

I remember playing the word game hangman with my children once and getting down to "_u_umber"; the unfortunate man was nearly hung and they just couldn't guess the missing letter—even though cucumber was one of their favorite foods! I worried about their future but we laugh to this day about it and often refer to the long, green vegetables as "_u_umbers."

This recipe is a great way to use up small amounts of leftover spiced vinegar or cucumbers from your vegetable patch. This version is based on Lynda Brown's recipe from her *Preserving Book*. I like to make it in small batches because it is quick to make and I don't want to take up too much room in the freezer. For best results, defrost the cucumbers the day before you need them and use in homemade burgers, with sausages and sauerkraut, or in a sandwich with Cheddar cheese.

makes approx. 1½ lbs (enough for 3 portions each serving 4 people)

approx. 1lb cucumber
2 shallots, very thinly sliced
1–2 teaspoons salt
¼ cup sugar
1 teaspoon mustard seeds
a small handful of dill leaves
½ cup white wine vinegar or Quick spiced vinegar (see page 19)

Thoroughly wash the cucumbers and cut into approx. ¼in slices. Layer the cucumber slices with the shallots in a glass or plastic bowl, sprinkling each layer with salt. Cover and set aside in a cool place for 2 hours; this process will draw out the moisture from the cucumbers and help to keep them crisp. Tip into a colander and rinse under very cold water. Drain well, pressing out any surplus liquid with a small saucer.

Transfer the slices to a clean bowl and layer them up with the sugar, mustard seeds, and dill leaves. Pour in the vinegar and weigh down the cucumbers with a small saucer. Cover and set aside in the fridge overnight.

The following day, divide the mixture into small containers, cover, and freeze. Do not overfill your containers as the liquid will expand in the cold. To use, thaw overnight in the fridge. Once defrosted, store in the fridge and consume within a week.

SIMPLE SMOOTHIES AND FROZEN DESSERTS

I remember watching an Eddie Izzard sketch about fruit bowls being a place where we watch fruit rot, and how we actually end up throwing all of it away apart from the oranges. However, since learning this trick, I never throw out fruit any more. No more soft, black bananas and wrinkled apples in our house, thank you! We used to make smoothies with ice cubes and fresh fruit, which does water the taste down, but this version uses just pure, cold fruit, so it has a great flavor.

THESE ARE SOME OF OUR FAVORITE SMOOTHIE COMBINATIONS

Katie's Breakfast in a Glass: banana + avocado + ginger + orange + cinnamon + oats + kefir.

Giancarlo's Memories of Tuscany: melon + pear + peach + honey + milk.

Giorgio's Red Sky in the Morning: plum + blood orange + apple + ginger + apple juice.

Flavio's Extravaganza: strawberry + raspberry + banana + vanilla ice cream + strawberry ice cream + apple + ginger + orange juice + yogurt + vanilla extract!

freezing fruit for smoothies

You can use all sorts of fresh fruit for smoothies. For larger fruit, such as apples, oranges, mangoes, clementines, plums, kiwis or bananas, I chop the fruit into 1in cubes and freeze it on baking sheets in the freezer. I leave the skins on for apples, but peel the rest. For grapes, raspberries, blueberries, and strawberries, freeze whole on open baking sheets to stop them from sticking together. Once your fruit has frozen solid, bag it up into freezer bags or boxes. I always use separate bags or boxes for individual fruits so that I can offer choices to fussy children— mentioning no names of course.

When you want to make a smoothie, choose the fruits you like and put them into a food processor (still frozen). You can either process them on their own or combine them with other fresh fruit, fruit juice, milk, yogurt, or a dash of honey and blend until smooth. I like to add vanilla seeds and/or cinnamon to yogurt-based smoothies. A little lump of fresh or frozen ginger works well with either fruit or dairy smoothies. Avocados and carrots work well, too.

frozen desserts

FROZEN YOGURT

Frozen fruit is great to blend into yogurt for a healthy frozen dessert. I wouldn't recommend freezing bananas or strawberries for desserts in general, because their texture suffers, but it is fine to freeze them to combine with yogurt. Just take a handful of frozen fruit and mix with ⅔ cup of yogurt per person. Sweeten to taste with honey or drizzle some over the top. Serve right away.

MAKING ICE CREAM AND SORBET IN THE FREEZER WITH NO ICE-CREAM MACHINE

Thanks to the ingenious trick of a chef friend of ours, Stuart Green, we can now make wonderfully smooth ice creams and sorbets without an ice-cream machine. All you need to do is freeze your mixture in ice-cube trays or small yogurt cups and then blend it in a blender once it has frozen to form a smooth, soft fluff. I find flexible silicone muffin molds work well too because they are easy to turn out and make a small enough quantity to be ground easily by the blades of the food processor.

NO-CHURN SEVILLE ORANGE SORBET

This makes a great last-minute dessert. Serve in chilled glasses.

serves 6–8
6 Seville oranges, washed
1 cup sugar
1⅔ cups cold water

Grate the zest of two of the oranges into a saucepan. Add the sugar and water and dissolve the sugar over medium heat. Remove from the heat and allow to cool. Cut all six oranges in half and squeeze out the juice. Stir the juice into the sugar syrup and strain into a pitcher. Pour into flexible ice-cube trays or silicone muffin molds and transfer to the freezer.

Once the sorbet has frozen solid, remove from the freezer and turn out the molds into a food processor. Process to give the texture of a soft but firm sorbet. Either serve right away in chilled dishes or refreeze in a sealed container and store for up to 3 months.

NO-CHURN STRAWBERRY ICE CREAM

This is a quick ice cream recipe that doesn't require a custard base. Feel free to the same weight of raspberries, mango, blackberries, or cherries for the strawberries.

serves 10–12

2lbs strawberries
1⅓ cups sugar
2 cups heavy cream
½ cup milk

Remove the green stems from the strawberries and cut each one in half. Put them into a saucepan with the sugar and bring slowly to a boil, stirring to dissolve the sugar. Reduce the heat and simmer for 10–15 minutes until the strawberries soften.

Pass the strawberries through a fine sieve into a bowl; you should end up with approx. 2 cups of fruit purée, depending on how juicy your fruit is. (If you have more than this amount, reserve some to serve as a sauce.) Add the cream and milk to the purée, stir well, and set aside to cool.

Pour the mixture into small silicone molds or ice-cube trays and place in the freezer. Once frozen, you can bag up the frozen cubes into plastic bags and store them for up to 3 months or use them right away. To serve, put the cubes or molds into a food processor and whizz until soft. (A dash of milk can help to get the cubes going through the blades.) Serve right away in chilled dishes or shot glasses.

and now for something completely different— cold lemons for the ultimate hot bath full of essential oils.

When you have lemon halves left over after you have juiced them, don't throw them away: freeze them! Then at the end of a fulfilling day's preserving, throw a handful of them into a hot bath. The temperature will drop slightly—so allow for that—but the essential oils in the skins of the fruit will be released, the smell will be amazing, and you will feel wonderful afterward.

suppliers & bibliography

Suppliers

cooking equipment

Canning Supplies
www.canningsupply.com

Kilner Jars
www.pacificmerchants.com/kilner

Le Parfait
www.leparfait.com
Wide range of preserving and glass jars.

sausage making supplies

The Sausage Maker
www.sausagemaker.com

The Sausage Source
www.sausagesource.com

dehydrators

Excalibur Dehydrator
www.excaliburdehydrator.com

You not only can buy directly from the manufacturer, but tehe webstie offers recipes and support.

smoking equipment and wood chips, dust etc.

Big Green Egg
www.biggreenegg.com

A US-made, versatile egg-shaped barbecue that grills, makes excellent pizza, and hot smokes meat, fish and vegetables. Try the maple-roast chicken, salmon on a cedar plank, and alder wood chips for cooking pizza. Loved by smoking enthusiasts.

Bradley Smoker
www.bradleysmoker.com

Still the only hot and cold smoker on the market. It makes life easy and takes the uncertainty out of smoking.

Weber
www.weber.com

These familiar dome-shaped barbecues will also act as smokers, working to infuse flavor throughout your meat with varying strengths, depending on the wood type or herb. If using the charcoal indirect method of smoking, keep the vents open and position the top vent on the opposite side to the wood, this will draw the smoke over the meat. We enjoyed succulent ribs that cooked long and slow over 9 hours. The website also provides grilling lessons and advice.

BBQ Guru
www.thebbqguru.com
A that is great for gadgets such as the DigiQ DX2 and CyberQ Wifi, which is the ultimate in temperature control information supplied to your phone.

cheese-making suppliers

The Cheesemaker
www.cheesemaker.com

water and milk kefir grains and kombucha mothers

Cultures for Health
www.culturesforhealth.com
Great advice and a good range of these sought-after products.

pressure canners and information

National Presto Industries, Inc.
www.gopresto.com
Pressure canners, lots of helpful advice, and pressure canner testers.

Bibliography

useful books

Agricultural and Food Research Council
Home Preservation of Fruit and Vegetables
Stationery Office Books, 1989
An essential bible for jam and chutney makers originally published in 1929 and still accurate and reliable today.

Darina Allen
Forgotten Skills of Cooking
Kyle Books, 2009
A huge and definitive guide to traditional cooking skills. A well-thumbed bible in our house that is never out of the kitchen.

Ball's *Blue Book Guide to Preserving*
Alltrista Consumer Products, 2012
A really reliable guide to canning either in a waterbath or pressure canner.

C. J. J. Berry
First Steps in Winemaking
Nexus Special Interests, 1997
The essential place to start for anyone interested in country wines. It started as a collection of recipes from the amateur winemaker and has since sold over 3 million copies.

Margaret Briggs
Practical Household Uses of Salt
Abbey Press, 2012
A fascinating read all about the history and uses of this essential ingredient.

Sherri Brooks Vinton
Put 'em up!
Storey Publishing, 2010
Sherri has included good step-by-step instructions and some really unusual recipes as well as the favorites.

Lynda Brown
The Preserving Book
Dorling Kindersley, 2010
A simple and clear guide to buy if you are starting to preserve.

Pam Corbin
Preserves: River Cottage Handbook No. 2
Bloomsbury, 2008
Pam the Jam, as she is known, has used her vast experience to produce this book full of ideas of what to do with fruit and vegetables.

The Culinary Institute of America and John Kowalski
The Art of Charcuterie
John Wiley & Sons, 2011
For enthusiasts and professionals, this book is a must for anyone who wants to cure and dry meat, or make sausages, pâtés and more. Good step-by-step photographs make this subject much easier to understand.

Maynard Davies
Secrets of a Bacon Curer
Merlin Unwin Books, 2007
An amusing and touching insight into the life of the last apprentice bacon curer, with recipes scattered throughout.

Keith Erlandson
Home Smoking and Curing
Hutchinson 1977
One of the earlier books written on this subject but still a good source of information from an experienced writer.

Excalibur Products
Preserve it Naturally: The Complete Guide to Food Dehydration
Prentice Hall Trade, 2010
An essential book if you get a dehydrator, they are usually sold together.

Marc Frederic
Le Charcutier Anglais
Moorish Foods, 2011
Tales and recipes from a gamekeeper
turned charcutier.

The Good Cook
Preserving
Time Life Books, 1981
A before-its-time collection of preserving
recipes from around the world.

Janet Greene, Ruth Hertzberg and
Beatrice Vaughan
Putting Food By
Penguin, 2010
Plenty of instructions, safety advice, and
recipes for canning, freezing, pickling,
and curing.

Jane Grigson
Charcuterie and French Pork Cookery
Penguin, 1970
A brilliant book that is as relevant today
as when it was written, which describes
how to use all parts of the pig.

Andy Hamilton
Booze for Free
Eden Project Books, 2011
A clearly written and fun guide on
how to turn the produce from your
garden or foraging trips into all types
of alcohol and soft drinks.

Wardeh Harmon
*The Complete Idiot's Guide to
Fermenting Foods*
Alpha, 2012
A no-nonsense, clearly written guide to
making your own fermented foods.

Anissa Helou
Lebanese Cuisine
Grub Street, 2003
A wonderful collection of 250 authentic
and accurately written Lebanese recipes
that make your mouth water just
reading them.

Ikuko Hisamatsu
Tsukemono: Japanese Pickling Recipes
Japan Publications Trading Company,
2010
A small book packed with information
for how to pickle vegetables Japanese-
style. The step-by-step photos and clear
instructions take the mystery out of this
form of food preparation.

Ghillie James
Jam, Jelly and Relish
Kyle Books, 2010
A beautiful book of inspiring preserves
and recipes.

Sandor Ellix Katz
The Art of Fermentation
Chelsea Green Publishing Company,
2012
A must-read, mainly information rather
than recipes, but it will change the way
you think about food and possibly life.

Sandor Ellix Katz
Wild Fermentation
Chelsea Green Publishing Company,
2003
If it wasn't for Katz, none of us would
be discussing fermentation. This will
give you the history, the reasons behind
why fermented foods should be a part
of our lives, plus great recipes, too.

Alex Lewin
Real Food Fermentation
Quarry Books, 2012
A book that will hold your hand
when you are beginning to ferment
foods. Lots of step-by-step photos
and clear recipes.

Vivien Lloyd
First Preserves
Citrus Press, 2011
A really clear guide to making
marmalade, jams, and chutney by
the lady who teaches the judges
how to judge.

Deborah Madison, Eliot Coleman, and
Centre Terre Vivante
*Preserving Food Without Freezing or
Canning*
Chelsea Green Publishing Company,
2007
An unusual collection of quirky recipes
from around the world.

Marisa McClellan
Food in Jars
Running Press, 2011
A beautiful book of inspiring recipes.
Great for fruit butters and pickles.

Harold McGee
*McGee on Food and Cooking:
An Encyclopedia of Kitchen Science,
History and Culture*
Hodder & Stoughton, 2004
Every chef and eager cook should own
a copy. McGee explains the science
behind foods and cooking in an easy-to-
understand manner.

Paul Peacock
The Smoking and Curing Book
The Good Life Press, 2009
A no-nonsense guide and an amusing
read. I would like to meet Paul, because
he makes me laugh out loud.

Michael Ruhlman and Brian Polycn
Charcuterie
W. W. Norton, 2005
A comprehensive book written by
experienced enthusiasts for those
interested in salting, smoking, and
curing meat. Great sausage and pâté
recipes, as well as some for pickling
and smoking.

Ed. Helen Sabieri
*Cured, Fermented and Smoked Foods:
Proceedings of the Oxford Symposium
on Food and Cookery 2010*
Prospect Books, 2010
A serious and astonishing tome made
up from papers written by culinary

luminaries for a symposium about global preserving techniques.

Nick Sandler and Johnny Acton
Preserved
Kyle Cathie, 2009
A great book with loads of information and ideas for preserving all kinds of food.

Oded Schwartz
Preserving Through the Year
Dorling Kindersley, 2012
This was a bible when it was first published in 1996, but it still stands the test of time because Oded is a master of jams, jellies, chutneys, bottled fruits, and pickles.

Sue Shephard
Pickled, Potted and Canned
Simon & Schuster, 2000
Everyone should read this book. It is fascinating and helps you understand how food preservation shaped the world we live in today.

Dick and James Strawbridge
Made at Home: Curing & Smoking
Mitchell Beazley, 2012
A useful little book packed with techniques and lovely recipe ideas.

Kate Walker
Practical Food Smoking
Angels' Share, 2012
Loads of information for those who are going to take up smoking seriously.

Lindy Wildsmith
Cured
Jacqui Small, 2010
Lindy's book is great for techniques and recipes for salting, drying, smoking, potting and pickling.

Beryl Wood
Let's Preserve It
Vintage, 2010
Plenty of recipes for those that already know how to make jams, jellies and chutneys.

US Department of Agriculture
Complete Guide to Home Canning and Preserving
Dover Publications, 1999
Everything you need to know about canning.

useful blogs and sites

Bradley Smoker
http://forum.bradleysmoker.com
Smoking recipes shared and queries answered by other enthusiasts, mainly in the US.

The Cottage Smallholder
www.cottagesmallholder.com
Fiona Neville has created this inspiring site and blog about her journey into self-sufficiency. I love her pickles, chutneys, and jam recipes.

A Gardener's Table
www.agardenerstable.com
This is a fascinating read from Linda Ziedrich. She answers so many queries with her in-depth well-researched writing.

Hunter Angler Gardener Cook
http://honest-food.net
Good recipes and advice on wild game and charcuterie.

Meat and Sausages.com
www.meatsandsausages.com
Originally called wedlinydomowe.com this was set up by some Polish guys eager to preserve their sausage-making

skills. It is a huge site full of science, good sense, and recipes. A valuable resource for doing any form of curing.

Nourishing Days
www.nourishingdays.com
Shannon writes from her homestead in Texas about self-sufficiency. I love the recipes and her journey in fermentation.

Wild Fermentation
www.wildfermentation.com
A great site for ideas, news, recipes, and problem solving for fermented foods.

index

Index

Acknowledgments

The experts we learned from and the courses that got us started......

Jasper Aykroyd, aka The Bacon Wizard. What can I say, you are talented, clever, fun, and your cured meats are the best. I don't think anyone has ever shown me the patience you did over the Salt and Air chapters. For bacon and all forms of curing solutions as well as curing courses, Jasper Ackroyd is a fantastic consultant, contact him at: jasper@baconwizard.co.uk.

Marc Frederic, The English Charcutier, for his enthusiasm, passion, and knowledge. And a good laugh, too.

Christine Ashby—cheese-maker extraordinaire—she simply makes people want to make yogurt and cheese. For more information see www.abcheesemaking.co.uk.

Katy Rodgers, for showing us her award-winning dairy produce and helping us produce amazing yogurt and crème fraîche – www.knockraich.com.

Sally Morgan and Marc Frederic, for getting us started in sausages and smoking at Empire Farm.

For Foraging walks in London, contact www.urbanharvest.org.uk.

Debi King, for her knowledge and patience in helping make country wines.

Vivien and Nigel Lloyd, what a pleasure to have gotten to know you this last year. Your knowledge is phenomenal; thank you for sharing it and your years of experience with us.

Sukie and Bill Barber taught us how to smoke and have answered questions and queries ever since. Their fascinating courses and demonstrations cover many food-related topics from rearing their own livestock, growing fruit and vegetables, to breadmaking, preserving, and smoking – billandsukie@gmail.com.

Reiko Hara, teacher of Asian cooking for her help on Japanese foods.

Iain Spink makes fantastic Arbroath Smokies in the traditional way— available by mail order at www.arbroathsmokies.net.

Jane Milton and Maxine Clark, for their advice on our Scottish tour of smokers.

Brian McLeod, for helping with research, planning our Scottish trip and generally making us laugh a lot.

A huge, heartfelt thank you from us both to.......

Kyle Cathie, when you took me out to lunch and quietly mentioned writing a book about preserving, I had no idea of the enormity of the journey we were about to embark upon. It has been a fascinating if hair-raising ride; we have loved it and wouldn't have missed the opportunity for a moment. It really has changed our lives for the better.

Sheila Abelman, thank you for introducing me to Kyle all those years ago and getting this book started.

Vicky Orchard, we've discussed, laughed, disagreed, fussed, tweaked, and above all cared for and loved this book—may it live long and give years of pleasure to all those who read it. Thank you to you and your assistant, Laura Foster.

Chris Terry, we fell for your sensitive, artfully lit, stunning photographs when we first saw your portfolio. We didn't know we would also find a friend, a wit, and wonderful duck confit! Thank you so much for those great shoot days and all the beautiful photos in this book.

Props stylist Pene Parker did us proud with her imaginative sets, backgrounds, cloths, cutlery, and care. I loved working with you.

Copyeditor Catherine Ward, thank you so much for painstakingly reading the text and correcting my awful grammar without patronizing me once.

Sheila Keating, you are an amazing and talented lady. Thank you for making this so much easier.

Manjula Samarasinghe, I couldn't have had a better assistant to help me on this journey. You have endlessly cooked, tasted, learned, washed, eaten yogurt with jam, too much sourdough, drank tea, and discussed fermentation with me!

Jim Davies, for taking over my work without moaning even once while I wrote the book.

My brother, Philip, for building our meat boxes, getting smoked out, and chopping logs with a blunt axe in 26°F. True dedication and brotherly love.

Gemma Harris, for giving up your day to us to teach us about fermenting, drying, and making amazing cordials.

John Watkins from Bradley Smokers for your advice and support.

Pernilla Daniels for her Swedish recipes and translation.

Ian Bethwaite and Carrie Darby for all your knowledge, research and support. From supplying the "gherkin advice line" to answering "what is a bean weevil?" you were always there for me.

Designer Carl Hodson, for the beautiful book that this has become.

Sian and Steve Adams, for introducing me to the Big Green Egg and letting me smoke cauliflowers, pulled pork, and peppers on theirs.

Livia and Nello Ceccuzzi whose lifestyle on their farm in Tuscany is an inspiration to us.

Andrew Fairlie at Gleneagles, who let us into his kitchen and shared his recipes with us.

To our chefs, Gregorio Piazza, Antonio Sanzone and Stefano Borella for helping us research and test the recipes over and over again!

Important Note
The information contained in this book is intended as a general guide to preserving and is based on the authors' own experimentation, experience, and research. Guidelines for safety and warnings of dangers are presented throughout and should be heeded. Neither the authors nor the publishers can be held responsible for the consequences of the application or misapplication of any of the information or ideas presented in this book.

First published in 2014 by Kyle Books
www.kylebooks.com
generalenquiries@kylebooks.com

Distributed by National Book Network
4501 Forbes Blvd., Suite 200
Lanham, MD 20706
Phone: (800) 462 6420
Fax: (800) 338 4550

First published in Great Britain in 2013 by Kyle books, an imprint of Kyle Cathie Limited

ISBN: 978-1-909487-08-6

Library of Congress Control Number: 2014931346

Katie and Giancarlo Caldesi are hereby identified as the authors of this work in accordance with Section 77 of the Copyright, Designs and Patents Act 1988

Editor: Vicky Orchard
Editorial assistant: Laura Foster
Design: Carl Hodson
Photography: Chris Terry
Props styling: Pene Parker
Illustration (page 83): Esther Coombs
Copy editor: Catherine Ward
Production: Nic Jones and David Hearn

Color reproduction by ALTA London
Printed and bound in China by C&C Offset Printing Company Ltd.